Killing the White Man's Indian

Fergus M. Bordewich

Killing the White Man's Indian

Reinventing Native Americans at the End of the Twentieth Century

D O U B L E D A Y
New York London Toronto Sydney Auckland

PUBLISHED BY DOUBLEDAY
a division of Bantam Doubleday Dell Publishing Group, Inc.
1540 Broadway, New York, New York 10036

DOUBLEDAY and the portrayal of an anchor
with a dolphin are trademarks of Doubleday,
a division of Bantam Doubleday Dell
Publishing Group, Inc.

Library of Congress Cataloging-in-Publication Data

Bordewich, Fergus M.
Killing the white man's Indian: reinventing Native
Americans at the end of the twentieth century / by Fergus M. Bordewich.
    p. cm.
Includes index.
1. Indians of North America—Politics and government. 2. Indians
of North America—Ethnic identity. 3. Indians of North America—
Government relations. I. Title.
E99.T77B67   1996
323.1′197—dc20   95-23069
CIP

ISBN 0-385-42035-8
Printed in the United States of America
First Edition
February 1996

10   9   8   7   6   5   4   3   2   1

For Laverne Madigan Bordewich

My Mother
1912–1962

From her faith in a just society
sprang her unstinting devotion
to the cause of the American Indian.

Contents

Introduction

IN THE SUMMER of 1991, I spent several days in the small city of Salamanca, in western New York State. The blocks of low, gritty late-Victorian shops and wood-frame homes gave the impression, largely accurate, that almost nothing new had been built for decades. The railroads that made Salamanca's fortune around the turn of the century had virtually abandoned the city years ago, taking with them most of the industry and leaving behind the descendants of the Irish, Polish, and Italian workers who had come when times were flush. It was the kind of place where people enjoyed boasting about their lawns, and fish they had caught, and the prowess of school teams. But instead, that summer, they were talking bitterly and endlessly about Indians.

In 1892, sharp-dealing speculators had extracted a ninety-nine-year lease to Salamanca's site from the headmen of the Senecas, whose reservation snakes along the narrow valley of the Allegheny River. The way they accomplished it was by sequestering the Senecas in a local hotel and lubricating them with alcohol until they agreed to sign. The tribe agreed to accept $17,000 in combined rents annually, a pittance even by the standards of that time. Although decades later the Indians managed to renegotiate the total upward to $57,000, at the start of the 1990s many whites were still paying ground rents as low as $1 per year.

For one year short of a century, Salamancans had lived their lives as if the Senecas did not exist. Then, in 1991, the lease ran out. The Senecas made it plain that there would be no renewal and that the city's 6,600 inhabitants were about to become the residents of an Indian reservation. Whites were nearly hysterical with fear and rage. That there would be disruptions, there was no doubt. Rents, for the first time ever, would rise to market levels. There were all sorts of rumors: that the Indians would invade private homes, that they would evict the elderly wholesale. People kept telling each other that their parents and grandparents had drained and developed the land, that it had had no value at all until the white man came.

"The Indians are just after the money," I was informed by a retired farmer, who, like many others, seemed personally offended that Indians were showing the most elementary commercial sense. "They're trying to punish us because their land was taken away from them years ago. There was need for civil rights, but it's going too far now. They'll run everything down and close it up, that's what they'll do!"

The Senecas, meanwhile, were strictly business. "When they negotiated the original leases, they thought we weren't going to be here at the end," Dennis Lay, the president of the Seneca Nation, told a reporter from the *New York Times*. "I guess we fooled them."

In one sense, it was easy to see Salamanca simply as a small town struggling to cope with the unintended fruits of its history. But in fact no place in the United States offered a more vivid image of the dilemma faced by an entire nation confronted by hundreds of revitalized Indian tribes insistently demanding attention, power, and compensation for both the real and imagined wrongs of the past. It was equally clear that, not only in the Allegheny valley but throughout the United States, Indians could no longer be ignored with impunity.

In the course of numerous journeys that I made through the great inland archipelago of the nation's reservations during the first half of the 1990s, it became increasingly evident that a revolution was under way in Indian Country. It is an upheaval of epic proportions that encompassed almost every aspect of Indian life, from the resuscitation of moribund tribal cultures and the resurgence of traditional religions, to the development of aggressive tribal governments determined to remake the entire relationship between Indians and the United States. In almost every respect, it was challenging the worn-out theology of Indians as losers and victims and was transforming tribes into powers to be reckoned with for a long time to come. It was, moreover, a revolution that had gone largely unrecorded by the national media and unnoticed by a public that still sees Indians mainly through the mythic veil of mingled racism and romance.

For the first time in generations, Indians were shaping their own destinies largely beyond the control of whites. Talented tribal leaders were seeking innovative ways to define the place of the tribes in the modern world. Inspired individuals were reinventing Indian education, rewriting tribal histories, helping to bring about a remarkable resurgence of traditional religions, and coming to grips with the alcoholism and social pathologies that blight reservation communities. The ferment was not unalloyed, however. Alongside inspired idealism, I also found ethnic chauvinism, a crippling instinct to confuse isolation with independence, and a chronic habit of interpreting present-day reality through the warping lens of the past.

Indians were playing an entirely new game, and it often seemed that no one but the Indians understood the rules. In Connecticut, and elsewhere, tribes were exploiting a principle of sovereignty unknown to the average American in order to build gambling casinos that sucked colossal sums of money from neighboring regions. Landowners in southern California discovered that they had virtually no way to prevent the minuscule Campo Band of Indians from building a huge commercial waste facility on top of their watershed. New Mexicans found that they were equally helpless in the face of the Mescalero Apaches' determination to establish a nuclear waste facility on their reservation outside Alamogordo. In Wisconsin and in Washington State, recurrent violence had accompanied the judicially mandated enlargement of Indian fishing rights in accordance with nineteenth-century treaties that no one but the Indians remembered. In Nevada, farmers found themselves on the brink of dispossession as the Paiutes of Pyramid Lake gained political leverage over the watershed of the Truckee River, upon which their survival depended. In some states, Indian claims to land, water, and fishing rights and their demands for the return of sacred lands posed seismic threats to local economies, including, most prominently, the entire Black Hills region of South Dakota. Nor was science exempt. Tribal claims upon ancestral bones and artifacts were wreaking havoc upon many of the most valuable anthropological collections in the country, while a handful of Apaches had managed for years to stymie development of one of the most important observatories in the United States by asserting that the mountain upon which it was to be constructed was sacred land whose true nature could never be divulged.

Perhaps most far-reaching of all, it seemed by the mid-1990s that Indian aspirations to political autonomy were threatening to create a new third sphere of sovereignty that was never contemplated by the U.S. Constitution, along with a multitude of dependent statelets, some as poor and ill-governed as Chad and Haiti, where civil liberties taken for granted by other Americans were only arguably recognized and largely unenforced. Tribal officials were already invoking the principle of "sovereign right" in debates over everything from highway maintenance and fishing quotas and reservation gambling to law and order, toxic waste disposal, and the transfer of federal services to tribal administration. Echoing the sentiments of many tribal leaders, Tim Giago, the publisher of *Indian Country Today,* the most widely read Indian newspaper in the United States, likened state legislation that affects Indians to "letting France make laws that also become law in Italy."

The Indians of the 1990s were no longer the doomed warriors of the nineteenth century but politically astute men and women bent upon creating a new, vital Indian world within the modern United States. Moreover, in a striking reversal of policies that remained in force through the 1950s, which reflected a firm conviction that Indians must be either convinced or compelled to integrate themselves into mainstream America, Indians were now being abetted in their drive toward tribal autonomy by the United States government itself. Even as popular culture was unquestioningly embracing the fuzzy New Age myth of the Indian as the innocent child of nature, tribal politicians and the federal government were collaborating in the development of a concept of tribal sovereignty that exponentially increased the power of Indian tribes and guaranteed tribal authority over reservation communities.

In 1970, Richard Nixon declared that federal policy would henceforth be guided "by Indian acts and Indian decisions" and would be designed to "assure the Indian that he can assume control of his own life without being separated from the tribal group."

It is a promise that has, so far, been only partly fulfilled. As one of the nation's most influential tribal leaders, Chief Phillip Martin of the Mississippi Band of Choctaws, has said, "Nothing, or next to nothing happens on an Indian reservation without it being a result of, a reaction to, an attempt to get around, or a violation of, an action or policy of the federal government or of its employees. Said another way, the federal government always has an effect on the reservation and its development, either a positive effect or a negative effect, but always an effect." By the 1990s, the nation's commitment to Indians was costing taxpayers about $3 billion each year in federal appropriations (accounting for 70 percent of all tribal dollars), channeled primarily through the Bureau of Indian Affairs, whose legendary mismanagement has included, according to numerous recent investigations, the inability to account for $95 million, or 10 percent of its 1990 budget; lackadaisical oversight of tribal lands that has resulted in the loss of at least hundreds of millions of dollars in oil royalties; and the mishandling of $2 billion in tribal trust funds, which a Congressional report in 1992 termed "a national disgrace."

Framed against such inefficiency, not to mention the historical destruction wrought upon the continent's Indians by disease, warfare, and the misguided policies of the past, tribal autonomy seemed only just, a reasonable step toward restoration of the proud independence and cultural glory that every American child weaned on *Dances With Wolves* and the homilies of Chief Seattle by now surely knew that Indians were heir to. However, the new national commitment to tribal sovereignty was bestowing practical autonomy upon groups of people whose very identity was, at least arguably, based on obsolete ideas of race and ethnicity, even as Indians continued to blend into the larger population through intermarriage at a faster rate than ever before. As the retired farmer in Salamanca wondered aloud, as much in sheer confusion as resentment, "How long does it take to become just a plain American?"

In the course of writing this book, I visited a Lakota woman, now in her late eighties, whom I had known well when I was a child. It was not easy to find her home in the straggling lanes of the village where she lives on the Pine Ridge Sioux reservation, in South Dakota, and I had to stop several people to ask for directions. Suspicion of outsiders is common at Pine Ridge, and it was some time before I found anyone willing to point out her cottage. Although nearly thirty years had passed since we had last met, she recognized me instantly. We were soon sitting at her kitchen table, eating cheese sandwiches and drinking Coke. We talked, first of all, about my mother.

Like the Association on American Indian Affairs, which she managed as its executive director during the 1950s, my mother believed passionately in both social justice and the creative ability of government to solve human problems. It was a difficult era for Indians. Federal policy was officially committed to terminating Indian tribes and breaking up the reservations. More than a dozen tribes had already been legally abolished, and nearly every other one feared that it might be the next. Officials of the Bureau of Indian Affairs (BIA) governed the reservations more or less as colonial satraps, sometimes deciding if and when tribal leaders should visit Washington and then accompanying them there like political chaperones. Until her death in 1962, my mother worked tirelessly—twelve- and fourteen-hour days were commonplace—to forestall termination and to prod the federal government to improve reservation economies, education, health care, and safety. The men and women she recruited to work with her were often among the first in their communities to participate in public affairs outside the BIA's rubber-stamp tribal governments.

Thanks to her work, I had the privilege of spending much of my childhood and youth around Indian communities of all sorts. Several times each year, I could look forward to being lifted out of the predictable rounds of life in suburban New York and taken along on field trips to Montana or Nebraska, Washington State, Alaska, Florida, or the Dakotas, almost anyplace where Indians lived. Vivid experiences were plentiful: participating in a nightlong peyote rite in a tepee on the Montana prairie, a journey by pirogue deep into the Louisiana bayous to meet with a forgotten band of Houmas who wanted Washington to take notice of their existence, walking the Little Big Horn Battlefield with an aged Cheyenne who, as a small boy, had witnessed the annihilation of Custer's command. More generally, those years left me with a sense of the tremendous diversity of the lives that lay submerged within the catchall label of "Indians."

Of all the places that I came to know, none left a stronger impression than Pine Ridge. To a youngster, it was an undeniably exciting place, with its vastly rolling prairie, spectacular skies, Indian cowboys in pearl-buttoned shirts and ten-gallon hats, and thrilling memories of the frontier wars. Poverty, however, seemed to insinuate itself into every encounter and could be unnerving. Staying with friends meant wind fingering its way through gaps in the walls, a cheese and baloney sandwich for dinner, sleeping three or four in a bed with broken springs. It seemed to me that there was always someone talking about an uncle who had frozen to death drunk on a lonely road or a cousin who was already pregnant at sixteen.

My mother's friend told me that some things had changed for the better. Now there was a modern supermarket in Pine Ridge. Public housing had replaced most of the log cabins and tarpaper shacks. A tribal college had been established at Kyle, and a tribal radio station now broadcast from Porcupine Butte. Lakota officials now ran many of the programs that had been operated by the BIA. And, astonishingly, hundreds of Lakotas now came together every summer to perform the dramatic exculpatory rite of the sun dance, whose performance had within living memory been punishable by imprisonment. In other respects, however, little seemed to have changed at all. Shannon County, which included the reservation, had the highest percentage of poor people of any county in the United States. Fewer than three in ten had jobs, and most of those who did worked for the tribal government. Per capita income was less than $3,500 per year. Crime was worse than it had ever been. Stoically, she told me that a few years earlier vandals had wrecked her shop, one of the few private businesses on the reservation. She had let the building go to ruin; she was too old to start over, she said.

Something else had changed, too. Pine Ridge had been placed firmly on the nation's mental map. Perhaps it had begun in 1973, when a virtual civil war between armed radicals of the American Indian Movement and more conservative Sioux elements had led to the bloody and widely publicized standoff at Wounded Knee. Whatever the reason, the reservation had become a national metaphor for the perceived plight of all Indians, quintessential victims in a nation that increasingly seemed to venerate victimhood as a badge of honor. Just before my visit, there had been a major report on Pine Ridge by ABC-TV news that dwelled on the ravages of alcoholism. Soon after it, there were major stories in the *Wall Street Journal* and the *New York Times,* both in much the same vein: "a mean and despairing place," the *Times* had called it. Michael Dorris's heart-rending 1989 book on fetal alcohol syndrome, *The Broken Cord,* had focused at some length on Pine Ridge. In 1992, two films by Michael Apted, *Incident at Oglala,* a documentary, and *Thunderheart,* a thriller, heroized the radicals of 1973 as third world–style revolutionaries struggling against a fascistic tribal leader and the tyranny of the United States government, in the form of the allegedly corrupt Federal Bureau of Investigation. Still another polemical rendering of that period, *Lakota Woman,* became a best-seller and in 1994 was made into a TV movie by Ted Turner.

In some ways, this is understandable. In terms of statistics, Indian Country does seem to present a daunting and monotonous landscape of insoluble social problems. Indians are twice as likely as other Americans to be murdered or to commit suicide, three times likelier to die in automobile accidents, and five times more likely to die from cirrhosis of the liver. Rates of alcoholism on reservations commonly range higher than 50 percent. On some reservations, unemployment surpasses 80 percent. In spite of progressively increased access to education, 55 percent of Indian young people drop out of high school. Although the number of Indians who graduate from college has increased from less than 1 percent in 1960 to 7.4 percent today, it is still less than half the proportion of other Americans. Exactly what all this means, however, is less obvious. Seen from one angle, it suggests a massive failure of government to remedy generations of mistreatment; seen from another, an equally massive failure of Indians to cope with life in present-day America.

All this poses many deeply provocative questions: Are Indians so fundamentally different from other Americans, so historically and culturally unique, that they occupy a special category over which conventional American values, laws, and criteria of ethics should not apply? Or are they simply one more American ethnic group, whose special pleading is yet further evidence that the United States has become, in the words of Arthur Schlesinger in *The Disuniting of America,* "a tangle of squabbling nationalities . . . a quarrelsome spatter of enclaves, ghettos, tribes"? Are we discriminating against Indians by failing to encourage them to participate in the national mainstream? Or is the very notion of "mainstreaming" Indians so inherently racist that it should not even be contemplated as a component of national policy? Are Indian reservations and the way of life they preserve a precious national resource that must be preserved without the taint of contact with non-Indian America? Or is tribal self-determination perpetuating a form of segregation that merely preserves decayed tribal cultures like ghettoized versions of Colonial Williamsburg? Will tribes remain forever dependent on the tolerance and generosity of American taxpayers? Or do Indian tribes have the inner resources to become self-sufficient and, if necessary, to reinvent themselves to compete in the increasingly complex twenty-first-century economy? Who, ultimately, are Indians in the 1990s? What are they to other Americans, and we to them?

Curiously enough, the implications of the upheaval that is taking place have drawn comparatively little scrutiny; it is almost as if a culture that is literally saturated with allusions to fictional Indians had no interest in living Indians at all. We drive "Cherokees," "Winnebagos," and "Pontiacs." During the Gulf War, American troops flew "Kiowa" and "Apache" helicopters and shot down Iraqi planes with "Tomahawk" missiles. Sports fans, in the nation's capital of all places, think nothing of cheering a team called the "Redskins," while Atlantans wave foam-rubber tomahawks for the "Braves." Schoolchildren write on "Big Chief" tablets. Pipe smokers light up with "Red Chief" tobacco. New Age bookstores are chock-a-block with spiritualizing treatises on supposed traditional native beliefs, while gurus urge repressed modern males to flee to the woods, to become "real" men by howling and drumming, by becoming "warriors." By acting "like Indians," it would seem, we may become noble, free, authentic: we may discover our true selves. As the lonely soldier played by Kevin Costner in *Dances With Wolves,* that fable of twentieth-century angst projected back into the Dakota Territory of the 1860s, says, "I had never known who John Dunbar was, but as I heard my Sioux name being called, I knew for the first time in my life who I really was."

Beneath the shallow patina of popular culture, ideas of mythic force lie rooted in the American psyche, fundamental not only to our perception of Indians but also, perhaps, of ourselves. Like no other inhabitants of the United States, Indians have for centuries nourished our imagination, weaving in us a complex skein of guilt, envy, and contempt; yet, imagining that we see "the Indian," we often see little more than the distorted reflection of our own fears, fancies, and wistful longings. Meanwhile, live Indians are, in a sense, our national nightmare, figments of a guilty imagination, like Fritz Scholder's sly portraits of flag-draped and feathered warriors, reminders of a history that we would prefer not to remember and confusing our fantasies with real-life demands.

Until not long ago, Americans were generally taught to view the nation's westward movement as a saga of heroic pioneering and just wars that carried European immigrants from the shores of the Atlantic to those of the Pacific. At the center of that essentially mythic vision stood the Indian, simultaneously noble and barbaric, man of nature and bloodthirsty savage, and destined for tragic extinction. The epic of the Indian wars added color and grandeur to the saga of national expansion: in their apparent savagery, Indians dramatically underscored Euro-Americans' notions of civilization, while their repeated military defeats seemed unchallengeable proof of the white man's technological and moral superiority.

More recently, revisionist scholars and educators have tended to portray that same history as one of deep, unredeemed tragedy, of which the destruction of the Indians is a central, equally mythic example, apparent proof of the barbarism of Euro-American civilization. Numerous books suggest the flavor of the changing times: *The Conquest of Paradise: Christopher Columbus and the Columbian Legacy; American Indian Holocaust and Survival; Facing West: The Metaphysics of Indian Hating and Empire Building; Forgotten Founders: How the American Indian Helped Shape Democracy;* and *Indian Givers: How the Indians of the Americas Transformed the World* are but a few of an ever-growing genre. At the same time, a transformation in popular attitudes has prompted hundreds of thousands of Americans to take new pride in real and supposed Indian ancestors. Since 1960, the number of Americans claiming to be Indians on United States census forms has tripled, to more than 1.8 million, while scores of groups in virtually every part of the country have flooded the Bureau of Indian Affairs with appeals for recognition as official tribes.

In this book, I have endeavored to peel back some of the layers of distortion that blur our vision of American Indians in the 1990s and to show that the transformation of Indian Country is much more than a passing phenomenon at the margins of American society. Readers who expect a single uncomplicated portrait of the modern Indian will not find one, for "the Indian," as such, really exists only in the leveling lens of federal policy and in the eyes of those who continue to prefer natives of the imagination to real human beings. There are, however, certain common threads that link the broader experience of modern Indian tribes as they pursue their quest for political, economic, social, and spiritual renewal. I have unraveled these threads mostly in the form of stories, sometimes of individual men and women, sometimes of entire tribes, in an effort to capture the human dimension of events whose sheer strangeness and complexity are unimaginable to people who have never had to make sense of what takes place in the maze of conflicting histories, jurisdictions, and identities that is Indian Country.

Some readers may protest that I have neglected the many Indians who spend at least part of their lives working in urban areas, but it is still reservations that define the unique status of Indians in modern America; without them, and the claim to separate government that they represent, Indians would, for all practical purposes, be no different from other ethnic minorities in the United States. Other readers will be surprised to find that one or another well-known tribe has been mentioned only glancingly, if at all, in these pages. In all, there are more than three hundred Indian tribes in the lower forty-eight states and more than five hundred if you count the various Indian, Aleut, and Eskimo, or Inupiat, communities of Alaska, each with its own unique history, traditions, political environment, and, in many cases, language. At the risk of what may seem to be glaring omissions, I have preferred to avoid a survey so comprehensive that it would risk dooming itself to encyclopedic tedium.

In referring to the aboriginal inhabitants of the United States and their modern descendants, I have for the most part used the term "Indian," which as every schoolchild knows by now is history's most fantastic misnomer, the hopeful guess of a Genoese mariner who thought he had reached Asia. The more formal "Native American" feels strained and unsatisfactory, and implies that other people born in the United States are somehow less "native" than, say, a Yaqui immigrant from Mexico or than someone who may be only one-thirty-second Cherokee by the measure of "blood quantum" but who nonetheless meets the criteria for membership in that tribe. "Indian" has the virtue of clarity; it remains by far the most commonly used term among natives themselves and the established form for organizations such as the National Congress of American Indians, the radical American Indian Movement, and the new National Museum of the American Indian, for such agencies as the Bureau of Indian Affairs and the Indian Health Service, and as part of the official name of most modern tribes.

Like "Indian," the word "tribe" also has a double and often confusing meaning. Anthropologically speaking, it generally refers to a cultural group defined by a set of shared beliefs, traditions, and language. In the narrower, political sense, however, tribes are only those groups that have been recognized as such by the federal government since the passage of the Indian Reorganization Act of 1934 and that, no matter what their cultural origins, are repre- sented by a single government elected in accordance with an approved tribal constitution. (There are a few exceptions to this.) It is for the most part in the latter sense that I use the term.

The story, the dilemma, of American Indians is, in a sense, a window into the American soul; through its cloudy and often confusing lens, we may see ourselves at both our worst and our best. The relationship between Indians and other Americans has continued for half a millennium, while as a nation the United States has struggled to craft Indian policy longer than it has any other— longer by far than for Soviet Russia, a bare seventy-five years, or for postwar Japan, a mere fifty. That relationship has sometimes been cruel and sometimes obtuse, but it has also been infused with an intense moral fervor and with a determination to make the United States live up to its highest ideals. "Like the miner's canary, the Indian marks the shift from fresh air to poison gas to our political atmosphere; and our treatment of Indians, even more than our treatment of other minorities, marks the rise and fall of our democratic faith," Felix Cohen, the foremost interpreter of Indian law, wrote in 1942.

Only by abandoning many long-held, often lovingly held, myths and fantasies are we likely to achieve a mutually productive modus vivendi with tribes that are destined to play increasingly important and self-determined roles on the national scene, and only then will we become able to shape a healthy national policy for peoples whose real life is far more complex, and interesting, than our persistent fantasies. I have written this book in the firm belief, unpopular in some quarters today, that Indians and other Americans share not only a common history but a common future as well and that the long-overdue revival of Indian life will bring a complete liberation of individual Indian people only if it also leads, eventually, to a more intimate, trusting, and self-confident participation of Indians in the larger American society. In that spirit, this book is not only about Indians but also about the nature of the United States itself as it enters the twenty-first century.

Killing the White Man's Indian

1

"The Very Dregs, Garbage and Spanne of Earth"

THE MAN in the baseball cap was standing in the lee of the museum, squinting across the Montana prairie. "There's just too much carrying on about Indians," he was saying, passing time until the rain let up. He was a veteran of World War II, and he had a soldier's respect for the warriors who had annihilated General George Armstrong Custer's command on this same ground, 115 years before, but he had no use for what he considered the selfish whining of modern Indians. "How long is the government supposed to take care of these people? I just plain simply don't think we owe anything to the Indians anymore. The only answer is to get them into the mainstream. It's time to let them go. They're going to have to change if they're going to survive."

Steamy rain slanted in iron-gray shafts across the prairie. Every few minutes, jagged sticks of lightning flashed against the steep hills, throwing the monument to the army dead into stark relief. The names engraved on the monument were mostly German and Irish, immigrants from poor and overpopulated lands who had been trained for nothing better than soldiering. Each man's name was faithfully recorded—Otto Hagemann, Adam Hetesheimer, T. C. Kavanaugh, Henry Klotzbucher, Bartholomew Mahoney, all 268 of them who had been cut down that June day in 1876—

proclaiming to the ages, in the self-confident way of the nineteenth century, that no person's life, ultimately, is wasted or forgotten.

Then something eerie and disconcerting happened. As the rain blew off to the east, men uniformed in cavalry blues began to appear on the ridge, as if the dead had risen from their graves and come back to life. Like apparitions silhouetted against the violent sky, they moved among the tombstones, pausing briefly and walking on, as if they were looking for lost friends. But it was of course just a momentary illusion. Nearby, a car started up, and then another, and another, until they moved off in caravans down the ridge. Cassette players blared "Garryowen," the battle song of the Seventh Cavalry, and the naked hills began to swarm.

Every year, thousands of history buffs, like the man at the museum, who owned businesses in California and who had not missed the occasion for more than ten years, converge on the battlefield to mark the anniversary of the "Last Stand." Scores come dressed festively in old cavalry outfits; a few even show up togged out like Custer himself, in white fringed buckskins and shoulder-length hair. They walk the battlefield, rehashing Custer's deployments and visiting the graves that lie scattered poignantly over the hillsides, where his men died in twos and threes. The more scholarly gather in symposiums to chew over such topics as the distribution of spent shells over the battlefield, while companies of uniformed "re-enactors" refight the Last Stand on a prairie outside the nearby town of Hardin, with local Crow Indians standing in for the Sioux.

The anniversary is normally a gala event, an uninhibited celebration of old-fashioned battlefield glory. But this year a sense of gloom overshadowed the theatrics. First of all, there was the plaque. In 1988, a group of Indian radicals had illegally entered the battlefield under cover of night and embedded the cast-iron plaque among the cavalrymen's graves. It declared: "In honor of our Indian Patriots who fought and defeated the U.S. Calvary [sic] In order to save our women and children from mass murder. In doing so, preserving rights to our Homelands, treaties and sovereignty." The National Park Service, trapped between Indians who threatened violence if the plaque was destroyed and veterans outraged at the desecration of a military cemetery, took the coward's way out. Three years later, the plaque still lay in an embarrassing limbo, propped against a wall in an empty room in the battlefield museum, a provocative and inescapable symbol of Indian rage, white guilt, and the power of the past to intrude, unwelcomed, upon the present.

Worse yet, Congress was on the brink of removing Custer's own name from what had been known officially since 1879 as the Custer Battlefield. (A few months later, the only Congressman to vote against changing the name to the more neutral Little Big Horn National Monument was the representative of Custer's hometown in Michigan.) The hobbyists, who had come from every part of the United States to honor their hero, sounded like men under siege. There were hard words said about the "reinvention" of once-moribund Indian tribes, about the resuscitation of forgotten treaties and the caving in of politicians to fashionable causes.

"Custer was on a legal mission to return the Indians to the reservation," protested Ron Nichols, a reasonable man who is the president of the Custer Battlefield Historical and Museum Association, a nonprofit group dedicated to maintaining the character of the site. "We can't go back and rewrite history. Should we change the names of the Washington and Jefferson memorials because they were slaveowners? What our grandpas did was by the norms and values of their time. This place was a symbol of a hostile environment that needed to be conquered, and that conquest gave a lot of poor people an opportunity to move into a new area and earn a lot of wealth. To force out people they called savages was the norm of the time. You just can't impose today's norms on the 1870s."

Every year, a quarter of a million people visit the battlefield, a particularly impressive number given its near dearth of tourist facilities and its isolation, ninety miles from the nearest city. Visitors come at least in part because it is an unusually evocative site and has changed very little since the summer of 1876. It is still, for most of the year, an empty, silent, fantasy-inspiring place. It is easy, standing alone on Last Stand Ridge, to imagine the overconfident hero of Gettysburg waiting anxiously for the reinforcements that would never arrive and to picture Sitting Bull's warriors dodging up through the silvery sage, on their way to ensure their nemesis an indelible place in history.

But there is something considerably more powerful that also draws people to this remote corner of Montana. It is a place that is inextricably interwoven with the mythology of Manifest Destiny. To generations of white Americans, "Custer's Last Stand" was a central icon of the grand drama of national expansion, which until

quite recently most Americans were taught to see as a cosmic struggle between civilization and barbarism. Just four years before
Custer's defeat, John Gast vividly captured the evangelical spirit of
the time in his immensely popular painting, titled "American Progress," which showed Winged Progress, clad in the Grecian robes of
enlightenment, gliding westward out of the sunrise, leading Cones-
toga wagons, a steaming railroad train, telegraph wires, and farmers with plows, while terrified Indians fled away into receding night.
In such a climate, there was the stuff of instant martyrdom, of a
prairie Golgotha, in the fate of the golden-haired general slain in his
prime at the Little Big Horn. In an age when Americans viewed
their history as a soaring story of unbroken successes, the battle
was a romantic, if tragic, punctuation that underscored the inevitability of the final American victory. The young hero might die, a
sacrifice to the National Purpose, but everyone knew that his spiritual resurrection would come with the final conquest of the West
and the ultimate rolling back of the forces of darkness.

Indians, with very few exceptions, see the same history as a far
darker tale, in which whites play the permanent role of predators
and Indians that of helpless victims. A fairly representative statement of such views was issued by Indian writers and artists who
convened at Taos, New Mexico, in 1992 to plan a response to the
quincentenary of Columbus's discovery of America:

> We, the Indigenous Peoples of this red quarter of Mother Earth, [have
> survived] 500 years of genocide, ethnocide, ecocide, racism, oppression,
> colonization and christianization. These excesses of western civilization
> resulted from contempt for Mother Earth and all our relations; con-
> tempt for women, elders, children and Native Peoples; and contempt
> for a future beyond the present human generation.

It is a history for which, the purveyors of such views usually imply,
there can be no possible moral response on the part of other Americans except unending guilt.

The Little Big Horn battlefield is no less central to the orthodox
Indian view of American history than it is to most whites'. Historians point out, quite correctly, that Custer was a man of both great
personal bravery and some intellect, who authored one of the more
thoughtful books about life on the Great Plains, and that the Sioux,
far from "defending their homeland," as the plaque in the museum
claims, were actually invaders in the ancestral lands of the Crows.

To many Indians today, however, such nuances seem beside the point. To them, Custer has become the incarnation of all that was most arrogant and cruel in the westward push of the United States across Indian Country. "To me, the man Custer had one thing in mind, that was to come into our land and commit genocide on the Indian race under the guise of Manifest Destiny," Hugh White Clay, a spokesman for the Crow Tribe, said in 1993, during a debate over the appropriateness of continuing to reenact the battle each year. He neglected to note that the Crows had embraced the United States as an ally against the Sioux and that their warriors had fought alongside the U.S. Army during the Little Big Horn campaign.

Lately, numerous revisionist works have portrayed American history as one of deep, unredeemed tragedy and failure, of which the destruction of the Indians is a central example and compelling proof of a fundamental ruthlessness at the heart of American civilization. Such beliefs have steadily percolated into the wider culture. They have been embodied in such New Age Westerns as *Dances With Wolves* and the latest romanticizing version of *Geronimo,* in such popular books as the best-selling *Indian Givers: How the Indians of the Americas Transformed the World,* which purports to show how practically every aspect of modern life, from potatoes to democracy, derives from the generosity of American Indians, and into the consciences of journalists, church leaders, and others who shape public opinion. Nevertheless, it may be fair to say that for the majority of Americans, immigrants all, from the sixteenth century through the twentieth, the baseline view of American history remains a triumphal narrative that traces a virtually unbroken chain of successes in national expansion, in which the fate of the Indians was a sad but inevitable part.

The past generation has seen the development of a national consensus on a number of aspects of the nation's history that were once long obscured by racism or shame; for instance, there is today little dispute among Americans of any ethnic background over the meaning of slavery or the internment of Japanese Americans during World War II. There is no such consensus, however, with respect to the shared and deeply complex history of Indians and whites. In essential ways, both Indians and whites see their common past as apocalypse, as a story shaped crucially by violence, competing martyrdoms, and the collision of irreconcilable opposites. But there the

similarity ends. Few other Americans, and perhaps none, have been
so reshaped and so crippled by the events of the past, and at the
same time so distorted in the national vision by myth and illusion.
In a nation that is often impatient with history, Indians are still
often dominated by it in a deep, visceral way that others find difficult to grasp. Indeed, it is impossible even to begin to understand
modern Indians without taking into account the lingering power of
events that the rest of the nation has never known or has pushed to
the margins of memory.

The monument on the shore of Humboldt Bay gives no hint of the
dreadful thing that happened there on the night of February 25,
1860. The plaque is mysteriously opaque: "Indian/Gunther Island.
This site possesses national historic significance in commemorating
the history of the United States of America." It says nothing more.
Not surprisingly, few of the tourists who pause to admire the bay
pay it much attention. The cheerful woman at the chamber of commerce in downtown Eureka has no information at all about the
island. Apologetically, she offers a booklet that tersely recounts the
official version of the city's history: "filled with hopes and dreams
for a new prosperity," it says, Eureka was founded in the spring of
1850 by miners who needed a more convenient alternate to the
tedious overland route from Sacramento to the northern California
goldfields. The city museum is silent, too. There is, among the Victorian gowns and frontiersmen's buckskins, a good collection of
stone tools and ceremonial objects excavated from Indian Island.
But there is not a word about the massacre.

Eureka was once the busiest port between San Francisco and
Portland. Prodigious quantities of timber were stripped from the
inland ranges and shipped out across Humboldt Bay, much of it to
Japan and other parts of Asia. In recent years, the old port has
remodeled itself as a destination for weekend holidaymakers, full of
puce- and buff-colored Victorian inns, cappuccino cafés, and the
sort of shops that sell stylish chocolates, music boxes, and ecologi-
cally correct camping supplies. It is soothing, even sedative, this
sanitized ideal of the past, promising a history without consequence, as if the Indians had never been there at all.

The truth, or at least part of it, lies buried in the microfilm
archive of the public library on I Street, in the blurry pages of the
Humboldt Times for the last week in February 1860. Straining, the

eye searches through columns of debate over the Southern states' imminent secession, through the ads for saddles and harnesses, and for plows newly arrived on the Boston clipper. Finally, there it is: "It may well be imagined that this unexpected attack on the diggers in their town produced unbearable excitement here Sunday morning . . ." "Digger," at that time, was the pejorative of choice for Indians on the Far Western frontier; it was no coincidence that it sounded much like "nigger," and it carried the same freight of contempt.

Sometime in the foggy predawn hours of February 25, a group of white men climbed into a boat at the foot of K Street. There may have been as many as seven men or as few as three; the reports were never clear about that. A mile across the water, on the island, the Wiyots had been dancing.

Little is known about the Wiyots. They were a small tribe of sedentary people who wove basketry skullcaps, traveled in red-wood canoes, fished for trout, salmon, and shellfish. Indian Island was the navel of their universe. Although whites had been flooding into Eureka for a decade, crowding the Wiyots, nudging them, occasionally killing them, the Indians still returned to the island year after year, drawn by the tug of the absolute, to perform the annual rite of renewal that shaped their collective identity. They awaited disaster with what, in hindsight, seems like eerie passivity. The dance had already gone on for a week, slow and balletic, a prayer in motion. Now they slept, without sentries, secure perhaps in the profoundly deluded conviction that the earth had been balanced, made stable for another cycle of the seasons.

The whites landed on a deserted part of the island and slipped silently through the cypress groves. When they reached the Wiyot village, they went methodically from hut to hut, killing every Indian they found. They killed indiscriminately, men, women, and children. Mostly they killed with hatchets and Bowie knives. Those who fled were slaughtered in the mud and surf. Others clumped instinctively, helplessly together and were hacked to death where they stood. A mile away in Eureka, people heard the Wiyots die. Robert Gunther, who would one day buy the island, recalled years later: "A scream went up from many voices, and I could plainly hear it was on Indian Island, for it was perfectly dark and still. Hearing no more, I went to bed again."

The next morning, curious whites ventured to the scene. Bret

Harte, then a newspaperman across the bay in Arcata, was among them. "Here was a mother fatally wounded hugging the mutilated carcass of her dying infant to her bosom; there a poor child two or three years old, with its ear and scalp torn from the side of its little head," Harte wrote.

> Here a father frantic with grief over the bloody corpses of his four little children and his wife; there a brother and a sister weeping and trying to soothe with cold water the pallid face of a dying relative. There an aged female still living and sitting up, though covered with ghastly wounds and dyed in her own blood; there a living infant by its own dead mother desirous of drawing nourishment from a source that had ceased to flow. The wounded, dead and dying were found all around and in every lodge the skulls and frames of women and children cleft with axes and hatchets, and stabbed with knives, and the brains of an infant oozing from its broken head to the ground.

In the space of a few hours, the world of the Wiyots had come to an end, cataclysmically and totally. Between sixty and seventy Indians were killed on the island. Another two hundred or more were massacred simultaneously on the south spit of Humboldt Bay and at the mouth of the Eel River, in what were presumably coordinated attacks designed to exterminate the Wiyots at a single stroke.

The immediate reason for the massacre is still a mystery. At the time, some whites maintained, not very plausibly, that the "hoarse, guttural sounds, interspersed with hideous yells" of the Wiyot rite sifting across the bay scared the citizens of Eureka into believing that an attack on the town was imminent. There is a second possibility. Just three days before the massacre, a certain Captain Moore had purchased the island from another white man. He may have seen practical advantage in removing its occupants. A grand jury was eventually impaneled to investigate the events on the island; it blandly reported that "after a strict examination of all witnesses, nothing was elicited to enlighten us as to the perpetrators." Nevertheless, for years afterward, the killers were pointed out on the streets of Eureka. They were, it was said, "men of intelligence," and nearly all men of family. The ringleader may have been an Indian-hating rancher named Larrabee, who had once built a raft, piled the corpses of ten Indians on it, and floated it down the Eel River with a placard addressed "To the bleeding hearts of Rohersville."

Staring at the blurred reels of microfilm, one struggles to make sense of the horror. What could the Wiyots have done to inspire such horrific retaliation? No one, in the weeks preceding the massacre, had accused them of any particular crime. And what kind of men could have coolly hatcheted families on their own hearths? What could they have been thinking as they raged through the Wiyot village that night? These "men of intelligence" were not, by most accounts, psychopaths or the shiftless louts of the frontier. They were good, settling Americans, who committed murder within earshot of an entire city. One would be grateful to be able to write it off as a random, tragic event, a terrible accident at the margin of American history. But it is not that. It lies at the core of things.

What the historian Robert E. Berkhofer, Jr., has aptly called the "white man's Indian"—the Indian of the Euro-American imagination—is as old as the continent's discovery. The continent that Christopher Columbus stumbled upon in 1492 was, to Europeans, a terra incognita inhabited by a vast congeries of unknown, and virtually unknowable, peoples. There were literally thousands of distinct native societies, each with its own unique history, its own systems of ethics and aesthetics, and its own cosmology, each speaking a language that, as often as not, was completely incomprehensible to groups that lived just a few miles away. Few of them were organized in their modern tribal form, and fewer still were known to each other by the names that we associate with them today. Some were migratory hunters, others tillers of the soil, others fishermen or communities of traders. Some inhabited cities that contained thousands of inhabitants; others scratched salt deserts for roots.

In an effort to explain to themselves this unexpected and bewildering human landscape, Europeans rummaged through the old trunks of their own mythic tradition. At times, Columbus seemed to believe that he had found the terrestrial paradise, and he assured his patrons at the Spanish court that the New World's inhabitants were "very gentle and without knowledge of what is evil; nor do they murder or steal." A few years later, Pietro Martire d'Anghiera described the natives of the newfound lands as "living in that golden world of which the old writers speak so much." As time went on, such fantasies became increasingly elaborate in the minds of Europeans who had themselves never visited the Americas. By the end of the sixteenth century, Montaigne had canonized the Indian for all time as the quintessential Natural Man, who existed in a state "so pure and simple," with "no kind of traffike, no knowledge of letters, no intelligence of numbers, no name of magistrate, nor of politike superiorite; no use of service, of riches or of povertie; no contracts, no successions, no partitions, no occupation but idle."

The Indian became the archetype of mankind's infancy at a time when European thinkers who hadn't the slightest idea of the difference between a Hottentot and Hoopa were attempting to define the meaning of civilization itself. "In the beginning all the World was America," John Locke asserted with remarkable self-assurance. As time passed, the invented Indian was made to serve the arbitrary notion that man had been born noble and good and had been corrupted only by monarchy and the constraints of sophisticated European society. "In proportion as he becomes sociable and a slave to others," Jean Jacques Rousseau wrote, "he becomes weak, fearful, mean-spirited, and his soft and effeminate way of living at once completes the enervation of his strength and of his courage." By contrast, "savage man" was a paradigm of pure instinct, of unity with nature, pristine and authentic, a reproach to the artifice of cultivated life, living proof that humankind's essential nature was one of instinctive harmony and goodwill. "If I consider him, in a word, such as he must have issued from the hands of nature," Rousseau opined, "I see an animal less strong than some, and less active than others, but, upon the whole, the most advantageously organized of any."

Like all versions of the "white man's Indian," Rousseau's idealizing flattened out the multitudinous realities of actual Indian communities, blurring their individuality and trapping them permanently in European fantasy:

> His imagination paints nothing to him; his heart asks nothing from him. His moderate wants are so easily supplied with what he finds everywhere ready to his hand, and he stands at such a distance from the degree of knowledge requisite to covet more, that he can neither have foresight nor curiosity. The spectacle of nature, by growing quite familiar to him, becomes at last equally indifferent. It is constantly the same order, constantly the same revolutions; he has not sense enough to feel surprise at the sight of the greatest wonders; and it is not in his mind that we must look for that philosophy, which man must have to know how to observe once, what he has every day seen. His soul, which nothing disturbs, gives itself up entirely to the consciousness of its

actual existence, without any thought of even the nearest futurity; and his projects, equally confined with his views, scarce extend to the end of the day.

This was not a description of a human being but of a creature of the forest, a stag or a bear, a quarry.

There was a second, equally powerful, darker archetypal vision of the Indian. In counterpoint to the "gentle" natives who foreshadowed all the "noble savages" of later folklore, Columbus placed the terrible Caribs, who "go to all the islands and eat the people they are able to capture" and whose name in one of its varied forms has given us the word "cannibal." Neither Columbus nor any other explorer ever found the elusive Caribs, but they hovered for generations on the edge of early narratives, serpents in paradise, the very antithesis of Arcadian innocence. Upon this imaginative foundation, the British settlers of North America added a distinctly apocalyptic edifice of their own. A Virginia poet writing in the aftermath of the Jamestown colony's war against the Powhatans, in 1622, declared the Indians to be irrevocably "Rooted in Evill, and opposed in Good; errors of nature, of inhumane Birth, The very dregs, garbage and spanne of Earth." In New England, zealots such as Cotton Mather encouraged the Puritans to regard the Indian as a principal actor in the cosmic drama that governed even the smallest details of life, a "spetiall instrument sent of God" to punish errant souls in the eternal struggle between good and evil. In such a climate, killing Indians became not merely warfare but the cleansing of sin itself. Although wartime atrocities were perpetrated against both the colonists and the Indians, those committed by whites were usually forgotten, while the natives' were long remembered and were attributed less to the awful nature of colonial war than to the moral failings of Indians as a race.

The degree of violence that was woven into the texture of early frontier life fairly boggles the mind of our, in some ways, far more delicate age. In the 1650s, Dutch colonists brought back eighty decapitated Indian heads from a massacre and used them as kickballs in the streets of New Amsterdam. In 1711, the Virginia House of Burgesses appropriated 20,000 pounds "for exterpating *[sic]* all Indians without distinction of Friends or Enemys." An English traveler in the northern colonies casually recorded in his diary, in 1760, that "some People have an Indian's Skin for a Tobacco

Pouch," while a Revolutionary War soldier campaigning against the Iroquois could note with equal dispassion that he had been given a pair of boot-tops made from the freshly skinned legs of two enemy braves.

To be sure, Indian hating was by no means either universal or unquestioned. Particularly during the early decades of European colonization, Indians and whites lived in a mostly peaceful, if often uneasy, patchwork of communities scattered along the frontier. From the earliest colonial times, there were intermittent attempts to gather Indians into "praying towns," where they were exhorted to know the Christian God through constant prayer. Roger Williams, the founder of the Rhode Island colony, was among the first in a long and enduring line of liberal idealists who actively opposed the racism of the frontier. Throughout his life, Williams continued to agitate for Indian land rights so successfully that purchase of Indian land, on the Dutch model, gradually became accepted practice up and down the coast in the English colonies. In the midst of the barbarism of the Pequot War of 1636, it took considerable courage for him to write:

> Boast not proud English of thy birth and blood,
> Thy brother Indian is by birth as good.
> Of one blood God made him, and thee, and all,
> As wise, as fair, as strong, as personal.

Despite the apologetics of modern romantics who like to portray Indians of the past as universally harmless ecologists, neither warfare nor sadistic cruelty was a white man's monopoly. Even as white settlers pushed inland from the Atlantic seaboard, the Iroquois were waging their own ruthless war of extermination against the Hurons, the Sioux were building an empire on the Great Plains at the bloody expense of numerous other tribes that had the misfortune to lie in their path, and the Navajos were aggressively colonizing the lands of the agrarian Hopis. Indians commonly considered only their own tribes to be the "Real People" and disdained others as "dogs," "snakes," or "man-eaters"; the Catawbas of South Carolina called the Tuscaroras "short-tailed eunuchs" and white colonists "Nothings," while the name "Comanche" derives from a Ute epithet meaning "Those Who Are Always Against Us," and "Apache" from the Pueblo word for "enemy." Although popular convention now blames whites for the invention of scalping, words for scalping and more imaginative forms of dismemberment existed in many Indian languages from the earliest times; for instance, the Timucuas of Florida collected arms and legs as well as scalps, while the tribes of the St. Lawrence stretched the skin of dead men's faces on hoops, like parchment. Whites, it is true, turned what may have been a custom with sacred associations into a commercial activity when they began offering bounties for enemy scalps.

Although many modern polemicists call upon Americans to regard the nation's treatment of the Indians as a pattern of deliberate "genocide," the physical extermination of Native Americans was never an official policy of the United States government. With more realism than racism, the new republic initially worried less about ridding itself of Indians than about how to protect them from the depredations of its own citizens. As early as 1788, Secretary of War Henry Knox had condemned in no uncertain terms the "unjustifiable conduct" of settlers whose actions had "been dictated by the avaricious desire of obtaining the fertile lands possessed by the . . . Indians." Laws were enacted to expressly prohibit whites from intruding on Indian land. When, for example, the Cherokees ceded large tracts of North Carolina to the United States in 1791, the Treaty of Holston guaranteed, in language similar to that employed in many other treaties of the time: "If any citizen of the United States, or other person not being an Indian, shall settle on any of the Cherokees' lands, such person shall forfeit the protection of the United States, and the Cherokees may punish him, or not, as they please."

But settlers flooded across the Appalachians as if treaties never existed. As Secretary of State, Thomas Jefferson at one point even contemplated sending federal troops against them. "Unless such crimes shall be punished in an exemplary manner," Knox presciently wrote to the governor of the Tennessee territory, "it will be vain for the government to make further attempts to establish any plan or system for the administration of Indian Affairs founded on the principles of moderation and justice." But the unbridled democracy of the frontier brooked little interference from Washington. "No people will sit and starve for want of land to work, when a neighboring nation has much more than they can make use of," declared John Sevier, a particularly combative leader of the Tennessee whites. Indeed, in a very real and tragic sense, it was democracy itself that would devastate the tribes, the proud contempt of ordinary Americans for central government in general and for the policies of politicians remote from the homespun greed of the frontier.

It is a mistake to imagine that white customs were always forced on unwilling Indians. Most Indians were also realists; as encroaching white settlement disrupted their old way of life, they often sought aid from whites who were willing to provide them with education and help them adapt to new technology. In 1791, the Seneca chief Cornplanter wrote, with both dignity and pragmatism, to friendly Quakers in Philadelphia, asking for the equivalent of foreign development aid:

> The Seneca Nation see, that the great Spirit intends that they shall not continue to live by hunting, & they look around on every side, and inquire who it is that shall teach them what is best for them to do. Your fathers have delt [sic] fairly and honestly with our fathers, and they have charged us to remember it and we think it right to tell you, that we wish our Children to be taught the same principles by which your Fathers were guided in their Councils.

National leaders struggled, at least at first, to craft a humane policy, predicated on the conviction that, given a chance, Indians would shed their "barbarism" and readily embrace the fruits of European culture. In an 1802 message, Jefferson, who was by then President, advised the Miamis, Potawatomis, and Weas of the Northwest Territory: "We shall with great pleasure see your people become disposed to cultivate the earth, to raise herds of useful animals and to spin and weave, for their food and clothing. These resources are certain, and they will never disappoint you, while those of hunting may fail, and expose your women and children to the miseries of hunger and cold." As the nineteenth century progressed, Jefferson's confidence in the civilizing power of agriculture would eventually become the most enduring cornerstone of federal Indian policy. It was a formula that, almost from the start, became intertwined with religious faith.

The Indians were destined "miserably to waste away," Jedidiah Morse of the Northern Missionary Society of New York warned in 1822, "unless we change our policy towards them; unless effective measures be taken to bring them over this awful gulf, to the solid and safe ground of civilization." This was the age of the Great Awakening; Protestant evangelism fused with the Jeffersonian ideal of the yeoman farmer in a vision that saw the conversion of the

Indian to property ownership as not merely a cultural but a spiritual transformation. Federal funds were allocated to supply tribes with plows, looms, and spinning wheels; with domestic animals; with carpenters to demonstrate cabin-building and blacksmiths to show them how to forge tools. Christian missionaries were encouraged, and later employed, to carry out the government's policy. "Those who come to Christ and join the church turn to agriculture and raising stock, keeping cattle, hogs and fowls," wrote David Zeisberger, who proselytized among the Delawares and who was but one among many remarkable men and women motivated to commit their lives to work among the Indians by a deep belief in the common membership of all peoples in the family of God. While this reflected yet another kind of white man's vision that was as arbitrary in its assumptions as Rousseau's noble savage or the poet's "errors of nature," it did at least promise that in return for abandoning their identity and traditions Indians would be received with respect into the Christian community and made American.

All along the frontier, Quakers and Methodists, Moravians and Baptists established model settlements that were explicitly intended to indoctrinate Indians, by means of example and persuasion, in the ways of settled Anglo-American life. It was the liberalism of its day, the confident forerunner of recurrent attempts, which persisted well into the 1950s, to assimilate Indians to the mores of mainstream America. The mysteries of property and private enterprise, the missionaries and their spiritual successors were firmly convinced, were the ultimate gifts that Americans had to offer. Few looked to the values inherent in Indian life itself. But churchmen such as Morse had reason to be optimistic; the Cherokees had already shown the way.

There are few places in the United States more poignant than New Echota. It lies about two hours from Atlanta, in the low red, pine-forested hills of northwest Georgia, hard by the sluggish flood of the Coosawattee. During a brief and extraordinary moment in history, this was the capital of the Cherokee Nation. Today it is a forlorn and lonely place, a monument to frontier greed and stupidity. Shallow troughs in an open field mark the grid of disappeared streets. Four or five buildings stand scattered among them. There is a farmstead, a tavern made of chinked logs, the clapboard courthouse that housed the Supreme Court, the whitewashed office of

Elias Boudinot's splendid newspaper, the *Cherokee Phoenix,* raised up on stone pilings. These are all reconstructions, modern apostrophes to the destruction of a nation that, had it been allowed to survive, would have changed American history and would almost certainly have ordained a very different fate for the nation's native peoples.

At the start of the nineteenth century, tribes almost everywhere east of the Mississippi were abandoning wigwams for cabins, buckskins for cotton clothes, and the hunt for the plow, but nothing quite compared to the speed and extent of the Cherokee transformation. Before New Echota's establishment, in 1817, the Cherokees were a pastoral people who spoke three separate languages and lived in more than sixty villages scattered from present-day Alabama through Georgia and Tennessee, as far as North Carolina. Now, in less than a generation, they had self-consciously redefined their nature as Indians, electing their own legislature, establishing a free press, inventing an alphabet in which they had begun to print their own literature, and cautiously beginning to trade their traditional religious practices for Christianity. To be sure, support for such innovations was by no means universal among the Cherokees. Full-bloods, in particular, were uneasy at the prospect of what in a later age would have been called wholesale Americanization. Missionaries were warned that the white man's religion would not be welcome in Cherokee country unless it was accompanied by education in the three Rs.

Although New Echota lay beyond the frontier of the United States, it did not lack sophistication. Wealthy Cherokees ate from Chinese porcelain and wore frock coats cut by a tailor recently arrived from New York; shoppers could purchase sugar from St. Croix, indigo from New Orleans, or the newest novel by Sir Walter Scott. By 1826, the nation, according to Boudinot, boasted "762 looms; 2,488 spinning wheels; 172 waggons, 2,943 ploughs; 10 saw-mills; 31 grist-mills &c," as well as eighteen schools and a similar number of ferries. Cherokee farmers who had taken up Euro-American farming methods cultivated orchards of apples and peaches. Others operated toll roads, blacksmith shops and taverns, and plantations that exploited the labor of black slaves. Under Boudinot's stewardship the *Cherokee Phoenix* published 733,800 pages of Bibles, hymnals, tribal laws, broadsheets, and novels in the new Cherokee "syllabary," along with a newspaper that carried

Boudinot's own eloquently written articles on Cherokee government as well as Washington debates, foreign news, Christian hymns, and brief moral tales. Visitors constantly remarked on the system of well-maintained public roads and on the orderliness of council meetings. Reform was everywhere in the air: polygamy had been outlawed, along with the custom of blood vengeance and the entrenched practice of putting aged persons to death for witchcraft. A traveler from the North reported, in 1830, "A spirit pervades the nation for amelioration, and in pursuit of economical and intellectual improvements and attainments." He found well-attended schools where students learned English, the New Testament, grammar, and geography. "Some have received instruction in higher grades of learning, with whom you can discourse rationally on most subjects."

Most far-reaching of all, the Cherokees had systematically remolded their loose tribal structure of clan chiefs into a modern government on the model of the United States itself. The Constitution that they adopted in 1827 self-consciously echoed that of their neighbor: "We, the Representatives of the people of the Cherokee Nation, in Convention assembled, in order to establish justice, ensure tranquillity, promote our common welfare, and secure to ourselves and our posterity the blessings of liberty . . ." Four delegates from each of eight districts were elected to a lower house, the National Council, which voted for the twelve members of the upper house, the National Committee, which in turn selected the three members of the executive branch, the Principal Chief, his assistant, and a treasurer. Sheriffs were appointed to execute the decisions of the eight district courts; appeals were taken to the Superior Court, which met every autumn in New Echota. The Constitution also provided for an independent judiciary, taxation, trial by jury, and protection from unreasonable search and seizure; true to the increasingly systematic racism of the age, it also explicitly excluded blacks and mulattos from citizenship.

If the Cherokees as a whole reassured liberal whites that all Indians might one day become civilized, Elias Boudinot was the very embodiment of the new Indian man: Christian, well mannered, brilliant, and stripped of Indian ambiguities. Boudinot, who eventually took the name of a white benefactor, was born as Kilikeena, or "Buck," to an influential Cherokee family in 1804. At the urging of Moravian missionaries, he was sent north, much as the future leaders of African and Asian countries are sent to Harvard or MIT today, to the school of the American Board of Foreign Missions in Connecticut, which trained young men "from amidst the darkness and corruptions and miseries of paganism to be sent back to their respective nations with the blessings of civilized and christianized society." There Boudinot read history, geography, philosophy, and Virgil, learned surveying, and corresponded on lunar eclipses with Jedidiah Morse, who taught astronomy at Yale. As a vivid symbol of his commitment to assimilation, Boudinot married a white woman, much to the shock of her Connecticut neighbors and to bigoted Cherokees, as well. After returning home to Georgia, he immediately threw himself into the defense of his homeland, as pressure steadily mounted on the Cherokees to open their land to white settlement.

In 1826, the nation's modernizing leaders sent Boudinot on a journey through the United States seeking support for the Cherokee cause. The speech he gave was later published as a pamphlet entitled "An Address to the Whites." "It needs not the display of language to prove to the minds of good men, that the Indians are susceptible of attainments necessary to the formation of polished society," Boudinot declared. "It needs not the power of arguement on the nature of man, to silence forever the remark that 'it is the purpose of the Almighty that the Indians should be exterminated.' It needs only that the world should know what we have done in the last few years, to foresee what yet we may do with the assistance of our white brethren, and that of the common Parent of us all."

Boudinot was a true visionary, with an enthusiasm rooted in both the evangelical optimism of the time and the self-confidence born from his own remarkable personal transformation. He was convinced that Cherokee survival depended on the abandonment of traditional culture, and for Indian tribes as a whole, he saw, coldly, only two alternatives: to become "civilized and happy" or extinct. His optimism is still infectious across a century and a half. "What are the prospects of the Cherokees? Are they not indeed glorious, compared to that deep darkness in which the nobler qualities of their souls have slept? Yes, methinks I can view my native country, rising from the ashes of her degradation, wearing her purified and beautiful garments, and taking her seat with the nations of the earth."

Boudinot saw the future of the Cherokees as irrevocably tied to the United States in a mutually beneficial relationship.

In times of peace she will plead the common liberties of America. In times of war her intrepid sons will sacrifice their lives in your defence. And because she will be useful to you in coming time, she asks you to assist her in her present struggles. She asks not for greatness; she seeks not wealth; she pleads only for assistance to become respectable as a nation, to enlighten and ennoble her sons, and to ornament her daughters with modesty and virtue.

It was a defining moment. With its commitment to democratic institutions, self-sufficiency, and private enterprise, the Cherokee Nation offered a precedent for change on Indian terms, and it might well have set the model for the natural evolution of other tribes, in partnership with the United States. Boudinot understood how much hung on the Cherokee experiment. "If the Cherokee Nation fail in her struggle, if she die away, then all hopes are blasted, and falls the fabric of Indian civilization." But if the Cherokees completed their transformation into a modern state, other tribes would surely follow, eventually shaping the West into "one continuous abode of enlightened, free and happy people."

But of course it never happened.

The United States had signed treaties with the Cherokees that guaranteed the nation's territorial integrity in return for a series of land cessions in Tennessee, North Carolina, and Georgia. But in 1802, the federal government cut a fateful deal. To get Georgia to agree to relinquish its claim to lands in present-day Alabama and Mississippi, Washington promised to remove all Indians from the state, as a prelude to white settlement. There were well-known precedents for such a solution. After the defeat of the last Stuart King of Scotland, in 1745, tens of thousands of Scots had been evicted from the Highlands and forced to emigrate to the American colonies. Thousands of French-speaking Acadians had also been uprooted from their homes in Canada and removed to Louisiana following the British victory in the French and Indian War.

The idea of systematic Indian removal originated with Thomas Jefferson, who at one point had actually contemplated a constitutional amendment that would provide for the exchange of Indian land east of the Mississippi for tracts within the newly acquired Louisiana Purchase. Not surprisingly, the idea steadily gained in popularity among land-hungry whites. Removal, President James Monroe asserted in 1817, would facilitate the nation's westward advance, for "the hunter or savage state requires a greater extent of territory to sustain it, than is compatible with the progress and just claims of civilized life, and must yield to it." But the prospect of uprooting the Cherokees and other tribes that had adopted the American prescription for civilization produced considerable unease. To use force against the "civilized tribes," Monroe asserted, would be "revolting to humanity and entirely unjustifiable." The Georgians were adamant. "There is no alternative between their removal beyond the state of Georgia and their extinction," an official state proclamation declared.

In the meantime, Washington dithered. Then, in 1828, gold was discovered at Dahlonega, in the heart of the Cherokee Nation. Prospectors flooded in from all over the world, overrunning Cherokee land with virtual impunity. Later that same year, the old Indian fighter Andrew Jackson was elected President; a month after his inauguration, Georgia passed a law formally annexing Cherokee country. In his first state of the union address, Jackson proposed the creation of an "ample district west of the Mississippi" where removed Indians might constitute "an interesting commonwealth, destined to perpetuate the race and to attest the humanity and justice of this Government." To force the Cherokees from their homes, if one believed the President, would be a veritable act of philanthropy.

In January of 1830, Georgia declared Cherokee laws null and void and banned Indians from testifying in cases involving whites, ensuring that the Cherokees could not legally protect themselves from the seizure of their land. They were also forbidden to engage "in digging for gold in said land, and taking therefrom great amounts of value, thereby appropriating riches to themselves." Other state laws outlawed meetings of the Cherokee council and prohibited Indians from gathering for any reason, including religious services, except for the purpose of ceding land.

"A few thousand half civilized men, both indisposed and incompetent to the faithful discharge of the duties of citizenship, and scattered over a territory so extensive, can never enjoy the inestimable blessing of civil government," Georgia's governor, Wilson Lumpkin, contemptuously declared, articulating for perhaps the first time the principle that was meant to justify the greed and violence of frontier whites for the rest of the century. "Our government over that territory in its present condition, in order to be efficient, must partake largely of a military character, and consequently must be more or less arbitrary and oppressive in character."

There was eloquent opposition to Georgia's ambitions. In a series of widely published letters, the chairman of the Board of Foreign Missions, Jeremiah Evarts, insisted that the Cherokees and other Indians be recognized "as human beings, entitled to receive the same treatment as Englishmen, Frenchmen, or ourselves." He added, "Long continued encroachments do not furnish a justification of those who make them, but they prove that the oppressors may possibly not perceive the true nature of their oppressive acts." It was a subtle perception, but unfortunately far ahead of its time. "If one man, however ill-deserving, may be removed from the protection of the law, it is impossible to tell who will be removed next," Evarts warned.

In the spring of 1830, Congress passed Jackson's removal bill. From a political standpoint, it was not ungenerous. The bill appropriated $500,000 to reimburse the Cherokees for improvements they had made on their lands, for emigration costs, and for financial support for the first year after removal. The only problem was, the Cherokees did not want to go.

What the Cherokees did then was utterly unprecedented. They sued the State of Georgia in the United States Supreme Court. They contended that as a sovereign nation like any other they were not subject to Georgia law and further that Georgia's acts were void because they contradicted federal treaties guaranteeing the tribe's territory in perpetuity. The decision that Chief Justice John Marshall handed down in *Cherokee Nation v. Georgia* affirmed that the Cherokees, and implicitly every other Indian tribe, were "a distinct political society, separated from others, capable of managing its own affairs and governing itself." Marshall nevertheless denied the Cherokees' plea for an injunction, arguing, with a tortuous ambivalence that has forever plagued attempts to define the nation's relations with the Indians, that tribes were not quite independent nations. Rather, they were "in a state of pupilage," Marshall wrote. "Their relation to the United States resembles that of a ward to his guardian."

The Cherokees once again sent their most eloquent spokesmen to beg for support in the North. In Philadelphia, Elias Boudinot's friend John Ridge declared: "You asked us to throw off the hunter and warrior state: We did so—you asked us to form a republican government: We did so—adopting your own as a model. You asked us to cultivate the earth, and learn the mechanic arts: We did so. You asked us to learn to read: We did so. You asked us to cast away our idols, and worship your God: We did so."

Scenting victory, however, Georgia forbade whites to reside in Cherokee country without a license. The state's aim was to expel Northern missionaries who had encouraged the Cherokees in their struggle. Two who refused to leave, Samuel Worcester and Elizur Butler, were arrested, with Butler marched to prison chained to a horse, with a padlock around his neck. Both men were sentenced to four years at hard labor in the state prison at Milledgeville. The missionaries, in turn, sued the State of Georgia.

The Supreme Court's decision in *Worcester v. Georgia* was one of the most important ever handed down in Indian affairs, and it continues to shape the relationship of Indian tribes to the United States government up to the present day. Indeed, it has become increasingly relevant in recent years as tribes have demanded greater sovereignty and de facto autonomy within the United States. The questions that the Court sought to answer still haunt the United States in the 1990s: Are Indian tribes "nations"? Or are they something else entirely? How do they fit into the United States? Do they fit at all? What, ultimately, is the nature of their relationship to the United States?

In March 1832, the Court ordered Georgia to release Worcester, in a decision that dramatically surpassed its earlier one. The Cherokee Nation, Marshall wrote, was "a distinct community, occupying its own territory, with boundaries accurately described, in which the laws of Georgia can have no force, and which the citizens of Georgia have no right to enter, but with the assent of the Cherokees themselves, or in conformity with treaties, and with the acts of Congress." The decision was a complete vindication of the Indian position and a ringing affirmation of the Cherokee Nation's right to exist. It should have meant that the United States would have to find ways to accommodate Indian nations and their rights as it grew westward. There was widespread elation in Cherokee country. But it was short-lived.

What happened after that is well known. Georgia simply ignored the Court. Jackson announced blandly that "the decision of the supreme court has fell still born, and they find that they cannot coerce Georgia to yield to its mandate." In private, the President was reportedly more blunt: "John Marshall has made his decision; let him enforce it now if he can." When Ridge and a delegation of stunned Cherokees begged him for an explanation, Jackson assured them of his friendship, then suggested they go home and tell their people that "their only hope of relief was in abandoning their country and removing to the West."

Although the Cherokees' defeat was now inevitable, the political struggle dragged on for a few years more. It tore the Cherokees apart. Boudinot, Ridge, and the other modernizers finally conceded that the nation could no longer survive in Georgia and signed Jackson's removal treaty. Chief John Ross, although he was of mainly Scottish descent and lived in the style of a white aristocrat himself, won the support of traditionalists by adamantly rejecting compromise with Washington. However, without even perfunctory consultation with the Cherokees, the State of Georgia parceled out Cherokee lands to whites in a grand lottery. The inhabitants of New Echota quite literally found white settlers moving into their cabins, slaughtering their livestock, and harvesting their crops. Disillusioned Cherokee traditionalists procrastinated, hoping desperately for a reversal of Washington's policy and denouncing Boudinot and his allies as traitors for even contemplating abandonment of their ancestral lands. In the end, seven thousand federal troops were mobilized to flush the Cherokees from their cabins, herding them at bayonet point into stockades, where some two thousand died from disease even before the march west began. In the autumn of 1838, they started for Oklahoma. Another four thousand Cherokees, 25 percent of the population, died en route from illness and exposure during the grueling winter march that has come to be known as the Trail of Tears. White farmers plowed up New Echota and planted corn. Never again did an Indian tribe venture to sue for its right to exist.

On the morning of June 22, 1839, Elias Boudinot was at his new home near present-day Tahlequah, Oklahoma. Several Cherokees approached him and asked for medicine. As he turned his back to lead them to the dispensary, they set upon him with tomahawks and left him for dead. It was as much an execution as murder. By advocating the cession of tribal land, Boudinot had committed a capital crime against Cherokee law.

As long as the Cherokee Nation survived in Georgia, the future of the tribes remained a dialogue among at least putative equals. That dialogue now abruptly ended. Not until our own time would the United States government again permit tribes even to pretend to have a voice in deciding their own fate. The fierce Plains wars of the 1870s were still to come, of course, along with the final closing in of the frontier, the penning-up on reservations, and the disaster of allotment. But with the destruction of New Echota, the political fate of Indian tribes far removed from the red-dirt hills of north Georgia had already been sealed. All the rest was, in a sense, anticlimax.

It was now obvious to almost everyone but Indians themselves that independent tribal life was doomed; it was less clear, but no less significant, that living Indians were increasingly to be consigned to the twilight realm of the white man's myths. Even as the Cherokee drama unfolded, popular writers were revising the Indian into yet another idealized fantasy that, like all those that had gone before, owed more to hoary European motifs than to close observation of actual Indians. *The Last of the Mohicans,* for example, published in 1826, has perhaps done more to give shape to our basic images of the Indian than any other single book in American history. In it, James Fenimore Cooper describes young Uncas, the ultimate incarnation of the noble savage, as "graceful and unrestrained in the attitudes and movement of nature" and handsome as "some precious relic of the Grecian chisel, to which life had been imparted by the intervention of a miracle." How much more complex a tale Cooper might have told, however, had he cared to imagine the moral dilemma of the venomous Magua, who like all Hurons of that time would have been a devout Catholic, or the mores of the Mohicans, who, rather than Rousseauian men of nature, would probably have been Protestants from the Indian "praying town" near Stockbridge.

By then it was widely assumed by Americans that Indians were destined to vanish before the onrush of civilization, a view of things that conveniently allowed cynicism to blend with sentimentality: "It is melancholy to see them melting away so rapidly; but it does not appear to be intended that civilization should prevent it," wrote a naval officer who witnessed the wholesale extermination of coastal tribes in the Pacific Northwest. Even as entire tribes succumbed to the epidemics that usually ran ahead of white settlement or to the occasional massacres that followed it, whites remote from the frontier pictured them perishing as gracefully as "snow before the vernal influence" or like "the leaves of the forest that are swept away by the autumn winds." It was as if the Indians' disappearance were the result of some force completely beyond the human power to stay, like a tidal wave or a change of seasons.

In the meantime, attitudes toward live Indians steadily hardened, and not only among hooligans on the frontier. The Harvard historian Francis Parkman, who shaped generations of Americans' perceptions of westward expansion, wrote of his encounters with the Sioux during a journey west in 1847, "So alien to himself do they appear, that having breathed for a few months the magic air of this region, he begins to look upon them as a troublesome and dangerous species of wild beast, and if expedient, he could shoot them with as little compunction as they themselves would experience after performing the same function upon him." Horace Greeley, the influential editor of the *New York Tribune,* who urged the young men of America to "go West," would be even more scathing: "Their arts, wars, treaties, alliances, habitations, crafts, properties, commerce, comforts, all belong to the very lowest and rudest ages of human existence . . . These people must die out—there is no help for them. God has given the earth to those who will subdue and cultivate it, and it is vain to struggle against his righteous decree."

By the time of the California gold rush, the disappearance of the Indian seemed a truth so absolute that few even thought to question it. Within two years after the discovery of gold at Sutter's Mill, in 1848, 120,000 white men had flooded into California. Extreme and pervasive violence was a fact of life: Mutual of New York ceased issuing life insurance for anyone headed for the goldfields, having ascertained that 25 percent of its policyholders who went there met violent deaths. The goldseekers were men without roots in the land, without women of their own, without accountability of any kind on a lawless frontier. They seized Indian lands without even the pretense of legality, abruptly diverted rivers to serve placer mines, and wiped out the game upon which Indian communities depended for survival. When such men spoke of the "Indian problem," they usually meant the existence of the Indians themselves. Indian killing became a way of life, a form of reliable, state-subsidized off-season work for ranchers and unemployed miners; between 1850 and 1859, the federal government reimbursed the State of California $924,259 for what was basically freelance murder.

In April of 1852, miners at Orleans Bar, "after a meeting to discuss the Indian problem, voted to kill on sight all Indians having guns," a local newspaper reported without comment. The next month, near Weaverville, 153 Wintuns were slaughtered in reprisal for killing five cows that belonged to a white man. In 1853, at Yontoket, several hundred Tolowas were murdered in the midst of their harvest dance. A survivor described it: "The whitemen built a huge fire and threw in our sacred ceremonial dresses, the regalia, and our feathers, and the flames grew higher. Then they threw in the babies, many of them were still alive." The following year, the rest of the Tolowas were exterminated, because one of them had stolen a white man's horse. "Cold-blooded Indian killing being considered honorable, shooting Indians and murdering even squaws and children that have been domesticated for months and years, without a moment's warning and with as little compunction as they would rid themselves of a dog," an Army officer assigned to Fort Humboldt noted, with a trace of unease. Dryden Laycock, an early settler in Round Valley, claimed that between 1856 and 1860, settlers went out "two or three times a week" and killed "on an average, fifty or sixty Indians on a trip." There was no redress for any of this, of course. Until the 1880s, California courts barred any kind of testimony from "Indians, or persons having one-fourth or more Indian blood in an action in which a white person was a party."

Professional slave hunters raided Indian villages with impunity, seizing women and children for sale to miners and to brothels in the gold rush towns. In the mid-1850s, a pubescent girl sold for about $300 and smaller children for as little as $50. Not even reservations were safe. "Some of the agents, and nearly all of the employees, we are informed, of one of these reservations at least, are daily and nightly engaged in kidnapping the younger portion of the females for the vilest of purposes," a San Francisco newspaper reported in 1856. "The wives and daughters of the defenseless Diggers are prostituted before the very eyes of their husbands and fathers, [but] they dare not resent the insult, or even complain of the hideous outrage." When immigrant women finally began to appear in the settlements, coastal Indians were heard to sing: "Thank God white women have come, they'll rape us no more . . ." Raiders also sold large numbers of Indians into the more southerly counties as agricultural slaves. For more than a decade, California law allowed whites to indenture Indians for up to sixteen years upon payment of a two-dollar fee. As many as ten thousand Indians may have been legally enslaved before the law was changed in 1863, as a result of the Emancipation Proclamation. How many Indians were killed outright or died from disease and the indirect effects of pillage and rape is anyone's guess. But it has been estimated that the Indian population of California before the gold rush of 1848 was probably over 150,000; in 1870, it was 30,000.

The truth is, Indian killing was genuinely popular, a matter of economic expediency. "The Indians are in a starving condition; they kill stock to live," the *Humboldt Times* editorialized not long after the Indian Island massacre. "The whites cannot afford horses and cattle for their sustenance, and will not. Ergo, unless Government provides for the Indians, the settlers must exterminate them." How logical the massacre of the Wiyots must have seemed in such a climate. Was it really a crime to kill someone whom God, Manifest Destiny, or the law of natural selection had condemned to die anyway? Might it not even have seemed more moral to serve as an instrument of plainly assigned fate? Who can blame Robert Gunther for rolling over and going back to sleep? Perhaps the "men of intelligence" who stalked through the Wiyot village that night did not even see men and women at all, but "errors of nature" who were "more brutish than the beasts they hunt." Perhaps, worst of all, they were sincere, knowing in their hearts that violence against Indians meant absolutely nothing at all.

"They probably got into their boats over there, where most of the docks used to be," Jack Norton says, angling his goateed chin across the channel, toward the gentrified Eureka waterfront. Norton, who is a historian of the settlement of northern California, teaches at the state college in Arcata. He is a craggy, graying figure, pecking at a tuna salad in the restaurant in the marina across the channel from Indian Island. "It's less than a mile to the island. It wouldn't have taken them very long to row there. The Wiyots knew that it was dangerous to gather so close to Eureka, but you have to remember that the island had been the center of their universe from time immemorial. The ceremony they had come to perform was comparable to the high mass. If you believe that you are responsible for keeping the world in balance, you have a duty to do it no matter what. They must have looked around themselves and seen the total collapse of everything they knew. The most natural thing for them was to go to the center, to go to God."

There is nothing about Norton's physical appearance—the beard, the lively blue-brown eyes set deep in the pink, bony face—that distinguishes him as Indian. In fact, like most modern Indians, he is a sort of multiethnic conglomerate. His Hoopa father was a chairman of that tribe, whose reservation lies northeast of Eureka, and his mother a Cherokee from Oklahoma. His veins also carry the burdensome blood of Alonzo Norton, a Yankee trader who came West with the gold rush, kept Hoopa concubines, and left his mixed-blood progeny to share the fate of the native people he had helped subdue. "I have always felt responsible for that man," Jack Norton says, with a gravity that belies his easy smile. "I could deny responsibility and say that Alonzo lived in 1860 and I live now, so that whatever he did it's no concern of mine. Or I can face the truth and the responsibility that comes with it."

Norton is the author of a book entitled *Genocide in Northern California,* a study of the impact of the gold rush period on the area's tribes. "Oddly enough, it was the Bicentennial, in 1976, that got me started on it. I was asked to represent the 'Indian point of view' on a committee that was planning some kind of commemoration. As I thought about it, I began wondering, what is it that Indians have to celebrate? Euro-Americans might want to celebrate the founding of the nation and the birth of democracy. But our vision of the same history, at least here in California, was nothing but massacre after massacre."

No one really knows how many Indians died as a result of the European colonization of North America, because no one knows how many inhabited the continent before Columbus arrived. For many years, historians believed that in 1500 the native population might have numbered about 1 million in the area of the present-day United States. More recent estimates vary widely, from fewer than 2 million up to 16 million. Precontact estimates for individual states range with equally dizzying latitude: for example, from 186,000 to 705,000 for California, from 24,000 to 700,000 for Florida, from 71,000 to 144,000 for all of New England, and so on.

Since there were no native census enumerators conveniently

counting heads, demographers rely on mathematical projection techniques that extrapolate a theoretical number of inhabitants based on assumptions about the numbers of human beings who could have been sustained by environments that no longer exist. One influential demographer, whose estimates are widely cited by Indian advocates, obtained an estimate of between 9.8 and 12.25 million simply by multiplying what he assumed to be the nadir Indian population of 332,397, based on the U.S. census of 1930, by depopulation factors of twenty and twenty-five. Most historians believe, however, that the nadir was actually reached around 1900, at about 250,000; applying the same depopulation formula to that figure nearly halves the totals. Douglas Ubelaker, a senior anthropologist at the Smithsonian Institution, has, perhaps more realistically, estimated the native population to have been between 1.9 million and 2.6 million at the time of contact.

There is an unstated assumption underlying at least some estimates that the Indian population was at its historical peak in 1492. In fact, the population of some regions, notably the Southwest, may have peaked centuries earlier and already have been in a period of long decline at the time of the European invasion. There is no dispute that tribes suffered staggering losses, however, often as much as 90 percent of their total, when they came into contact with white settlers. Premeditated massacres accounted for only a very small proportion of overall Indian deaths. The vast majority actually resulted from European and African diseases that spread wantonly through what was, in effect, a biological island of human beings who had lived for millennia in isolation from Old World infections. Nevertheless, what was perpetrated against the Wiyots and many other bands, particularly those that were small and isolated, was, by any reasonable definition, genocide.

From the marina, it is a short walk across a parking lot to the National Park Service's strange and evasive monument. Not far away, a more forthcoming obelisk lists, with a precision that is embarrassing by comparison, the names of forty-two fishermen who lost their lives to Pacific storms. Indian Island is a private enclave today, a low yellowish smudge of grass where the mayor of Eureka and three or four other wealthy citizens have waterfront homes. Herons stalk long-legged across the sand and black geese glide honking overhead; the Wiyots would have known them with the vivid intimacy of a people for whom the natural world was both church and larder, as they would have known the salmon that still, like clockwork, migrate across the bay and the blue fog that now, in late afternoon, rolls in from the open sea.

"We lose the sense that these terrible things happened to real people," Jack Norton is saying. Not only people died here, but with them an entire cosmology, a whole way of understanding the world, a complete miniature civilization. " 'For me, the dier, death is best,' " Norton says. He is quoting Sophocles. "When I look at Indian Island, I think of Antigone standing over her brother's un-shriven corpse, filled with horror. 'Friend shall I be with him, yes friend with friend, when I dared the crime of piety.' Antigone can-not live with herself, knowing that her brother's body lies violated, without it having been given a proper burial." He goes on to speak of the accounting that Americans must, in his view, still somehow make to their own unquiet Indian dead.

"It's easy to lie about the past, to say that our ancestors were just 'sharp bargainers' who cleverly got the land away from the Indians, when in fact they stole it, and cheated and killed for it. We are still paying the consequences of that today. When Indians killed whites, there was terrible retribution; but when whites killed, there was no accountability at all. The legacy to us is the belief that our actions have no consequences. But, in truth, all of us still suffer the conse-quences of what happened here. Indians have been wounded in their psyches, their economy, and physically. Other Americans have been cheated of the truth and therefore of a piece of their own identity."

It is nearly dusk now, and the chilling air is sour with the smells of salt and mud, and sawdust from the lumber mills across Hum-boldt Bay. Norton is watching the neat white triangles of sailboats slide past Indian Island, making for the sea. "There was no time for the Wiyots' spirits to move on," he says. "They are still here, you know, unshriven. They will stay to haunt us."

The Wiyots' killers read history all wrong. Indians refused to disappear. Since the 1970s, the United States census has steadily recorded huge increases in the number of Americans choosing to identify themselves as Indians, mostly in cities and suburbs far from reservations. Between 1980 and 1990, the apparent number of Indi-ans jumped by 78 percent in New Jersey, 66.1 percent in Ohio, 64 percent in Texas, 62 percent in Virginia, and 58.3 percent in New York, with similar figures recorded almost everywhere in the country. Although only about half of the nearly 2 million Americans who listed themselves as Indians in the 1990 census are members of federally recognized tribes, the definition of "Indianness" as far as Washington is concerned, the steady demographic recovery of Native Americans flies in the face of every assumption of nineteenth-century America. Among the most numerous of all are the descendants of the survivors of the Trail of Tears.

The hilltop near Tahlequah, Oklahoma, where Elias Boudinot lies buried can be found, with some difficulty, only by following an overgrown path across private land. The rusted fence, the vertigris that streaks the grave's rough-hewn slab, the undisturbed moss underfoot all suggest a place that is seldom visited today. A plain monument shaded by oak trees says: "Elias Boudinot. Kilikeena 'Buck' Watie. 1802–1839." Nearby lies the equally neglected grave of the Reverend Samuel Worcester, the missionary who left his name on one of the most far-reaching Supreme Court decisions in Indian history. But the hilltop is a fitting resting place for men who did so much to shape the fate of the Cherokees, for it looks out over a smiling landscape of rolling downs and distant farms that seem to shimmer in the humid heat, into the heartland of the modern Cherokee Nation.

When the Cherokees set out upon the Trail of Tears, they largely marched out of the unrelentingly tragic mythology that most Americans perceive as modern Indian history. But they did not, of course, disappear. With characteristic determination, after a few years of factional strife, they rebuilt the nation there in the foothills of the Ozarks. By the late 1840s, the tribe was enjoying a golden era of progress that far surpassed the provincial life of their closest white neighbors in frontier Arkansas. Political institutions were reestablished, and churches, missions, and improvement societies of all sorts thrived. Protestant seminaries were established for both women and men. Temperance meetings flourished all over the nation. The Cherokee public schools became the first free, compulsory, coeducational system west of the Mississippi. Tahlequah merchants, wheelwrights, and blacksmiths prospered serving Forty-niners on their way to the California goldfields.

Although the Cherokee Nation was formally terminated in 1906, along with other tribal governments in Oklahoma, as part of the preparation for statehood, the Cherokees as a people continued to thrive and to intermarry widely, as they always had, with their non-Indian neighbors. The official reestablishment of the tribe in 1971 enabled an enterprising new generation of Cherokee leaders to create jobs and to extend benefits even to the small population of full-bloods who had largely been bypassed by previous advances. They also abolished the long-standing criterion of having at least one-quarter Cherokee blood as a requirement for tribal membership. Instead, they opened the tribal rolls to anyone who could prove descent from a Cherokee who had received an allotment of land from the federal government at the turn of the century. As a result, tribal membership exploded from 12,000 in 1975 to more than 162,000 in 1995.

Tahlequah, the seat of Cherokee tribal government, is today a bustling town of 17,000. It is indistinguishable from most of Southern small-town America, with its familiar assortment of motels, malls, and fast-food restaurants—Hardee's, Taco Bell, Long John Silver's, the Sirloin Stockade—and trumpeting proclamations of evangelical faith. Popular bumper stickers say things like "My Boss Is A Jewish Carpenter" and "If you have lost your way, we have travel plans from here to eternity"; the slogan of a downtown secondhand clothing store named Twice Is Nice is "Have A Twice Is Nice Day In The Lord." There is nothing here of the haunted quality that taints Indian Island. Tahlequah is, after all, a community of survivors.

The Cherokee Nation is generally acknowledged to be among the best-managed tribes in the United States. Every year since 1985, the tribal government has received a Certificate of Excellence for Financial Reporting from the State Finance Officers Association, one of only four local governments in Oklahoma to receive it. Significant in Indian Country, where few tribes enjoy either separation of powers or adequate regulatory oversight, the tribe has adopted a model code of ethics that bars tribal employees from using any information generated within the tribal government for personal gain. Less than half of the tribe's annual $75-million operating budget comes from the federal government; the bulk is generated by the tribe's own enterprises, which include a motel, gift shops, a ranch, a lumber company, a greenhouse business with satellite stores in dozens of regional shopping malls, and several highly profitable plants that manufacture wire harnesses for IBM, General Dynamics, and the United States Army.

The Cherokees were among the first tribes in the country to embrace the Bush administration's "self-governance" initiative, which allows tribes to contract to manage federal Indian programs locally without the paternalistic oversight of the Bureau of Indian Affairs. Tribes receive grants directly from the federal government (about $6 million annually, in the case of the Cherokees), and may spend, and at least theoretically misspend, them as they see fit. While skeptics accused the federal government of shedding its responsibility to Indians, more progressive tribes, including the Cherokee Nation, saw the initiative as an important strengthening of the autonomy of tribal governments.

Principal Chief Wilma Mankiller reproached less venturesome tribes in a speech to tribal leaders gathered in Washington, in 1992. "Sometimes I really feel discouraged when I imagine our ancestors hearing us saying that we can't live without the BIA," she said. "We have gotten too used to the BIA doing everything for us. In spite of the fact that one-quarter of our tribe died on the 'Trail of Tears,' in spite of the bitter divisions that removal created in the tribe, we managed to reestablish our economy and our political system in Oklahoma on our own. Getting away from the BIA is a major step for Indians. Self-governance is an act of faith in ourselves."

Although Elias Boudinot could not have imagined the Hardee's or the bumper stickers or the sophistication of modern tribal administration, they probably would have pleased him, for in some sense they represent the fulfillment of his dream: a Cherokee Nation profoundly conscious of its specialness, but intertwined inextricably with the culture, economy, and people of the United States. "I look at Boudinot as being too far ahead of his time," says R. Bruce Ross, a tribal historian and a traditionalist deeply committed to the revival of pre-Christian Cherokee spiritual life. "He was very intelligent, no ifs, ands, or buts. Even the people who killed him liked him. But I do fault him, too, because he was trying too much to drop the old ways and become assimilated with whites. It would have meant the extinction of the race."

Ross is a huge and gregarious man in his early forties. With his bushy ginger hair and ruddy complexion, he lacks only a tartan to form the perfect image of the Highland Scots from whom, if he chose, he could certainly claim descent. He is, however, rather more than an ordinary citizen of the Cherokee Nation; he is also a direct descendant of Chief John Ross, Boudinot's political antagonist, who led the Cherokees West in the 1830s. But in an era when even the imputation of assimilation embarrasses, Ross is sensitive both to his physical appearance and to the ambiguity of his heritage. He says, somewhat apologetically, "On paper, I'm only three-sixteenths Indian. But by rights, I'm really five-sixteenths. My father lied about his blood. He was really three-quarters, but he said he was only three-eighths."

Ross pauses for a while in silence, watching a flock of schoolchildren swarm chattering through the elegant, mid-nineteenth-century drawing room of the Murrell House, the preserved plantation home of a prominent white family, into which John Ross's daughter married, and over which the chief's great-great-grandson now presides as resident historian. "Could the Cherokees have remained cloistered as a traditional society and still live in the world today?" he wonders aloud. "I don't think we could have. But how much choice did the Cherokees really have? If there was some kind of utopian solution, I just don't know what it might have been."

Not only the future of American Indians but also that of the United States hung in the balance a century and a half ago, as the Supreme Court pondered the fate of the Cherokees. Had the United States backed up the decision of its own highest court, Indian tribes could have been integrated naturally into the American economy and into the nation's political life either in some form of voluntary democratic association or, conceivably, as full-fledged states. It is no exaggeration to say that such a solution might have created a framework for tolerance and ethnic diversity that would have spared the nation much of the racial conflict that has tarnished its political landscape ever since. Regrettably, in the 1830s, the United States government had little more authority over its constituent parts than the government of Yugoslavia did 150 years later. When the Cherokees were driven from New Echota, an extraordinary national opportunity was lost.

There are almost as many variants to the historical experience of North American Indians as there are tribes. But if there is a central metaphor for Indian history, it is not the massacre at Indian Island, much less the Battle of the Little Big Horn, but rather the story of the Cherokees, a story of destruction and lost opportunity, certainly, but also one of persistence and renewal and of the ambiguous process of social and political transformation that has enabled Indians to adapt to life in modern America. It is fashionable today to lionize Indians, such as Crazy Horse and Chief Seattle, who seemed to reject everything that had to do with white, European culture. But there were many others, often far more complex figures, and Elias Boudinot was one of them, who understood that Indians would somehow have to come to terms with Euro-American culture and be changed by it, if they were to survive. The questions that Boudinot raised are still the defining issues of Indian Country today: Are Indians to be part of American society, and if so on what terms? How are Indians to make use of Western culture? And what, indeed, does it mean to be "Indian" in the modern world?

2

"We Ain't Got Feathers and Beads"

I
T IS HARD TO BELIEVE now that the plain and forthright flatlands of Robeson County could have hidden an entire people for generations. Most everything in this part of North Carolina used to be tobacco country, and in late winter the fields are glistening ebony where they're still soaked from the last rain, and chalky gray and brittle-looking, patched with white where they have begun to dry. But many, perhaps most, of the tobacco fields are abandoned now. The generation that has gone off to work the assembly lines in the Converse plant down at Lumberton, or at Kelly-Springfield in Fayetteville, or at Campbell Soup over in Maxton hardly even remembers the grueling handwork of plucking tobacco and twisting it up to dry in the gap-sided sheds that still stud the fields. The speckled-brick houses and the tidy mauve and aqua trailer homes, the new Chevy pickups, all speak of modest success and steady jobs, of a people suspicious of ornament, who take pride. Nothing here hints at secrets. But then the hiding of the Lumbees was not entirely (perhaps not even primarily) a physical thing as much as it was a concealment of blood, a deliberate and nuanced blending into the moral and cultural order of the place and into the violent racial chiaroscuro of the segregated South.

To see this land through Cynthia Hunt's eyes is to see not so much an economy, or a physical landscape, as a human text, an intricate web of relationships of the living and the dead, remembered to an infinitesimal degree. Hunt, who studied political science at the state college in Pembroke, the informal capital of Lumbee country, is a pert, thirtyish woman with the kind of round face, deep-set black eyes, and walnut complexion that distinguishes many Lumbees from their white and black neighbors. By profession, she is a paralegal with Lumbee River Legal Services, but Lumbee identity is her vocation. The clump of brick cottages beyond the pines, she says, "That's Crawley Locklear's people." Back there through that copse is the Major Locklear area, and then over there, across the swamp, the Brooks settlement "where you still find Daniel Lowry's kind," and then beyond the river, the Preston Locklear set, who have been on the same swamp for two hundred years, people say.

The Lumbees have done well. There is little of the gritty, shaming poverty that scars the human landscape of Indian communities in much of the United States. Lumbees run most everything in Pembroke: the Hardee's and the Piggly Wiggly, and the Rite Aid, and the filling station, and the store that sells Christian tapes and license plates that say such things as "Expect A Miracle!" They have been landowners since property records were first written up in the eighteenth century and may well be correct when they boast that they have produced more doctors, lawyers, and Ph.D.'s than any other Indian group in the United States. Many Lumbees hold local elective office, and a Lumbee currently represents Robeson County in the North Carolina legislature. At the same time, as long as anyone can remember, they have been a prickly and cantankerous folk, troublemakers, who drove off Confederate tax collectors during the Civil War and, perhaps unique in the South, forced the Ku Klux Klan to flee Robeson County after attacking the Klansmen in a pitched battle in 1958. Religious convictions are held with an equal ferocity; within recent memory, a doctrinal dispute at the White Heel Community Church provoked parishioners to tote shotguns with them to Sunday service. Hunt recalls blandly, "It was a plum riot."

Encounters here begin invariably with the swapping of genealogies, endless linkings of marriages and births, obscure couplings and linkings both legal and casual, of rivulets of blood that connect, divide, and then link up again, joining together in great streams, into the great sprawling clans that are the most vivid, and perhaps the only, hint of the remote tribal past. Locklears, Lowrys, Dials, Oxendines, Hunts, Maynors; the names repeat endlessly, like mantras. "People here believe in blood," Hunt says. "They know that bloodline." Blood, or at least the idea of blood, is the root of everything here, of character, history, identity.

Blood has always been the Lumbee problem; it was blood that provoked the Shoshones and Bannocks. Hunt is telling the story of her trip to Idaho, one of many that she has made to tribes around the country to lobby support for the Lumbees' quest for recognition. She is cheerful and effervescent by nature, but the remembered humiliation still radiates. "They were supposed to meet me at the airport," she says, her voice a honeyed drawl. "I waited and waited, but nobody ever showed up." The snub was by no means her first. "The Indians out West can't accept us because we ain't got feathers and beads. It really gets to me. You can't expect anything from non-Indian society, but you'd expect Indians to empathize, to understand what you're going through. But now they've got a chance to go down on somebody else. They don't accept you, and they let you know it."

Finally she rented a car and found her own way to the Fort Hall Reservation. But there the humiliation continued. As she walked through the tribal office building, Shoshones and Bannocks peered at her from doorways and from behind corners, staring, she realized, at her hair. "I guess they figured I was supposed to look black." The smooth voice betrays gradually mounting rage. "I'm as Indian as they are. I look exactly like them. I can quote every ancestor I had since 1790, and not one of them was black! I know I am an Indian, and I want them to acknowledge that I am an Indian."

Before she finished her speech to the tribal council, she instinctively knew that they would not offer support. As she spoke, she watched the Shoshones squirm, staring at the floor. At the end, facing her, a councilman said, "You can't be Indian—you've got no reservation."

Hunt's eyes dance now with triumphant irony. "What I said to him, what I said back was, 'Are you an Indian just because the feds gave you a reservation?' "

The Lumbees' century-long quest for identity is a story as serpentine as the jungled Lumber River, whose swampy course shielded, and perhaps even created, them and their ambiguous world, held it fast for centuries beyond the reach or understanding of the European settlers who flooded around them. It is in large part a guesswork story that says much not only about the contradictions of Indian identity but also about the deep ambiguities of race and ethnicity in late-twentieth-century America. The Lumbees challenge almost every preconception of what Indians should be; they are an anthropological no-man's-land located beyond the conventional boundaries of race and political organization that traditionally define Indians' identity. They run the physical gamut from blond hair and blue eyes to the nearly Negroid. They have no chiefs or medicine men and no reservation. They have no memory of the tribe from which their ancestors may have come, nor of the language they spoke, nor of any religion older than the pious and passionate Baptist faith that, to a person, they today profess. Even their present name is a neologism, coined in the 1950s from the way old folks pronounced the name of the Lumber River. There is, in fact, nothing at all about the Lumbees that fits conventional notions of what it means to be Native American. Yet for as long as any Lumbee can remember, they have possessed an unflagging conviction that they are simply and utterly Indian, a tenacious faith that is troubled only by the failure of most other Americans to recognize it. "Recognition psychosis," Cynthia Hunt calls it. "I feel as if I'm not a real Indian until I've got that BIA stamp of approval. You think, Maybe I'm not a real Indian if I don't wear feathers. Just thinking about it, I get all bent out of shape. You're told all your life that you're Indian, but sometimes you want to be that kind of Indian that everybody else accepts as Indian."

The Lumbees' ancestors seem to hover mysteriously on the rim of history, never quite coming clear. Early visitors to the region spoke curiously of "light-skinned Indians" who tilled the soil and dressed like Englishmen. In 1739, Welsh settlers complained of "Indians running amongst their settlements under pretense of hunting." In 1754, there were reports of truculent folk dwelling in the swamps, "a mixt Crew, a lawless people" who "filled the lands without patent or paying quit rents." In 1773, another report mentioned Locklears and Hunts, two of the most common present-day Lumbee clans, among "a mob railously assembled" against the colonial government. By the time they finally came into focus as a distinct people in the early nineteenth century, the Lumbees were already a people apart, confusingly and interchangeably described in censuses as "free persons of color," as "whites" and as "mulattos," a people who didn't quite "fit."

For more than a century, the Lumbees have sought official federal recognition as Indians with a single-mindedness, indeed a ferocity, unmatched by any other group in the United States. They have applied for certification nine different times, under almost as many names. In 1888, without any hard historical evidence, they applied as "Croatans," the alleged descendants of the "Lost Colony" of Roanoke, who, their petition stated, "during the long years that have passed since the disappearance of said colony have been struggling unaided and alone to fit themselves and their children for the exalted privileges of American freemen." In 1910, they lobbied to have Congress declare them "Cherokees" instead. In 1911, they successfully petitioned the North Carolina legislature to change their name to "Indians of Robeson County." They petitioned again in 1913 for another change, this time—over the protests of Cherokees in both North Carolina and Oklahoma—to "Cherokee Indians of Robeson County." In 1932, a bill introduced in the U.S. Senate called again for recognition of the Robeson County folk as "Cherokees," but just a year later still another bill sought to have them recognized as "Cheraw Indians." The following year, another new bill proposed recognition of the "Siouxan Indians of Lumber River."

In 1936, the Bureau of Indian Affairs sent a Harvard anthropologist by the name of Carl Seltzer to Robeson County to sort the Lumbees out once and for all. During a sweltering July week, while the world waited impatiently for the start of the Berlin Olympics, Seltzer sweated in a rented room in Pembroke, engaged in a federally funded "racial diagnosis" of 108 "Siouxans," as they then preferred to call themselves. His techniques were state of the art; in fact, they were similar to the ones that the Olympics' Nazi sponsors were employing to distinguish Aryans from Jews at just the same time. Using calipers and steel tape, Seltzer measured the prominence of chins, the thickness of lips, the droop of earlobes, the width of noses. He put a pencil in each subject's hair, meticulously noting down "Indian" blood if it slipped easily through and "Negroid" if it failed to. He reported in detail on every person he examined. For example: "Border line case. Doubtful diagnosis. Probability ½ or more Indian blood." And another: "Doubtful diagnosis. Probability towards less than ½ Indian."

Of the 108, Seltzer "diagnosed" just three as having at least one-half Indian blood. He later returned to Robeson County and, with equal precision, examined another 101 "Siouxans." The results were ludicrous. Children appeared on the approved list while their parents did not; brothers and sisters, parents and children fell on opposite sides of the racial line. "Diagnoses were based solely on the manifestations of physical characteristics of known racial significance as interpreted by the science of physical and racial anthropology," Seltzer informed the Commissioner of Indian Affairs. In the end, the Secretary of the Interior certified twenty-two "Siouxans" as Indians.

In 1956, the United States Senate finally voted to permit the Lumbees, as they now chose to be known, to call themselves Indians. But it was a hollow, even demeaning victory, for it came just as the Eisenhower administration was committing itself to terminate federal obligations to even well-established tribes around the country. The Senate explicitly declared: "Nothing in this Act shall make such Indians eligible for any services performed by the United States for Indians because of their status as Indians, and none of the statutes of the United States which affect Indians because of their status as Indians shall be applicable to the Lumbee Indians." The Lumbees were, in the most literal sense, Indians in name only. In 1985, the Lumbees began once again, lobbying this time with the longest and most exhaustive Indian petition ever submitted to the United States government for recognition as a legitimate tribe. By the early 1990s, the hopefully named "Lumbee Tribal Enrollment Office" had listed no fewer than 41,000 members who, if the community's application is ever approved, will become the country's ninth largest Indian tribe, more numerous by far than famed tribes such as the Seminoles, Cheyennes, Comanches, and Kiowas and a power to be reckoned with in national Indian politics.

Until quite recently, scarcely anyone thought to ask what is fast becoming an increasingly pertinent question: just who is an Indian? For centuries, the Indian seemed self-evident, like a natural force. When the young painter George Catlin saw a delegation of tribesmen from the West pass through Philadelphia on their way to Washington in 1824, he knew that he was seeing Indians because these "lords of the forest" were "arrayed and equipped in all their classic beauty,—with shield and helmet,—with tunic and manteau,

—tinted and tasselled off, exactly for the painter's palette!" They were myth come to life; the Indian was an Indian precisely because he looked like one and lived a life that was visibly different from that of white Americans.

Indians who did not conform to white expectations were harder to define. In 1869, the Supreme Court of New Mexico Territory declared that the Pueblos were not actually Indians, since they were "honest, industrious, and law-abiding citizens" and exhibited "virtue, honesty and industry to their more civilized neighbors." A few years later, the United States Supreme Court held that the Pueblos could be considered "Indians only in feature, complexion and a few of their habits." However, after receiving agents' reports of drunkenness, dancing, and debauchery, the Court reversed itself and declared that the Pueblos were Indians after all.

Today the answer, if there is one, is more problematic than ever. After generations of intermarriage and adaptation, the Indian is not an easy person to define. The United States Census Bureau simply allows anyone who believes that he is Indian to declare himself one, a convenient portmanteau for the fantasies of wishful-thinking wannabes that probably accounts for much, if not most, of the statistical near doubling of Indians over the past twenty years, to 1.8 million in the 1990 census. "There are a lot of just plain old Americans who want to belong to an ethnic group of some kind," says Holly Reckord, the ebullient anthropologist who heads the Bureau of Indian Affairs' Branch of Acknowledgment and Research. "Usually people claim to be Cherokee. Some say all the records were lost when the courthouse burned during the Civil War. We check and find that the courthouse is still there. Or some say, 'Grandma hid in a cave and couldn't declare her Indianness.' We check and find that they haven't a trace of Indian ancestry, yet they are still totally convinced that they are Indians. Even if you have a trace of Indian blood, why do you want to select that for your identity, and not your Irish or Italian? It's not clear why, but at this point in time a lot of people want to be Indian."

Indian identity remains naggingly elusive. Generations of Wild West shows and Hollywood films created an iconographic Indian modeled on idealized versions of the craggy-featured Northern Plains warrior of the mid-nineteenth century, but there is no typical Indian physique any more than there is a generic Caucasian, Asian, or African one: Pimas from Arizona look as different from Wascos from Oregon or Passamaquoddies from Maine as Greeks do from Norwegians or Czechs. Moreover, centuries of intermarriage have made countless Indians whose cultural credentials are unimpeachable physically indistinguishable from Anglo-Americans, Hispanics, or blacks.

Some Indians would make traditionalism the measure. "An Indian is one who offers tobacco to the ground, feeds the water, and prays to the four winds in his own language," the Crow poet Henry Real Bird has said. "Without language, you're nothing." This, however, excludes both Indian Christians, who comprise a large majority of Native Americans today, and countless members of long-established tribes who either have forgotten or were never taught their ancestors' tongue. The Pulitzer Prize–winning Kiowa author N. Scott Momaday suggests a more generous but still troublesome definition. "An Indian is someone who thinks of themselves as an Indian. But that's not so easy to do and one has to earn the entitlement somehow. You have to have a certain experience of the world in order to formulate this idea. I consider myself an Indian; I've had the experience of an Indian. I know how my father saw the world, and his father before him." This may be both subtle and true, but it is hardly adequate for the needs of policymakers and tribal leaders who are responsible for the allocation of nearly $3 billion worth of federal aid and services to Indians each year.

Some federal laws define an Indian as anyone of "Indian descent," while others require one-fourth or one-half Indian blood, a confusing state of affairs that produces more than a few individuals who may, for example, qualify as an Indian for educational benefits but not for medical ones. For the most part, however, the federal government now defines an Indian as someone who is an enrolled member of a recognized tribe. This has the virtue of simplicity as well as a certain reassuring force of logic, however circular. In the mid-1990s, just over 1 million men and women met the federal criteria. But Ross Swimmer, who headed the Bureau of Indian Affairs during the Reagan administration, estimated that as many as half a million ethnic Indians receive no federal benefits at all because for one reason or another they happen not to be members of a federally recognized tribe.

Absurd contradictions abound. A 1991 federal law—it was introduced by the only Indian member of Congress, and now Senator, Ben Nighthorse Campbell of Colorado—intended to protect native craftsmen from fraud made it illegal for artists who do not belong to federally recognized tribes to sell their work at Indian crafts fairs or to describe it as "Indian made," and provided that both the artist and gallery may be fined up to $10,000 for violations. As a result, the well-known Cherokee painter Bert Seabourn and various other artists whose Indian background is not in doubt have been barred from exhibiting because they do not happen to be enrolled tribal members. According to Seabourn, his Cherokee forebears were farmers in Texas, many days' ride from where the official rolls were being signed in northeast Oklahoma at the turn of the century. "I don't know if my ancestors even knew about it," he told a reporter. Similarly, when the tribal council of the Tonawanda Band of Senecas, in western New York, banished five political critics from the tribe in 1992, it in effect transformed them into whites. "Make no mistake—they are no longer citizens here," the council clerk declared to the local press. "They're to be treated as non-Indians. Their names have been removed from our rolls."

All this leads with majestic inevitability to an even more vexing question: what then is an "Indian tribe"? In earlier times, federal recognition was an arbitrary, hit-or-miss business. Tribes most often became legally recognized when they made treaties with the United States government and occasionally through executive orders or presidential proclamations, which usually specified the rights to which a tribe was entitled. Recently, one group has asked for recognition based on the fact that Andrew Jackson bestowed military dress coats on its chiefs in 1815, a gesture that the group's present leaders maintain constituted "acknowledgment" in the manner of that time. Groups that never made war on the United States seldom needed to make treaties, while others—and the Lumbees insist that they fall into this category—were so isolated that no one ever noticed them.

Indian thinking on the subject wreaks havoc with the Anglo-American craving for clear definition. A few years ago, testifying before a Massachusetts court that had been charged with determining whether the Mashpee community of Cape Cod was actually a tribe, the Sioux author Vine Deloria, Jr., declared, "As I use it and as I understand other Indian people using it, [tribe] means a group of people living pretty much in the same place who know who their relatives are. I think that's the basic way we look at things."

A lawyer for white property owners who feared that recognition of the Mashpees as a tribe would jeopardize title to neighboring land tried repeatedly to pin Deloria down:

Q: Can a group be a tribe without a political organization?

A: This is getting increasingly difficult to respond to, because we don't make the distinctions that you do in the Anglo world: religion, political and everything else. What you are talking about is a group of people who know where they are. They may have to respond to outside pressures and adopt political structures, religious structures, or economic structures to deal with the outside society.

In ethnology, a tribe has traditionally been understood to mean a community of people bound together by blood ties, who are socially, politically, and religiously organized, who live together, and who speak a common language. There is, however, no universal legal definition of a tribe, and no single statute that clearly describes what a modern Indian tribe is supposed to be. The federal government has deftly skirted the problem by means of language such as that enshrined in the regulations of the Department of the Interior, which describe "tribe" with splendid circularity simply as "any Indian or Alaskan Native tribe, band, pueblo, village or community within the continental United States that the Secretary of the Interior presently acknowledges to exist as an Indian tribe." No matter what tribes might once have been like, if in fact they ever fit European definitions, they vary so widely today that they defy generalization of any kind.

Early European colonists assumed that all societies fundamentally resembled their own, and they stubbornly insisted that native realities fit their preconceptions. They typically viewed clusters of vaguely related bands as immutable "nations" like the ones they remembered from the Old World. In fact, native societies included almost everything from the semi-urbanized theocratic communities of the Pueblos, to small villages of extended families in northern California, to powerful city-states along the Mississippi and the Ohio, to centralized chiefdoms along the Atlantic coast, not to mention the remarkable Iroquois Confederacy in the Northeast. More than a few "tribes," moreover, were almost wholly the product of white contact. Until 1700, for instance, the Catawba "nation" of South Carolina was no more than an assortment of neighboring groups that came together for mutual defense against colonial aggression, while in Puritan New England missionaries organized Christian Indians from various tribes, Mashpee among them, into so-called praying towns, which in the course of time evolved into tribelike communities in their own right.

Moving back in time, uncertainties proliferate. For instance, before the pressure of European encroachment compelled them to centralize in the eighteenth century, the Cherokees consisted of perhaps seventy villages speaking several different languages. The North Carolina Band of Cherokees is today demanding that the Smithsonian Institution return a collection of human remains that were excavated from what used to be tribal land in Tennessee. Federal law on the point seems plain: "The Secretary [of the Smithsonian], upon the request of the descendants of such individual or of the Indian tribe shall expeditiously return such remains (together with any associated funerary objects) to the descendants or tribe, as the case may be." The bones in question, however, date from the tenth century A.D., and it is far from clear that the natives who occupied the area then were in fact Cherokees.

"How far back were the Cherokees actually Cherokees?" asks Thomas W. Killion, an anthropologist charged with sorting out such questions for the Smithsonian, which in 1991 was required by federal law to inventory the millions of Indian artifacts in its collections and to invite tribes to apply for their "repatriation." "Are we dealing with proto-Cherokees, or with a totally different group? Is there any relationship at all between the two peoples? The Cherokees were living on mounds when De Soto encountered them in the 1500s. But we don't know whether they built those mounds themselves or had moved into other tribes' territory. The Assyrians and the Sumerians both built ziggurats, but it doesn't mean that they were the same people."

Throughout the long ages that preceded the arrival of the Europeans, native peoples migrated, blended, disintegrated, and reassembled in new configurations all over North America. In the nineteenth century, the unstoppable force of westward migration shattered Indian nations into fragments that eventually often became separate tribes: for instance, scattering Cherokees from North Carolina to Oklahoma, Winnebagos from Wisconsin to Nebraska, the Sioux to seven reservations in four different states, and the Chippewas over a veritable archipelago of tiny communities around the northern Midwest. War created still more new "tribes," such as the exiled remnant of Geronimo's band that became the Fort Sill Apaches of Oklahoma, while for the sake of administrative convenience tribes with little or no historical relationship were arbitrarily placed together, such as the Cheyenne-Arapaho Tribes of Oklahoma, or the conglomeration of Wascos, Sahaptins, and Paiutes who now make up the Confederated Tribes of Warm Springs, in Oregon.

Although the principle of tribal sovereignty rests on the premise that modern tribes are the direct continuation of nations that predate the founding of the United States, the governments of all but a few are wholly a twentieth-century invention. They are, in their essentials, the brainchild of John Collier, disillusioned social worker, friend of Isadora Duncan and Emma Goldman, sometime poet, visionary, and Franklin Roosevelt's Commissioner of Indian Affairs. Collier believed passionately in a sort of social gospel, a redemption through community, as an alternative to the "shattering, aggressive drone" of modern life. Having failed to create it to his satisfaction in New York City settlement houses, he discovered his ideal, or something that looked like it, among the Pueblos of New Mexico. (In old age, he would believe that it also existed in Mao Zedong's China and Castro's Cuba.)

Collier believed that Native American culture—"this Red Atlantis"—was morally and aesthetically superior to modern industrialized society and to its ethos of individualism and competition. Taos, his spiritual home, by contrast, was "a magical habitation full of magical people." Throughout the 1920s, he worked tirelessly to make others see that traditional Indian beliefs and ceremonies were a national resource that must be preserved at any price. Indeed, he was convinced that the future of Western civilization depended on saving the Indians. "They had what the world has lost," he wrote in the introduction to *Indians of the Americas*. "They have it now. What the world has lost, the world must have again, lest it die." Mysticism aside, Collier was a man of tremendous personal determination, and as the leader of the fledgling American Indian Defense Association, he gained national recognition by leading the successful campaign to prevent Pueblo lands from being sold off by the federal government.

Once in Washington, Collier initiated what came to be called the Indian New Deal. Its centerpiece was the Indian Reorganization Act of 1934, which halted the conversion of reservations to the private property of individual Indians (which had diminished tribal lands by two-thirds in less than fifty years), reversed the doctrine of assimilation that had guided federal policy since the 1880s, and committed the federal government firmly to the strengthening of the tribes. In the process, he committed the assimilationist's error in reverse. As the historian Brian W. Dippie has put it, "Collier assumed that inside every Indian, no matter how assimilated, there lurked a Pueblo waiting to be freed, a communal being eager to shuck off the trappings of individualistic, materialistic white civilization in order to recapture a long-lost communal past." Collier saw the act, characteristically, both in metaphysical terms, as a means of "awakening the racial spirit," and as a practical tool to enable Indians to learn how to manage their own affairs for the first time since the end of the Indian wars.

The act encouraged tribes to adopt constitutions and bylaws and to apply for charters of incorporation that would enable them to own and manage property and to conduct business. It also allowed them to establish their own governments, which, in a formula devised by Collier and his brilliant solicitor general, Felix Cohen, vested authority exclusively in an elected council and chairman. Although this was indeed a form of democracy, it was one that was rooted more in Collier's sentimental view of Indians and their supposedly spiritualized sense of common interest than it was either in political reality or in the basics of true American democracy, for it glaringly lacked the separation of executive, legislative, and judiciary powers that the founding fathers of the United States understood was essential for responsible government. This oversight continues to haunt tribes today.

The United States Supreme Court has affirmed that each tribe has the power to set its own criteria for membership: they vary widely, not to say dizzyingly. The Cherokee Nation of Oklahoma accepts anyone descended from a person listed on the rolls of the federal commission that liquidated the tribe's reservation in 1906, after a century of extensive intermarriage and cultural assimilation. The Onondaga and Seneca tribes of upstate New York restrict membership to individuals born of an enrolled mother. By contrast, in Arizona, all children born to members of the Tohono O'Odham, or Papago, Tribe who reside on the reservation automatically become members themselves. Although Yakima children need not be born on the tribe's Washington reservation in order to become members, their parents must establish residency by returning to the reservation once every five years; the Yakimas also insist that a member have at least one-quarter Yakima blood and belong to one of the fourteen original bands.

The concept of "Indianness" has long been rooted at least partly in the belief that blood is fundamental to identity. Nearly all tribes require proof of descent from a tribal member measured in the form of a "blood quantum," which quite literally means (or is at least believed to mean) the amount of Indian blood that runs through one's veins. Here again, criteria vary greatly. Not a single tribe requires full Indian blood as a criterion of membership; none could. In 1910, slightly more than half of the nation's 265,683 Indians were full-bloods; today, many tribes contain no full-bloods at all. The White Mountain Apaches of Arizona and the Uintah-Ouray Tribe of Utah demand a blood quantum of 50 percent or higher for membership. The Mescalero Apache Tribe of New Mexico, like most tribes, requires one-quarter tribal blood. Many, however, like the Citizen Potawatomi Band of Kansas, ask for just one-eighth, and others as little as one-sixteenth, or, in a few cases, none at all; the establishment of any blood quantum requirement, a tribal enrollment officer for the Seminole tribe of Oklahoma testified at a 1992 child custody hearing, would "in effect, cause the tribe to become extinct." Without proof of clear Indian lineage, the possibilities for abuse are self-evident. Since abolishing its blood quantum requirement in 1975, northern Michigan's Sault Ste. Marie Band of Chippewas has ballooned from 1,300 to 21,000 members and has earned a reputation, perhaps undeserved, for allegedly selling tribal membership and the valuable fishing rights that accompany it to fishermen who have little or no Indian blood.

Ethnographically, it is preposterous to consider an American whose extraction is, say, one-eighth Italian, one-eighth English, one-quarter German, and one-half Irish to be an "Italian." Indians, however, are quite commonly given to speaking with a straight face about being "seven-sixteenths Blackfeet" or "fifteen thirty-seconds Cheyenne," and the like. The tyranny of blood inevitably produces challenges to logic like the recently recognized Mashantucket Pequot Tribe of Connecticut, who have intermarried with both whites and blacks for centuries but who have arbitrarily defined their late-nineteenth-century great-great-grandparents as "full-blood for the purpose of enrollment." Given the dazzling casino profits that have made the Pequots totally self-sufficient (each Pequot is guaranteed a job with an annual salary of $50,000 to $60,000 per year), not to mention one of the most profitable business corporations in eastern Connecticut, such presumption is no more than a harmless indulgence. But it cannot be surprising that the Lumbees (and other mixed-blood groups) claim the same right and insist that the ancestors whose names are found on the so-called Croatan petitions of a century ago be treated as bureaucratic full-bloods too.

In their current petition for federal recognition, the Lumbees assert that their native ancestors, the "outlaws and fugitives" cited by the Welsh, the "pest and a nuisance," the "mixt Crew, a lawless people," the "mob railously assembled," were mainly the descendants of the Cheraw Tribe, a hazy grouping that may have been identical with the "Xuala" whom Hernando De Soto encountered on his trek through the Southeast in 1540. There is no doubt that until the 1730s the Cheraws were a real and continuing threat to the English colonies, appearing sometimes in Virginia, sometimes in South Carolina, stirring the tribelets of the frontier into war against the encroachments of white settlement. But then, suddenly, they disappeared from history.

If the Lumbees are now correct, and they may very well be, one should try to imagine the last Cheraws, probably diminished from smallpox and overcome by war, retreating family by family into the safety of the swamps, where they are joined by the enfeebled remnants of other bands—Waccamaws, perhaps, or Enos, or Keyauwees, three or four here, a dozen there. Beyond the horizon of colonial sight, the polyglot swamp dwellers adopt frontier traders' English as their lingua franca, along with the Christianity of their immigrant neighbors, in an effort to construct some kind of workable moral order in ruins of the old Indian world. They mingle uninhibitedly with frontiersmen, surveyors, and outlaws, with white, mulatto, and black, in an era before color consciousness became a national obsession.

Towering, slab-fisted, slowly crumpling with age, Claude Lowry suggests a mountainside that has slumped in the aftermath of an earthquake. Now in his mid-nineties, he serves as a sort of living archive for the Lumbees. He remembers when, seventy or eighty years ago, Lumbee preachers baptized in the swamp in front of his porch, before the engineers dried it out for tobacco fields. He also remembers history as the Lumbees wish it to be, a coarse but straightforward story of proud though predatory white and clannish Indian. "The whites who came down here, they were mutts, that's who they were. They were seeking their fortune, and they had to have a woman while they were at it, so they took an Indian. James Lowrie came down here from Virginia, about 1745. He stopped up on Long Swamp and got him a child by an Indian woman. There wasn't no marrying in those days, because there wasn't no law. He had three sons: Thomas, Will, and James. I descend from the Thomas clan." Nowhere but in Robeson County would a man as pale-skinned and blue-eyed as Claude Lowry be thought anything but white. But here where family, blood, and race are indelible, heritage has left him with a sense of deep-seated grievance, a lingering rage: "That's why I hate the whites, they don't want to recognize their own blood. The white man infiltrated, undermined, and divided." He brandishes, dwarfing it in his vast hands, a tattered surveyor's book dated 1836, containing proof, he says, of land stripped from Lumbees by unscrupulous settlers. "That's the way the white man purposed to take over the country. But the Indians survived by cunning and conniving, and sticking together. They were here when the white man come, and they're going to be here to the Great 1 A.M."

For generations, according to anthropologists who back the Lumbee petition, the swamps were a terra incognita without newspapers or schools; even churches were so rare that births, marriages, and deaths went unrecorded. By the time the modern Lumbees emerged, at the turn of the nineteenth century, they were already a demographic anomaly, dark-skinned but free, clearly not colonists yet farming, dressing, and praying like Europeans. But seeing no feathers, no beads, the white authorities, in effect, saw no Indians at all. Relations between whites and nonwhites grew steadily worse after Nat Turner's abortive slave uprising in Virginia, in 1831. In 1836, North Carolina stripped every "free negro, free mulattoe, or free person of mixed blood" of the right to vote, serve on juries, and to bear arms. The Lumbees had thus far survived in the interstices of race, but now they were faced with a cruel dilemma. Proclaiming Indianness risked expulsion to the West at a time when the United States government was routing the Cherokees and other Eastern tribes from their homes; acquiescence with the law, on the other hand, must lead inexorably to oblivion in the helpless "colored" underclass. The solution was simple and cruel: the Lumbees discovered that hating black people was a way to avoid being considered black themselves. But they became slaves of a different kind, to the terrible tyranny of genes, to the spread of a lip, the accidental angle of a nose, the tint of flesh that sealed one's fate for life.

Within Claude Lowry's memory, even white-skinned Lumbees were barred from buying a Coke in the Red Springs drugstore and from "whites-only" barbershops in Lumberton; they were required to sit with blacks in Lumberton movie houses, and when Lumbee mothers gave birth at the community hospital, their newborn infants were banned from the nursery and had to sleep in the bottom drawer of their mother's dresser instead. At the same time, Lumbees who married blacks or mulattos were shunned; they were said to have "crossed the border," to have passed into a country from which there was no return. Lumbee "blood committees" investigated, to the fourth generation, the race of every child and teacher who applied to enter the segregated "Indian" schools. Even today, people still speak without shame of the Lumbee who kept his own sister's children out of school because she had married a half-black Indian and about the school inspector who was sent all the way to Georgia to find out if a child had black ancestors. Sophisticated notions of identity were academic; to be Lumbee meant, simply, not to be black.

"Indians started out white, you know. It was climatic change over a number of years brought about a change in their pigmentation." Lowry is poking through wads of family photos, of two nephews who were bombed at Pearl Harbor, of another who was shot down over the Pacific, of a grandson who flew in the Persian Gulf war. From among them, he plucks one that shows students at a Lumbee school. It is a charming picture; the boys are posed uncomfortably in the stiff suits of three or four generations ago, staring with a quaint intensity at a camera that may still have been an unfamiliar object to some of them. "They say you can tell it down to the eighth generation, nigger blood, that is." Lowry is pointing to two boys with very dark skin, tapping them with huge fingers. "It's easy to tell whether he's got that dark blood from an African or not. You look at his lips, look at his nose, look at his curly things up here." Lowry ruffles his own straight white hair. "We got them little niggers out of there."

Mention African blood even to younger Lumbees, and there is still a tensing, a narrowing of the eyes. It is the old terror of blood taint, an almost physical loathing. A young Lumbee woman in a T-shirt and stonewashed jeans stands, palpably ill at ease, in front of a class on North Carolina Indian Culture at Pembroke State College, struggling to say something about her own family's history. Clearly annoyed at the girl's vagueness, the teacher, also a Lumbee, struggles to draw her out.

Coaxing, she asks, "Why are origins so important?"

"Because people don't know who they are anyway."

"What do you mean by that?"

"Oh, I don't know."

The girl's discomfort is painful to watch.

"Try."

"There are people in my family who crossed the line one way or the other. But nobody ever talks about it. People said we were black; we had to get away from that."

"People get scared when you mention the word 'black,' " says Cynthia Hunt, honey-voiced. "I have this thing with blood quantum. I went a long time, I wouldn't enroll. You hear all your life you're not all Indian, that you're mixed with black. You keep thinking, reckoning, if I've got any black blood there, I think I don't want to know about it. Finally, it became real important to me to know whether I really am an Indian. When I enrolled, I was really surprised to see that I had a good blood quantum—it was quite high—I was so relieved!"

Like their ancestors of two centuries past, the Lumbees remain "a mob railously assembled," troublemakers at the gates of race, defying the categories that for generations have hemmed in Native Americans, blacks and whites alike. They not only undermine Americans' dubious preoccupation with the mystique of blood; they wreak havoc with our custom of treating race as a distinction cast in genetic concrete. If blood is at all a meaningful measure of Indian identity, the Lumbees probably possess as much as at least some established tribes. Indeed, the historical experience of the Lumbees' ancestors probably roughly paralleled that of various other Eastern groups—falling somewhere between that of the federally recognized Pequots of Connecticut and Narragansetts of Rhode Island, and more problematic groups such as the Ramapoughs of New Jersey and the "Sandylanders" of North Carolina—who were overwhelmed by the early waves of colonial immigration and who gradually blended with the newcomers in unpredictable ways as the frontier moved beyond them to the West.

"The Lumbees bring into question all our assumptions about Indians, and about whites and blacks," says James H. Merrell, who teaches American history at Vassar and whose study of the Catawba Tribe of South Carolina ranks among the best examinations of Indians in the Southeast during the colonial period. "They are simultaneously none of these and all of these. They can stand as a lesson to us; by understanding them, we can see that racial categories are not innate. People certainly didn't think in those terms when the Lumbees were being formed. In that sense, the Lumbee story tells us that the way the United States turned out, with the conquest of the Indians and the enslavement of blacks, was not a foregone conclusion, but the result of a whole range of individual decisions; in turn, it gives us hope that our present racial problems can be remedied by a similar host of individual decisions."

The Lumbees may, in fact, foreshadow the biological future of American Indians more closely than many established tribes must care to imagine, or admit, as Indians nationally continue to marry people of other races far faster than any other ethnic group in the United States. In 1970, more than 33 percent of all Indians were married to non-Indians (compared to just 1 percent of all Americans who married outside their race); a decade later, the number had grown to 50 percent, and it has continued to climb. A 1986 congressional study estimated that the percentage of Indians with one-half or more Indian blood would decline from about 87 percent in 1980 to just 8 percent by 2080. Similarly, in 1970, before the upsurge in Americans choosing to identify themselves as "Native Americans" in the U.S. census, only 32 percent of Indians declared a tribal language as their mother tongue. Two centuries from now, the Bannocks and Shoshones may well seem as ethnically ambiguous as the Lumbees do to Shoshones and Bannocks today.

The current Lumbee story of origins suggests that there was a time in American history when both biological and social integration took place free of the artificial barriers erected by later generations and when neither the conquest of Indians nor the enslavement of blacks seemed foreordained. On that plane, it offers at least some hope that today's seemingly intractable racial problems may someday be shoveled into the dustbin of history by generations as uninhibited as those that populated frontier North Carolina two or three centuries ago. Such concerns are, to the Lumbees, largely beside the point. In essence, they want their story to be understood to mean that it is possible for Native Americans to lose their language, their traditions, and even their name, without losing the fundamental fact of their being Indian.

The Lumbees' problem has always lain, in part, in the Euro-American tendency to see Indian tribal identity as something immutable, as a sort of ethnic Maginot Line that may be fatally breached by new blood or alien culture. Instead, as the Lumbees would have it, true tribal identity may reside less in the buried secrets of seventeenth-century bloodlines than in the very process of cultural change and reinvention that has been the defining experience of their community for more than two centuries as, generation after generation, it has coalesced in moments of community crisis, faded away, then reappeared once more under a different name. "Lumbees are not looking for themselves, rather, they are trying to understand themselves, to see how we fit in with the rest of the Indian world," says Linda Oxendine, an anthropologist who heads the department of Native American studies at Pembroke State College. Oxendine, a more phlegmatic woman than many of her fellow Lumbees, sees the campaign for recognition less as a quest for fundamental identity than as a way to shape an identity that the outer American society can accept. "Lumbees know who they are. But they don't know why they are. A lot of people define Indian identity as traditional religion, tribal land, and language. Along with that, there is a tendency to believe that when Indians adapt they become less Indian. Lumbees are Christians, private landowners, and speak English. But adaptation is the essence of being Indian. Before contact, tribes borrowed from each other. After contact, they borrowed from the whites. Tribes were always changing. Total adaptation was not the goal, but people did what was necessary to make life good for themselves, or what they had to do to survive."

The fate of the Lumbees' aspirations lies, in all probability, at the end of a beige corridor in the Department of the Interior's headquarters building on C Street, in Washington, D.C. Dreams, fantasies, and frail hopes lie thick on the plain metal shelves where the bureau's Branch of Acknowledgment and Research stores the more than 150 petitions that it has received from groups around the

United States that are seeking official status as Indian tribes. Here, packed into green and brown file folders, wads of yellowing news clips, dissertations, old censuses, jargon-laden reports by hired academics, consultants' tomes and scribbled sheets of family lore, outright frauds, neurotic claims for identity and validation, lie side by side with the fragile hopes of genuine Indian communities that were brushed aside and forgotten in the traumatic helter-skelter of American expansion. There are petitions from the Mashpees of Cape Cod and the Shinnecocks of New York, from the San Juan Paiutes of Arizona and the Houmas of Louisiana, from Creeks left behind in Alabama when the tribe was forced West in the 1830s, from two California women who claim to be the last of their tribe, from new and doubtful entities such as the "Cherokees of Hoke County," the "Revived Ouachita Indians of Arkansas and America," and the "Delawares of Idaho." Among the largest of all, the Holy Grail of North American ethnography, filling two entire shelves, is the Lumbee petition.

Here, Holly Reckord's staff of nine genealogists, anthropologists, and historians sort through these parenthetical remnants of the continent's native peoples, deciding which Americans, in the cold official eye of the United States government, have the right to a relationship with the federal government. Petitioners must prove that they are the descendants of a historic tribe that inhabited a specific area, that they have been identified as a cohesive Indian group throughout history, and that the group has exercised tribal authority over its members without interruption since its first sustained contact with non-Indian settlers. In addition, they must exhaustively document such evidence of common identity as the rates of marriage and the amount of shared ritual activity within the group, the degree to which most of the membership is swayed by actions taken by the group's leaders, how its disputes are settled, and how effectively the group sets and enforces standards of behavior for its members. Not surprisingly, the process is painfully slow. Since the Branch of Acknowledgment and Research was established in 1978, only ten groups have won recognition; thirteen others have been denied. "These histories are deceptively complex," says Reckord. "You can't make any assumptions based on what people tell us when they come into our office. There were often pressures that encouraged groups to select different identities under different circumstances in the past. Documents often conflict with what they believe about themselves and about their history."

It is no revelation to anyone that the Lumbees clearly fall short of the federal criteria. The language of the petition strains to convince: "The Lumbee tribe has maintained a continuous social and political existence in Robeson County since at least the early part of the eighteenth century. The Lumbees are, and have always been, a clearly bounded, distinctive community with its own political leadership." However, no trace remains of culture that is usually considered "Indian" but for the faintly remembered use of horn spoons and vague talk of "rootwork," or witchcraft, deep in the backcountry. Although they have tacitly been recognized as Indians by their neighbors, and officially by North Carolina statute, they have never had a central government of any kind; decision making has always taken place in the household, within the labyrinthine and interlocking clans that are, in effect, Lumbee society.

Jack Campisi, an anthropologist who teaches at Wellesley College and who has served as a consultant to the Lumbees, argues that the federal requirements for acknowledgment simply fail to provide for groups that do not fit conventional notions of what an Indian tribe is supposed to be. "First, you must show that you are related to a specific tribe. Eighteenth- and nineteenth-century records are often unable to show a clear connection between old and contemporary Indian groups. Should the Indians be burdened because the records were destroyed? Tribes in North Carolina had three language stocks and a high degree of mobility. How do you deal with populations that moved away from their original area of settlement? Moreover, there was a conscious, racist effort on the part of white society to remove any evidence of the native population. You also have to show political continuity. But there is just no standard for what constitutes this. One native group was turned down because it couldn't demonstrate continuity between 1945 and 1970, partly because whites worked on building their church, but the department recognized another group that had no tribal records of their own up to the 1980s." The federal process, Campisi says, assumes that tribes always followed a similar historical trajectory, from complete independence to a treaty relationship with the national government, a pattern based mainly on the country's experience with the Plains tribes in the mid-nineteenth century. "What could a tribe do to assert its identity in a state like North Carolina in the 1800s? Very little."

Established Indian tribes have, virtually without exception, refused to support the Lumbees' claims, however. "If Congress creates Indian tribes at will, without meaningful criteria or substantial evidence that a group is in fact a tribe within the normal meaning of that term, then the government-to-government relationship and the trust responsibility will be enormously weakened," the Southern Pueblo Governors' Council warned during congressional hearings on the Lumbee question. Others have been more brutal. "There is no Lumbee tribe," says Phillip Martin, Chief of the Mississippi Band of Choctaw. "Indians are a tribal people who have historically been together, who have their own form of government, their own language and their own artifacts, things that are their own and nobody else's. The Lumbees cannot come up with those things. We paid the price of being Indians, and we're still maintaining our identity. It just don't seem right that the feds should make someone Indian by legislation. No one can do that. Maybe God can, if even He can." The most vigorous opposition of all has come from the Eastern Band of Cherokees, at present the only federally recognized tribe in North Carolina. Citing "extensive inter-marriage with various races," Principal Chief Jonathan L. Taylor told Congress: "How then can the Indian people of this country (or the non-Indian community for that matter) seriously be expected to accept these people as full-blooded Lumbees?"

Principles aside, Taylor and the other tribal leaders are well aware that recognition of the Lumbees would mean significantly less federal money that could be spread around among other tribes. The cost to the BIA of providing federal services for the Lumbees would be an estimated $90 million annually, equivalent to about 10 percent of the bureau's budget. Moreover, recognition of the Lumbees would undoubtedly lead to a landslide redefining as Indians of most of the other groups of uncertain origin whose petitions are now gathering dust in the BIA's archives. That, in turn, would mean the general extension of the full panoply of federal support and protection to scores of groups that were never tribes in any traditional sense, just at the time when established tribal governments are demanding enhanced powers as semiautonomous nations.

Recognition would automatically entitle the Lumbees to all the rights and privileges that are enjoyed by established tribes. The inhabitants of an obscure corner of rural North Carolina would instantly be lifted up into a direct government-to-government relationship with the United States that would allow them largely to bypass the State of North Carolina. Freed from state regulations, for instance, they theoretically could turn a tract of their swampland into the site for a gambling casino or, for that matter, a nuclear waste dump. In accordance with its mandated trust responsibility to Indian tribes, the federal government would be bound to help the Lumbees set up a formal tribal government as well as tribal courts and police and schools from which non-Indians legally could be excluded, and to provide free health care through the Indian Health Service. The Lumbees would also enjoy "Indian preference," a form of affirmative action that requires that members of recognized tribes be granted special consideration for federal jobs and in the allocation of public contracts. The tobacco farmers, the Sheetrock men, the plant workers from Pembroke and Maxton, the descendants of the "mixt Crew" and the putative heirs to the myth of the Lost Colony, would, in short, at last have the right to describe themselves as a "sovereign nation."

For the past quarter century, federal Indian policy has been driven largely by principles that were laid down by Richard Nixon in July of 1970. "Both as a matter of social justice and as a matter of enlightened social policy, we must begin to act on the basis of what the Indians themselves have long been telling us," declared the President, whose reputation among grateful Indians remains largely untarnished by the stain of Watergate. "The time has come to break decisively with the past and to create the conditions for a new era in which the Indian future is determined by Indian acts and Indian decisions." Nixon went on to state that the goal of any new national policy toward Native Americans must be "to strengthen the Indian's sense of autonomy without threatening his sense of community. We must assure the Indian that he can assume control of his own life without being separated involuntarily from the tribal group. And we must make it clear that Indians can become independent of Federal control without being cut off from Federal concern and Federal support." The glaring contradiction in his words —that Indian "independence" could somehow be reconciled with continuing "Federal support"—would continue to bedevil both tribes and policymakers, just as it had since the days of John Marshall.

Nixon's words ushered in one of the most active periods of Indian legislation in American history. By the end of the decade, the political landscape of Indian Country would be profoundly altered, less by the attention-getting dramatics of the radical American Indian Movement, whose occupation of the Bureau of Indian Affairs' offices in 1972 and armed standoff at Wounded Knee in 1973 captured headlines around the world, than by the deliberations of the United States Congress. A steady flow of new laws mandated increased spending for Indian schools and health care, established a federal responsibility for the protection of traditional religious practices, recognized long-moribund fishing rights, and conveyed large tracts of federal land to native corporations in Alaska. In 1972, the Nixon administration also began the transformation of the Bureau of Indian Affairs into an agency staffed almost exclusively by Indians, by authorizing the preferential hiring of natives at all levels, a measure that had the dubious distinction of institutionalizing racial discrimination for the first time as a criterion for federal employment. Additional legislation redefined the very nature of the relationship between Indians and the federal government by strengthening both the concept and the powers of tribal governments. The Indian Self-Determination Act of 1975 initiated a continuing shift of practical authority to tribal governments that still continues today. Declaring that "Indian people will never surrender their desire to control their relationships both among themselves and with non-Indian governments," Congress directed the Secretary of the Interior to help tribes in contracting to administer federal grants and programs for financial management, construction, the maintenance of tribal facilities, the planning of federal programs serving the tribe, and the development and management of health services.

In 1977, the American Indian Policy Review Commission, the most thorough study of Indian policy to date, carried the concept of sovereignty another step further, asserting in its final report that "the relationship of the American Indian tribes to the United States is founded on principles of international law"—a somewhat arbitrary assertion given the great diversity in the character of the tribes, but one that has become an article of faith among Indian leaders and polemicists around the country. All future policymaking, the commission proclaimed, must be guided by two fundamental principles:

1. that Indian tribes are sovereign political bodies, having the power to determine their own membership and power to enact laws and enforce them within the boundaries of their reservations, and

2. that the relationship which exists between the tribes and the United States is premised on a special trust that must govern the conduct of the stronger toward the weaker.

In a cutting dissent, the commission's vice-chairman, Congressman Lloyd Meeds, a Washington Democrat, accused the commission of trying "to convert a political notion into a legal doctrine," arguing that

the assertion of inherent tribal sovereignty . . . would mean that whenever there is a group of American Indians living together on land which was allocated to them by the Federal Government, they would have the power to exercise general governmental powers. The source of those powers would then be some magical combination of their Indianness and their ownership of land. Governmental powers do not have as their source such magic. Governmental powers in these United States have as their source the State and Federal Constitutions.

He added, "It is one thing for the Congress to permit tribal Indians to make their own laws and be ruled by them without State interference. It is quite another for the Congress to permit tribes to exercise general governmental powers without general Federal supervision."

Nevertheless, the principle of "tribal sovereignty," ill-defined though it may often be, has since then become the cornerstone of federal Indian policy, and of right-minded political discourse. Senator Daniel K. Inouye, who as chairman of the Senate Select Committee on Indian Affairs has been a driving force in Indian policymaking since the mid-1980s, embraced the doctrine of sovereignty wholeheartedly. "Sovereignty, the inherent right of self-government and self-determination, is the focal point in all Indian issues," he told a White House conference of Indian leaders, in 1992. "I stand with you to receive your marching orders."

In 1968, two years before Nixon's speech, Congress had enacted the Indian Civil Rights Act in an effort to ensure that the freedoms enjoyed by other Americans were also respected by tribal governments. Essentially, it required that tribal governments enforce most of the basic principles of the Bill of Rights, including free speech, freedom of the press, freedom of assembly, the right to a speedy and public trial, and due process; no tribal court, the act declared, shall "deny to any person within its jurisdiction the equal protection of its laws or deprive any person of liberty or property without due process of law." However, Congress significantly modified the provisions of the bill to take account of certain tribal customs—for example, guaranteeing the free exercise of religion but not prohibiting its establishment. Nor, with deference to limited tribal budgets, did Congress require tribes to provide free counsel for the accused or a jury trial in civil cases.

Congress failed to take into account the practical application of the act's provisions in the bare-knuckle arena of tribal politics. Nor did it appropriate any money for its enforcement. Even with its limitations, the Indian Civil Rights Act was an important step in extending the principles of civil rights across Indian Country. But the act became a virtual dead letter just ten years after its passage, with the Supreme Court's landmark decision in *Santa Clara Pueblo v. Martinez*. Perhaps more than any other single event, this decision revealed the fundamental moral contradiction that lies at the heart of modern Indian policy as well as the practical dilemma of a government that has simultaneously committed itself to civil rights and to the inexorable logic of tribal self-determination, in which the rights of individual Indians (who also happen to be U.S. citizens) are secondary to the will, and to the increasing power, of the tribe.

Ostensibly at issue in the Martinez case was a tribal law of the Santa Clara Pueblo, near Santa Fe, which barred from tribal membership children of female tribal members who were married to nonmembers; reflecting the patriarchal tradition of the pueblo, the law did not apply to the children of male tribal members. In denying tribal membership, the law deprived individuals who may have been born and lived their entire lives in the pueblo such privileges as the rights to vote, to hold office, to take matters before the tribal council, and even to live on the reservation. Julia Martinez, a skilled potter who was married to a Navajo, brought suit against the pueblo, arguing that the law discriminated against her daughter by violating her rights to equal protection and due process under the Indian Civil Rights Act. The pueblo maintained, however, that since its membership laws were rooted in its traditional culture, control over the criteria for belonging to the tribe was basic to its exercise of tribal sovereignty.

To the Martinezes' dismay, the federal district court in Phoenix upheld the pueblo's argument. The court wrote:

> Much has been written about tribal sovereignty. If those words have any meaning at all, they must mean that a tribe can make and enforce its decisions without regard to whether an external authority considers those decisions wise. To abrogate tribal decisions, particularly in the delicate area of membership, for whatever "good" reasons, is to destroy cultural identity under the guise of saving it.

On appeal, the Supreme Court later used the case as a vehicle to extend the power of Indian tribes generally by ruling that the Indian Civil Rights Act could not be interpreted to authorize a lawsuit against a tribe or its officers in the federal courts. In other words, simply providing a federal forum for civil rights litigation would constitute interference in tribal self-government. Reasoning that the application of the conventional constitutional standards of equal protection and due process would undermine the tribe's status as a "culturally and politically distinct entity," the Court ruled, in a decision penned by Thurgood Marshall, that the promotion of Indian self-determination was more important than "providing in wholesale fashion for the extension of constitutional requirements to tribal governments."

Dissenting from the majority of the Court, Byron White wrote, with a skepticism that is ever less frequently heard in a political climate which increasingly regards tribal claims as inviolate and beyond debate:

> Given Congress' concern about the deprivations of Indian rights by tribal authorities, I cannot believe, as does the majority, that it desired the enforcement of these rights to be left up to the very tribal authorities alleged to have violated them. In the case of the Santa Clara Pueblo, for example, both legislative and judicial powers are vested in the same body, the Pueblo Council.

He went on to add, with emphasis, that "the extension of constitutional rights to individual citizens is intended to intrude upon the authority of government."

The impact of the Martinez ruling was soon felt, and nowhere more vividly or grotesquely than in the case of Tom Shortbull, a

Lakota educator who sought to run for president of the Pine Ridge tribal council in 1980. In a community where elected officials often had no more than an eighth-grade education, Shortbull's credentials were impressive: he held a master's degree in public administration and had served as president of Oglala Community College from 1975 to 1979. Like Martinez, the Shortbull case conflated questionable criteria for tribal membership with blatant discrimination in a way that is comparatively commonplace on many Indian reservations but that would very likely have shocked other Americans had it ever been publicized outside western South Dakota.

No one suggested that Shortbull was not Lakota. His father had been an enrolled member of the tribe and had bequeathed him land on the reservation; Shortbull's wife was also an enrolled member. Rather, his first and knottiest problem was that he fell into the ambiguous category that tribal bureaucrats designated "NE," for "not enrolled," along with about five thousand other Lakotas who had been born off-reservation. NEs were, in principle, disqualified from voting or running for tribal office, even though they met the tribe's blood quantum and residency requirements for membership. However, tribal politicians had in fact manipulated the NE class for more than forty years, distorting the entire electoral process, either by depriving thousands of Sioux of their right to vote or else by granting it only capriciously when it suited the interests of the party in power.

Shortbull's second problem was that he was a political insurgent and a threat to certain powerful members of the tribal council. Citing his status as an NE, the tribal election board refused to certify him as a candidate, with the specious excuse that it would require the personal approval of the Secretary of the Interior. When Shortbull requested a ruling from the department, the BIA declared that the criteria for candidacy were a matter that lay wholly within the ambit of tribal sovereignty. Undaunted, Shortbull next sued in federal court, arguing that he was being denied his right to run for office because there was no official panel to hear election complaints (even though one was required by the tribal law) and that the next existing level of appeal on the reservation was the tribal court—which included two members of the same election board that had disqualified him in the first place.

Citing the Martinez decision, lawyers for the tribal council insisted that the tribal court had no jurisdiction to hear civil rights cases because of the tribe's sovereign immunity from lawsuits lodged under the Indian Civil Rights Act. With some courage, the tribe's own senior judge, H. Clyde Red Shirt, threatened to issue an injunction against the council unless it reconsidered Shortbull's right to contest the election and immediately placed his name on the ballot. One week later, the council's executive committee ordered Red Shirt to rescind his actions. Red Shirt, in turn, found the executive committee members in contempt of court and ordered them arrested. The executive committee thereupon ordered a more pliable appellate court judge to quash Red Shirt's orders and simultaneously suspended Red Shirt and replaced him with its own appointee. Although the tribal code required that charges be filed and a hearing be held before a judge could be removed from the bench, none were. On February 4, 1980, the new chief justice rescinded all of Red Shirt's orders. One month later, a tribal restraining order was served against Shortbull, enjoining him from relief in either tribal or federal court. "Martinez set Indian law back thirty years," says Ramon Roubideaux, Shortbull's attorney, who in 1950 became the first Indian certified to practice law in South Dakota.

Twelve years later, little had changed at Pine Ridge. When Harold Salway, frustrated in his efforts to reform the tribal government, decided not to run for reelection as tribal president in 1992, he left office with a harsh blast, declaring, "The system is weak, deficient, and creates an arena of corruption. There's no code of ethics, no responsibility. Without accountability, the system supports corruption." Pine Ridge, it must be said, with its extreme poverty, overpopulation, and a political culture that is still badly damaged by the civil war of 1973, is by no means typical of all reservations. It should also be said that tribal governments as a whole are probably no more mismanaged or corrupt than many municipal administrations elsewhere in the United States. However, no other governments have such ill-defined and ill-regulated powers, coupled to the court-sanctioned right to discriminate and sheltered beneath the principle of tribal sovereignty.

In 1986, the Department of Justice informed the U.S. Civil Rights Commission that in the seven years prior to the Martinez decision, the department had received some 280 complaints of violations of the Indian Civil Rights Act by tribal governments. After Martinez, the number dropped precipitously, not because there were fewer abuses but because the department had made clear that it would do nothing to address them. Between 1978 and 1985, the department received only forty-five complaints against tribal governments, typically accusing tribal officials of failing to allow defendants' attorneys to appear in tribal court, failing to allow defendants to be heard in court, denying trial by jury, interfering in elections by tribal councils, as well as fraud, nepotism, and discrimination in tribal housing. The victims needn't have bothered. James M. Schermerhorn, an official of the department's Civil Rights Division, informed the commission, "No effort has been made, post Santa Clara, to invoke the jurisdiction of the federal court."

"Not one Federal dollar has been spent on the enforcement of fundamental civil rights of American citizens domiciled on reservations since the 1978 Supreme Court decision, *Santa Clara Pueblo v. Martinez,*" the U.S. Commission on Civil Rights reported in 1991.

> The government of the United States has failed to provide for Indians living on reservations guarantees of those fundamental rights it is obliged to secure for all U.S. citizens living on territory controlled by the United States and under the laws of the United States. In abandoning by act of Congress individual U.S. citizens to the indeterminate control of tribal governments without recourse to Federal courts of judicature the United States thereby fails to provide the just constitutional claims for which all citizens may pray.

Ramon Roubideaux is a small, rotund, almost elfin man whose eyebrows remain perpetually raised in an expression of mock surprise and who enjoys describing himself, rather disingenuously, as "just a little old barefoot boy from the Rosebud Indian reservation." While his view of tribal sovereignty is a minority one, it bears listening to, for, in contrast to that of most of the advocates of sovereignty, it has been gleaned from observing the behavior of tribal governments from the outside for nearly half a century. "We have people with eighth-grade educations running what are, in effect, multimillion-dollar corporations," he says, leaning over his desk in his office in Rapid City. "It's so ridiculous, I can't even cry! Indians can do anything harmful to their own people, and nothing happens. The federal government has given up its responsibility to guarantee their rights to Indian people—not only from the federal system, but also the tribal system, by hiding behind the idea that this is tribal sovereignty. What we've done is let the worst thing that was created by the white man in the last one hundred years—tribal governments—have a power that they simply do not deserve."

For the Lumbees, however, such concerns remain the luxuries, or the curse, of the future. The recognition that they crave is still a chimera that lies just beyond reach, on a political horizon that seems forever to recede from them as they struggle toward it. In 1989, under pressure from the established tribes, the Bureau of Indian Affairs recommended against recognition of the Lumbees, asserting that they had failed to document convincingly their descent from a historic tribe. Since then, they have lobbied tirelessly for direct recognition by a vote of Congress. In 1994, a bill for recognition passed in the House of Representatives, but failed on the floor of the Senate.

Down the road from the Pembroke Gym, with its hand-painted ads of muscled and feathered Indians, the Lumbee enrollment office may be found in the cavernous interior of a former supermarket. It is here that the Lumbee tribe has painstakingly come into being, name by name, year by year, a sisyphean endeavor carried out by people whose dedication approaches an act of transcendental faith. Amid a welter of battered file cabinets, desks, and Kmart chairs, two or three women are wading through the tidal wash of Locklears and Lowrys, Dials and Oxendines, matching remembered genealogies against old census rolls and photocopies of century-old petitioners' lists. Applicants for membership must also be approved by the Lumbee Elders Review Committee. What that means, says its chairman, the Reverend Weldon Lowry, is that "there's got to be somebody here that remembers their daddy."

At seventy-nine, Lowry still stands well over six feet in height. His face is large, wedge-shaped and walnut-brown, with eyebrows like inverted vees. He speaks in lofty cadences like a man who is accustomed to being listened to, as he is, by all accounts, with trembling attention, when he brings hellfire to the doors of the church where he preaches each Sunday. Like many Lumbees of his generation, he perceives the fate of his people in terms of powerful metaphors of exile and redemption.

"The difference between us and Israel in the land of Egypt is that they were transported for four hundred years into a foreign country, while we've been in bondage in our own land. They were allowed to go home one day, but we're still not free. They don't have us conquered financially or politically but, spiritually speaking, they've got us down. You can compare us to those children in Egypt. They had two rivers to cross, the Red Sea and the Jordan. We have already crossed the Red Sea. Now we stand on the banks of the Jordan, looking at the promised land." His voice undulates fervently, with the charging pitch of a church organ, heavy with biblical resonance. "We changed our name many a time. It doesn't bother me. I've been a Croatan. I was a Cherokee at one time, how many years ago? Another time we were Siouxans. That other one, what was it, 'Indians of Robeson County'? The name is more important to white people than it is to us. We have lived to see the day when we've got our own appliance store, our own bank, our own medical doctors. We're climbing the ladder. We've just got to get this noose removed from our necks. Recognition will make us free. We'll be just like other Indians."

3

The Reinvention of Indian Country

A FEW MINUTES before 8:00 P.M. on June 15, 1984, fourteen-year-old Biscuit Brown and his younger brother Donovan mounted their bicycles and rode out of their mother's yard on the Salt River Pima-Maricopa reservation, just outside Scottsdale, Arizona. Biscuit wanted to borrow a tape cassette from his friend Wade Hays, who lived a half mile away, in the settlement known as Victory Acres. They pedaled due south down Country Club Road through the spare and graceful landscape of sand and sage. Just before they reached Indian School Road, they turned east onto the dirt track that cut through the cotton fields.

Victory Acres is, as it was then, a compact settlement of half a dozen homes whose residents have attempted to overcome the desolation of the desert by painting their solid but otherwise austere cinderblock houses in an assortment of cheerful, eye-catching colors. There is a straining for suburban effect in the struggling lawns, the white-painted rocks that line the curb, the satellite dishes. There is also a basketball court. That evening, four or five young men were idling on the ball court, drinking and arguing about cars. One of them was a thirty-year-old Cahuilla Indian from California named Albert Duro. He had come to Salt River three years earlier and shacked up with a local woman. He was known as a troublemaker and as someone who "liked to party." People later said they always knew that he would do something terrible.

The tribal police eventually pieced together what happened next. Duro was shouting that his Chevy could beat anyone's car on a straightaway. Listo Ramirez took offense. There was a scuffle. Duro walked to the Chevy, leaned in, and took his 30.30 out of the backseat.

Biscuit and Donovan were now crossing the drainage ditch behind the Pachecos' house. They were about 250 feet short of Wade Hays's place when Albert Duro began shooting at Ramirez. The boys immediately realized the danger they were in. Donovan would remember Biscuit shouting, "Hurry! Hurry! You might get shot!"

Perhaps what occurred then was merely an act of alcoholic insanity. Possibly, though less likely, Duro recognized Biscuit and remembered some real or imagined slight. Duro surely could not have failed to see the two boys on their bicycles. The summer solstice was only a few days away, and the sun was still well above the horizon, casting pink shadows across the cotton fields and the desert. Duro lifted the 30.30 and fired directly at Biscuit as he pedaled frantically toward the Hayses' yellow house.

Donovan told the tribal police that there was "a zinging noise and then a kind of thud." He looked back and saw Biscuit lying on the ground. The bullet had hit an artery in his stomach. He bled to death on the ground.

Duro fled in his souped-up Chevy. He got as far as Riverside, California, where he was found and arrested by the FBI, in accordance with the federal government's statutory responsibility for investigating major crimes committed on Indian reservations. He was charged with homicide in the United States District Court in Phoenix and remanded to the tribal jail at Salt River. The case seemed cut-and-dried. But, in July, the tribe was informed by the federal district attorney that the government had decided to drop the indictment for lack of evidence. The decision did not come as a complete surprise at Salt River. Few Indians believe that any courts take crime committed on reservations seriously; indeed, not one of the eight homicides committed on the Salt River reservation that year resulted in a conviction.

The tribe decided to prosecute Duro on the most serious charge that lay within its jurisdiction, the "unlawful discharge of firearms," which carried a maximum sentence of only one year in the tribal jail but which would buy time to enable the tribal police to develop a stronger case on the murder charge. The five-thousand-member tribe was affluent, by the standards not just of Indian Country but of the rural Southwest. The tribe leased water from the Salt River to the city of Phoenix and large tracts of land to non-Indian farmers; it also operated several quite profitable enterprises, including a golf course, a trailer park, a storage facility for recreation vehicles, and one of the largest sand and gravel companies in the United States. The tribal police department was widely reckoned to be more professional and better equipped than those in most non-Indian Arizona towns of comparable size. Given its reputation for efficiency, the tribe had reason to be self-confident.

But it was now that events became slippery, that human concerns, plain things like punishment and retribution and the fact of a small boy's violent death, disappeared amid the baroque complexities of Indian law. In the ensuing months, Biscuit's murder became transformed into the Duro case, one of the most bitterly fought Indian issues of the 1980s. Duro's court-appointed lawyer filed a writ of habeas corpus in federal court, challenging the tribe's right to try him on any charge, arguing that since Indian tribes were sovereign entities, like nations, no tribe had inherent legal jurisdiction over a member of another tribe. To the astonishment and dismay of the tribal officials at Salt River, the court agreed. So, on appeal and in accordance with the prevailing philosophy of tribal sovereignty, did the United States Supreme Court.

Biscuit's mother, Martha Whitman, works as a dispatcher for the tribal police department. Not surprisingly, even years later, the devastating impact of the tragedy can still be read in her broad, otherwise smooth-featured face. She takes Biscuit's junior high school graduation picture out of her purse. In the picture, the boy's face is fleshy and still unformed; there is a shock of black hair, dark eyes, and the lopsided smile of a class clown. "Those puffy cheeks," she says. "That's why everyone called him Biscuit. His real name was Phillip." Then, after a while, weeping now, she says, "I went to the hospital. He had dirt in his face, in his mouth. He was determined to get his eighth-grade diploma. It arrived in the mail two weeks after he passed away."

Haltingly, she tells how she rode in a tribal police car that followed the one carrying Albert Duro off the reservation after the federal court ordered his release. The cars stopped at Pima Road, the Scottsdale city line. There a policeman unlocked Duro's handcuffs. Duro then turned and looked Whitman directly in the face. "He smiled at me," she says in her girlish, numbed voice. "He just smiled at me. Then he crossed the traffic into Scottsdale and walked away."

On the face of it, the Supreme Court's ruling seemed preposterous. It appeared to say that a crime committed against an Indian by a member of a different tribe was no crime at all. The ruling effectively prevented Indian courts from prosecuting crimes as elementary as domestic abuse involving spouses who belong to different tribes. The implications for law enforcement were obvious and nightmarish. The predicament was especially acute in Arizona, which has one of the most intricately mingled tribal populations in the United States. The Salt River reservation, for example, and the reservations of the nearby Gila River and Ak Chin tribes are all inhabited mainly by ethnically identical Pimas and Maricopas. Entire families who are members of the Salt River Tribe have lived for generations on one or another of the other reservations. There are Gila River members who own land at Salt River. There are Salt River women married to Ak Chin men and living at Gila River. To complicate matters still further, about one thousand members of more far-flung tribes—Navajos, Apaches, Sioux—also reside on the Salt River reservation, along with hundreds of whites who live in the tribe's trailer park.

Duro's release was greeted with shock by the tribe's leaders. Like Indian officials across the country, those of the Salt River Tribe correctly saw the Duro case as a major test of tribal powers and, by extension, of modern Indian identity. "The guy was guilty of a crime—he killed a kid," says Ivan Makil, the tribe's current chairman, a youthful, intense man who operated a discount cigarette shop before entering politics. "He shouldn't have been allowed to go free. That was just plain wrong. He ought to have been tried by our court and our judge. No one wants to admit it, but the only difference is that we are Indian. The government says it wants us to practice self-determination, to govern ourselves, but they still don't let us out of the box. The essence of self-determination is to decide things for yourself."

Micki's Café is, in its modest way, a last bulwark against the encroachment of history and a symbol, amid the declining fortunes of prairie America, of the kind of gritty (and perhaps foolhardy) determination that in more self-confident times used to be called "the frontier spirit." Seen in that light, Micki Hutchinson's rage might even seem heroic. To her, the Indian problem seems as plain as the grid of streets that white homesteaders optimistically laid out here in 1910, on the naked South Dakota prairie, in the middle of what they were told was no longer the reservation of the Cheyenne River Sioux Tribe. It was not difficult for her to decide what to do when the tribal government ordered her to purchase a $250 tribal liquor license, in the winter of 1991: she ignored them.

"You've got to take a stand. You can't just roll over and play dead. They have no right to tell me what to do—I'm not Indian!" The tension shows on her face; it is a handsome face, tanned and chiseled, fortyish, but aloof with the wariness of someone who obviously dislikes the attention of strangers. "If this were Indian land, it would make sense. But we're a non-Indian town. There is no Indian land here. This is all homestead land, and the tribe was paid for it. I already pay taxes to the State of South Dakota. The tribe doesn't provide us with any services. There's no tribal law enforcement here. I can't vote in tribal elections or on anything else that happens on the reservation. What they're talking about is taxation without representation."

Even now, it may not be clear to Hutchinson how irrevocably things changed on the morning of March 27, 1991, or that what happened had a meaning beyond rural South Dakota, that it was but a small part of the much larger drama that is being played out between defensive whites and resurgent tribes almost everywhere in Indian Country. Hutchinson knew, of course, that the tribe would react somehow. But she was unprepared for the public spectacle or for the guns. Like everyone in the town of Isabel, she remembers the screech of the warning siren that someone set off when the tribal police reached the edge of town, as if they were some kind of natural disaster, a tornado or a fire.

People said later that it was "like something out of *L.A. Law*." The convoy of gold-painted prowl cars rolled in from the prairie and then, when they had come abreast of the café, swung sideways across the road, blocking traffic. Thirty-eight tribal policemen surrounded the yellow brick building. After extracting his considerable weight from his car, the tribe's police chief, Marvin LeCompte, told Hutchinson that she was in contempt of tribal court. A truck

backed up to the front of the café. Cops pulled off sheets of plywood and began nailing them over the picture windows. Inside, one
group of officers ordered the morning breakfast crowd away from
their fried eggs and coffee. Another group went back into the pine-
paneled bar and confiscated Hutchinson's stock of beer and liquor
—"contraband," as LeCompte described it—and drove off with it
to the tribal government's offices at Eagle Butte.

Ten days later, Hutchinson's lawyer, Steve Aberle, obtained a
federal restraining order that enabled the café to reopen. Hutchinson and five other white bar owners argued in tribal court that the
tribe had no authority to enforce its laws upon them. They argued
that, like much of Indian Country, the reservation's nominal
boundaries were an illusion, a cartographic sleight of hand. They
pointed out that virtually all Isabel's three hundred inhabitants
were white, as were more than one-third of the six thousand people
who lived inside the reservation's official limits. They quoted the
allotment acts of 1887 and 1889, which had explicitly given ("right
there in black and white") the Secretary of the Interior the authority
to buy reservation lands and resell them to settlers, who would then
"have the benefit of and be subject to the laws, both civil and
criminal, of the State or Territory in which they may reside," and
the 1908 law, which with equal clarity referred to the reservation as
"thus diminished" by the sale of land to white settlers.

"Homesteaders still wanted more land," says Aberle, a mild-
mannered and earnest man who is the state's attorney for Dewey
County as well as an enrolled member of the Cheyenne River Sioux
Tribe. "At the same time, there was a feeling that the Indians
weren't using all their land and that it could be put to better use. All
the old maps show that the reservation was a patchwork," he explains, spreading out a 1967 map ("information courtesy of the
Cheyenne River Sioux Tribe") showing large portions of Dewey
and Ziebach counties free of the cross-hatching that identified land
as part of the reservation. "The Indians were told that if they gave
up this land for homesteading, whites would be kept off the rest
forever." With a toothpick Aberle draws a swath from Glad Valley
in the west, through Isabel, to Firesteel, and Timber Lake and Glencross, and then another through the center of the reservation,
around Dupree and Lantry as far east as Eagle Butte. "This area is
as large as Rhode Island, and 95 percent of the people who live in it
are not Indian."

The tribe, at least at first, maintained that alcohol rather than land was at the heart of the problem. When Gregg Bourland, a young businessman, was elected chairman of the Cheyenne River Sioux Tribe in 1990, he inherited the previous administration's pledge to end alcoholism on the reservation by the year 2000. "It affects everyone and everything on this reservation," he says. Bourland can recite any number of dismal statistics: The reservation has an estimated rate of active alcohol addiction of 53 percent and rates of liver disease and of death from the direct effects of alcohol eight times higher than the national average. Virtually every one of the average of sixty-three suicide attempts on the reservation each year involves alcohol in some way; 95 percent of the tribal police budget is spent fighting alcohol-related crime.

"Too many people on the reservation see alcohol as a staple, like bread and potatoes. We say it is a luxury and that it should be taxed like one. These non-Indian bar owners have taken advantage of Indians too damn long. They think this is still the Wild West. As far as they're concerned, as long as you have a dollar, you're good for a drink in those places. They've had free run on the reservation ever since alcohol was legalized. They think it's fine to let Indians drink themselves to death. Well, they're socially irresponsible and we're going to make them pay tax. They are within reservation boundaries, and they will follow reservation law."

Not surprisingly, the tribal court found against Hutchinson and five other white-owned bars that had defied the tribe. The court ruled that the tribal government's jurisdiction extended throughout the reservation from border to border and over everyone who lived within its boundaries, Indian and white; the following year, the tribal appeals court upheld the lower court's judgment. Then, in separate briefs, the bar owners and the reservation's predominantly white towns sued the tribe in federal court with the support of the State of South Dakota, which viewed the tribe's actions as an encroachment upon its own authority. It was clear to everyone that the liquor license was meant to set a precedent; it was to be followed by a tribal gas tax and other levies that would benefit members of the tribe only. "The tribe's goal is to seek control over the entire area through taxation," says Aberle. "Our position is that when the area was opened up for settlement, the tribe lost its regulatory control over non-Indian people residing in this area, who cannot vote or hold office." One by one, the bar owners eventually capitulated. Finally, only the towns and Hutchinson still held out.

"Once you give them what they want, they just want more. I'll close up the business before I buy that license." Hutchinson is leaning forward warily over the bar; glass cowboys buck across the long frosted mirror behind her. Her voice is as hard and flat as a weathered plank. "If they get away with this, they'll be able to do anything they want to anyone who comes on the reservation. Nobody here is rich. We're all just hanging in. Now people are scared the Indians are going to come into their homes and take them away." The flat, defiant voice is suddenly edged with a note of anxiety. "Who'd come in here and buy this place from me now? Who'd ever open a new business in this town?"

A century ago, it took a considerable leap of faith to imagine any business here at all. The Cheyenne River reservation had been deemed eligible for allotment only a few years before, in 1889, as the climactic act in the dismantling of the Great Sioux Reservation, which once encompassed the entire western half of the Dakotas. "Allotment" today has become merely another confusing term of art in the jargon of Indian affairs, but then it was perceived as the final, brilliant solution to what white Americans called "the Indian problem." Half the reservation was to be broken up among Indian freeholders, who were expected to abandon the life of the camp and government handouts and to be transmuted into solid citizens within a generation by the alchemical power of the family farm. The land that remained was to be offered for sale to land-hungry white settlers, who until then had been held at bay east of the Missouri River.

Agriculture was, in effect, imposed on the land by main force. Soon federal surveyors were squaring the open prairie into an ordered, rectilinear realm of acres and sections. It was an unquestioned technique that had been in use since the end of the American Revolution and that paid no attention at all to the availability of water. That meant little in New Jersey or Wisconsin, but on the northern Plains a single quarter section might contain all the water to be found for miles around. Immigrants came from as far away as Norway and Ukraine with the extraordinary delusion that they could grow rich tilling soil that received an average of just fourteen inches of rainfall per year. A promotional brochure of the era gushingly described the region as "the fairest and richest portion of the national domain, blessed with a climate pure, bracing and healthful, while its undeveloped soil rivalled if it did not surpass the most productive portions of the Eastern, Middle, or Southern states."

They were undaunted when they saw the dipping and rolling, coppery green landscape of the Dakotas. It was the golden age of American farming. Wheat was selling for the astronomical price of ninety cents a bushel. Soon great steam-driven threshers were chugging over the prairie like brontosauruses come to life. Before long, however, the settlers found, as Wallace Stegner put it, "that the 160 acres of a dryland homestead were a hand without even openers." The Depression was mere anticlimax. Busted farmers went West in droves, "to California," people in Isabel say, more as if it were a kind of oblivion than a real place. There were some who somehow made the mortgage payments, who endured the plagues of grasshoppers that sometimes lay three deep underfoot, and the wind that blew off all that soil that never should have been tilled in the first place and that sometimes hung so thick in the air that people put lamps on in the daytime to see inside their homes. The survivors bought up their neighbors' spreads, mechanized, managed finally to put together enough land to be economically viable.

Micki Hutchinson's father came up from Bennett County after World War II to make his fortune in cattle. There was plenty of good rangeland then, millions of acres of it, where all the busted homesteaders' places lay baking in the sun. Some of what they left drifted back into tribal ownership: "Most of your heavy soil, your gumbo, your poorer land, what couldn't be farmed, that was returned to the Sioux Tribe," says Aberle. When Micki Hutchinson was growing up in the 1950s, Indian Country seemed no more than a distant land that lay somewhere far beyond the horizon of rolling prairie.

There were signs that things were not all well. The coal mine down the road at Firesteel shut down; building lots there that sold for $250,000 apiece in 1910 reverted to prairie. In the 1960s, the railroad that linked the immigrants' towns was torn up and the rails sold off as scrap. In Isabel, the movie house closed and then the last restaurant burned to the ground. But the boom of the 1970s temporarily masked decline. Farmers who ought to have known better borrowed massively to buy $100,000 harvesters and to erect $50,000 silos.

When the bills came due in the 1980s, the effect was catastrophic. In 1988, precipitation on the northern Plains dropped to less than seven inches. As pastures withered and feed rocketed in price, the bottom dropped out of the cattle market. Land that had sold for $700 an acre at the start of the 1980s had lost half its value by the end of the decade. Foreclosure signs appeared around Isabel, as they did all over the Plains; banks began to repossess the grandiose harvesters and tractors, the silos, and the ambiguous land upon which they stood.

On the surface, Isabel still embodies the style of small-town life that Americans often wish to think was once the national paradigm. People leave their keys in their cars and their doors unlocked; it is the kind of town where people try hard to put a good face on things. Petunia beds are kept up in front of the Community Clinic; faux fieldstone was recently added to the façade of the Dewey County Bank. The fat rolls of hay in the fields, the vivid rows of new corn, the split-level farmsteads speak of hard work and the illusion of prosperity. But when you look more closely, you can see the slippage: the empty shell of the gas station that failed, of the place where the grocery store used to be, of the old state highway office. Young people move away and don't come back; since 1970, the high school graduating class has dropped from twenty-eight to five. Since the tribe's raid on the café, Isabel's population has dropped by half, from almost six hundred.

Micki's Café is, in a way, an answer to all this, the finger in the dike. When the old restaurant burned, ranchers and farmers chipped in their own money to build a place where they could have eggs and bacon, a sundae, a beer in the evening. Hutchinson took it over in 1984, after her husband broke his neck breaking a horse on the ranch where they lived; with their savings, she bought the knives and forks, crockery, tables and barstools, the alcohol. By the early 1990s, it was the place, since there was no other, where folks held their baby showers, proms, wedding receptions, and harvest dances, the quotidian events that, if only temporarily, reknit a disintegrating town into a community. When the tribal police appeared at the door that March morning in 1991, not just one woman's pride was felt to be at stake, but a way of life.

By then it was no longer the Indians but the whites who had come to seem but a ghostly presence on the land and destined for oblivion. As things slipped, it was perhaps tempting to blame the Indians, as if their assertiveness, their insistent specialness, was a kind of betrayal. "Once you give them what they want, they just want more. If they get away with this, they'll be able to do anything they want to anyone who comes on the reservation. People just don't understand!" In the midst of Hutchinson's bitterness lies, unexpectedly, the innocent notion that if Americans "out there" simply knew what was happening in Isabel, they would quickly put a stop to it. She cites evidence that is meant to shock: the federally purchased school band instruments that are reserved for Indians alone, the annual $70 federal allowance for Indian children's gym shoes, the checks bounced by tribal cops. "Indians have all the advantages. They have all these grants and benefits, and welfare checks. We build their roads, their schools. We build beautiful homes for them, and they kick out the walls, demolish them. Every year a billion dollars goes down that rat hole, and it's all destroyed. It's our money that pays for it, and it's really disgusting. They should go out and work like us. But they can't run a business. We're the ones who work hard. I put in ten or fifteen hours a day here to earn what I have. Nobody gives me anything. We need to abolish the reservations and make them get out and work. They should all be like us."

Beneath the crust of Micki Hutchinson's rage lies the fear and bewilderment of a hard people who mistook their isolation for independence and who no longer recognize the world in which they find themselves. "I was born and raised here, and I want to stay here. I don't want to go anywhere else. But the tribe will destroy us. They will destroy this town. It's going already, but at least it's our own."

Many Sioux hold that their ancestors originally lived in darkness beneath the earth and that it was a deception that brought the People up into the sunlight. In the world above, Iktomi, the Trickster, who carried his penis in a box and who had learned from the mice how to juggle his eyes, assembled the wolves and whispered to them that the flesh of those who dwelled below was much tastier than that of muskrats or deer. "I shall bring them to you for food," he promised. He then loaded a wolf with a pack of soft robes and choice meats. Following Iktomi's instructions, the wolf made its way underground through a cave until it encountered a young man by the name of Tokahe. The wolf told him, "I have come from the world to give people what they most desire." Tokahe delightedly shared the meat with his friends, who gazed at him enviously when he put on the clothes he had gotten from the wolf. "There are plenty more such things in the world," the wolf said. "I shall be happy to take you there." Although Tatanka, the holy man, warned the People that the gifts were merely illusions conjured by a wizard, they begged Tokahe to lead them upward. In a vision, Tatanka saw that those who entered the cave would never be able to find their way back and that he must follow them, even though he would be irrevocably transformed. When the People emerged from the cave, their illusions soon fell away. They were hungry and cold. Slavering wolves dogged their steps. When all seemed lost, a shaggy beast appeared from the cave and led the People to where there was water and fruit. But the People had become different. They had forgotten the language they spoke in the darkness of the cave and had to invent a new one. Only Tatanka, the buffalo, the holy man, remembered the language of the Spirits and could talk to the other creatures of the world. Those who came up through the cave became the Ikce Oyate, the Real People, and many of their descendants say today that the place where they emerged from darkness was Wind Cave, in the Black Hills.

Anthropologists believe that the Lakotas originally inhabited the forests and grasslands of central Minnesota. Their enemies the Crees bestowed upon them the pejorative that produced the name by which they have long been known by whites: Nadoweisiw, or "Snakes," which the pidjin of French frontiersmen transmuted into "Sioux." In the late 1600s, Crees and Chippewas armed with European guns forced the Sioux westward, where they underwent the remarkable transformation that was to make them into the greatest power on the northern Plains. They were a profoundly ethnocentric people, with a passionate faith in their natural superiority; they made no concessions and few alliances. Until they finally collided with the power of the expanding United States, they seized land with virtual impunity from the Ioways, Omahas, Arikaras, and Mandans, inventing as they went the nomadic, horseborne way of life that has become emblematic of all Indians in the American imagination.

By 1700, the Sioux had abandoned their canoes and forest homes and had become buffalo hunters, mounted on tough horses traded northward by tribes that had acquired them from the Spanish settlers of the Southwest. In 1776, they reached the Black Hills on the western edge of the Dakotas and early in the nineteenth century decisively expelled the Kiowas and Cheyennes, establishing a claim to the Hills that remains a potent element of Sioux identity and tribal politics down to the present day. At its apogee, in the mid-1800s, the Lakota empire encompassed a vast portion of the central buffalo range and stretched from the Missouri River to the Bighorn Mountains of Wyoming, and from the Platte River in the south to the Heart River in the north.

"That's just racism, that's just bull," says Gregg Bourland, the chairman of the Cheyenne River Sioux Tribe, who prefers to believe the story of Tokahe and that the Lakotas have occupied the Dakotas since time immemorial. Bourland has undeniable presence, combining square-jawed good looks, charm, and the edgy self-confidence so characteristic of the Sioux; he may be the only man in Eagle Butte who wears a tie and jacket to work every day. There are no windows in Bourland's office, which is perhaps just as well, since there is not much to look at in the tribal capital of Eagle Butte except a congeries of silos and corn cribs, trailers interspersed with split-level HUD homes (ten of the twenty-five are boarded up), and a feeble commercial strip, where not far from the Dairy Queen and the Super Pumper you can find the video store that was Bourland's springboard to power. In a place where private enterprise seems to many to be a kind of white man's conjury, success made him a man to be reckoned with.

Barely forty, Bourland is widely reckoned to be one of the most effective tribal chairmen in the region. With a B.A. in business from the state college in Spearfish, he is also one of the best educated. On trips to Washington, he has called for legislation that would establish an enterprise zone on the reservation and would provide the same support for American companies willing to invest there as they would receive if they were breaking into a new foreign market. In 1992, he initiated an overhaul of the tribe's constitution, which made the tribe's courts independent for the first time from the political power of the tribal council. Pressed to name the people he admires, he offers all in one breath: Crazy Horse, "because his motto was 'total defiance' "; Jesus Christ, "the absolute master of peace and forgiveness"; and the inhabitants of the Amazon rain forest, who "are all role models for us: free, honest—what everyone should be."

More than Micki Hutchinson or than any of the frightened

whites in their crippled hamlets, it is Bourland who sees what is really at stake, that all this is about much more than small-town politics on the prairie, that it implicates the very nature of the United States itself. The tax, the ostentatious convoy, the lawsuit are less about alcohol than about power and the promises that the nation has made to its citizens, both white and Indian. Hutchinson and the other inhabitants of Isabel never noticed during the downward spiral of harvests, proms, and foreclosures that America had changed. A generation of legislation and court action had remade Indian Country, canonizing ideas about tribal sovereignty that would have appalled the lawmakers who, a century ago, saw the destruction of the reservations as the salvation of the American Indian.

"Let them talk about 'taxation without representation,'" Bourland says dismissively. "We're not a state: we're a separate nation, and the only way you can be represented in it is to be a member of the tribe. And they can't do that. They're not Indians. These folks are trespassers. To say that Isabel is a non-Indian community is a redneck argument. They are within reservation boundaries, and they will follow reservation law! The United States government induced and seduced people to come out here to settle, and never informed them that the tribes had sovereign rights. Maybe the government owes them an apology for not telling them what they were getting into. They've now had one hundred years with no tribal authority over them out here. Well, that's over."

Increasingly, Indian leaders speak of "sacred national sovereignty" as if its meaning were incontrovertible and self-evident. Their rhetoric can be jarring. "Indian Nations are not now, nor have they ever been, a part of the United States or its federal system," Rudolph C. Ryser, a Cowlitz Indian and chairman of the Center for World Indigenous Studies, declared at a 1988 conference on Indian self-government. "The settled reality is that Indian Nations have original or inherent sovereignty, in many ways more sure and certain than many of the states in the world." Dismissing the argument that the Constitution allows no place for autonomous Indian nations, Ryser said, "No Indian Nation ever ratified the U.S. Constitution, but then, neither did France, Canada, or China . . . That the United States has unilaterally restricted Indian self-government does not mean that Indian Nations lack the right and power to exercise full self-government—the same as any other peoples in the world." For sovereignty to be meaningful, he asserted, Indian Nations must be recognized as the sole governing authority inside their respective reservation boundaries. "The only alternatives to this arrangement are continued jurisdictional chaos on Indian reservations or tribal suicide."

At a minimum, tribes demand legal parity with the states. Within the spectrum of Indian politics, Bourland is comparatively restrained: "We are simultaneously citizens of two nations, the United States and our own, although we may be closer to Puerto Rico than to Canada." More extravagant declarations of tribal independence abound. "We, the members of the Confederated Tribes of the Warm Springs Reservation of Oregon hereby declare our national sovereignty," that tribe's council proclaimed in 1992. "We declare the existence of this inherent sovereign authority—the absolute right to govern, to determine our destiny, and to control all persons, land, water, resources and activities, free of all outside interference—throughout our homeland and over all our rights, property, and people, wherever located." Although claims to sovereignty are sometimes based on treaty stipulations or court rulings, they frequently appeal to a kind of divine right that flies in the face of modern American ideas about law. "Our sovereignty is based, not on the laws of human beings, but on natural laws given to us by our Creator; these natural laws are as they are, not as human beings may find them," the Confederated Tribes declared mystifyingly. Increasingly, tribal officials invoke the principle of "sovereign right" in wide-ranging debates with state governments over everything from law and order, highway maintenance, fishing quotas, and toxic waste disposal to, most visibly in recent years, the phenomenal proliferation of tribal gambling casinos.

Tribal "gaming," as it is rather delicately called these days, began with the establishment of the first high-stakes bingo game in Indian Country by the Seminoles in Florida in 1979. However, the current boom was initiated by the Indian Gaming Regulatory Act of 1988, a Reagan-era initiative that was designed to promote tribal self-sufficiency as an alternative to the federal dole. At the same time, however, it exacerbated the fraught relationship between tribes and the states by giving Indians the exclusive right to regulate any gambling on their lands that was already permitted in any form within a given state, enabling tribal lawyers, for instance, to argue successfully that occasional church-basement "Las Vegas Night" fund-raisers formed a precedent for permanent casino gambling on reservations. Not surprisingly, states reacted with almost universal hostility to legislation that created untaxable competition for their own lotteries and racetracks and, more significantly, compelled other state residents to tolerate an industry that they might find repugnant and over which they had no control. "What happens within a state ought to be decided by that state's citizens," Governor Roy Romer of Colorado, then chairman of the National Governors' Conference, declared in 1992. "A state ought to make that decision for itself, and it ought not to have a dictate from the federal government as to what should be the form of gaming and gambling within the state."

States were barred from prohibiting Indian gaming and were required to negotiate an agreement defining the terms under which tribal gaming would be conducted. Many states tried to resist: in 1990 in California, and in 1992 in Arizona, state governors ordered the confiscation of hundreds of tribally owned electronic gambling machines that they said failed to conform to state law. In both cases, the states were ultimately overruled by federal courts. Elsewhere, governors cut the best deal they could. Governor Lowell P. Weicker, Jr., of Connecticut dropped his adamant objections to the establishment of a casino by the Mashantucket Pequot Tribe in return for the tribe's commitment to voluntarily pay 25 to 30 percent of its gross gambling revenues into a special state fund to aid local governments, which now amounts to more than $100 million annually.

As an economic development tool, the act achieved considerable success. Since 1988, tribal gaming has grown into a $6-billion industry, accounting for about 2 percent of the $330 billion that Americans legally bet each year. By 1994, more than 160 tribes were operating some form of gambling activity, including forty full-fledged casinos, in twenty states. "Gaming is all that many tribes have today that can work," Gaiashkibos, the Ojibwe president of the National Congress of American Indians, told a congressional subcommittee. "The harsh reality is that the financial world has not historically looked towards locating business on Indian reservations. We had no competitive edge to attract non-Indian business nor the financial resources to create our own businesses and employ our people. But that window of opportunity which opened the way for gaming has given us the competitive edge and opened the door for other economic ventures as well."

Success is by no means evenly distributed. Gambling halls on remote or badly governed reservations are often as unprofitable and poorly managed as other tribal enterprises, while casinos fortunate enough to be situated near large cities have sometimes reaped astonishing profits. Some tribes have dissipated their earnings in lavish per capita payments to tribal members that evoke the squandered oil and land-sale windfalls of earlier eras. Others have invested in the kind of infrastructure that most American towns take for granted, but that many Indian communities conspicuously lack: fire and police departments, clinics, child care centers, roads, sewerage systems and power plants, and new housing. The Sycuan Band of Mission Indians, near San Diego, has used the profits from its casino to establish a health clinic and a fire department, while the nearby Cabazon Band built a new power plant and 950 units of housing. The Menominee Tribe of Wisconsin endowed a community college. The Oneida Tribe of Wisconsin funded a $9-million project to extend the city of Green Bay's sewer and water system to the reservation. The tiny Shakopee-Mdewakanton Dakota Community, which owns one of the biggest casinos in Minnesota, has wiped out unemployment, established a revolving fund for home mortgages, provided every one of its members with trust funds and every student with a full college scholarship, and appropriated as much as $80,000 per year in per capita payments for some families.

By far the most profitable tribal gambling operation of all lies among the steep, oak-forested hills of eastern Connecticut, on the reservation of the 320-member Mashantucket Pequot Tribe. The Pequots, who barely more than 20 years ago were not even recognized as an Indian tribe by the federal government, now own one of the largest casinos in the world, grossing about $800 million annually, half again as much as Donald Trump's Taj Mahal, the biggest casino in Atlantic City, and comprising nearly 15 percent of all the money taken in by Indian gaming nationally. Foxwoods Casino has also made the Pequots the largest single employer in eastern Connecticut, with a staff of more than 9,000, only a handful of them Pequot. Since its establishment in 1991, the casino has become a mecca for gamblers from throughout the Northeast, and on any given day, up to 35,000 gamblers crowd the casino's 7.6-acre gambling floor to play blackjack, craps, roulette, acey-deucey, and nearly 4,000 slot machines. The forty-seven-table poker room remains open around the clock, while the football-size bingo hall seats 3,100 players at two sittings a day. Amid all this, there is little that could be called "Indian" besides the kitsch of "wampum" betting cards and the beaded tunics worn by the cocktail waitresses.

Since tribal finances are not open to public scrutiny, the full disposition of the Pequots' profits is unknown. (Although they are exempt from federal and state taxes, they contribute $130 million to the state annually as stipulated by a negotiated compact.) It is well known that they have repurchased hundreds of acres of land that once belonged to the tribe, provided housing and full medical coverage for all tribal members and preschool-to-Ph.D. scholarships for each student, and developed a wide range of public services, including a tribal police force and court system. The tribe has also financed a number of cultural endeavors that are designed to endow the Pequots, who have been totally assimilated for generations, with some form of culture that is recognizably "Indian," including, most visibly, an annual powwow that lavishes $500,000 in prize money on competition dancers, nearly all of whom sport the feathered regalia of the Plains tribes. Terry Bell, a spokesman for the tribe, says, "We want to build a community and pass what we've built down to future generations. We want to rebuild what was taken from us three hundred years ago."

Downstairs in the casino, past the Las Vegas–style indoor waterfall, the tribal museum displays some examples of basketry, the only surviving Pequot traditional craft, along with some photographs of twentieth-century Pequots and a narrative text that describes what is called the tribe's "persistent struggle to maintain tribal identity and to hold onto tribal land." It is a formulation that implicitly links the Pequots with the histories of the better-known Western tribes. However, the Pequot story is not quite so simple. From one angle, the "retribalization" of the Pequots can be seen as a soaring example of the persistence of the human spirit. But from another, it might equally be seen as a disturbing illustration of the strange coinages that may result from the combining of gambling wealth and the ideology of tribal sovereignty in groups that in an ethnographic sense are, at most, only marginally Indian.

The Pequots, once powerful along the Connecticut coast, were crushed by troops from the Massachusetts Bay Colony in 1637, in one of the first, and most devastating, colonial Indian wars. The survivors were eventually resettled on a reservation near the town of Ledyard. They gradually accepted Christianity and intermarried among their neighbors, both white and black. By the mid-nineteenth century, they had become so invisible within the general population that Herman Melville could write, in *Moby Dick:* "Pequod, you will no doubt remember, was the name of a celebrated tribe of Massachusetts Indians, now extinct as the ancient Medes." The reservation, by then just a few acres in extent, was managed with the minimum of interest by the State of Connecticut, which periodically sold off portions of land to pay for the Pequots' upkeep. By the end of the century, the tribe had shrunk to a single extended family with fewer than two dozen members; by the 1930s, only two elderly women still lived on tribal land.

The tribe's current incarnation is largely the handiwork of Richard L. "Skip" Hayward, a former pipefitter for Electric Boat, who became chairman in 1975. Hayward, who by all accounts was inspired by a personal vision of tribal revival, tenaciously tracked down scores of distant relatives from all over the Northeast and as far away as Michigan and Florida. For nearly a decade, lawyers for the Pequots argued that on the basis of their genealogy and their continued occupancy of the land, however tenuous, the federal government was duty-bound to grant them recognition. Early in 1983, Congress did recognize the Pequots as an Indian tribe and appropriated $900,000 as compensation for lost lands. "They are now making the difficult transition from an extended family into a political organization," says Kevin McBride, the Pequot tribal archaeologist and an anthropologist at the University of Connecticut. The present-day Pequots are thus, in effect, a sort of family condominium that has reconstituted itself as an official Indian tribe, and which has in turn become a corporation that is also a "sovereign" state.

"The sovereignty issue won't go away," Timothy Wapato, a member of the Colville Confederated Tribes of Washington and then–executive director of the National Indian Gaming Association, has written.

> What needs to occur is an educational process, so the governors will deal with their local tribes on a government-to-government basis, not a government-to-special-interest basis. Many of the state and local politicians want to treat tribes as if they were Donald Trump's Taj Mahal or Caesar's World—as a commercial special-interest group as opposed to a

government . . . [T]he states that have been successful in resolving their issues on gaming have come to a recognition that a true negotiation has to occur between the two governmental sovereigns.

Federal policy has only cautiously embraced the fraught rhetoric of sovereignty. With perhaps deliberate ambiguity, George Bush described tribes in 1991 as "quasi-sovereign domestic dependent nations," whose "government-to-government relationship is the result of sovereign and independent tribal governments being incorporated into the fabric of our Nation." In practice, since the 1970s, the courts and Congress have tended to sustain Indian aspirations for increasing control over their reservation homelands. In 1978, the Supreme Court affirmed that tribes "still possess those aspects of sovereignty not withdrawn by treaty or statute," and it proclaimed four years later that "sovereign power, even when unexercised, is an enduring presence." Recent Supreme Court decisions have upheld the right of tribes to define their own criteria for membership, levy taxes, and, unfortunately for Micki Hutchinson, regulate the conduct of non-Indians on non-Indian land within the reservation boundaries, "when that conduct threatens or has some direct effect on the political integrity, the economic security, or the health or welfare of the tribe."

Predictably, the integrity of reservations has become an issue of paramount importance, for sovereignty can have no meaning without homelands where Indian governments may exercise their political will. "Without a land base, how can we keep from eventually being swallowed up?" Georgia C. George, the executive director of the Suquamish Tribe of Washington, rhetorically asked the annual Tribal Leaders Conference in Washington in 1991. "Without land 'sovereignty' becomes just an old word that our grandfathers told us about." The fate of tribal sovereignty is thus inextricably bound up with the future of that uncertain and balkanized land known as Indian Country.

In 1948, Congress decreed that for purposes of the law, "Indian Country" included all land within any reservation, including privately owned land. Technically speaking, Indian Country thus consists of slightly more than 2 percent of the land area of the United States, including 50.4 million acres in the lower forty-eight states and another 40 million acres in Alaska. But such statistics are deceptive. So are maps. For instance, the brown patches that mark off the Indian reservations on Rand McNally's map of South Dakota seem solid and logical, as neat as the plats that federal surveyors laid out for hopeful homesteaders a century ago all across the coppery green prairie. But like so much in Indian Country, the superficial impression of integrity is an illusion. Indian Country in the 1990s is, in a sense, less a physical landscape than it is a confusing snarl of jurisdictions and conflicting powers that nearly defies human ability to unravel.

Since colonial times, federal policy successively treated Indian tribes as independent nations, wards in need of protection, and finally, for the most part, semiautonomous governments. Each epoch left its indelible mark on Indian Country, like layers of crippling palimpsests, as vast regions of unsurveyed land contracted to become the congeries of present-day reservations. Most modern reservations are confusing checkerboards of tribal land, land held in trust for individual Indians by the federal government, land privately owned by Indians, homestead land owned by non-Indians, federal public land, and state and county land; in some areas, to complicate matters still further, the land surface is owned by an individual and the subsurface by a tribe, the United States, or a private concern.

Not surprisingly, law enforcement of any kind presents nightmarish problems. Tribes have clear-cut civil jurisdiction over Indians on tribal land but only patchwork authority over non-Indians on other parts of most reservations. "In white towns like Isabel or Timber Lake, we can detain a white guy, but we have to turn the suspect over to the local cops," says Cheyenne River police chief Marvin LeCompte. "The white cops, on the other hand, can detain an Indian, but they must turn him over to us. We can arrest anyone on tribal land and put him in our jail, but if he proves that he isn't Indian we have to hand him over to the state or county police." Serious crimes—including murder, rape, incest, arson, burglary, larceny, and certain forms of assault—present even more intricate problems. Investigation may be the responsibility of the state, the FBI, or the Bureau of Indian Affairs police, depending on the ethnic algebra of the parties involved.

In coming years, it may be on the Mashantucket Pequot reservation that large numbers of non-Indians, including Foxwoods employees and the 140,000 bettors who visit the casino each week, find themselves for the first time subject to tribal judicial processes.

The Pequots' wealth has enabled them to hire well-qualified attorneys and judges to staff their new legal system, however their standards of civil justice differ from those of their off-reservation neighbors. There are, for instance, no jury trials in the Pequots' tribal court, which has jurisdiction over all civil disputes, accidents, and injuries occurring on the reservation, except inside the casino, where the tribe has granted the state police jurisdiction as a bulwark against infiltration by organized crime. Moreover, although the tribe offers comparatively generous benefits to its employees, union activity is explicitly forbidden; according to tribal law, labor disputes cannot be appealed to state or federal court, thus making the tribe simultaneously employer, judge, and jury in such cases. "The legal rights of someone on the reservation, a non-Indian, are drastically different," the Connecticut attorney general, Richard Blumenthal, told the *New York Times* in 1994. "The state really has very little leverage."

For many white Americans, "Indian Country" still perhaps evokes less a real place than it does an atavistic sense of the wild and free, a Hollywood land where adventuring souls might court danger and glory; as recently as the Vietnam War, American soldiers used it instinctively to refer to enemy territory. When John Wayne gazes across the Texas prairie in *The Searchers,* he sees a land where he believes that civilization and savagery, good and evil, beauty and foulness collide in a clear and apocalyptic struggle. That is, of course, the Indian Country of the white man's imagination. The Indian Country that modern Americans have actually wrought is a far different, a more ambiguous place. Indeed, there is probably no other piece of American real estate that is so freighted with the historical detritus of opportunism, neglect, and good intentions gone awry.

Try to picture the man in black broadcloth as he rides up through the arbutus and the azaleas, the birch and the laurel, the hemlocks, chestnut trees, maples, and pines that October day in 1886, knowing that the future of the American Indian lies in his hands. When he reached the ridgecrest, Senator Henry L. Dawes, the chairman of the Appropriations Committee, looked down across a panorama of white farmsteads and the bounteous autumn fields of the Hudson Valley, with their cargo of corn, pears, apples, and plums. Beyond the river's glistening ribbon he could see the Berkshire Hills, blue on the horizon, containing in their shallow folds the memory of his impoverished childhood. His life was a quintessential American story. By dint of sheer hard work, he had put himself through Yale University, become a teacher and then a lawyer, gone on to Congress, and was now among the most influential men in the Senate. Gazing down, Dawes thought of the vast, recumbent plains of the Dakotas. Someday they would be as fecund as the valley spread out before him, and their fertility would transform the Indian forever.

Despite the silvery beard that lent it a hint of statesmanlike grandeur, Dawes's face was an indisputably ordinary one, with its heavy brow, blunt nose, and steady, inexpressive eyes. But it could not conceal his pride as he thought about the speech that he was soon to deliver to the eminent men and women who called themselves, without self-consciousness, the Friends of the Indian. They were even now assembling for their annual conference at the Mohonk Mountain House, which nestled far below the Senator's perch, towered and gabled like some fantastic Oriental confection. Their mission, as they saw it, was to guide the Indian "from the night of barbarism into the fair dawn of Christian civilization." As liberal Christians, they were certain that the Indian had, like themselves, been made in the image of God and that the Indian's ultimate transformation into a white man was part of a grand cosmic plan. They were equally convinced that the reservation system was tantamount to racial segregation and that it bred unhealthy dependence on the federal government. They believed that tribal life imposed an "absolute conformity" and a "uniformity of action and feeling" upon tribal members; if the Indian was to be saved, this repressive "tribal mass" had to be destroyed. Total immersion in "American ideals, American schools, American laws, the privileges and pressure of American rights and duties," they were sure, could accomplish in a single generation what biological evolution, left to its own devices, might have taken centuries or millennia to achieve.

Dawes was one of the most powerful men among them, the pivot upon which Washington's Indian policy turned. As a New Englander, he knew that the first Indian reservation had been established in Connecticut, in 1638, for the Quinnipiacs, a Christianized tribe that had been devastated by epidemics, and that small pieces of land had occasionally been set aside for Indians in other colonies. Until the eve of the American Revolution, however, whites and Indians generally lived mingled together in an uneasy symbiosis

almost everywhere along the Eastern seaboard, frequently marrying, trading household manufactures and weapons for game and
furs, and sometimes slaughtering each other with bloody abandon.
In 1763, the British Crown proclaimed that the main cause of trouble with the Indians was the encroachment of whites on native land
and that it would not end unless a "clear line of demarcation was
drawn between the two races." The King forbade settlement, land
grants, or surveys west of the Appalachian watershed and formally
reserved to Indians "all the Lands and Territories lying to the Westward of the Sources of the Rivers which fall into the sea from the
West and North West." Defiant settlers for the most part ignored
the proclamation, but it had established ethnic separation for the
first time as the keystone of government policy.

The creation of reservations eventually became the primary tool
in the national effort to remove Indians from the path of settlement
everywhere along the frontier. In its original usage, a reservation
meant land that a nominally independent tribe reserved to itself
when it ceded land to the United States and agreed to end hostili-
ties. It was usually agreed that the tribes would be left alone to
govern themselves but would receive federal protection against in-
truders and government support in the form of goods and services.
Tribal lands were guaranteed in perpetuity. Such assurances were
standard by the time the chiefs of the Sioux gathered at Fort Laramie in 1868. They were promised that roughly half the land in
present-day South Dakota, as well as portions of Nebraska, Wyoming, Montana, and North Dakota, had been "set apart for the
absolute and undisturbed use and occupation of the Indians, and
for such other friendly tribes or individual Indians as from time to
time they may be willing, with the consent of the United States, to
admit amongst them." The government promised that no unautho-
rized persons "shall ever be permitted to pass over, settle up, or
reside" on Sioux lands and agreed to provide the Indians with food
and clothing, livestock, medical care, and other assistance for the
next thirty years.

No sooner had the treaty been signed than an armed expedition
under General George Armstrong Custer set out to explore the
Black Hills, which lay deep within acknowledged Sioux territory.
Custer's discovery of gold there made the agreement virtually a
dead letter. The Army fended off prospectors for a time, but the
popular press proclaimed that Black Hills gold could pay off the

national debt, which then stood at $2 billion. The killings of miners who penetrated the halfhearted military blockade led to increased hostility with the Sioux and finally, in 1876, to war. Although history recalls the annihilation of Custer's command at the Little Big Horn as a victory for the Sioux, the war as a whole was a disaster for the Indians. Within months of Custer's defeat, they sued for peace. An act of Congress the following year deprived the Sioux of the Black Hills, but still left them with a vast portion of Dakota west of the Missouri.

Dawes had long believed that reservations were essential to protect Indians from rapacious whites. Although he shared the ethnocentric assumptions of his age, he was determined, like many other Americans who did not claim to understand Indians, to do the right thing by them nonetheless. He considered the history of white and Indian relations as one "of spoliation, of wars, and of humiliation," and he firmly believed that the Indian should be treated "as an individual, and not as an insoluble substance that the civilization of this country has been unable, hitherto, to digest." He estimated that it had cost the United States nearly a million dollars for every Indian it had managed to kill. To a hardheaded Yankee from the Berkshires, it made no sense.

Dawes had traveled personally to the Dakota Territory. What he learned about reservation conditions there appalled him. Rations were often short and inedible. In lieu of woolen clothing, each Sioux received a canvas suit that even government officials described as "devoid of appearance, warmth or durability." The government-issue blankets intended to replace the buffalo robes that used to keep the Sioux warm in winter were made of "wool shoddy apparently mixed with a cheap adulterant." Shoes, tools, and other materials were no better. Nevertheless, with the buffalo gone and their traditional economy in ruins, the Sioux clung with pathetic ferocity to the government handouts. "They promised to feed us till the very last dog died," one old man recalled. Dawes calculated that since the establishment of the Indian bureau sixty years earlier, the United States had spent $600 million to keep Indians "in darkness, heathenism and ignorance"—more than it would have cost to have sent every Indian in the country to college.

At the same time, Dawes also could not help taking note of the fact that a mere 28,000 Indians occupied 30,000 square miles in the heart of Dakota while 500,000 frustrated white settlers were swarming at the reservation boundary. Two railroads were stopped dead at the Missouri, unable to go forward across Indian Country. There was terrific pressure to break up the reservation, and the land-hungry settlers had strong support in Congress. At one point a bill to strip 11 million acres from the Sioux reservation had been just "a squirrel's jump" away from passage.

Dawes was convinced that with the correct policy and political will, Indians had the same capacity for civilization as anyone else. Like many of his contemporaries in the golden age of capitalism, Dawes perceived private property as an almost magical force, a severe but benevolent taskmaster with transformative power. He had told an audience in Washington: "When the Indian begins to understand that he has something that is exclusively his to enjoy, he begins to understand that it is necessary for him to preserve and keep it, and it is not a great while before he learns that to keep it he must keep the peace; and so on, step by step, the individual is separated from the mass, set upon the soil, made a citizen." In Nebraska, where the Omahas had allotted tribal land to individual members, he had seen Indian farmers selling their corn to the markets of Omaha, and at Devil's Lake Agency in Dakota, he had discovered that Indians who learned farming had raised 18,000 bushels of wheat, more than enough to feed themselves for the year. They were harbingers of a glorious future.

But Dawes's visit to the Cherokee Nation, in what would eventually become Oklahoma, was more troubling. He was impressed by the Cherokee government, with its written constitution, elected legislature, supreme court, compulsory education, and hospitals. And he was pleased to learn that there was not a pauper in the nation. On the other hand—and it bothered him deeply—he found no great wealth, either. To Dawes, it was obvious that this was because they held their land in common. There was no incentive for a man to strive to make his home better than his neighbor's; there was none of the selfishness that the Senator, like most of the educated men of his time, was convinced lay at the root of advanced civilization. He returned to Washington convinced that until tribes agreed to give up their lands and divide them among their people, they would make no more progress.

Dawes knew that there was despotism in the allotment idea. He wondered how his neighbors in Pittsfield, Massachusetts, would feel if the city voted that it would be for their own good to move somewhere else and then took away their homes. But he had come to believe passionately that with the bestowal of citizenship all the vexing problems of reservation life would "disappear like an April cloud before the sunrise." It was time to stop treating Indians as a foreign people incapable of becoming part of the nation. They must be brought under the secure shelter of the Declaration of Independence and the Constitution. The pressure for settlement was politically irresistible and must sooner or later destroy the reservations in any case. Dawes made up his mind to accept the inevitable and to secure the best deal for the Indian that he could get. The quicker he was mingled with the whites in every particular, the better it would be for all concerned. The means of the Indian's salvation was to be the family farm, the ultimate repository of American individualism and the democratic spirit.

In all this, Dawes never considered the question of tribal sovereignty. But then no one did. Only a few weeks earlier, the Commissioner of Indian Affairs had dismissed notions of separate Indian nationality as mere sentimentality. "It is perfectly plain to my mind that the treaties never contemplated the un-American and absurd idea of a separate nationality in our midst, with power as they may choose to organize a government of their own," he wrote. To maintain such a view was to acknowledge a foreign sovereignty upon American soil, "a theory utterly repugnant to the spirit and genius of our laws, and wholly unwarranted by the Constitution of the United States."

It was a sober, not to say solemn, crowd that met to hear Dawes's speech the next afternoon. A religious atmosphere permeated the genteel cherrywood lounge in keeping with the sentiments of the Mountain House's Quaker owners, who permitted no card playing, dancing, or alcohol anywhere in the establishment. As Dawes rose to speak, he saw before him the collective liberal conscience of the nation. He recognized General Whittlesley, the secretary of the Board of Indian Commissioners; Herbert Welsh of the Indian Rights Association; Merrell Gates, the president of Rutgers College; H. Q. Houghton, the publisher of the *Atlantic Monthly;* and many of the most influential church leaders, educators, lawyers, and journalists in the United States.

"To me, it is no matter of consequence at all whether the reservation system is to be abolished and the treaties abrogated, or whether the civil service system reform should be applied to the appointment of agents, or whether it should not," the Senator declared, standing behind the small prayer table that served as a podium. "If you make the Indian a self-supporting citizen of the United States, all these things disappear of themselves. The work is accomplished when the Indian has become one of us, absorbed into this body politic." He then proudly described the legislation that he had introduced in the current session of Congress, the most far-reaching ever proposed in Indian affairs. Enthusiastic white supporters likened it to the Declaration of Independence, even the Magna Carta. It would give the President discretionary power to order reservations to be surveyed, to allot land to each Indian who lived there, and to offer the remainder for sale to white settlers. Each Indian allottee would receive 160 acres of land and eventual United States citizenship, along with money for seed, tools, and livestock. Allotment would effectively remove individuals from the oppressive authority of the tribe. Every member of the tribes to whom allotments had been made would have the protection of and be subject to the laws of the state or territory in which they lived, while no territory would be permitted to pass any law denying any Indian the equal protection of the law. For twenty-five years, the Indian could not sell or lease his allotment, or have it seized from under him by local authorities. By then, he would surely understand the mysteries of modern farming and property ownership and could be trusted to dispose of it like any other American.

Dawes was a clumsy speaker in an orotund age. But as he went on he gathered force. "If you will prepare the Indian to take care of himself upon this land that is allotted, you will find the solution to the whole question," Dawes told the Friends of the Indians. "He shall have a home and be a citizen of the United States; shall be one of us, contributing his share to all that goes to make up the strength and glory of citizenship in the United States."

The law was not supposed to take the Indian "by the collar, if he has one, or by the blanket, and force him to be a farmer." Money would have to be allocated to educate him, teach him how to plant and reap, how to read and write and compute, how to fashion the tools that he would need in order to survive. "We need great patience, perseverance and kindness before the Indian will become a self-sustaining citizen of the United States." But there was also a desperate urgency.

Our work must be done now and without delay, for the greed for the Indian's land is growing every day, and it is as impossible to resist it under the forms of our government as it is to stop the flow of a river. We may guide and direct it, but we cannot stop it. We are blind, we are deaf, we are insane if we do not take cognizance of the fact that there are forces in this land driving on these people with a determination to possess every acre of their land, and they will lose it unless we work and declare that the original owner of this land shall, before every acre disappears from under him forever, have 160 acres of it when he shall be fitted to become a citizen of the United States.

Dawes was the star of the conference. His place in history seemed assured. Walter Allen of the Indian Citizenship Association of Boston articulated the sentiments of many when he declared, "I have more than once spoken of Senator Dawes's severalty bill as the act of emancipation for the Indian. I believe when it is passed it will enroll his name with that of Lincoln as an Emancipator of those in bonds." There were few, that day in the crisp October light of the Hudson Valley, who would gainsay him.

In February 1887, Congress passed the General Allotment Act, which quickly and universally became known as the Dawes Act, in honor of the man who had given it birth. Separate acts were passed for each reservation. The Sioux Act required each head of family to select his own allotment; if he failed to do so within five years, the local Indian agent was directed to do it on his behalf, regardless of his wishes. Each family was to receive $50 in cash to erect a house and seed for two years, along with "two milch cows, one pair of oxen, with yoke and chain, or two mares and one set of harness in lieu of said oxen, yoke and chain, as the Secretary of the Interior may deem advisable, one plow, one wagon, one harrow, one hoe, one axe, and one pitchfork." Finally, $3 million would be deposited in the United States Treasury as a permanent fund "for the promotion of industrial and other suitable education among said Indians." The Secretary of the Interior was empowered to make the remaining Sioux land available for settlement; when he finished, approximately half of the Great Sioux Reservation still remained in Indian hands. Two days after the bill was passed, five thousand homesteaders gathered at Chamberlain, South Dakota, made a flying rush across the frozen Missouri River to obtain the choicest sites.

For the next half century, allotment was the cornerstone of Indian policy. In spite of Dawes's promise that no Indian would be "seized by the collar and forced to become a farmer," that is in effect what happened on many reservations. On the Yuma reservation, Indians who refused to accept their allotments were jailed, and others threatened until they agreed to submit. Although Indians were supposed to be free to select the best land for themselves, agents often reserved the best pasture and timber for whites. On the Papago reservation, where land without water was worthless, the Indian Office allotted each Indian only ten acres of irrigable land. On the Fort Duchesne reservation, allotments were made on high country that could never be irrigated at all. On the Colorado River reservation, allotments were so sloppily surveyed that they overlapped previously allotted land.

In spite of mounting evidence that allotment was crippling the very people it was intended to help, Western Congressmen pressured the government to accelerate the process so that "excess" land might be opened to further white settlement. In 1903, the year of Dawes's death, the *Sioux Falls Press* editorialized: "The Cheyenne River Reservation is ripe for opening. The white people need the lands and the Indians are making no good use of them and would be infinitely better off without them." Five years later, the Secretary of the Interior was permitted to waive the twenty-five-year waiting period for any Indian whom he deemed "competent" to sell his land. So-called competency commissions were sent out to meet Indians who had not yet accepted allotments and to convince as many as possible to apply for deeds to their land. Half the remaining land at Cheyenne River was thrown open for homesteading almost immediately, while the rest was reserved for Indian allottees. The competency commission assigned to the reservation pursued its task aggressively, issuing deeds not only to the relatively few Sioux who sought them but also to illiterates, convicted criminals, Indians who did not want them and had not applied for them, and others who pleaded for exemption for fear that the speculators who swarmed at the edges of the reservation would find ways to get hold of their land.

An outdoor ceremony was staged at Timber Lake to impress the allottees with the importance of citizenship. They stood resplendent in the feathers and fringed buckskins of a bygone age, facing Major James McLaughlin, a shrewd and hard man who was known to all Sioux as the Indian agent who had ordered the arrest of Sitting Bull in 1890. Ramrod-stiff, cigar in hand, McLaughlin watched as each Indian solemnly stepped from a tepee and shot an arrow to signify that he was leaving behind his Indian way of life. Moving forward, he then placed his hands on a plow to demonstrate that he had chosen to live the farming life of a white man. He was next handed a purse to remind him to save what he earned. Finally, holding the American flag, the Indian repeated these words: "Forasmuch as the President has said that I am worthy to be a citizen of the United States, I now promise this flag that I will give my hands, my head, and my heart to the doing of all that will make me a true American citizen." It was the culminating, transformative moment of which Dawes had dreamed.

To the crowds of white and Indian spectators, it seemed like grand theater, but it might as well have been a comedy on the New York stage. Unscrupulous speculators soon infested the allotted reservations, offering worthless securities and credit in return for land. "Grafting has become in a measure respectable," one superintendent openly confessed. Moreover, vast tracts of allotted land were totally unfit to the kind of farming that the East Coast visionaries believed in. Indians who tried often saw their corn burn up beneath the prairie sun or turn into fodder for grasshoppers. Within a few years, it was found that of those who had received patents to their land at Cheyenne River, 95 percent sold or mortgaged their property. It was much the same everywhere. Seventy percent lost their land on the Fort Peck reservation, 75 percent on the Umatilla reservation, 90 percent on the Turtle Mountain reservation, 90 percent on the Crow reservation, 93 percent on the Yankton reservation, 95 percent on the Omaha reservation.

On that October day in 1887, when Henry Dawes delivered his ringing oration to the Friends of the Indians, there were 138 million acres of Indian land in the United States. By the time allotment was finally brought to a halt in 1934, Indian Country had shrunk by 63 percent, to 52 million acres. Two-thirds of Indians were either completely landless or did not have enough land left to make a living from it. In 1931, the average monthly income for a family of five on the Pine Ridge reservation was $152.80; a decade later it was only $120.00, one-sixth the figure for the rest of South Dakota and one-third that of Mississippi, the poorest state in the nation.

Dawes had never even considered the possibility that the Indian population would expand or the nightmare that several generations of inheritance would lead to. Throughout Indian Country, most allotments have been subdivided and redivided so many times that they are worthless to the nominal owners. In the early 1990s, Doran Morris, Sr., then chairman of the Omaha Tribe, which pioneered allotment more than a century ago, was receiving a total of $2.40 annually for his share of a family allotment whose ownership is splintered among more than two hundred heirs. Much land that is Indian-owned on paper has in fact become so fragmented that to be made economically viable at all, it has had to be leased out by the Bureau of Indian Affairs to white farmers and ranchers.

John Collier, Franklin Roosevelt's Commissioner of Indian Affairs, called allotment "the greatest single practical evil" that has been committed against the American Indian. There is no question that allotment was a disaster whose effects still shape the physical, legal, and human landscape of Indian Country today. A land policy that was intended to emancipate Indians from federal supervision promoted the growth of a vast bureaucracy to manage the certification of competency, the sale of Indian lands, the issuance of deeds, and, as time went on, the leasing of fragmented Indian lands to whites. What was supposed to be an educative process that would transform Indians into yeoman farmers instead paralyzed the development of modern economies on lands that might, had they been left intact, have better sustained tribal farms, ranches, and timber or mining industries. Allotment devastated the Indian land base, sapped the vitality of traditional tribal government, and terminated the last possibility that Indian societies might be able to evolve at their own pace according to their own standards. Dawes had dreamed that allotment would destroy the tribes once and for all. In that, it very nearly succeeded.

The spirit of the allotment era is splendidly, and now rather embarrassingly, captured in a vivid mural that hangs in the State Capitol in Pierre, South Dakota. It was painted in 1910, at the height of the land fever that swept the state. It shows armed pioneers accompanied by a Grecian figure brandishing a book, trampling the bodies of fallen Indians as the cloaked figure of Ignorance slinks away before them. Not surprisingly, Indians have demanded that the mural be removed. But in the 1990s, it was still hanging in the governor's reception room, although a new plaque underneath it said, somewhat grudgingly it seemed, in a state where the politically correct does not go down well at all: "This mural 'Spirit of

The People' symbolized the history of the period. To appropriately reflect the changes in the times and the attitudes of the people, it has been retitled 'Only By Remembering Our Mistakes Can We Learn.' "

It is hardly surprising that impoverished tribes cling tenaciously to the strictest reading of treaties that promised that vast lands would be reserved forever for their exclusive use. "I still consider the boundaries of the Great Sioux Nation intact," Gregg Bourland says. "Everyone else is a trespasser." But allotment radically changed the human landscape of Indian Country. While shysters did swindle many gullible Indians of their allotments, it is also true that homesteaders went West in pursuit of honest dreams, secure in the promise of equal rights under American law. "It defies common sense to suppose that Congress would intend that non-Indians purchasing allotted lands would become subject to tribal jurisdiction when an avowed purpose of the allotment policy was the ultimate destruction of tribal government," the Supreme Court declared in 1981, in *Montana v. United States,* a decision that is often cited by state governments in defense against assertions of tribal sovereignty.

"Historically, Indian policy may be some of the worst policy ever made in this nation," said Governor George Mickelson, a Republican who had generally pursued a conciliatory course with the state's several Indian tribes, a few months before his death in an airplane crash in the spring of 1993. "The whole concept of the reservation was segregation—keep Indians and non-Indians separate. Promises were made to the Indians, and they were broken. Then, under the Dawes Act, we promised that we were going to assimilate Indians into white society, and that non-Indian settlers would not be subject to tribal governments. Now the promises to non-Indians are being broken. The reservation system is not going to go away. A generation ago, tribes did not need to be taken seriously; now they do. But whites are not going to go away either."

Lawyers for the Salt River Pima-Maricopa Tribe kept at the Duro case, or at least at the legal principle that lay at the bottom of it, with bulldog tenacity. In October of 1991, the tribe's persistence was finally rewarded. The United States House of Representatives closed the void that had been opened by the Supreme Court's ruling by voting explicitly to extend a tribe's jurisdiction over all Indians who commit misdemeanors on reservation land. For a time, the Senate had hesitated, in a halting effort to ensure protection for the civil rights of the accused. But the spirit of compromise, and official commitment to the principle of tribal sovereignty, prevailed. Tribal leaders were elated, and with good reason. "This is a great victory for Indian Country," Navajo President Peterson Zah declared. "This is a victory for tribal sovereignty and the powers of self-government and self-determination."

By then, a great deal had happened at Salt River that seemed to diminish the Duro case by comparison. Prosperity was in the air. People were justifiably proud of the tribal police department's new state-of-the-art computer-aided dispatch system, and the new tribal kidney dialysis center, and the new shopping center that had just been opened in the northwest corner of the reservation, at Indian Bend Road. It was the largest shopping center in Indian Country, handsome in the sleek style of the suburban Southwest, replete with palms and well-watered lawns and a representative complement of middle-range and low-budget merchants: there was a Target store, a Marshall's, Toys "R" Us, Athletic Express, a PharMor drugstore, a bookstore, and numerous others.

The mall's creation had been a brilliant stroke. In order to accomplish it, the tribe had been obliged to lobby Congress itself, a measure of the herculean labors that attend almost any attempt to attract serious investment into Indian Country. The tribe had found a developer who wanted to lease the site. But because reservation land is legally federal trust land, it can neither be sold nor repossessed by creditors. "But no one wants to do business with you unless you can be sued," says Richard Wilks, the tribe's longtime attorney, whose office overlooking downtown Phoenix seems a world away from the sagebrush emptiness of the reservation. The Salt River Pima-Maricopas became the first Indian tribe in the nation to request Congress to waive its sovereign immunity to lawsuit. At the time, there was sharp criticism from other tribes, which saw it as a dangerous precedent, a surrender of precious and fragile power that they were convinced had to be husbanded if it was to be preserved. "It was, in fact, an exercise of sovereignty," Wilks argues. "Sovereignty is not what some philosopher hypothesizes. Sovereignty is a vessel, a concept, that you put reality into. Sovereignty is about taking power and using it."

And what of Albert Duro? In August of 1991, barely two months before Congress closed the loophole that had allowed him to escape justice, he was arrested by the Sheriff's Department in Riverside, California. He had been "partying" with several men, non-Indians this time. There had been a fight. Duro beat up one of his erstwhile drinking partners, robbed him of $200, and then left him in a vineyard to die, a crime for which he was at last caught and convicted, and eventually sentenced to prison.

Victory Acres has not changed much either since 1984. "This is where it happened," Martha Whitman is saying, a fragile figure in a white dress printed with chrysanthemums and a blue windbreaker, huddled more perhaps against the force of memory than the premature November chill. "He fell right here." She is standing on the ball court. Nearby, there is a seesaw and a swing; pieces of broken plastic and old cans are scattered on the gravel. Someone has left a mysterious graffito on the backboard: "X Slayer." If it offends Whitman, she doesn't let on. But her voice quivers. "He liked wrestling. He wanted to grow up to be a lawyer."

Beyond the ball court, the naked desert stretches away in its vastness toward red-gray mountains that in the fading afternoon light seem like the vertebrae of some strange, half-submerged creatures of the Pleistocene notched against the sky. The feeling of tremulous desolation, of a land in which human beings have only a small and humble role to play, is almost eerie in its intensity. At the same time, in the fragile presence of Martha Whitman, the invisible grid of law and illogic that modern government has imposed upon the land is no less inescapable. Like the rest of the vast and scattered archipelago that is Indian Country, it is a strange and confusing maze of jurisdictions, laws, communities, and identities, a landscape of almost unrelenting ambiguity.

Still, in other and important ways, it is a landscape redolent with success and the fruits of Indian achievement and with examples of innovation that may eventually give the hackneyed slogans of self-determination and tribal sovereignty real meaning. By the early 1990s, profits from the tribe's various enterprises and investments were generating nearly three-fourths of its budget; only 27 percent still came from the federal government. Of course, the tribe was fortunate in its proximity to Phoenix and Scottsdale; without the shoppers, and the golfers, and the "snowbirds," it would probably have remained as inhospitable and depressed as central South Dakota. Nonetheless, largely by force of its own will and imagination, it had converted the landscape into power and, in turn, into money, and then again into jobs, clinics, police protection, and new homes —in short, into the elementary landmarks of the kind of life to which nearly all Indians, like other Americans, aspire.

Whitman is quietly weeping now, struggling to keep her soft voice clear enough to be understood. Her family has broken up since the killing. Her husband began drinking heavily and finally left. Biscuit's younger brother Donovan was still in counseling. "They said there wasn't enough evidence. But how much do you need to have? I can feel how this case just wasn't important to them. Maybe they thought, 'It's just an Indian, so what?' If an Indian had killed a white man, I guess the system would have jumped. To me, it seems like it just got to be a battle between politicians, about who was going to give the better argument. I guess I just kind of feel like I was cheated."

4

The Shadow of Chief Seattle

FEWER THAN two hundred Campo Indians live on the tribe's tiny reservation in the scrubby hills that lie an hour's drive east of San Diego. The landscape is a profoundly discouraging one. It offers nothing to comfort the eye, produces nothing of value, and provides almost nothing to sustain life as it is enjoyed by most Americans at the end of the twentieth century. The single resource that the Campos possess is wasteland. In 1987, the band learned that the city of San Diego had identified the reservation as one of several potential dump sites for the city's refuse. "At first, we thought, 'Why take others' trash?' " recalls Ralph Goff, the band's chairman. "But if you look at it from a business standpoint, that's irrelevant. It's like serving other people in a restaurant. Garbage is garbage."

Goff is walking through the redshank and yucca and the ocher sand where the first trenches have been cut for what is to be the new landfill. He talks hopefully about the future and trash. "We just need this one little thing to get us started. With it, we can create our own destiny." Goff is a formidably built man with little formal education. When he was growing up in the 1940s, the only work available was as a cowhand or day laborer for whites. When there was no work, people went hungry. "You just had to wait until there was some more food." In the 1960s, most of the unskilled jobs disappeared and nearly every Campo family went on welfare. "We needed it, but it really wrecked us as people. It created idleness. People didn't have to do anything in order to get money."

By the end of the decade, Goff expects daily freight trains to be carrying loads of municipal waste and possibly sewage from San Diego to a 300-acre site on a hilltop at the southern end of the reservation. For the privilege of leasing the tribe's land, Mid-American Waste Systems will pay the Campos between $2 million and $5 million per year. Goff argues that the dump will put an end to the tribe's dependence on federal largesse: it will create jobs for every adult Campo who is willing to work; provide long-term investment capital for the tribe and money for full college scholarships for every school-age member of the tribe; and finance new homes for every family that now lives in substandard housing. The dump will, in short, give the tribe financial independence for the first time in its modern history.

The landfill will be one of the most technically advanced in the United States; to regulate it, the tribe has enacted an environmental code more stringent than the State of California's. Nevertheless, the dump has generated fierce opposition in towns near the reservation, where thousands of non-Indians live. Geologists hired by the dump's opponents have suggested, but not proved, that there are fissures in the rock and that seepage could contaminate the water supply of ranches that lie outside the reservation boundary and of Mexican communities across the international border, a half mile to the south. Environmentalists have accused the tribe of irresponsibility toward the earth and charged that the Campos have been targeted as part of a general assault on reservations by "renegade" waste-dumping companies. State and local officials demanded the authority to approve the tribe's plans. A bill was even introduced in the California state legislature that would make it a crime to deliver waste to the Campo landfill. Goff shrugs away the protests. "It's a sovereignty issue: it's our land, and we'll do what we want to with it."

"How can you say the economic development of two hundred people is more important than the health and welfare of all the people in the surrounding area?" The white woman and her husband run cattle and horses on the scrubby land downhill from the dumpsite; she is not yet forty, but years of toil and the desert sun have taken their toll on her crisp good looks. "It's hard making a living here," she says. "You just get by. If our water is spoiled, then everything's spoiled. The vegetation will be gone. The livestock won't have anything to eat." From the mobile home where she and her husband live, she sees the dumpsite all day long, every day. The thought of it never leaves her mind. "The fissures will carry that stuff right through here. Then we'll have all that stuff in our water and stuff blowing down on us off the hills."

There are predictable elements to her rage: the instinctive resistance of most Americans to any waste dumps anywhere near their home, and the distress of white Americans when they realize the implications of tribal sovereignty for the first time and find themselves subject to the will of a government in which they have no say. But there is something more, something that is at the same time both subtle and overarching, a sort of moral perplexity that Indians have failed to behave according to expectation. "Before all this, I had this ideal about Indian people and all they've been through. I used to think that they had this special feeling about the land." The imputation is that the Campos are suckers, that they have been conned by smart operators or that, even worse, they are guilty of self-interest.

It is really the ranchers, she seems to be implying, who are the land's best caretakers, who are the true "Indians," so to speak, and that it is the Campos who have become the predators. On the wall of her trailer there is a poster decorated with Indian motifs. It is entitled "Chief Seattle Speaks." It begins, in words that are becoming as familiar to American schoolchildren as those of the Gettysburg Address once were, "How can you buy or sell the sky, the warmth of the land?" Here, in sight of the dump, they are meant to be a deliberate reproach to the Campos, an unassailable argument rooted in what the rancher believes to be Indians' profoundest values.

No document more completely encapsulates the feeling that modern Americans suppose Indians universally have for the earth than the 1,200-word speech that Seattle is said to have delivered in response to President Franklin Pierce's offer to buy the tribe's land near Puget Sound in 1854. "The idea is strange to us," the apparently dismayed chief is said to have responded. "If we do not own the freshness of the air and the sparkle of the water, how can you buy them? Every part of this earth is sacred to my people." Gracefully defining the antithesis between "European" and "Indian" attitudes toward the earth, he declares,

> The white man's dead forget the country of their birth when they go to walk among the stars. Our dead never forget this beautiful earth, for it is the mother of the red men. We are part of the earth and it is part of us. The perfumed flowers are our sisters; the deer, the horse, the great eagle, these are our brothers. The rocky crests, the juices in the meadows, the body heat of the pony, and man—all belong to the same family.

The speech goes on to recapitulate history as the familiar drama of Indian innocence and white greed. The chief speaks with bitter irony of seeing countless dead buffalo rotting on the prairie, "left by the white men who shot them from a passing train. I am a savage and I do not understand how the smoking iron horse can be more important than the buffalo that we only kill to stay alive." He then sadly observes, "The white man does not seem to notice the air he breathes. Like a man dying for many days, he is numb to the stench." The loud noises of the white man's world "insult the ears," he laments. "There is no quiet place in the white man's cities. No place to hear the unfurling of leaves in spring, or the rustle of an insect's wings."

More than any other single document, Seattle's words lend support to the increasingly common belief that, to Indians, any disruption or commercialization of the earth's natural order is sacrilege and that the most moral, the most truly "Indian," relationship with the land is a kind of poetic passivity. Seattle has achieved prophetic stature among environmentalists; his speech has been translated into dozens of languages and is widely reproduced in school texts. In 1991, a spokesman for the Iroquois cited Seattle to a United Nations conference on the environment, in Geneva, as the authoritative source for Indian values, declaring, "Perhaps in these pockets of ancient wisdom there may be some direction . . . that could help guide us in these perilous times. We believe a spiritual perspective is important for balance to deal with the aggressive nature of industrial states." The following year, the organizers of Earth Day urged religious leaders across the United States to read Seattle's words to their congregations, while a children's book based on the speech, *Brother Eagle, Sister Sky,* was number five on the *New York Times* best-seller list. Then vice presidential candidate Al Gore quoted the chief in his best-selling book on the environment, *Earth in the Balance,* calling Seattle's speech "one of the most moving" Native American ideas about man's relationship to the earth. In 1993, Greenpeace used the text as the introduction to a scarifying report on alleged plans by waste companies to store toxic refuse on Indian lands, calling the chief's words "the most beautiful and profound statement on the environment ever made."

None of this has much to do with the historical Seattle, who never saw a white man's city, since there was none in Washington Territory in 1854. Nor was there any industrial pollution, since there were no factories. The chief's people never saw buffalo, either, for there were none within hundreds of miles of Puget Sound. The great buffalo slaughter to which he seems to refer took place far to the east, on the Great Plains, nearly twenty years after his death, and no railroad came anywhere near the chief's home in his lifetime.

If Seattle's musings sound surprisingly modern, it is not a coincidence. The earliest version of the "speech" was composed in 1887, from memory, by a white doctor named Henry Smith, who claimed to have been present at its delivery twenty-three years before. However, the most commonly reproduced version of the speech was actually written in 1972, by Ted Perry, a Texas scriptwriter, to serve as narration for a film produced by the Southern Baptist Radio and Television Commission, which wished to give its audience a warning about the environment. Soon afterward, Perry's text was reprinted in *Environmental Action* magazine as Seattle's own words; it was then distributed around the world by the in-flight magazine of Northwest Airlines, under the title: "The Decidedly Unforked Message of Chief Seattle." The speech as it is known to most Americans is, quite simply, an invention, a fact that seems to make little difference to well-meaning whites who are determined to portray Indians as icons of ecological correctness. When a reporter from the *New York Times* broached the question of the speech's authenticity to the illustrator of *Brother Eagle, Sister Sky,* she replied, "Basically, I don't know what he said. But I do know that the native American people lived this philosophy, and that's what's important."

If all the Indian reservations in the United States could be combined into one, Indian Country would be among the richest nations in the world, measured by the opulence of its natural resources. At least 50 percent of all the uranium, between 5 percent and 10 percent of all the oil and gas reserves, and one third of all the strippable low-sulfur coal in the United States lie on Indian lands. The Navajo reservation alone produces almost as much coal as the entire State of Utah. Many tribes own rights to water whose value is dramatically expanding along with the increasing urbanization of the West. More than ninety tribes have land that is densely forested, while millions of acres of leased tribal grassland provide pasturage for ranchers, and millions of acres more are leased to farmers. Freedom from state regulation has even made some tribal lands, like that of the Campos, at least potentially valuable to firms searching for places to store nuclear waste and garbage from expanding cities.

Until quite recently, the Bureau of Indian Affairs managed this vast patrimony like a private condominium. The bureau set the terms of leases for mining, grazing, and the sale of timber; it collected the fees, paid its own expenses, and distributed what remained as it thought fit to the Indians themselves. All too often, this "trust responsibility," as it is formally called, was carried out with a slovenly disregard for tribes' long-term interests. With a dogged persistence rooted in the bureau's history of paternalism, the BIA consistently failed to defend tribes' water rights against the encroachment of white farmers and ranchers, while its forestry officials encouraged the widespread clear-cutting of tribal timber. Elsewhere, the bureau typically negotiated leases for the extraction of minerals for flat or fixed rates, instead of percentage royalties, which meant, for instance, that the Navajos continued to receive only ten or fifteen cents per ton for their coal even as the market price rose from two dollars per ton in the 1950s to twenty dollars per ton in the 1980s.

For years, Indians were explicitly prohibited from deciding upon the disposition of their own land and even from hiring their own lawyers to negotiate leases and contracts without the bureau's approval. In 1921, when Paiutes from the Pyramid Lake reservation in northern Nevada attempted to organize a delegation to protest legislation that threatened to wreck the fishing industry upon which they depended, the local superintendent ordered the Indians back to the reservation, telling his agent on the spot: "You must discourage 'meetings' of Indians that take them away from their work and do nothing but unduly excite them . . . The 'talk habit' must be stopped wherever possible."

Federal paternalism officially came to an end in 1975 with the Indian Self-Determination Act, which called for a "transition from Federal domination of programs for and services to Indians to effective and meaningful participation by the Indian people." In practical terms, the act laid the foundation for the eventual turning over of many federal programs to the management of tribal governments. It also enabled tribes, for the first time, to create their own resource policies and regulatory agencies. Since then, to cite just a few typical examples, the Navajos and the Jicarillas of Arizona have established their own tribal oil and gas commissions to regulate production on their lands. The Jicarillas and the Blackfeet of Montana decided to take part in risk-sharing joint ventures with petroleum companies. The Southern Ute Tribe of Colorado has set up its own oil production firm. The Colville Confederated Tribe of Washington trained a professional staff to manage timberland that provides 90 percent of the tribe's income; logging is now done on a sustained-yield basis, which means that trees are never harvested more rapidly than they can be replaced. The Confederated Tribe of Warm Springs, in Oregon, obtained ownership of three hydroelectric dams and now sells power to the state grid. In one of the most dramatic turnabouts of all, the Pyramid Lake Paiutes have gained what may prove to be a controlling influence over the distribution of water in much of northern Nevada.

"We're going through a major sea change," says A. David Lester, a Creek from Oklahoma who is the executive director of the Conference of Energy Resource Tribes, a tribally supported organization based in Denver that provides assistance to tribes in resource management, engineering, and business development. "Especially in terms of minerals, tribes have rewritten the rules that govern their relations with the federal government and industry. Basically, the historical thrust is toward gaining land-based control—as proprietors, managers, and governments in charge. Tribes are either already in the driver's seat or on the way."

The ability to draw profit from the earth is compelling tribes not only to recognize the economic potential of their natural resources, in many cases for the first time, but also to confront the moral consequences of exploiting them for profit. Tribes are being forced to come to terms with the practical nature of their relationship to the land, to decide as a matter of policy whether the earth is primarily a form of wealth to be converted into goods, services, community welfare, and personal income, or whether it is something wholly different, as much a thing of spirit as it is plant and mineral. It is a debate that ultimately touches upon the disquieting question of what it means to be Indian, and to behave like an Indian, in modern America.

Many Indians worry that, having been freed from the dead hand of the BIA, tribes may simply be continuing an assault against the earth that rapacious whites initiated long ago. Others wonder if commercial development, modern economics, perhaps even change itself may be inherently un-Indian. "The whole idea of logging is opposed to our Indian ways," Louie Pitt, a tribal forestry official, has insistently told members of the Warm Springs Tribe, which owns vast tracts of valuable timberland in the Oregon Cascades. "Being Indian means that you stay home and take care of your people, and that you're not out to max profits." Other tribal leaders argue with equal force that passivity toward the land merely perpetuates economic dependence on the federal government and that aggressive development is in the best ancestral tradition of self-reliance.

Similar voices may be heard within almost every native community where there is water, land, or ore that can be leased or sold. The imperatives of development are pitting tribes against both non-Indian neighbors and, in some places, against other, less well-endowed native communities. In Alaska, the oil-poor Gwich'in Indians of the Brooks Range have lobbied aggressively against the more northerly Inupiats, or Eskimos, who want the Arctic National Wildlife Refuge where they live opened to oil exploration. Sarah James, a spokeswoman for the Gwich'in, told a Congressional subcommittee, "It's the whole ecosystem that we are concerned about. It's about all the animals and plants, ducks and geese and other birds, and fish too. Also, we still have clean air and clean water . . . It is our responsibility to keep this land pure." A representative of the Inupiats, Brenda Itta-Lee, retorted that oil royalties had already enabled the Eskimos to build schools, to keep the elderly at home instead of sending them away to institutions in distant Anchorage, and that jobs in the existing oilfields had reduced unemployment to less than 7 percent. "No one should dictate policy over our own natural resources," she protested without success to the Congressmen, who have so far declined to open the refuge to development. "We have no other economy except oil. We're headed toward economic depression if there is no more gas development. We don't want to go backwards. We never want to go back to being wards of the government, or a welfare society."

In the years to come, tribes that control valuable resources are likely to become powers to be reckoned with. Some, at least, will be able to shape not only their own destinies but to an increasing extent that of non-Indian communities, as well. The economic future of entire regions may well hinge on both the willingness of tribes to cooperate with non-Indian neighbors who for generations have been perceived as enemies and the ability of mainly white municipalities and states to accommodate long-ignored Indian concerns. The need for compromise is especially acute in the arid West, where water is the key to both wealth and political power and where still-unexploited Indian water rights may total more than 45 million acre-feet per year, an amount three times greater than the annual flow of the Colorado River.

It hardly seems plausible that the fortunes of cities and Indian tribes, of farms a hundred miles distant, and of countless waterfowl could depend on the trickle of water that debouches through the thistles and the purplish oatgrass, the foxtail, and the gay yellow cinquefoils that clump along the northern shore of Lake Tahoe. Anywhere east of the hundredth meridian, the Truckee would scarcely be considered a river at all, but this is dry country, and every acre-foot of water that seeps past the Tahoe Yoghurt Factory and Izzy's Burger Spa, and the chalets and condos, toward the Nevada desert carries with it a freight of contention that is unsurpassed by any waterway in the nation. Just below Donner Summit, the Truckee doglegs abruptly eastward. Falling more than 2,500 feet in the space of ten miles, it snakes back and forth beneath the asphalt lanes of Interstate 80, gathering force as it drops, tumbling past billboards that shriek "Megabucks!" and "Lotsa Slots" finally to enter the concrete channel that is the main source of water for the cities of Reno and Sparks.

Without the Truckee, there would be no Harrah's or Harold's Club, no hotels, no sprawling suburbs with opulent lawns and sculpted shrubbery that pretend, even in the midst of the worst drought in memory, that water is as easy to come by, and to waste, as if they lay in Ohio or Connecticut. By the time the Truckee exits the cities for the desert to the east, its water has passed through the plumbing of tens of thousands of homes, scores of factories, and dozens of casinos, and has been so thoroughly scrubbed, sifted, and aerated in the cities' treatment plants that it is purer, the public officials of Washoe County like to boast, than a bottle of Perrier. Beyond Sparks, the Truckee rejoins its ancient bed to continue its journey eastward toward Derby Dam, the symbol, the Paiutes bitterly say, of everything that went wrong.

As hydraulic architecture, Derby Dam is a trivial thing, hardly more than a concrete plug in the river between the gravelly black shoulders of the Truckee Gorge. But its iron gates still enshrine the dreams of an age that aspired to transform the most inhospitable desert in the United States into a blooming garden. Derby Dam is the linchpin of the Newlands Project, a plan of grandiose ambitions and disastrous results, whose history has become a morality tale of the West, a story in which a living relic of the Pleistocene plays the role of a secular grail, and water is the elixir of a tribe's political resurrection.

In the late nineteenth century, the arid West was perceived not only as a physical challenge but also as one of the spirit, a problem that many Americans approached much as the pragmatic idealists of the Mohonk Conference did the Indians, as a kind of moral desolation that could be rapidly converted into an earthly Eden, given a sufficient amount of political determination. One such man was Francis Griffith Newlands, a straitlaced and balding lawyer from Quincy, Illinois, who believed fervently in the transformative power of big government and in the role that water was to play in the reinvention of the West. He was an American type that seems to have been unusually common in that self-righteous century, who managed to weave opportunities and good intentions into a seamless web of unbreachable self-confidence. The vision that he was determined to impose on the Truckee seemed like a fine and noble one to the white men of his own time. However, for the small tribe of Paiutes who lived on the shores of Pyramid Lake, life would never be the same again.

Newlands had come to Nevada in the 1880s to manage his in-laws' share of the legendary Comstock Lode. When the mining economy declined, he used his wealth to buy his way into politics, winning election to the United States Congress in 1893 and then to the Senate a decade later. It was an era when big government was a novel idea; in the eyes of Newlands and other Progressives, it was destined to serve as the great engine of national development. As the century waned, he came to believe with a truly religious fervor that the irrigation of land that received barely nine inches of rain each year held the key to the territory's future. He was convinced that it bordered on the criminal to let the natural environment go to waste; man had a moral duty to harness it, to make it productive. "Nevada was born in the deeps of the darksome mines, and irrigation will now bring it out into the open sunshine," he declared.

The manipulation of water was what made the modern West possible; it was the magic liquid that infused what Wallace Stegner called "the vast speculative real estate deal that is American and western history." Delegates to the first International Irrigation Congress, held in Los Angeles in 1893, were told by speaker after speaker that 1 million new farms could be created by means of vast irrigation works throughout the West. It was the old Jeffersonian vision of a national yeomanry now writ on a truly grandiose scale. It was also a delusion. According to the geologist John Wesley Powell, who probably knew the West better than any man alive at that time, only a small fraction of the 850 million acres in the federal domain could actually be irrigated. "I tell you gentlemen," he said, "you are piling up a heritage of conflict and litigation over water rights for there is not sufficient water to supply the land." It was a prescient prediction. But it was a message that no one in Los Angeles wanted to hear. His thanks was to be booed off the stage.

Newlands eventually found the ally he needed in President Theodore Roosevelt, who saw massive land reclamation as an integral part of the West's Manifest Destiny. With his encouragement, Newlands drafted landmark legislation that was to become the Land Reclamation Act of 1902. Newlands saw it as one of the great populist documents of his time. "The aim [of irrigation]," he declared, "is to prevent monopoly of every form, to open up the public domain to actual settlers who desire homes, and to disintegrate the monopolistic holdings of land that prevail on the Pacific coast and in the intermountain region." In a speech to Congress, he proclaimed that his legislation would "nationalize the works of irrigation," which, as a modern environmentalist, Marc Reisner, has wryly pointed out, is rather like saying today that one intended to nationalize the automobile industry.

The Newlands Project was the first to be initiated under the new act. It was the forerunner for the eventual reclamation of vast tracts of the West, and for one of the costliest and, in the view of many modern environmentalists, one of the most unnecessary federal programs in American history. Derby Dam was a test run for the monumental barriers that would one day dam the Colorado, the Columbia, the Missouri, and scores of other Western rivers. It would divert half the flow of the Truckee into a canal that would carry it across thirty-two miles of desert to the new Lahontan Reservoir. There it would combine with the waters of the Carson River and be redistributed into a network of canals that would irrigate 323,000 acres of sagebrush desert around the town of Fallon. Flyers proclaimed: "The Land is Free. Water rights furnished by the U.S. Reclamation Service at $60 per acre, payable in 16 installments in 20 years . . . WITHOUT INTEREST . . . the Opportunity of a lifetime for the homeseeker exists RIGHT NOW." No one even considered the fate of the Paiutes of Pyramid Lake.

The Paiutes' early history is obscure. They probably reached what is now northern Nevada about one thousand years ago, pushing out an earlier people who had preceded them. The most fortunate of the many Paiute bands were those who settled by the shores of Pyramid and Winnemucca lakes, which since time immemorial had been the natural termini of the Truckee. Pyramid Lake lies in a deep crack in what was once the lowest part of the drainage of the vast primeval lake, known to modern geologists as Lake Lahontan, that once covered much of present-day Utah and Nevada. The lake today has a surface area of 115,000 acres and measures 360 feet at its deepest. It is surrounded by a strange and barren landscape of bulbous tufa outcrops and jagged, reddish-gray jagged ridges that, in the hazy heat of an autumn day, seem to hover eerily over the turquoise surface of the water. One of them, a pyramidal crag that rises up through the water near the eastern shore, was regarded by Paiutes as a protective deity and gives the lake its modern name.

The desolation that characterizes Pyramid Lake today—the naked shores, the scrub-choked delta, the sterile hills—offers no hint of what the first Paiutes might have seen. It was, for many centuries, a fortunate and generous environment, an oasis in the dreary emptiness that was the Great Basin. Around the lakes there was everything that a foraging culture needed to sustain life. Arrows could be fashioned from the cane that grew along the Truckee, mats made from cattail fibers, and baskets, sandals, and bags woven from marsh reeds. Geese, heron, and ducks provided game, while chokecherries and piñon nuts, wild rye and rice grass could be harvested with ease.

But nothing compared to the truly stunning profusion of fish that swam out to spawn in the Truckee, when the annual spring floods roared down off the Sierras. Of the two species that inhabited the lakes, the steel-colored Lahontan cutthroat trout was the larger, often growing as big as forty pounds. The blunt-snouted cui-ui (pronounced "kwee-wee") was utterly unique; it was the last surviving denizen of Lake Lahontan. At spawning time, the cui-ui crowded the Truckee as far upstream as the site of modern Reno, so thick in the water that they could be plucked out by hand. So seemingly inexhaustible, so predictable in their habits, and so profoundly interwoven with the lives of the people of the lakes were the cui-ui that the Paiutes took the fish's name as their own: they called themselves the Kuyuidokado—the "Cui-ui Eaters."

The Kuyuidokados' story of origin held that mankind had once been a single family of light- and dark-skinned children. After a quarrel, the light-skinned children were sent into exile and told to find another land to live in. It was prophesied that their descendants would one day return and heal the ancient rift. That miraculous day came in 1833, in the minds of at least some Paiutes, when they spied a caravan of white-skinned men approaching from the east. Word spread that the long-lost children had come home. Hundreds turned out to greet them, dancing and singing, and begging the strangers to share the pipe of reconciliation.

The trappers, of course, had no interest in Paiute mythology. They wanted to kill Indians. "A number of our men had never been engaged in any fighting with the Indians, and were anxious to try their skill," one of the trappers reported later. Several dozen riflemen went forward to give the Paiutes "a severe blow." Instead of halting when they saw the whites pointing their guns, the Paiutes smiled and danced faster. Having never heard gunfire, they thought it was merely the clap of thunder. "We closed in on them and fired," the chronicler reported, "leaving thirty-nine dead on the field—which was nearly the half—the remainder were overwhelmed with dismay—running into the high grass in every direction, howling in the most lamentable manner." A modern Paiute has dryly written of the same event, "After a few volleys, the Paiutes knew the white men did not want to be friends."

With the discovery of gold in California, the Truckee basin became part of the overland trail. Settlers trekked through the Paiute lands by the tens of thousands, shooting game and bringing with them herds of cattle that devoured the fruits and grasses upon which the Indians depended for food. Sawmills in the Sierras contaminated the Truckee with vast quantities of sawdust. When silver was discovered at Virginia City, the white population of the territory swelled from a few hundred to thousands overnight. Many of them, like their counterparts in northern California, viewed the extermination of Indians as a kind of public service. A government agent reported matter-of-factly that settlers "are in the habit of shooting the Indians whenever and wherever they can find them, whether the Indians are molesting them or not."

A brief war in 1860 made it clear to the Paiutes that armed resistance was futile. The Indians tried to accommodate themselves peacefully to a difficult new reality. They soon learned that survival depended on obedience. At that time, federal Indian agents frequently "bought" their reservation appointments like the tax farmers of the Roman Empire, repaying themselves by extorting every third bale of hay, say, or every fourth sack of grain from Indian-run farms. Indians who protested corruption, or who resisted the pressure to become farmers or to send their children away to distant schools, were punished with short rations, bad work assignments, or, in extreme cases, banishment from the reservation. Even when the harsher aspects of federal control abated, the habit of paternalism ensured that Indians would never learn the skills necessary to manage their own financial affairs. As late as 1930, when the government allocated money for the Paiutes to buy cattle, the resident agent reassured concerned white citizens, "The money will not be loaned outright to the Indians for them to use as they wish, because you can see how such a plan would not meet with success. We will use our discretion in making purchases for them."

Measured against the vision of Francis Newlands, the fate of the Paiutes was at best a minor concern. Pyramid Lake, Newlands grandiloquently asserted, existed "only to satisfy the thirsty sun." When Derby Dam was completed, the effects were catastrophic. Deprived of water, Lake Winnemucca eventually disappeared completely. Marshes dried up. Wildlife disappeared. Pyramid Lake's level eventually dropped almost eighty feet, to its lowest point in four thousand years. Its alkalinity increased by 50 percent. The spawning runs failed. The cui-ui and trout beached themselves and died on the delta that spread across the mouth of the Truckee. The precipitous decline in the fish population kicked away what had for a thousand years been the steadiest prop of the Paiutes' fragile economy.

Meanwhile, the reclamation program that had begun with such fanfare soon revealed unforeseen problems. When the soil around Fallon was finally tested, much of it proved to be so sandy and alkaline that cultivation would be fruitless. That was just the beginning. The government had estimated the annual cost to white settlers at $5 per acre for machinery, fertilizers, and water-use fees. Farmers discovered that their actual expenses ran as much as twenty times higher per acre, including chemicals to control the salination that irrigation forced up into the root zones of their crops. Reclamation officials were eventually forced to install more than one hundred miles of drains, at a cost of nearly $750,000, an astronomical sum at the time. In the end, barely 73,000 acres were irrigated, less than a third of what Newlands had promised.

There was an even grander delusion which has been chronicled by Marc Reisner in *Cadillac Desert,* a vivid deconstruction of federal water policy in the West. The entire national reclamation program was supposed to pay for itself. Projects throughout the West were financed by a public fund, which was initially to be filled by revenue from the sale of federal land and then reimbursed through the sale of water to farmers. Farmers were exempted from paying interest on any of their repayment obligations, a public subsidy that compounded with time as interest rates topped 10 percent. Even so, by 1922, twenty years after the reclamation program began, only 10 percent of the money loaned from the Reclamation Fund had been repaid. Irrigators defaulted everywhere, even though they paid no interest, and, in 1924, Congress increased the repayment period from twenty years to forty. During the Depression of the 1930s, the government gave up trying to collect entirely.

Meanwhile, the Paiutes of Pyramid Lake pleaded for water to sustain the shrinking population of cui-ui. The Bureau of Reclamation took the position that the fishery issue was outside its jurisdiction. It was an open secret that the farmers downstream were simply siphoning off as much water as they wanted, but officials responsible for controlling the flow of the Truckee argued that settlers would never consent to giving up any of their water and that, in any case, it was impossible to save Pyramid Lake. Although the Supreme Court had declared as early as 1908 that Indian tribes had a prior right to the use of water that flowed through their reservations, the Bureau of Indian Affairs consistently declined to defend the Paiutes' claims. In 1921, a federal inspector blandly observed, "The Indians have a water right, but being at the tail-end of the river, so to speak, they are unable to obtain their proper share of the water, all other water users on the river having first chance and there is no one in authority to make a just and fair distribution."

Glorene Guerrero remembers what must have been one of the last cui-ui harvests. It took place sometime in the early 1940s, when Guerrero, who is now a lab technician employed to monitor the quality of the lake water, was still a small girl. The reservation was then a place without even the hope of a future. The Paiutes had been virtually forgotten by everyone, buried in their open-air tomb in the hills north of Wadsworth, a people of utterly no consequence and virtually no means of support. Guerrero's mother took in laundry. It was counted as good work in those days. "I was always told," Guerrero remembers, " 'You're not going to be anything, and you're not going to do anything.' " She remembers the humpy gray shapes of the fish crowding against the shore, and the turquoise water that spread as far as she could see, it seemed, between the naked tufa hills. She remembers men hauling in the fish, women scraping them clean, the fish drying on shore by the hundreds, and then feasting. She remembers joy, the coming together of families and of a tiny nation. It was also very nearly the cui-ui's final appearance on the stage of history.

In 1944, the Department of Justice ruled that the Paiutes had a right to enough water to irrigate the 5,400 acres of land that tribal members then had under cultivation. But the same ruling specifically asserted that water for fishing did not constitute a sufficiently "beneficial use" to be worthy of consideration. Six years later, Commissioner of Indian Affairs Dillon Myer forced the transfer of an agent who dared even to suggest that the bureau had failed to protect the tribe's right to more water. When the Paiutes prepared to initiate a lawsuit on their own, Myer refused the tribe permission to renew its contract with its own attorney and denied an official

Paiute delegation the use of tribal funds to travel to Washington to lobby Congress in their own behalf.

With some difficulty, the delegates managed to borrow enough money to buy bus tickets to Washington. The sight of the Paiutes that October day in 1951, dressed in cowboy boots, Stetsons, and their best jeans and pearl-buttoned shirts, crowded into a Greyhound heading east across the numbing desolation of the Nevada desert is perhaps a quintessential image of Native Americans at midcentury: hobbled by poverty, driven by quixotic pride, stumbling off on a crusade that they were too naive to realize was politically unwinnable. The Paiutes stayed on in Washington for several weeks, living on borrowed money, talking to any member of Congress who would listen to them. "We intend to squat here in the Capital . . . until we get our rights," Avery Winnemucca, the tribal chairman, wrote home to a friend in Reno. But the trip was, of course, like everything else that the Paiutes had put their trust in, a complete failure.

At the tribal hatchery where Glorene Guerrero works, on the lakeshore near Sutcliffe, one can see minuscule cui-ui fry by the thousands, paddling aimlessly in 150-gallon green fiberglass vats, waiting to be released into the salty water of Pyramid Lake, where their ancestors lived, like a population of ecological hermits, for at least the last 40,000 years. The cui-ui is not a pretty fish. Its body is thick and graceless, and its blunt snout endows it with an unpleasant, rather thuggish appearance. Fishermen who once traveled from all over the United States to catch the lake's mammoth trout disdained the cui-ui as a junk fish, too bony to bother with and unpleasant to the palate. But to the Paiutes, the fate of the cui-ui was indistinguishable from their own survival. Paul Wagner, who has managed the hatchery for most of the last twenty years, says, "The cui-ui were their flag, their nation, their identity."

By midcentury, it seemed clear to everyone that the cui-ui's extinction was only a matter of time. In the 1960s, it was estimated that no more than a few tens of thousands of cui-ui might still exist. Fortunately, it was just at this time that the national conscience began to regard the fate of disappearing wildlife as a matter of moral concern. The cui-ui was one of the first species to be placed under protection by the Endangered Species Act of 1966, becoming a founding member of a company that would include such famous political irritants as the snail darter and the spotted owl. It seemed an innocuous enough decision at the time. However, it was at this point that the snub-nosed relic of the Pleistocene became the fulcrum upon which the fate of the Paiutes began to turn. No one imagined that it would lead to the effective demise of the Newlands Project and, in the process, overturn the entire balance of power in northern Nevada.

Virtually overnight, the redefinition of the cui-ui from a junk fish into an endangered species transformed the question of its survival from a matter of chance into a political imperative. By the mid-1970s, a hatchery financed by the Bureau of Indian Affairs was raising 1 million trout and cui-ui fry each year. In the view of fishery experts, however, a steady supply of clean water was essential to stabilize the shoreline for the cui-ui's reproductive cycle; the only possible source of more water was the Truckee. In 1973, a federal district court ruled that the federal trust responsibility required the government to maintain the level of Pyramid Lake and ordered the Department of the Interior to reduce the diversion of water to the farmers of the Newlands Project. Next, a federal court ruled that Stampede Reservoir, which the city of Reno had constructed to supplement its own water supply, would instead have to be managed to ensure that enough fresh water was available to guarantee the cui-ui's survival in times of drought.

The renaissance of the cui-ui was not taking place in a vacuum, of course. The entire Truckee watershed was undergoing a transformation that was in many ways a microcosm of changes taking place all over the West, as traditional economies withered and gave way to urbanization and to new values that demanded a balance between the needs of man and the natural environment. The historian Patricia Limerick has aptly described the typical Western water conflict as resembling "an old-fashioned showdown, but with the rivals converging from ten directions instead of the more traditional two." The Paiutes wanted more water to sustain the spawning run of the cui-ui and to raise the level of Pyramid Lake. The State of California was demanding more water for development around Lake Tahoe. The State of Nevada was determined to defend its claims to the Truckee against California's. Politicians in Reno and Sparks were desperate to guarantee a more predictable flow of water to a population that was growing at a rate of 33 percent per decade. Environmentalists were insisting upon more water for wetlands that had been created by runoff from the farms around Fallon. The once-unassailable farmers of the Newlands Project were determined to prevent any further erosion of their already diminished water supply.

In 1987, representatives of these various interests began face-to-face negotiations, in a sort of slow-motion version of the gunfight at the O.K. Corral. When it was over, four years later, the farmers were finished as a political power on the Truckee. The pivot of this transformation was a wholly unforeseen collaboration between the region's most powerful utility and the Kuyuidokado, an alliance that, in retrospect, seems perhaps as quintessential a creature of the new West as the Newlands Project was of the old. The Sierra Pacific Power Company (now Westpac Utilities) had supplied water-generated power to Reno and Sparks since the 1930s. But the 63,000 acre-feet of water that Sierra Pacific controlled was barely adequate to serve a population that was approaching 200,000 by the end of the 1980s and that was likely to continue to grow well into the next century. On the cusp of the worst water crisis in half a century, split-level developments with names such as Spanish Springs, Desert Springs, and Springwood were still sprawling northward along Route 445 as if their incantatory names had the power to make water magically appear. As reservoirs shrank, spurring fearful talk of rationing and shortage, the pressure to find a comprehensive solution reached fever pitch.

The view from Sue Oldham's office on the southern edge of Reno is enough to remind anyone of the hubris of settling a land as dry as northern Nevada. From her immaculate desk, she can look through a large picture window across a flat and sunbaked landscape that stretches as far as the naked, chalky blue summits of the Washoe Hills. Oldham is Sierra Pacific's director for government affairs; in the late 1980s and early 1990s, she was one of the utility's chief negotiators. "At first, it was everyone against the Indians," she recalls. "Everyone was really ticked off at the tribe." The Paiutes were then insisting adamantly on being given first claim to the Truckee's waters, a right that, if agreed to, could jeopardize the entire region's economy. The tribe was also engaged in four separate lawsuits against Reno and Sparks, in an effort to compel the cities to improve the quality of the water that flowed downriver toward Pyramid Lake.

"Everyone thought the Indians wanted the rest of us to just dry up and blow away," Oldham says. "They thought the tribe was outrageous. The fear was that if Indians had first right to the water, then there would be none for anyone else." For three years, the talks remained at an impasse. With self-conscious irony in her softly cadenced, lawyer's voice, Oldham says, "If you can't figure out why someone is saying what he is saying, you create your own explanation. Everyone thought, all the Indians really want is money. The fact is, we were talking about a twenty-year planning horizon, when the Indians were talking about a thousand-year planning horizon. We kept talking about the minimum needs for their fishery. They didn't like that. They kept looking for improvement."

The Paiutes were blessed with a skilled negotiator in their then-tribal chairman, a civil engineer in his early thirties by the name of Joe Ely. In February 1990, he testified on the tribe's behalf before the United States Senate's Subcommittee on Water and Power. Ely is an athletic man with aquiline features and dark, intense eyes. His trimness and concentrated intelligence, the impression of restless energy, evoked the style of an ambitious young academic or an up-and-coming young businessman rather than a tribal politician. He was crisp and convincing. "When we talk of the water it must be understood that it is a major component of our identity and way of life. Those components are the people—*cui-ui tuccatta,* the lake—*cui-ui pah*—and the fish, *cui-ui.* These are inseparable components and one does not exist without the other. I know one might make light of this significance or write it off as romance, but to us it is everything."

Ely was no sentimentalist, however. He was impatient with the widespread Indian preoccupation with loss, defeat, and vic-timhood. "We lived successfully for thousands of years," he says. "There was only a brief time that the tribe was on the downslide. I'm not going to whine about the last three hundred years—those years are over." He was determined to make the Paiutes a player in the expanding regional economy. Like the Campos of southern California, the Paiutes had only one resource, a single commodity that might conceivably be converted into power that could be used to create a future for the tribe. It occurred to Ely that water could be used to leverage power, just as the cui-ui had been used to leverage water rights. He was convinced that the defensive isolation in which the tribe had existed for so long was a dead end and that to make sovereignty meaningful, the Paiutes would have to engage the world outside the reservation. "This is a capitalist society, and if you want something you've got to buy it," he repeatedly told the Paiutes as he lobbied for their support. "Tribes that expect to live in isolation from the rest of the world are going to fail. You've got to get off the reservation and get involved in commerce out there, in the economics, and bring money back to the reservation. We need to participate in the outer world, to retain who we are, and also to pick up the best of [the white man's] world, and perhaps make our society a better one."

Ely had a plan. With a guaranteed supply of water, Pyramid Lake could become a natural attraction; tourists could be drawn from Reno and beyond for fishing, boating, and swimming. Tourism would generate new Indian-owned businesses—tackle shops, service stations, grocery stores. "Once our people have some money in their pockets, they'll want to spend it, so you could put in video stores and so forth." Meanwhile, tribal development money could be invested in industries in Reno or in California, and the profits used to operate the public services that the tribe now received from the federal government. Dependency would become a thing of the past. "In the past, the Paiutes exploited a wide region, not just what is now the reservation," says Ely, who, having been precluded by tribal law from succeeding himself as chairman, left Pyramid Lake in 1991 to join an engineering firm based in Phoenix. "That's what we need to do again. Like our ancestors, we can exploit the region far beyond the lake. At the same time, the reservation would be preserved as a sanctuary for our way of life."

"When we gradually came to realize that what the tribe really wanted was water for the fishery, we began to make rapid progress," Sue Oldham recalls. Sierra Pacific began to look at the Paiutes as an asset instead of an adversary. The Indians and the power company were, in fact, natural allies. Thanks to the cui-ui, the Paiutes had control over the water in Stampede Reservoir. If that water could somehow be made available to the utility in times of need, the cities' supply would be assured. There would have to be a quid pro quo: there would be no alternative to giving the tribe decision-making power over the redistribution of its water. "We are all alone up here in northern Nevada," Oldham explains. "We have to be self-sufficient. We have to know where our water supply is coming from." But there was a catch, of course. The Truckee's water was finite. Whatever additional water was allocated to Pyramid Lake would have to come from somewhere else. That meant that there would be less water for dams, less for energy, less for farming—less for something. It gradually became apparent that the something was going to have to be the Newlands Project.

Farming was no longer the sacred cow that it had been in Francis Newlands's day. To urban politicians, to suburbanites, to power company executives, to environmentalists, water for farming was increasingly seen as wasted water that could be used more efficiently to support people and wildlife. By conservative estimate, the Newlands project used at least 45 percent of the water available in the Truckee basin while it accounted for only about 3 percent of the region's gross economy. By contrast, the cities of Reno and Sparks, which comprised by far the largest proportion of both population and economy, used only 10 percent of Truckee water and returned almost one third of that to the river. The farmers whom Newlands had struggled so hard and long to entice onto fields reclaimed from the desert were now expendable.

"The tribe's bottom line was that our water had to be down around 300,000 acre-feet per year," says Lyman F. McConnell, the manager of the Truckee-Carson Irrigation District, the farmers' co-operative that manages the distribution of water in the Newlands Project. "That's 40,000 to 60,000 less than the project uses annually. We just couldn't do it. We were forced out of the negotiations. There was no way we could meet that kind of efficiency without federal funds to rehabilitate and upgrade the system."

It is not hard to sense the hurt and confusion behind Ted de Braga's easy smile and truculent turns of phrase. "They forced us against the wall. They ambushed us." That is perhaps the way he really sees what happened to him and to the other farmers, who never imagined that the Paiutes would one day be able to shut the tap on their way of life. De Braga stands well over six feet in height and has prematurely white hair and the kind of ruddy, light-skinned complexion that suffers in the riveting, shadeless sunlight of Nevada. He is wearing workboots and jeans, and a shirt that is soaked with sweat after a day cutting hay in 104-degree heat.

De Braga's grandfather came to Nevada from the Azores at the turn of the century to work in the mines. "He seen a sign: 'Settle on forty acres,' it said. And he did." The small frame house that he built for his family is the same one that Ted de Braga was born in, in 1947. Ted now lives down the road in a modern ranch house with white vinyl siding and a slate-floored living room with a picture window that looks out on withering fields of alfalfa. But you can tell that he is proud of the small house, which he still keeps up, and of his grandfather, and of the fortitude it required to start a life, even with the help of irrigation canals, on these baking plains.

Out here beyond Fallon, the vision that Francis Newlands and Theodore Roosevelt had is no abstraction, no pipe dream. At tremendous cost to taxpayers elsewhere in the United States, they did make the desert bloom. But this year there has only been enough water to irrigate a fraction of the seven hundred acres that de Braga used to till, and broad, scabrous gray patches of bare ground mark what, in wet years, would have been rich fields of alfalfa and corn. Because of the drought, water flow to Newlands was reduced by 30 percent in 1990, then by 26 percent in 1991, then by 28 percent more in 1992.

"Take water out of here, and nobody will want to live here," de Braga says. Without adequate water, the farms will inexorably shrink. The services that depend on agriculture will begin to disappear; the pig farms, the hay cubing outfits, the dairies, the equipment suppliers, they will all go, one by one. Some farmers have already begun selling acreage back to the federal government, to be given over to wetlands, for the waterfowl that, on the scale of late-twentieth-century values, rate higher than men who till the land. Banks are reluctant to lend to the farmers who remain. "It's the uncertainty of litigation, mandates, federal legislation, and stuff."

De Braga squints across the failing fields and beyond them over the desert speckled with thigh-high greasewood, stretching away depressingly, mile after mile, toward the toothed, pale-gray shadow of the Stillwater Mountains, suggesting, subtly and cruelly, the future that may lie in store for most of these farms of which Francis Newlands so floridly dreamed. "Whether we can be compensated for the blood, sweat, and tears we put in here, well . . ." His voice trails quietly off.

On November 16, 1990, the United States Senate voted to approve what everyone in the Truckee basin calls simply "the settlement." The twenty-five-page, single-spaced document utterly reinvented the economic geography of the Truckee. It reapportioned the division of waters from the Carson River and Lake Tahoe between California and Nevada and precluded California from diverting the

Truckee outside its own basin. It authorized the Secretary of the Interior to acquire water rights to sustain the Stillwater wetlands as a refuge for migratory waterfowl. It gave Sierra Pacific the authority to move water around the region through exchange and sharing, thereby guaranteeing drought protection for Reno and Sparks. It appropriated $43 million to the small Fallon Tribe of Paiutes for the acquisition of additional water rights and the improvement of the tribe's irrigation system.

To ensure the survival of the cui-ui, the act authorized the Secretary of the Interior to acquire both water and water rights from the Newlands Project to promote the recovery of the tribal fishery. The Secretary of the Army, as the head of the Corps of Engineers, was directed to undertake the rehabilitation of the Truckee, including the delta at Pyramid Lake, with a view to improving the spawning habitat for both the cui-ui and the cutthroat trout. A $25-million fund was created to operate the tribal fisheries at Sutcliffe, and another $40 million was set aside for economic development on the Pyramid Lake reservation.

On one level, the settlement was a philosophical watershed. It decisively rejected the old Jeffersonian faith that agriculture was the highest form of civilization and that it must be protected at all political costs. Instead, it embraced what Charles Wilkinson, an eloquent theorist of the shape of the new West, has termed a "new ethic of place," which strives to balance stable, improving economies with respect for the environment and the rights of Indian tribes. "An ethic of place," Wilkinson has written, "respects equally the people of a region, and the land, animals, vegetation, water and air . . . and includes a dogged determination to treat the environment and its people as equals, to recognize both as sacred, and to insure that all members of the community not just search for but insist upon solutions that fulfill the ethic."

Joe Ely saw the settlement as a kind of historical redemption. It finally vindicated the frustrated dreams of Avery Winnemucca and the hopeful tribal leaders who set off across the desert for Washington in 1950 and of those forgotten Paiutes who were contemptuously ordered back to the reservation and condemned for their "talk habit" thirty years before. "The agreement represents a bonding with the past, but a release from it at the same time," Ely says. "Through the settlement, we are now linked securely with the past, and we are assured of our identity. We no longer need to focus all our energies on struggle. Now we are able to work to ensure the tribe's longevity and the economic well-being of our people."

The settlement invited the Paiutes to participate as equal partners in the management of the Truckee basin. It required that they be consulted in all water decisions involving the river, including the right to sit on the committees that make water policy for Nevada and California, in order to ensure that the states' use of water was not impairing the Pyramid Lake fishery. The water stored in Stampede and Prosser Creek reservoirs was to be used solely to restore and maintain the lake's fishery and could be exchanged or loaned to other users during a drought emergency only with the approval of the tribe. Any other water that remained in the Truckee system was to be allocated automatically to the lake for the support of the fishery, as well. In effect, the settlement gave the Paiutes leverage over the most important sources of water in a region where the future of all development hinges on the flow of the Truckee. More problematically, it asked them, for the first time in their history, to choose to risk engagement with the outside world.

"There has been a very definite paradigm shift, but this community still has not fully grasped the situation, the role that the tribe is now in," says John McIntyre, the chairman of the Washoe County Commission. "Because this community has got to rely on the Truckee system, it makes the tribe a very significant player. Historians may say that the significance of the tribe's role is so great that they controlled our destiny. They can dictate the kind of water treatment facilities that are acceptable to them, which means that they can control the timing and location of growth itself. I think that it is they who will tell us what our growth rate is going to be."

It is a sultry Friday in August of 1992, and the tribal water committee is meeting to consider what would seem, on the face of it, to be an innocuous proposition. For five years now, northern Nevada has been in the throes of the worst drought in generations. The Truckee has shrunk to one-fifth of its normal flow. Reservoirs are going dry. The level of Pyramid Lake has dropped ten more feet. Shallow water cooked by the hundred-degree-plus heat is killing fish wholesale. The fourteen thousand acres of the Stillwater wetlands have contracted to barely six hundred; birds are dying there by the thousands. If the drought continues, people are saying, emergency water reserves may be wiped out by 1995. "Maybe a few hundred additional acre-feet of water can be scrounged from somewhere else," writes an editorialist at the *Reno Gazette-Journal*. "But maybe they can't, or only at a horrendous cost. And what happens if all the scenarios go bad? What happens if all this whistling in the dark produces not safety but a demon in the end? What happens if we wake up some day and the water . . . is gone?"

Almost alone on the Truckee, the Paiutes have water to spare. But it sits now, out of reach of anyone else, in the reservoirs in the high Sierras. Panicky in the face of the deepening drought, Washoe County's Board of Supervisors has asked the Paiutes for the loan of five thousand acre-feet. It is the kind of transaction that the settlement specifically mandated, with the tribe's permission, the kind of innovation that was intended to prevent shortage and to create among longtime enemies a sense of shared responsibility. The county has promised to pay the water back in time for the cui-ui's next spawning run, which can occur only when the drought ends.

Robert Pelcyger, the tribe's attorney, had negotiated the settlement alongside Joe Ely. He is now trying to convince the Paiutes to horsetrade, to deal with the whites, to trust them. "This is an opportunity," he is saying. Pelcyger is a brilliant lawyer, but he is also a white, and his style is self-consciously deferential. He tells the Paiutes that lending water to Reno and Sparks would prove that the tribe was willing to act in partnership. "That water is not doing anything but evaporating if it just sits there. It's not doing the tribe any good where it is. The question should be, what else can we get by giving the water? You tell Reno-Sparks, 'Okay, if you take our water, then what will you do for us in return?' "

It is a smart presentation, but the faces around the table—the tribal bureaucrats, the sunburned Paiute farmers in their billed caps —are cool and appraising. "All this talk and stuff," says one of the farmers. His voice is filled with contempt. "It sounds to me like they're just going to pay us back with our own water. It's always been 'to hell with the Indians.' It's always been that way. It'll always stay that way."

Outside the tribal office building, the dusk light has thrown the greenish scarps into relief across the baking surface of Pyramid Lake. Overheated air is blowing in gusts with a cargo of rasping dust past the general store, the boarded-up school, the Episcopal church, the mobile homes, and the HUD houses scattered with no apparent order over the sagebrush desert. Inside the air-conditioned committee room, the mood is sullen.

Although the new tribal chairman, Elwood Lowery, shares Pelcyger's sentiments, he lacks the lawyer's eloquence and conviction. He is easily overshadowed by the young director of the tribal water department, a quiet man with tightly wound braids named Mervyn Wright. Although Wright holds a B.S. in agriculture from California State College at Chico, he has little interest in the world beyond the reservation. When he speaks of having lived "out there," among non-Indians, it is as if he means an altogether foreign country, a harsh and sterile land in which he has no place.

He sees water in terms that defy the logic of economic development. "Water is life. If you waste it, it's like throwing life around. Upstream, they don't respect water. They see only money. But you can't throw hundred-dollar bills at the ground and make something grow. Only water can do that." To trade water, to exploit it for gain, seems to him a sacrilege. The lake, he says, is a mother to the tribe, and water a gift that must be restored to her care. "When I think of filling the Truckee, it's a way of giving the lake back to itself." The potential political gains of sharing water are beside the point.

Wright regards the whole water-sharing proposal as "white man's thinking," premised on the assumption that there is something to be gained by participating in the white man's world. To compromise is to risk corruption, to risk becoming like whites. "Why should we let them have water? The way I see it, we just stand to lose what we've already got." It is a blunt rebuttal to Joe Ely's optimism and pragmatic confidence. Wright's flat voice is calm at first and then gathers an edge of sarcasm as it goes on. "They'll take what they want, at any expense. They always make it look good on paper, but it will always nullify whatever benefits you're supposed to get."

The tenor of the meeting grows increasingly more hostile. Ultimately, the debate becomes less about water than about fear and distrust, and the legacy of racism. There is a feeling of steadily rising anger at the white farmers who for so many years stole the tribe's water, at Reno's continuing suburban sprawl, at the intractable facts of history. "I want to know how much of this water goes to growth," Wright asks rhetorically. He is talking about the new housing tracts that are spreading northward from Sparks, toward the lake. "They're still building even though there's no more water available. It's just running wild. Why should we be responsible for their growth?"

One can feel, almost minute by minute, the growing impulse to withdraw, to shy away from risk and entanglement, to slip back into ancient enmities. Someone from the tribal fish hatchery says, "We're going to lose either way. No matter what we say, they're going to get that water." In the contemptuous voices, one can hear the resignation of people still accustomed to defeat, and incomprehension that, for the first time in their modern history, the Paiutes hold the stronger hand, the power to dominate and thwart their white neighbors, if they wish, and to exert power through negotiation and cooperation.

"A lot of people in the county want the tribe to reject this agreement, so they can say, 'See, you can't work with the tribe, you can't trust them.' " Pelcyger is pleading now. "If you reject an agreement, you'll be playing right into their hands. If you don't negotiate the problem, an agreement will be reached without the tribe." He is telling the Paiutes that water is power, that it can be transmuted directly into political leverage. But he has failed to sway.

The moment to act, if it ever existed, is now lost. It slips away without decision or commitment into the miasma of paralyzing resentment that lies over the room like the suffocating Nevada heat, and from which it seems, this night at least, among the sullen bureaucrats and the farmers in their gay billed caps, that there will never be any surcease or redemption.

There is a surreal quality to the highlands that enfold the reservation of the Confederated Tribes of Warm Springs, in central Oregon. It is a dramatic and lonesome country of black basalt buttes that drop away into canyons thick with junipers, hemlocks, Douglas firs, and pines. The first paved road reached Warm Springs only after World War II, and there are still people who remember when most everyone lived in tepees and when mail came only twice a week by horsedrawn wagon. Even now, although the reservation is linked to the outside world by a good highway and modern communications, the feeling of separateness remains palpable. It is vividly symbolized by the volcanic cones that preempt the western horizon and that, in certain kinds of light, suggest a boundary of grandiose significance, the edge of a continent, or of a world from which one might drop off not merely to the fertile plains of the Willamette Valley, but into oblivion.

"This area is a battlefront," Louie Pitt, the director of the tribe's natural resources department, is saying. He is staring at the bare red soil, studying it, observing it as if it were alive. Beneath the lip of the ridge, clear-cuts have left wide, desolate swaths of earth jagged with snags and rotting stumps. Pitt speaks for a while about the fish, and elk, and insects whose habitats have been destroyed by logging, and of the fresh tracts of forest scheduled to go under the ax. "It's a crime to log an area like this. Soil is alive. When you clear-cut, you cook it, you shock it. You just kill that soil. It would have been an excellent watershed to leave as it was. But the tribe kicked it out of protected status into logging status. There was no impact statement, nothing."

Pitt lived for a time, in the 1960s and 1970s, in different cities on the West Coast, working on construction sites. "I pushed a wheelbarrow, all the time trying to figure out where I fit in this big mess. Mostly I fed my drug and alcohol habit." In 1973, Pitt's father died and he came home. "I spent a lot of time sitting in my driveway, beating a drum with the boys. I tried to get off the bottle." He watched tract after tract of virgin timber sold off by the tribal government. In 1984, there was talk of opening another watershed. "I went up there and walked around. There was all this solitude. I could smell the elk. I thought, this is my home. I thought, there is nothing here that will hurt me."

He remembered the uncle who had led him into the mountains when he was a boy, to this very vale, in fact, to teach him how to see the earth. "I was twelve years old. Uncle Andrew picked up a handful of dirt. 'What is this?' he asked me. I said, 'Just dirt.' 'Wrong answer!' Uncle Andrew said. 'Dirt is alive. It's where we came from.' Then he spent two or three hours telling me about all the magic and wisdom in the earth, and then all about the water, and its magic, and about its interplay with the earth. He drew a circle in the dirt. He said it was the circle of life. He told me, 'No one point in the circle is more important than another point. Everything is tied together.' He told me to listen to the things that had no mouths. He said, 'We have a duty to speak for the things that can't speak for themselves.' "

Ever since then, Pitt has been one of the most effective critics of the tribe's business-oriented leadership. "The corporate culture has totally won out in this tribe," Pitt says, staring at the red earth. "It's a kind of sickness—just cut the trees and run. We hired people to tell us what reality is—they call it 'facts,' or 'data.' But it is an illusion. They say, 'Hell, those trees are going to waste, we got to do something about it.' Now, instead of having a relationship with the resource, with the forest, we're having the relationship with a piece of paper, an allocation, a budget. When you think like that, you're throwing out whole pieces of reality, the whole magical element of what makes a tree grow. We can make money from these areas, but we don't know what we'll be doing to the land. By not looking at the connections among all the parts, we may be throwing out the ability to generate the next generation of the forest."

From a certain intellectual angle, Louie Pitt might seem a classic icon of the American Indian at end-of-century, poised gravely, even sacramentally, in his denims and dusty boots over the doomed earth, like Chief Seattle come to life. But Warm Springs defies such facile images, as it does all conventional assumptions about the hopelessness of reservation life. To be sure, it is possible to find pockets of poverty within just a mile or two of Agency, the reservation's administrative center, where most of the tribe's three thousand members live. But the broken windows and abandoned cars, the screes of broken furniture spilling across bare yards, troubling as they may be, are increasingly more the exception than the rule.

Thanks mainly to the tribal timber industry, which harvested and sold more than 100 million board-feet annually for most of the last decade, Warm Springs enjoys a degree of economic success that the Paiutes of Pyramid Lake, the Campos, and scores of other tribes can still do little more than dream about. More than seven hundred members of the tribe work in the forestry trades. Others, at the tribal textile plant, produce sportswear for Nike and Janson and beadwork for export to Europe. The tribe operates a luxury vacation lodge and three hydroelectric dams, and, with characteristic innovativeness, recently began manufacturing fireproof doors from diatomaceous earth, or fossilized sea creatures. However, more than half of the $80 million that tribal businesses earn each year still derives from timber sales. In the early 1990s, two-thirds of the tribe's workforce was fully employed, a very high percentage for almost any reservation, much less one as geographically isolated as Warm Springs.

For a generation, the driving force behind the tribe's economic advancement has been Ken Smith, who has been chief executive officer—the title is significant—since the early 1970s. An accountant by training, Smith is physically compact and dapper, with a pale, spade-shaped face and the appraising eyes of a man who has little patience with time-wasting and inefficiency. He was raised by illiterate grandparents on a ranch that had neither electricity nor plumbing. "They taught me," he says, " 'Be honest, don't lie, be responsible for yourself. If something goes wrong, look in the mirror.' " Years of wrestling with the tribal bureaucracy has left him with a Thatcherite faith in the transformative power of individual initiative, a view that, along with his managerial talent, led to his appointment as head of the Bureau of Indian Affairs during Ronald Reagan's first term.

Smith readily acknowledges that the forest has been overcut. By the end of the decade, he says, due at least in part to Louie Pitt's protests, the annual cut will have to be reduced by half. But Smith regards pressure to reduce the cut by a further 16 million board-feet as an unacceptable sacrifice for what he considers a "third world nation" that is struggling to modernize. "There's some kind of balance, but you've got to weigh it against economics," he says. From his office in the handsome new redwood tribal office building, he can look out across Agency's sheltered valley toward the clusters of new semidetached suburban homes and well-tended lawns that increasingly set the standard for life at Warm Springs. "You argue over 16 million board-feet. Well, that's $7 million worth of jobs lost to the community. Is it worth that much to us to save a couple of elks and fish? Each time you see an elk out there, remember that it's a $10,000 elk, and that each fish is a $400 fish. Is it more worthwhile to save jobs or to save a spotted owl? We need the timber to pay our bills, to pay for our schools, to keep the mill going. Suppose you've got to cut some education programs, or suppose it means that some kids won't be able to go on to college?"

Although the legend of "Chief Seattle" has indeed become a central part of modern Indian mythology, it no more represents universal native attitudes toward the earth than the Confucius of fortune cookies does the ambiguities of Chinese civilization. Many Indians of earlier ages may well have believed, as Seattle (or Ted Perry) did, that "the rocky crests, the juices in the meadows, the body heat of the pony, and man all belong to the same family." It is probable, however, that like any other human beings, their ideas were a diverse and often contradictory mix of the idealistic, the self-serving, and the pragmatic. If there is any lesson at all to be drawn from the amazing popularity of the chief's speech, it is that Americans still prefer fictional Indians to real human beings. For if there is truly a basic Indian attitude toward the earth in the 1990s, it is less one of sentimental passivity than of profound ambivalence. In the voices of Joe Ely and Mervyn Wright, of Ralph Goff, Louie Pitt, and Ken Smith, one hears the cacophony within the modern Indian psyche, where equally eloquent voices wrestle over the moral course of the tribal future, searching restlessly for a balance between the natural human craving for opportunity and affluence and the reluctance to disturb and disrupt.

It is a difficult balance to find when prosperity seems to imply the betrayal, the abandonment of fundamental Indian identity. "Our goal was a self-sustaining lifestyle, but we forgot who we were supposed to be," Louie Pitt says, digging his fingers into the red Oregon soil. "Being Indian is what you have in your heart. More money isn't the answer." But tribes that shun modern economics risk condemning themselves to a limbo of permanent underdevelopment that will satisfy no one but the kind of romantics and spiritualizers who chronically mistake poverty for pastoral bliss. Ken Smith's vision may lack Pitt's sense of mystery, but in its embrace of the outer world's challenge and complexity it is no less earnest. "This is a world of many races and cultures, and the sooner we understand that and learn how to cope with each other, the better off we're going to be. Sooner or later we're going to have to push our people out into that world, and when it happens they have got to know how to be self-reliant and self-supporting."

Nevertheless, it would be facile to dismiss Indian passion for the earth as a kind of exaggerated sentimentality. Where so little of the old native world has survived the collision with European civilization, the truncated land continues to retain a unique and fragile potency. For some, the land's power is actually rooted in the lingering religious feelings of earlier times, but for many more, it appears to lie more in the overwhelming, largely irrational fear of yet more loss and betrayal. However, like the current popularization of long-disused religious rituals and ubiquitous efforts to recover sacred artifacts from museums, the resanctification of the earth has become for a great many Indians a medium of salvation that far outweighs its economic cost, a way to reconnect with the tribal past and with the lives of ancestors who, during generations of systematic cultural repression, seemed beyond reach across a vast divide. It may thus not be so far from what Chief Seattle had in mind after all.

Although the "Seattle" whom Americans have come to love may be in large part a figment of the white man's imagination, the historical chief was real enough. Seattle, or more accurately Seathl, was a minor warlord of the Duwamish who had subdued several tribes in the neighborhood of Puget Sound, and who was quite willingly accepting the protection of American troops against his Haida and Tlingit enemies. He was also the presumably proud owner of a number of Indian slaves. In the late 1960s, William Arrowsmith, a professor of classical literature at the University of Texas, attempted to reconstruct the chief's speech in accordance with the actual syntax of the mid-nineteenth-century Duwamish.

Arrowsmith's version is much less melodious than either Smith's or Perry's, but it has the ring of accuracy. It is probably as close to what the chief might actually have said that day in 1854 as we are ever likely to get. In it, one can hear the chief picking his words without bombast, groping for ideas, searching his own thoughts for the meaning of the land that he was about to sell to the United States. The thrust of the speech was not, in fact, a scathing indictment of white civilization, which Seattle knew nothing about; it was more particular, and considerably more poignant. Free of rhetorical adornment, in Arrowsmith's version, one can hear Seathl struggling to explain the fusion of the earth and the tribal dead. "The ground beneath your feet responds more lovingly to our steps than yours," he told his listeners, "because it is the ashes of our grandfathers. Our bare feet know the kindred touch. The earth is rich with the lives of our kin."

5 ᵃᴿ

Listening for the Ancestors

IT IS A FINE MORNING for anyone to be going home, crisp with the kind of decisive light that frames silos and water towers like bright exclamation points against the golden, corn-stubbled landscape of eastern Nebraska. At 9:10 A.M., the anthropologists begin loading up from the dock behind Nebraska Hall. Tom Myers hands off each neatly marked box—"Infants," "Adults," "Infants and Grave Goods," thirty-six in all—to Hugh Genoways, who settles them with exaggerated care on the bed of the Dodge Ram. Then, at 10:25, with Genoways driving, the van turns up 17th Street and eventually out Cornhusker Highway through the suburbs of Lincoln and across rich plains studded with towns where hand-lettered signs advertise church suppers and ball games between high school teams called Homesteaders and Pioneers. Genoways, a cautious man, cruises precisely five miles per hour below the speed limit, heavy with the knowledge that with every mile one of the most valuable collections of human bones in the United States is slipping more irrevocably from scientists' hands.

Three hours' drive to the northeast, in Macy, Dennis Hastings is rounding up the crate that once held a nuclear warhead and will now take the ancestors on their final journey. It is a harsh and fragile place, this hamlet that is the capital of the Omaha Nation, a place that speaks eloquently of both the astonishing persistence and the grim burdens of countless Indian communities in modern America. Interspersed among the gloomy detritus of burned-down and fallen-down cottages are tidily kept trailers and frame homes that suggest the persistence of community against all odds; there is the new primary school, and the new tribal office building, the law courts, the health center and the tribal nursing home, all of them hard-won by a generation of tenacious tribal leaders. But even the most casual visitor can see that there are also too many idle people with nowhere to go, too many flaccid men tinkering halfheartedly at cars that will obviously never run again, too many children with the feral look of neglect, too many boarded-up stores in what, a couple of slightly more prosperous lifetimes ago, was once the center of town. But if the tribal historian is thinking of failure today, it isn't evident.

For Dennis Hastings, this is a day of heroic culmination. By the time Genoways and Myers arrive, Hastings has already been out on the bluffs for hours, showing the tribe's backhoe where to cut the trench in the sod. Genoways backs the van to the edge and then, opening the rear door, begins handing the boxes to Hastings and Myers, who carry them two at a time down the sloping end of the trench, to lay them on the wooden skid at the bottom. The site is dramatic; to the east, hills and forested autumnal vales roll down ruggedly toward the Missouri and the blue plains of Iowa beyond. But it is far from the paved road, and the lumbering old Chevys and Oldsmobiles that have been arriving, one by one, creep with the caution of age over the tricky sod. There is, at first, an almost holiday mood among the elderly men in tooled Western boots, and the women in jeans or lumpy, seldom-worn suits, and the small, yelping boys who scramble at the edge of the trench, inventing wars with toy soldiers.

Hastings is visibly tense. Wearing khaki trousers and a mauve polo shirt, he is in the trench, guiding the missile crate's cover as it dangles by a chain from the shovel. Accustomed to working out of sight, by telephone, he is in the open now, exposed. He is a man from the tribal margin, without family, a visionary in a place of pervasive apathy, where success of any sort is rare. He is desperate to get everything right.

With an imperceptible shift of mood, the milling and chatter at the edge of the grave have become ceremony. Almost unnoticed, a poker-faced man in a billed cap has moved to the head of the trench. This is Dennis Turner, a onetime accountant who came home from Los Angeles thirty years ago to have a kidney removed and stayed to become eventually the tribe's treasurer. Almost casually, he rolls a wad of tobacco into a stogie and puffs it, encouraging the smoke to waft over the trench that has now, with this gesture, become a grave, become sacred. He stands with head bent and arms akimbo. Then, speaking into the trench to the dead, he prays in slow cadences.

"I ask you to forgive me. You had your own way of doing things. You had your medicine men. Today we don't have those ways or any of those people around anymore. So I ask your forgiveness if I do something wrong."

What seemed impromptu has quickly become riveting and intense. The ancestors are being given back to the earth. Several women begin to weep. Soon Turner is weeping, too, tears streaming over his pitted cheeks. Hastings's ponderous frame is fairly quivering, whether with emotion or from exertion it is impossible to know.

The anthropologists realize that they no longer matter now, that this is the real burial, the sacred event, and that, for the Omahas, the public gathering tomorrow will be almost beside the point. They exchange pained glances, thinking of Karl Reinhard, who has teased so many secrets from the bones in the trench, who knew the people they once were better than anyone on earth.

Turner puffs smoke toward the four corners of the Omaha heavens. Then he kneels and grinds the stogie out in the raw soil. "From this day on, we remember that we have ancestors lying here. We are going to pray for them, take care of them. They may be our brothers, mothers, aunts lying here. That's what we're praying for. Mr. Genoways, Mr. Myers, thank you for taking care of them for us down in Lincoln. Now we're putting them back in Mother Earth. Now we've got them home here on the reservation, where they belong. The circle is just about completed."

The Omahas' origins are obscure and tantalizing. The meaning of their name, "People Who Go Against the Current," memorializes the tribe's trek up the Missouri River from somewhere far to the east, perhaps the Ohio valley, where they may have been among the builders of the mound complexes that have long intrigued archaeologists. Less literally, the name aptly suggests the unpredictable individualism of a small and vulnerable people who have defied the long odds of history. By the time white explorers encountered them, the newcomers had already reinvented themselves as horseborne prairie folk, having learned to cultivate corn in the fertile bottomland of the Missouri and to chase buffalo, and to celebrate the hunt in their varied and complex rituals.

The site of Tonwantonga, the so-called Big Village that the Omahas occupied in the late eighteenth century, lies on a flat plain a dozen miles north of Macy, on the other side of the Winnebago reservation. There is nothing much there now, just wet fields that on a chill autumn day are foamy and black with newly turned soil; a few cottonwoods, a farm half hidden by trees and mist. Here the Omahas first met the Spanish tentatively probing northward from their base in Mexico, and the French trappers from the north with their eye for furs, and finally, more fatefully, the Americans. At least some of the inhabitants of Tonwantonga probably watched Lewis and Clark pass by on their way West. In the years that followed, a remarkable transformation took place as the Omahas, with considerable skill, piloted their way into the modern world of their era. Tonwantonga became a bustling entrepôt whose inhabitants learned to trade in guns, and lead pots, and thimbles, and casked wine, and the rest of the ambiguous freight of Western civilization. They shipped the white man's manufactures to upriver tribes and beaver pelts and buffalo hides downriver to the whites in return, and for a time they prospered.

Then something mysterious and awful happened. In the space of a single lifetime, between 1780 and 1820, the inhabitants of Tonwantonga passed from a nation of some affluence and growing political importance to enfeebled victims for whom mere survival was an achievement. The nature of the cataclysm was not wholly unknown. Traditions of great suffering, of epidemic, of seeping despair were passed down orally from generation to generation. But as time went on these became amorphous things, increasingly generalized and remote. By the time the Omahas adopted a written culture toward the end of the nineteenth century, the details had largely been lost, and with them the human dimension, the particularity of events. The ravaged people of Tonwantonga seemed condemned to eternal silence. If a clear understanding of the past is essential to a people's self-knowledge and self-acceptance, as it is to an individual's, it was an understanding that the Omahas were to a large extent denied.

In 1935, workmen employed by the Work Projects Administration began turning up human remains as they widened a road near the town of Homer, where the bluffs drop off abruptly to the flood-plain of the Missouri, just south of the site of Tonwantonga. It was obvious from the artifacts that were unearthed with them that most of the bones belonged to people who had lived and died around the turn of the nineteenth century, and that they were Omahas. It was still the era of what many Indians now derisively call "frontier archaeology," when no one even thought of asking permission from tribes for digging up Indian graves. In all, the jumbled bones of 107 individuals were collected and offered to the University of Nebraska, where they lay in storage and largely forgotten until the 1980s.

In August of 1989, in accordance with the state's stringent new law pertaining to the reburial of Indian remains, the chancellor of the university, W. A. Massengale, sent an official letter to the Omaha tribe. In it, Massengale wrote:

> Many years ago the University of Nebraska in Lincoln came into pos-session of the skeletal remains and burial goods of some of your ances-tors. They have been kept here under the auspices of the University of Nebraska State Museum. I regret that this occurred, and it will not reoccur. We would like to take the appropriate steps necessary so that your ancestors may be reburied on the Omaha reservation.

To some Omahas, the disposition of the bones seemed of small consequence in a place where sweeping the floor in the tribal office building was counted a good job. Others feared the spirits of the dead and warned that because the old ways of burying had been lost, there was no way to channel their power safely. But there was a widespread feeling among the people who lived in the battered trailers and cottages around Macy that the spirits of their ancestors were lost and suffering, wandering the bluffs in search of their looted bones, as some said, and needed to come home; there was, as if for family, the instinctive wish to nurture, to shelter, to protect. In short, they wanted the bones back.

In a rural community where eighth-grade education was the norm, the concerns of anthropologists were held in no special re-gard. When Omahas thought of scientists at all, it was often as thieves, as scheming interlopers who, according to tradition, had somehow illicitly gotten hold of collections of objects that the Omahas had held to be of apocalyptic significance to the tribe: numerous pipes and medicine packs, burial goods sanctified by their presence in the graves of the ancient dead, and even *Waxthe'xe,* the True Omaha, the sacred cottonwood pole that was the living embodiment of the Omaha people and that had lain since the 1880s in Harvard's Peabody Museum. There was almost no one who understood, or for that matter much cared, what use the anthropologists down in Lincoln might have for bones and artifacts. One of the few who did was Dennis Hastings.

In his mid-forties, Hastings has the broad-chested, full-bellied frame of a prizefighter starting to go slack. His heavy-lidded, almost Oriental eyes are ironic and appraising, a counterpoint to the ready smile that hovers perpetually around his lips. His speech (like, perhaps, the self-perception beneath it) oscillates between the language of two cultures; in one breath, he will refer to himself as "only an academic instrument" and in the next as a warrior in the old tribal tradition. "It was the warrior's role to protect his people. Now I ask, what can I do in the scholarly sphere to protect the tribe?"

His early years must have been painful. He speaks with reserve of a mother of whom he will only say, "She had kind of a hard time," and even more vaguely of a father who lived, years ago, in Sioux City. A neighbor remembers "a sad little kid" who had nowhere to live until he was taken in by a grandmother. Like most Indian children of his generation, he was sent away to a government school far from the reservation, in Minnesota. "I kept asking myself, 'What did I do wrong to be put here?' I tried to hold on to the way my grandmother cooked, the smell of milkweed soup, fry bread, fried potatoes. When she died, the school wouldn't let me go to her funeral. They told me there was no budget for it. There was no more meaning for you to survive," he says, slipping into the second person, as he sometimes does at difficult moments, detaching. "You thought you were a bad character. So you joined the Marines." There was the tour of duty in Vietnam and then later a bachelor's degree in anthropology earned through an extension program at Berkeley; still later, a failed marriage and an unlikely stint running an antique shop in northern California.

Hastings returned to the reservation in 1981, intending to stay for a year. He had come home to one of the most distressed communities in the United States. The reservation was devoid of natural resources and far from the nearest city. Virtually all the tribe's land base had effectively passed out of Omaha control early in the century as a result of allotment. What little was still owned by the Omahas had been almost totally leased out to white farmers. Of the tribe's 4,700 members, more than half had left the reservation in search of work; 80 percent of the families that remained were on public assistance. Infant mortality was triple the national average, and more than half the adult population, by conservative estimate, was suffering from active alcoholism. It was a bruised and fragile world, this minuscule nation of Omahas, but it was Hastings's own. Like many Indians disillusioned by life in the American "mainstream," he never left. "I felt, you can't clean everybody's yard up if you don't clean your own."

Working from borrowed tribal telephones and finagled computers, Hastings's drawling, gregarious voice nagged at scholars, journalists, and legislators, demanding that attention be paid to the Omahas. The upshot was a storm of imaginative programs that is probably unmatched by any other small and equally impoverished tribe. Winkling small grants and volunteer scholars from institutions around the country, Hastings initiated an oral history project to collect memories of fading tribal tradition. "We go into each family, get an anthropologist to record everything right from how you wake up in the morning." Hundreds of historic photographs of early reservation life were collected and deposited with the State Historical Society in Lincoln. A friendly scholar from the University of Indiana recovered a trove of forgotten Omaha songs recorded in the 1920s on wax cylinders. Another at the University of New Mexico, at the instigation of longtime tribal activist Pauline Tyndall, undertook a collective genealogy that would trace the lineage of more than five thousand Omahas back to the eighteenth century. "Until now, everything was oral," Hastings says. "Some people knew the names of their ancestors, and some knew nothing at all. There was a loss of connection with the past. Now people can come back and find out who their ancestors were." In 1989, perhaps astonishing even themselves, tribal leaders brought home the Sacred Pole along with a hoard of sacred materials that, after years of negotiation, had been relinquished by the Peabody Museum. Hastings likes to describe all this as a "cultural renaissance."

"Our people live in a limbo culture that is not quite Indian and not quite white, either," Hastings is saying, sprawling on a lawn chair, surrounded by books, peering through the window of the sky-blue trailer where he lives in a cow pasture near Macy, out toward the Iowa plains. "It's like living in a house without a foundation. You can't go back to the old buffalo days, stop speaking English and just use our own language, and ignore whites and everything in white culture. If we did that, we'd become stuck in history, become dinosaurs. We want the benefits of modern society. But America is still a dangerous place for us. The question I put is: how do we take the science that America used against us and make it work for us? The answer is, we try to build on the past. It's like a puzzle. First you see where the culture broke and fragmented. Then you try to build on it where people have been practicing it all along. Then people start to think in a healthy way about what they were in the past. If you can get each person to be proud of himself, then, little by little, you can get the whole tribe to become proud. We're going to dream big, and be consistent with that dream."

In 1990, the tribe's economic development plan unsentimentally reported that "Family violence, child abuse, teen-age suicide attempts and sexual abuse instances are increasing," and noted that between 1984 and 1987, the Omahas' life expectancy actually fell, from fifty-eight to forty-eight years, two-thirds the state average. No one, least of all Hastings, expected that *Waxthe'xe,* or century-old medicine packs, or boxes of ancestors' bones could solve such problems by themselves. Yet this instinctive grasping, this tropism, toward the tribal past was by no means an insignificant thing. In Hastings's eyes, and in those of tribal chairman Doran L. Morris, Sr., and of elders such as Dennis Turner and Clifford Wolfe, Sr., it represented the first steps in a slow, incremental advance toward the recovery of Omaha identity, a process rooted in the conviction that the tribe's soul had somehow slipped away and that in seizing history lay a kind of redemption.

Morris, a laconic and guarded man, succinctly articulates Omahas' anxieties and fragile aspirations. "We want our children to know themselves. We're losing the right way to carry out our dances. We'd like to get back our language, to speak fluently again. In the past, our people got along, they helped one another, pitied one another. We'd like to be like that again. We're marrying into the Caucasians, the Spanish. We hate that. Already, there is not one full-blood left. We fear that day when there will no longer be an Omaha Indian."

With Massengale's letter, the University of Nebraska officially relinquished its claim to the bones of the Omahas' ancestors. In the bitter political climate of the time, nothing but reburial of the bones seemed conceivable. In the eyes of anthropologists, the bones were but the victims of a self-defeating polemic: Indians everywhere in the country were demanding the return, the "repatriation" they usually said, of their ancestors' remains as if they were prisoners of war. But the Omahas wrote Massengale back with an unexpected offer: they invited the university to carry out any kind of study of the bones that it wished for one year, but at the end of that time the bones were to be buried forever. "In the end," Hastings says, "we felt that maybe science could help us. Maybe it could give us a vision of who they were and how they died. Without it, we'd never know."

In 1989, President Bush signed into law a measure that redefined the responsibility of the country's most prominent museum, the Smithsonian Institution—and by implication the nation itself—to American Indians. One part of the act, hailed universally by Indians and museum people alike, transferred an unmatched collection of more than 1 million artifacts from New York's cramped and rarely visited Museum of the American Indian to the Smithsonian, where they will eventually be housed in a new Indian museum to be built on the National Mall, a significant symbol in itself of the quickening resurrection of Indians in the national mind. Of more immediate importance to Indian traditionalists, the law also required that the Smithsonian undertake a complete inventory of all the Indian human remains and funerary artifacts in its possession (collectively, they numbered in the hundreds of thousands) and make them available for "repatriation" to the native peoples to whom they had originally belonged. The act was the culmination of years of lobbying by Indian advocates who argued that such a mandate was essential to the regeneration of native communities that had been devastated by generations of assimilation and deliberate cultural repression.

The following year, the Native American Graves Protection and Repatriation Act extended a similar mandate to all museums that received any form of federal funding—in effect, virtually every museum in the United States—declaring that upon request, "sacred objects and objects of cultural patrimony shall be expeditiously returned" to the descendants of the original owner, or to existing tribes if they were the owners, or to a tribe even if no living descendant can be identified. Other provisions made trafficking in human remains and cultural items a federal crime, and stated that all native objects that were found in excavations on either tribal or federal land automatically became the property of whatever Indian group could reasonably lay claim to them. A few months later, in 1991, the new board of trustees of the National Museum of the American Indian radically expanded its own repatriation policy to cover ceremonial artifacts, "duplicate or abundant objects," objects that had been "acquired by the museum illegally or under circumstances that render the museum's claim to them invalid," and a murky category defined as "communally owned objects." Any "culturally affiliated" Indian or Native Hawaiian group that could base a claim to an object in the museum's collection through evidence of descent, "historical patterns of ownership," or "oral tradition" would be entitled to apply for its repatriation, upon approval of the trustees, half of whom are Indian.

Collectively, these actions, along with similar legislation in many states, some of them requiring immediate reburial of any Indian remains in museum collections, represented the clearest extension yet of the principle of tribal sovereignty into the realm of American culture. "We are talking about a renaissance," says W. Richard West, the politically astute director of the Museum of the American Indian. At the time of his appointment in 1990, West, a Harvard- and Stanford-trained lawyer and a member of the Cheyenne-Arapaho Tribe of Oklahoma, spoke of building a "sharing, collaborative future relationship" with modern Indians, and declared that his highest aspiration for the new museum was to "reanalyze, redirect and, in many cases, reformulate entirely the concepts and presentations of the past concerning Indian culture . . . In a very real sense, the walls of the museum must come down." Adding to that, West says, "Repatriation is the most potent political metaphor for cultural revival that is going on at this time. Political sovereignty and cultural sovereignty are linked inextricably, because the ultimate goal of political sovereignty is the protecting of a way of life. As separate polities, tribes can tax and regulate, and exercise jurisdiction. But it is equally important, perhaps even more important, to protect Indian ways of life and ways of thinking."

To many Indians, unredeemed artifacts and the bones of the ancestors had become potent symbols of conquest and cultural rape. In a sense, repatriation thus represents a campaign to regain contact with the dead, to draw strength from them and from the material remains of what idealistic traditionalists and others regard as an all-embracing way of life whose potency has been all but lost. As they see it, repatriation often means the "liberation" of still-living things that have been trapped in museum basements, in a limbo between the spirit world and the human. "These medicine bundles are the heartbeat of the Navajo Nation and they have their origins there," Albert Yazzie, a Navajo chanter, protested to officials of the Field Museum on a visit to Chicago in 1993. The Holy Ones, he said, were "longing for their people" and needed to be returned to the Navajo reservation. "It's not right to have these bundles locked up here. We need them for our ceremonies."

Such thinking is paralleled by that of some provocative anthropologists, who in recent years have redefined the acquisition of many of the nation's most important Indian collections as a facet of nineteenth-century colonialism. "Collecting was part of the nation-state building process," Curtis Hinsley, chairman of the history department at Northern Arizona University and the author of numerous studies of the Southwest, told a symposium on the ambiguities of collecting that was held at the Brooklyn Museum in the fall of 1991.

> These collections were not representations of reality, they were "hostages," constant reminders of the nation's new imperial power. One way alien territory was reconfigured to fit into the national imagination was by the removal of objects from the conquered landscape. The idols, masks, baskets and clothing that were carried back to Eastern museums were the 19th century equivalents of the dancing bears and barbarian slave girls that conquering generals paraded through the streets of ancient Rome. Things were ripped out of their context in a simultaneous exercise of political and aesthetic will. The most prized objects of all were the most secret.

Indian spokesmen often define repatriation as an issue of fundamental religious freedom, asserting as a general principle, for example, that native bones remain imbued with the spirit of the dead even after hundreds or thousands of years, and that keeping bones in a museum is a permanent desecration that produces ongoing spiritual ailments among the living. Some go so far as to blame alcoholism, AIDS, and social disintegration on the wandering spirits of the unshriven dead. In this view, contemporary Indians are deemed to be responsible for the spiritual well-being of all deceased Indians, a moral duty that compels living Indians to ensure that the remains of their ancestors are buried in the ground, because retention of the remains in museums and elsewhere is regarded as disturbing to the ancestors' spirits. So long as the spirits are suffering, living Indians will continue to suffer a myriad of adverse consequences.

Beyond this, however, lies an often quite explicit, and for anthropologists unnerving, assault upon the customary right of free scientific inquiry. "The bone robber barons, as some archaeologists would be apprehended, are academic neocolonialists and racial technocrats who now seem to posture as liberal humanists," Gerald Vizenor, a Chippewa journalist and academic, has written. "These bone barons protect their 'rights' to advance science and careers on the backs of tribal bones. The tribal dead become the academic chattel, the aboriginal bone slaves to advance archaeological technicism and the political power of institutional science." Similarly, the Lakota author Vine Deloria, Jr., asserts that Western science has "always been available as apologists for the majority who wished to dehumanize minorities for commercial and political purposes." But only American Indians, he says, have "become the exclusive province (and property) of scholars to the extent that the bones of their dead can be disinterred with impunity to be displayed in museum cases or used in speculative scientific experiments." Like many activists, Deloria argues that the scholarly analysis of bones has no value for contemporary Indians, charging that "no explanation has been given regarding the peculiar characteristics which make Indian remains more valuable than the remains of other races. What could possibly be learned exclusively from Indian bones which could not also be learned from the bones of other races?"

"This is an issue of racism," asserts Bob Peregoy, an attorney for the Native American Rights Fund, which represented the Pawnee Tribe in its successful effort to recover some three hundred sets of its ancestors' bones and thousands of burial artifacts from the Nebraska State Historical Society in the mid-1980s. The Nebraska law that resulted from the Pawnee victory was the first of its kind in the United States. It soon became a model for similar laws and voluntary museum policies around the country, as well as for the federal legislation that imposed repatriation upon the Smithsonian Institution. Adds Peregoy, "Indian people have been treated in a very discriminatory manner by the anthropological community. No other groups were targeted for massive grave robbing. In Nebraska you've got to get a court order to open a non-Indian burial. But no archaeologist ever thought he had to get one to open an Indian grave."

Somewhat defensively, anthropologists attempt to counter Indian arguments by pointing out that individual Indians frequently sold their artifacts to collectors as a matter of individual choice or, concerned about their tribes dying out, willingly entrusted their ritual objects to whites to ensure that they survived into the future. Similarly, it is often noted that native beliefs about the sanctity of human remains varied quite widely; neither corpses nor graves held special significance for every tribe. At one extreme, some tribes simply disposed of remains in communal refuse heaps. Others did not bury their dead at all, but rather placed them ceremonially in trees or on raised platforms where, eventually, their bones would be devoured by animals. At times, Indians also showed appalling contempt for other tribes' dead; the historian Francis Parkman recorded an instance in which five corpses of Sioux placed in trees were thrown down and kicked into fragments by a war party of Crows, who then held the muzzles of their rifles against the skulls and blew them to pieces.

Although the ultimate impact of the spreading repatriation movement on American society is still far from clear, passionate protests around the United States have already led to the dismantling of important collections of human remains and to an often rancorous struggle between some of the nation's most prestigious research institutions and Indians who assert that their spiritual beliefs must supersede science's determination to brook no obstacle to its right of free inquiry. Scholars have argued, to little effect, that objects destined for repatriation may be the only extant historical documents of groups that kept no written records and whose past is obscured by the vagaries of oral tradition, and that large skeletal collections are crucial for studying the effects of disease and diet on past populations. More than twenty states have passed laws requiring the immediate reburial of Indian remains, in many cases with no provision at all for study by scientists or historians. For some, it is a prospect that resembles the torching of a major archive. "This is going to affect every museum, and it may tip the balance for smaller ones," says Donald J. Ortner, chairman of the anthropology department at the National Museum of Natural History in Washington. "Basically, it could close down physical anthropology and archaeology in North America."

In a 1989 article in the *Yearbook of Physical Anthropology,* Douglas H. Ubelaker, a senior anthropologist at the National Museum of Natural History, attempted to articulate a moral defense of scientific research on human bones:

> I explicitly assume that no living culture, religion, interest group, or biological population has any moral or legal right to the exclusive use or regulation of ancient human skeletons since all humans are members of a single species, and ancient skeletons are the remnants of unduplicable evolutionary events which all living and future peoples have the right to know about and understand. In other words, ancient human skeletons belong to everyone.

It was an essentially idealistic argument, with roots that lay in the driving curiosity of the Enlightenment. But such expressions have attracted comparatively little support in an era that seems more prone to honor passion and guilt than speculative science, and in which the politics of repatriation, no less than the politics of tribal sovereignty, trades on the fundamental self-doubt that gnaws at the heart of American culture.

The Omaha remains soon became an academic minefield, the kind of entanglement that stalled promotions and withered careers. Responsibility for them fell to Karl Reinhard, a soft-spoken thirty-five-year-old anthropologist who had recently arrived in Lincoln with a Ph.D. from Texas A&M, where he had written a thesis entitled "Diet, Parasitism and Anemia in the Prehistoric Southwest." Campus radicals were demanding immediate reburial (never mind what the Omahas said), while historians attacked anthropologists for even presuming to reconstruct Indian history, and certain anthropologists prepared to condemn anyone at all who collaborated in reburial. Reinhard was the right choice, bruised colleagues said; he was new and therefore had less to lose.

Reinhard had grown up among Indians, in Montana and later Alaska and Arizona, the son of a peripatetic medical doctor with the Indian Health Service. He was not a bone man; by bent, he was a coprologist, a student of the mysteries that may be wrested from human waste. But he was moved, more than he expected, by the tribal delegation that traveled down from Macy to meet him and by the elderly man who offered a prayer in the Omaha tongue and then said, "There is a lot our ancestors have to tell us. We have to listen to them, to learn their story before we put them into the ground." Reinhard recalls, "I don't even like bones in the first place. But I could see that we were in the role of bringing them information they couldn't get anywhere else."

From the start, the remains were eloquent. In their worn-down teeth, Reinhard and his team of graduate assistants could see the intimate evidence of the tribe's trade in buffalo hides, whose processing required long hours of pulling and stretching, with the front teeth used as anchors. When university geologists determined that pigments found soaked into an infant's ribs had come from a site a thousand miles away in Utah, it hinted at the existence of vast, previously unknown networks of native commerce. Tests of bone surface with a mass absorption spectrophotometer unexpectedly revealed the almost universal presence of lead, in enormous and often lethal doses. Somehow the Omahas were absorbing it through their intestines, unconsciously poisoning themselves. But how? But why?

Reinhard became increasingly intrigued with the nameless dead. There was the woman whose femur and tibia had fused together at the knee, the result of some terrible accident. She had fallen on her hip, perhaps in a riding disaster, perhaps catching her foot in a stirrup as she fell, then twisting her leg apart and savagely wrenching her pelvis as she went off the horse; her wrist was fractured, as well. Few other events could have caused all three things at once. She began to live again in Reinhard's imagination. He imagined her that day, a century and a half ago, instinctively putting out her hand to break her fall, landing in a way that left her crippled for life. He pictured her living on for years, dragging the fused leg behind her, knowing that if Sioux raiders came she would never be able to escape.

Then there was the oldest of the group: the jagged tips of his ribs suggested that he was in his late forties when he died; a younger man's ribs would still have been smooth. He had obviously been a horseman; only the jarring effect of riding would have broken the cartilage away from the sternum that way. Pitting at the base of the radius told Reinhard that he had suffered an infection in the wrist that had gone far enough to penetrate and corrode the bone. It must have been excruciating, but somehow he had recovered. There was evidence that a hatchet had left a deep scar—a battle wound?—across his brow. He had survived that, too. Reinhard decided to call him "the archer."

And there was the enigma he named "the merchant." Traces of opulent burial ornaments indicated a man of considerable wealth. Most tantalizing, however, was the maroon cross-hatching across the cranium, the unmistakable imprint of a turban. The thing was, Omahas never wore turbans. The elder was almost certainly a foreigner; the shape of his cranium suggested that he might have been raised in one of the cultures that deliberately flattened infants' skulls while they were strapped to cradleboards. But where had he come from? And what was he doing among the Omahas?

For long hours, Reinhard studied the skull of a small child of about five, peering into the terrible, ragged cavity at the bottom of the temporal bone, at the signature of the infection, the otitis media, that had killed him. He followed the infection as it migrated through the child's body from its start in an ear canal. First, it had eaten away the cartilage and then the bone, leaving it warped and melted like warm taffy. Then it had entered the skull down the canals, devouring them inch by inch. Reinhard could see the telltale, foamy-looking pitting even on the little ribs, on the tibias, on the vertebrae. The infection could have gone on inexorably for years. He imagined the child in almost constant pain, shrieking helplessly.

Larger patterns gradually took shape. Testing of the bones for proportions of carbon and nitrogen surprised Reinhard with the fact that the men of the tribe lived largely on meat, while the women subsisted mainly on vegetables. "The differences were so great that had I seen the males and females in different collections, I would have said they represented different cultures. What it meant was that the women were deprived of adequate protein, and maybe of calcium, too." Reinhard also observed that the women's vertebrae were weakened and cracked from the pressure of heavy labor in numbers far out of proportion for a normal population. Few of them, moreover, lived to reach thirty. "By the age of twenty, women were showing arthritic stresses that they shouldn't have shown until after forty. They were working so hard, probably carrying loads like beasts of burden, that their spines were compressing, that their bones were quite literally breaking with the stress."

Certain conclusions seemed inescapable. The disparity in diet weakened females from the start, while the physical stresses of women's traditional work sapped their remaining strength until disease finally took them off. The children's ravaged skeletons told Reinhard that, at ever younger ages, they were struggling to do the work of their dead and dying mothers, and that it was killing them, too. Fewer than 50 percent, and maybe only 20 percent, had managed to attain reproductive age. Reinhard even found one case of a child of eight or ten years suffering from a spinal condition that normally appears in forty-year-olds.

The Omahas were a people under siege by disease. Reinhard began to see the disintegration of an entire people in the crumbling spines and joints, in ribs, and ulnae, and crania corroding from rampant infections, an entire history of a tribe's headlong rush to apparent extinction. The irony was, the dying Omahas were not at all poor. Even a cursory look at the silver gorgets and crosses, the brass pendants, the bracelets and armbands, copper pots and tin pans, iron buckets and guns that had been interred along with their bones told Reinhard that they were a tribe of considerable wealth. "There were no signs of malnutrition," says Reinhard. "These were not hungry people. But they were sick people, very sick. Scores, hundreds of them must have been sick at any given time, everywhere, in almost every tepee. And when they got sick, they died."

In the era before contact, the tribes of the Great Plains were, like the other North American peoples, biological islands, sealed off for millennia from the diseases of the Old World. Although fungal infections, cancers, tuberculosis, arthritis, and staph infections were common, the peoples of the Plains were comparatively healthy. When European traders arrived in their bateaux and pack trains, however, they also brought devastating new illnesses. Later, when westbound white settlers found what seemed an empty continent lying before them, it was not infrequently because disease had raced invisibly and cataclysmically ahead.

Historians generally hold that the onset of European illnesses took the lives of as much as 90 percent of native communities. From about 1780 on, smallpox epidemics repeatedly swept the Great Plains—between 1778 and 1783, then again between 1800 and 1803, and again between 1836 and 1840. In between, there were more epidemics, of influenza in 1798 and 1799, of measles and whooping cough between 1818 and 1820, and then whooping cough and cholera from 1832 to 1834. The worst of all was the smallpox epidemic that swept the Great Plains in the late 1830s, killing Indians in staggering numbers: between 6,000 and 8,000 each of Blackfeet, Piegans, and Bloods, 2,000 Pawnees, half of the 2,500 Arikaras and Minitarees, one-third of the 3,000 Crows, more than half of the 8,000 Assiniboines, along with countless Dakotas, Choctaws, Chickasaws, Osages, Winnebagos, Kiowas, Apaches, and Comanches.

The artist George Catlin described what happened when small-pox was carried to the Mandans of the upper Missouri by crewmen of the American Fur Company steamer *St. Peter*. The tribe, which numbered between 1,500 and 2,000 in June of 1837, was reduced to 138 by October. The Mandans, under attack by the Sioux at the time, were unable to flee to the open prairie, where some might have escaped infection.

> They were necessarily inclosed within the piquets of their village, where the disease in a few days became so very malignant that death ensued in a few hours after its attacks; and so slight were their hopes when they were attacked, that nearly half of them destroyed themselves with their knives, with their guns, and by dashing their brains out by leaping head foremost from a thirty-foot ledge of rocks in front of their village. The first symptom of the disease was a painful swelling of the body, and so virulent had it become, that very many died in two or three hours after their attack, and that in many cases without the appearance of the disease upon the skin. Utter dismay seemed to possess all classes and all ages, and they gave themselves up in despair, as entirely lost. There was but one continual crying and howling and praying to the Great Spirit for his protection during the nights and days; and there being but few living, and those in too appalling despair, nobody thought of burying the dead, whose bodies, whole families together, were left in horrid and loathsome piles in their own wigwams, with a few buffalo robes, etc. thrown over them, there to decay and be devoured by their own dogs.

For relatively small and self-contained communities, the consequences of such catastrophes can scarcely be imagined. It meant devastation far worse than that wrought by warfare. Epidemics meant not only the sudden loss of parents, of children, of beloved friends, but the destruction of entire cultures and economies. When warriors died, the entire nation became more vulnerable to predatory neighbors. When hunters died, the food supply shrank. When medicine men died, the spiritual world disintegrated. When young women died in large numbers, the community lost the capacity to reproduce. When the elderly died, collective memory went with them.

Smallpox attacked the Omahas at the peak of their prosperity, most disastrously in the epidemic of 1800, when the tribe's population plummeted from perhaps three thousand to fewer than three hundred. Tonwantonga became, quite literally, a village of the dying and the dead. According to Reinhard's estimates, close to 50 percent of the children born there died by the age of ten, only 8 percent of all people lived past age thirty, and just 2 percent survived to forty. So traumatic was this that the Omahas resolved to attempt a kind of collective suicide rather than face the future. As Alice C. Fletcher and Francis LaFlesch (himself an Omaha, and one of the first true American anthropologists) wrote in their classic turn-of-the-century study of the Omahas, "It is said that when the enfeebled survivors saw the disfigured appearance of their children and companions they resolved to put an end to their existence, since both comeliness and vigor were gone." The survivors determined upon a heroic death before even they perished in sickness and shame. They agreed to form a village-wide war party to attack their traditional enemies. Marching west, they fought their way through the Poncas, the Cheyennes, the Pawnees, and the Otoes, until the survivors began to realize that some of them might survive the disease after all, and straggled back to Tonwantonga and to an uncertain future.

The Omahas would never really recover. A series of treaties with the encroaching United States would eventually whittle the Omahas' lands down to 36,000 acres. After the 1880s, the Allotment Act would systematically break up what was left into private holdings, most of which would soon slip from Indian hands. With the disappearance of the buffalo, the complex organization of marshals and hunters that underpinned the Omaha economic order would unravel. The hymns and prayers that were the glue of the old religion would be forgotten, and no longer would children be introduced in ritual to the Cosmos or consecrated to the spirit of thunder. With the loss of *Waxthe'xe,* the Sacred Pole, the tribe's very soul would disappear. Lore would fade as elders died, and with them, devastatingly, the knowledge of what the Omahas once had been.

One of the victims of the great epidemic of 1800 was the despotic chief Blackbird, who, Borgia-like, was widely rumored among his own people to have poisoned his rivals with strychnine purchased from the downriver traders. Blackbird was buried with considerable pomp atop a bluff overlooking the Missouri, upright upon his favorite horse, with enemies' scalps hung from his bridle and an eagle-feather headdress on his head, and a supply of tobacco and pemmican to carry him into the next world. Chunks of sod were piled up around the steed's legs and back, and finally over the chief himself, until he was covered from head to toe.

For decades, the chief's tomb, which could be seen from fifteen miles away, served as a landmark first for the voyageurs and then for the steamboats that carried the white man's world with ever-increasing speed into the heart of the Plains. George Catlin paused there in 1832, during his journey north. "Whilst visiting this mound in company with Major Sanford, on our way up the river," the painter noted in his journal, "I discovered in a hole made in the mound, by a 'ground hog' or other animal, the skull of the horse: and by a little pains, also came at the skull of the chief, which I carried to the river side, and secreted till my return in my canoe, when I took it in, and brought it with me to this place, where I have it, with others which I have collected on my route."

So casual is Catlin's account that it takes several readings for the impact to fully register. Catlin, in fact, plucked off what he believed to be Blackbird's head and walked away with it as a souvenir, happily adding it to a growing collection. In a person who often showed deep sympathy for Indians, such behavior seems almost unbelievable. It is difficult to imagine a man with Catlin's education and sensitivity robbing a white frontiersman's grave, much less the tomb of, say, the deceased mayor of his native Philadelphia. To the painter, there was clearly nothing sacred about the Omaha chief's last resting place. But he was, after all, merely a man of his time: Indian skeletons, like their traditional clothing, handiwork, and religious artifacts were increasingly perceived not as things that belonged to living cultures, but as collector's items, as loot. Later, Catlin would spend years touring the cities of Europe as the impresario of a traveling exhibition that included live Indian dancers, a gallery of his paintings, and the numerous artifacts that he had amassed during his travels, among them Blackbird's skull.

Two years before Catlin began his journey up the Missouri, a fellow Philadelphian, a Quaker physician of mild disposition by the name of Samuel G. Morton, was asked to lecture on anatomy in the medical department of Pennsylvania College. He chose for his subject "the different forms of skull as exhibited in the five races of men." Later, having achieved fame as the leading craniologist of his day, he wrote of this seminal event: "Strange to say, I could neither buy nor borrow a cranium of each of these races . . . Forcibly impressed with this great deficiency in a most important branch of science, I at once resolved to make a collection for myself." Morton subsequently devoted the next twenty years of his all-too-influential life to the statistical analysis of skulls, mainly those of Native Americans.

Morton has been called the father of American physical anthropology. He sired it in the intellectual back alley of phrenology, that bogus "science" which held that the brain was composed of tidily distinct organs that determined personality, thought, and moral action. Phrenologists believed that the strength of those faculties was determined by the shape of the skull and that each race manifested its cultural traits through the distinct form of the cranium. Such beliefs derived from blurry theological assumptions that would be laughable had they not exerted so much influence upon serious thinkers. The German theorist Johann Friedrich Blumenbach, writing in 1775, for instance, reasoned that since the Caucasian skull was the "most symmetrical" and since the circle was the "most beautiful" shape in nature, it naturally followed that the white race had been the first created by God. It is difficult today to imagine how reasonable such "scientific racism" seemed to many serious thinkers in the nineteenth century. By Morton's day it was already beginning to provoke a virtual mania for the excavation and collection of human bones. For American phrenologists, the nearest to hand were Native Americans'.

Beneath all the craniological mumbo jumbo lay a genuinely important question, one that continues to preoccupy biologists even today: what was man's relationship to other forms of life, and especially to other primates? But in an age that tended to take the most virulent racism largely for granted, another question dangerously followed: were different races of men actually different species? To many in the early nineteenth century, the answer seemed by no means obvious. Indeed, to Morton and his disciples, the scientific pursuit of racial distinctions embodied the loftiest spirit of free inquiry.

Morton was especially admired for his innovative technique. He measured brain size by sealing the holes in a skull with mustard seeds or lead shot and then weighing it to determine volume. Purely on the basis of such calculations, he determined that Indians were inherently endowed with a "peculiar and eccentric moral constitution" in which "wildness" was an indelible racial trait. "They are not only averse to the restraints of education, but for the most part incapable of a continued process of reasoning on abstract subjects." Since, he asserted, American Indian brains were smaller than those of Malays and Mongolians, Indian intelligence must therefore be correspondingly inferior. "However much the benevolent mind may regret the inaptitude of the Indian for civilization, the affirmative of this question seems to be established beyond a shadow of a doubt." Those who opposed such assertions were dismissed by Morton's many supporters as "fuzzyheaded" and anachronistic. This was no ivory tower debate. Morton's work had important political implications, for it logically followed that if Morton's conclusions were right, slavery might be a perfectly moral destiny for some races, and extinction for others—namely the Indian.

In order to make convincing generalizations, Morton naturally needed large numbers of skulls, and he appealed to military and civilian physicians in the West to send him all the Indian crania they could find. One collector wrote to Morton from the field:

It is rather a perilous business to procure Indians' skulls in this country —The natives are so jealous of you that they watch you very closely while you are wandering near their mausoleums & an instant & sanguinary vengeance would fall upon the luckless—who would presume to interfere with the sacred relics . . . There is an epidemic raging among them which carries them off so fast that the cemeteries will soon lack watchers—I don't rejoice in the prospects of death of the poor creatures certainly, but then you know it will be very convenient for my purposes.

The systematic looting of Indian remains outlasted Morton's death in 1851 and the unlamented demise of phrenology itself. In 1865, the eminent Harvard zoologist Louis Agassiz, who was stocking a natural history museum, wrote personally to Secretary of War Edwin M. Stanton: "permit me to recall to your memory your promise to let me have the bodies of some Indians . . . I should like one or two handsome fellows entire and the heads of two or three more." During the Plains wars of the 1860s and 1870s, soldiers under orders from the Army Medical College collected bodies from Western battlefields, pulled them from scaffolds, dug up fresh graves, and boiled the skin off the freshly dead. Even the great anthropologist Franz Boas took such activities for granted. He noted in his diary, in 1888: "It is unpleasant work to steal bones from a grave, but what is the use, someone has to do it."

By the end of the nineteenth century, museums and universities were competing to amass collections of human remains, some of them eventually numbering in the hundreds and thousands. Beginning at least by 1862, however, when the Surgeon General ordered the bodies of soldiers to be brought back from Civil War battlefields in an effort to understand the then-unknown process of infections, institutions began gathering non-Indian bones as well, from hospital dissection rooms, archaeological sites, and, on occasion, disused graveyards stumbled across during road-building and housing construction. Although bone collections serve as valuable benchmarks for measuring physical differences among peoples, and as evidence for the study of migrations, trade cycles, and population size and density, they are used primarily by medical researchers who study the history of disease. Studies of ancient Eskimo remains, for instance, uncovered clues about the causes of osteoporosis, the weakening of bones brought about by the loss of body minerals, while lesions discovered in other prehistoric native bones disproved the belief that rheumatoid arthritis developed in modern times. While Indian polemics commonly assert that anywhere between 300,000 and 2.5 million native ancestors may be "held hostage" in institutional collections, in the early 1990s the total number of all types of skeletal remains was probably closer to 75,000, of which Indians may comprise somewhat more than half. The nation's largest collection belongs to the National Museum of Natural History in Washington, D.C. Of the 35,000 human remains that it held at the start of the decade, just over 18,000 were Native American.

• • • •

"Ours is a New World where things speak as in time primeval, and our museums become books and histories or should become so, for the History of Man in America is, thank heaven, a natural history and an unwritten one!" the pioneer ethnographer R. Stewart Culin declared at the turn of the century. Soldiers, missionaries, and others like George Catlin had always collected Indian "curios" during their travels. But it was only when anthropology diverged from craniology and other racialist theories that Indian artifacts came to be perceived as texts that revealed important truths about cultures whose individuality and complexity were just beginning to be appreciated. By the end of the nineteenth century, the country was experiencing a virtual mania for collecting pottery, buckskins, beadwork, masks, idols, shields, bows, indeed, for Indian artifacts of every conceivable kind, a phenomenon that encompassed both maturing curiosity about Indians and a more ambiguous attempt to impose order on exotic peoples by categorizing and assigning value to the things they made. Culin, a self-taught authority on Chinese games of chance before he turned his considerable intellect in the direction of American Indians, was one of the most exhaustive, not to say compulsive, collectors in his supremely acquisitive age. In 1903, the Brooklyn Institute of Arts and Sciences, now the Brooklyn Museum, sent him West with a mandate to acquire a "valuable and representative" collection. For a decade, he ranged over Indian reservations in the Southwest and California, and by 1912 would install more than nine thousand objects in the museum's new Halls of American Ethnology.

Culin's first destination was the remote pueblo of Zuni. Although the Zunis had been among the first Indians to encounter Europeans, in the form of the hapless Coronado expedition of 1540, the pueblo's isolation on the western edge of the Spanish colony of New Mexico enabled its inhabitants to preserve their customs intact longer than most other tribes. Culin already had a detailed picture of Zuni from his friend Frank Cushing, one of the earliest true field anthropologists, who had immersed himself in the Zuni way of life during his residence there from 1878 to 1884. Cushing had vividly described the "strange city" whose otherwise placid life was stunningly enriched by an intense religiosity characterized by dazzling ceremonies, witchcraft, and intricate taboos.

With the advent of the railroad in the 1880s, increasing numbers of tourists began making their way to Zuni in search of what Curtis Hinsley has wryly called the Apollonian Southwest. Visitors to the pueblo habitually insisted upon describing its inhabitants as "innocent" and "intensely poetic," while art dealers advertised Zuni pottery as resembling ancient Greek ascos and rhytons; even Frank Cushing could not resist characterizing a certain Zuni mythological cycle as "the Zuni Iliad." As one journalist fairly typically put it, a single "lovely trait" pervaded the Zunis' lives "like an interwoven golden thread, gleaming through every fabric—the idea of the ultimate good existing in everything."

Culin himself was convinced that Indian cultures belonged to a world "where things speak as in times primeval," and that by penetrating the mysteries of their world it would be possible to peer, as if by magic, into mankind's childhood. He was only echoing the dominant scholarly view of his time. The German art historian Aby Warburg wondered in an 1896 lecture, "To what extent can these remnants of pagan cosmology still obtaining among the Pueblo Indians help us to understand the evolution from primitive paganism, through the highly developed pagan culture of classical antiquity, down to modern civilized man?" To collect artifacts from such people was to own a piece of eternity. Between 1879 and 1884 alone, an average of five objects was acquired from every Zuni man, woman, and child. Even so, when Culin first set eyes on Zuni's "solid, substantial" agglomeration of adobe houses beneath the flat-topped mesas of the New Mexico desert in 1903, he regarded it as a virtually untapped reservoir compared to other reservations that had already been "picked clean" by collectors.

While travelers and ethnographers rhapsodized upon visions of the Golden Age miraculously transported to the American frontier, the real Zuni world was falling apart before their eyes. Repeated epidemics of smallpox, measles, diphtheria, and whooping cough carried away young and old by the hundreds, reducing the pueblo's population to about twelve hundred by 1900. Culin, like so many others, considered the Indians' decline irreversible. "The process of disintegration, now started, will progress rapidly, and old Zuni as it exists today, will soon disappear," he wrote. But it hardly mattered whether the Indians themselves survived or not. Culin was convinced that the essential truth of culture lay not in the living society, but in objects that seemed to embody the "timeless" quality of traditional life. Meanwhile, the Zunis were continuing to adapt to

Anglo-American civilization just as they had to the Hispanic for 350 years: by adopting wheeled transport, by using trade cloth in place of hides, by sending their children to government schools, by blending elements of Catholicism with their traditional faith, and by learning English (as they had formerly learned Spanish). Ironically, just as Americans were insisting that Indians had to change and become acculturated, museums were doing their best to freeze Indian culture in place. Says Hinsley, "Americans literally took the clothes off Indians' backs and put them on museum mannikins while they dressed up the Indians in the white man's own clothes."

Culin bought anything he could lay his hands on, leading the Zunis to slyly nickname him Inotai, or "Old Thing." To his sponsors in Brooklyn, Culin wrote: "The people were crazy to sell, and for many things 5 cents, the smallest coin, was enough. I got all the games . . . all the musical instruments . . . all the agricultural implements, all the weapons." He had a much harder time obtaining "the things which the scientific collector most admires," namely ceremonial masks and other objects that were central to the practice of Zuni religion. Such items, he recognized, "are usually the property of a society and cannot be legitimately disposed of." Indeed, the pueblo's religious authorities specially deputized men to see that no one sold Culin ceremonial materials of any kind. At one point, "a cryer was sent around, who called out to the people and cautioned them against selling me any masks, and I was told that the sale of masks was punished by death."

Culin was determined to acquire examples of the *Ahayuda*. Also known as the "Terrible Two" and the "Boy-gods of War," these were slender, humanoid figurines about eighteen inches in length, with stylized chins, beards, noses, and hair, who were the living embodiment of the twins who had led the Zunis out from the primal underworld and had ever afterward protected the tribe against everything that threatened its well-being. The twins' otherwise benign nature was distorted by a sort of subversive ambivalence; like human children, they were mischievous and unpredictable, capable of wreaking havoc upon anything, or anyone, that thwarted their will. Once a year, at the winter solstice, members of the Bear and Deer clans carved new pairs of *Ahayuda* and placed them in clumps around the Zuni lands. Americans who encountered them thought they resembled nothing so much as bunches of weathered fence posts. To the Zunis, they were supernatural light-

ning rods which attracted and dissipated the multifarious forces of
evil as long as they remained on guard in their assigned shrines.
They proved powerless, however, against the irrepressible curiosity
of twentieth-century Americans.

Culin made it known that he would pay well for what he wanted.
When all else failed, he hired Indian carvers to mass-produce
kachinas and other items in the basement of a nearby trading post.
Eventually, with the assistance of the trader, a former missionary
named Vanderwagen, he finally managed to get hold of dozens of
forbidden masks and idols, including no fewer than thirteen War
Gods, which would form the largest single group of them anywhere
outside the Zuni lands. Although the details are unrecorded in
Culin's copious notes, it appears that some if not all of them were
looted from unattended shrines. For more than eighty years, they
could be seen by any visitor to the Brooklyn Museum's imposing
beaux building on Eastern Parkway, itself a splendid artifact of an
age when all the world seemed like a treasure chest open to the
enlightened citizens of a nation that had little doubt of its own
moral and spiritual superiority.

Over the years, dozens more *Ahayuda* disappeared from sites in
the New Mexico desert, to finally wind up widely scattered in museums and private collections. For a time, in the 1920s and 1930s,
Zuni War Gods enjoyed a certain chic in Europe, particularly
among the Surrealists, who hailed them as a symbolic repudiation
of the canons of conventional Western art. Speaking of African
tribal idols, the anthropologist James Clifford has written: "A mask
or statue or any shred of black culture could effectively summon a
complete work of dreams and possibilities—passionate, rhythmic,
concrete, mystical, unchained: an 'Africa.' " The same thing might
well be said about the appeal of the *Ahayuda* and many other
sacred Indian objects that have come to be regarded in the West as
"high art." Paul Klee owned a War God; so, later, did Andy
Warhol.

In time, the looting of native sites became big business. A skilled
pot hunter in parts of Arizona or New Mexico is said to be able to
earn $10,000 for a weekend's work. In 1990, it was reported that
as much as two-thirds of Hopi sacred clan articles had been stolen,
including pieces of a construction known as the *taalawtumsi,* or
Dawn Woman, whose loss made it impossible for Hopi boys to
undergo ritual initiation. In the underground art market in Santa Fe

or New York a stolen mask might sell for as much as $100,000. Before the repatriation movement made it too risky for art dealers to handle them in the mid-1980s, *Ahayuda* fetched as much as $40,000 apiece in the open market; it has been alleged that in Europe they still sell for more than $100,000 each.

The Zunis that Stewart Culin was so sure would disappear from the earth did not, of course, disappear at all. Like tribes everywhere, the Zunis rebounded demographically far beyond anyone's imagination, and in the mid-1990s numbered more than nine thousand. Although it lies just forty-five miles from the city of Gallup, New Mexico, Zuni even today retains a strange atmosphere of wary isolation. Physically, it is a sprawling place of long, low buildings made of dark brown cut stone and cinder blocks roofed with tin and tar paper, and organized according to some indiscernible principle around a maze of sandy lanes and small plazas. On a November day when the wind blows dust in reddish-brown gouts through the kinked lanes, boys in T-shirts scramble in the red dust playing with plastic tanks and APCs marked "Desert Storm." A remarkably high number of Zunis are full-bloods and still speak Zuni as their first language. A few of them are brilliant silversmiths with international reputations. "The rest," a young priest at the rectory down the road from the restored Spanish church says, with the uneasy reticence that is common at Zuni when speaking to strangers, "are always poor and busted and trying to pay the bills."

There had always been Zunis who said that the connection between the people and the spirit world had been ruptured when the War Gods were taken away, that the pueblo had become vulnerable to evil, and that if they could be brought home, maybe the community's problems—the broken families, the suicides, the alcoholism, the epidemic diabetes—could be overcome. The prospect of actually recovering any of the *Ahayuda* seemed dim, to say the least, until a member of the Bow Priesthood was elected to the tribal chairmanship in 1968. In the ensuing years, the Zunis began systematically contacting museums and private collectors, auction houses, and eventually the FBI, requesting that the *Ahayuda* be returned to the pueblo. Shunning publicity, they explained that the War Gods' "captivity" had dire ramifications not only for the Zunis themselves but for all mankind. "The War Gods are living things, whether they were in a museum basement or the New Mexico desert," explains Edmund J. Ladd, a Zuni who is curator of ethnol-

ogy at the Museum of Indian Arts and Culture in Santa Fe and who
has sometimes represented the tribe in its efforts to recover the War
Gods. "The only difference is that in a basement they suffer from
not being able to do what it is they are supposed to do, which is to
be put in a shrine under the elements and disintegrate." Many of
the world's wars, earthquakes, floods, and tornadoes, the Zunis
suggested, might well have been due to the destructive mischief of
the imprisoned *Ahayuda*. Wouldn't it be in everyone's interest to
see that they got home?

"The Zunis' goal is an apocalyptic one, to reestablish the balance
of the universe not only for the good of their own people but for the
whole world, which far transcends the artificial modern boundary
of the reservation," says Ladd. A handsome man with corrugated
features and jet-black hair, Ladd self-deprecatingly describes himself as an "accidental anthropologist." His cluttered office at the
museum looks out toward the cubist adobe roofs of Santa Fe, a few
miles distant beyond slopes studded with sage and junipers. Having
grown up at Zuni, Ladd was prepared to spend his life herding
sheep until he hired on temporarily as an excavator during an
archaeological dig in the 1940s. Fascinated by the unlayering of the
past, he went on to college under the G.I. Bill and eventually became a specialist in Samoan and Hawaiian archaeology. Seated
beneath a bumper sticker that reads "Mutton Stew—The Breakfast
of Champions," he says, with force, "We Zunis are not a dead
culture that stopped evolving in the 1880s. Our culture is still viable. Putting a War God under glass is not preserving culture. The
way you preserve Zuni culture is by using the War Gods in the
ritual for which they were created. The War Gods are still part of
living ritual and their function in Zuni society is specifically not to
be preserved. They are not meant to be collected or interpreted."

The Zunis' argument, absurd as it sounded in the 1970s, foreshadowed what has become a tidal shift in the way in which museums and anthropologists have begun to regard the morality of owning many types of Indian artifacts, no matter what their aesthetic or
scientific value in the larger society. Zuni reasoning implied that
aesthetics was simply irrelevant to objects with sacred associations
and that preserving them was not only a fraud but immoral. "To
exhibit a War God because of its aesthetic beauty is like taking the
Host from a Catholic Mass and putting it in a museum and saying,
'Isn't that beautiful?' " Ladd says with sarcasm. The Zunis were

asking museum officials, anthropologists, and collectors to voluntarily give up not only their cherished right to possess, study, and admire certain artifacts but also the objects themselves. Furthermore, they were insisting that the *Ahayuda* had always been the property of the entire tribe and that no individual Zuni had ever had the right to give them away or to sell them; any War God found outside Zuni lands was therefore stolen property by definition, no matter whether it had been acquired in good faith.

The Zunis' campaign was being played out against a larger international landscape of changing cultural values that increasingly regarded artifacts collected during the colonial era as the fruits of imperialism, and techniques such as Culin's as unethical if not downright criminal. Especially in the third world, national governments were going to court to retrieve art objects and heirlooms that had long graced museums and private collections. In 1978, the American Association of Museums adopted a code of ethics requiring that its members not support the illicit trade in antiquities. That same year, federal agents for the first time halted the auction of a Zuni War God at the Parke-Bernet Gallery in New York City. Encouraged, the Zunis began pressing the Denver Art Museum for the repatriation of a War God that it held in its collections. The museum's trustees eventually capitulated to the Zunis in what may have been the first instance of a museum officially proclaiming that a fundamental distinction exists between art and objects of religious veneration. "It is true that the war god is a deity and a present, animated object of worship rather than a symbol or an art object," the press release that accompanied the War God's return in 1980 stated. It is intriguing, and scarcely far-fetched, to wonder what the eventual consequences may be for the world's museums if, say, Orthodox clerics and Christian fundamentalists begin lobbying for similar rulings on the display of icons and other Christian imagery.

In 1983, ethical restrictions on the handling of antiquities were given added force when the United States signed the UNESCO treaty on cultural property, which banned the import of cultural patrimony pillaged from archaeological or ethnological sites. In 1989, New York State handed over twelve wampum belts dating from the colonial era to the Onondagas, accepting the argument of the tribe's representatives that even though the state had purchased the belts in good faith years before, it could never be more than a "temporary custodian" of items that were of sacred value to the

tribe. In July of that year, *Waxthe'xe,* the Sacred Pole of the
Omahas, the white buffalo robe, and about 150 other artifacts that
had lain for more than a century in the Peabody Museum were
flown home to Nebraska, where Ian Brown, the curator of the
Peabody's Native American collection, likened the pole's return to
"finding the cross upon which Jesus had been crucified."

Several dozen *Ahayuda* had now been returned to the Zunis from
dozens of institutions in New York, Washington, Massachusetts,
Oklahoma, Arizona, and elsewhere. Under quiet pressure from the
Zunis, the Brooklyn Museum had removed its War Gods from
public display in the mid-1980s; then, in 1991, after polite but
insistent requests from the Zunis, the museum's trustees voted
unanimously to return them to the tribe. That spring, curators were
waiting in an atmosphere of subdued apprehension the arrival of a
Zuni delegation to take them back to New Mexico.

"I began to wonder at one point, is it insensitive to even handle
things that are so powerful to others? Do I have a right to lay my
hands on them? How deferential should I be?" Diana Fane was
walking along the metal shelves in the museum's basement where
the War Gods lay swaddled on beds of white plastic foam. As
curator of African, Oceanic, and New World art, she was in the
process of organizing an exhibit of objects collected by Stewart
Culin from around the world that would serve as an unofficial
envoi to the departing *Ahayuda.* An attractive woman with a dramatic head of silver hair, her eyes were appraising and inquisitive as
she lifted the slender figures one at a time, wondering aloud about
problems of proportion, dating, pigments. Picking up one that was
slightly more rounded than most, she asked, "What did this carver
have in his mind? What did tradition tell him? How much discretion did he have to innovate?" Examining another that was more
summary in execution, with hair that had been painted on rather
than carved: "This one really looks to me like a misinterpretation of
a War God. People were making fake sacred things left and right. Is
it a fake, or just a different carver?" Later Fane said, "There is a
tremendous amount to be learned from these. But they're going to
go away."

The War Gods' stylized faces peered enigmatically from the
musty gloom. It was easy to see how they intrigued the aesthetic
radicals of the 1920s, for whom the primitive was a kind of liberation from the pretensions of the bourgeois. But here in the gloom of

the basement, alongside the Ethiopian, West African, and Malagasy masks, it was equally apparent that they were trophies, loot, the prizes of power. In a few weeks they were to be sent back to New Mexico to eventual, certain destruction. They would be placed with the dozens of other repatriated *Ahayuda* in a shrine roofed only with barbed wire somewhere on a mountain outside Zuni, where they would inexorably crack and splinter in the rain and rasping desert wind, infusing the earth and the universe with their power and touching the drunks and the unemployed, the hopeless, the bitter, and the forlorn.

Their fate is simultaneously a redemption, a travesty, and a provocation. Like that of countless other objects that once graced the halls of American museums, the repatriation of the War Gods has exploded the notion that it is possible to know a culture through its objects alone and has made it far less possible to contemplate non-Western "art" without understanding something about the people who created it. Beyond that, it threatens the deeply rooted assumption that to be art an object should have no other function than to exist, be pleasurable to look at, carry an aesthetic message. It has also made the experience of art a more problematic, more morally fraught experience. "Repatriation is the tip of an iceberg of a much larger issue, which is the representation of peoples of all kinds by museums, and of who has the power to control the stories that make those things come alive," says Peter Welsh, chief curator of the Heard Museum in Phoenix, which possesses one of the largest collections of native materials in the United States. "This is only the beginning. We have to face the question of what all those religious objects are really doing in our museums. We say that we need to hold on to these works as part of the patrimony of mankind because of their aesthetic value as works of art. But what are the moral constraints on our ability to have an aesthetic appreciation of something? Is it immoral to deny the sacred potency of the object within the culture that produced it? If you respond to an object aesthetically and then discover that it is religious, have you done something that is immoral? Can an aesthetic response to an object be immoral?"

The location of the War Gods' shrine is kept secret from strangers by the Zunis. It is visited with some regularity by members of the tribe. "[It's] not just the Bow Priests [who use the shrines], but people like I and others who do jog, or who just may be out walking, and they have that religious feeling, that faith, and they will put some offerings in that place where the War Gods are enshrined," Tribal Councilman Edward Beyuka explained in an article in *Native Peoples* magazine. Members of the Zuni football team regularly make offerings of cornmeal to the War Gods before their games. Others burn sage and offer prayers. Beyuka added, "[It] is very hard to find—the real meaning why those offerings were made —because the different people, they don't tell you, but they have it in themselves." When a Stealth bomber on a test flight crashed on the reservation near Pia Mesa in May 1995, there were some who said it was the *Ahayuda* that had prevented it from coming down into the nearby pueblo.

Nor is it simple to say precisely what the return of countless extremely diverse sacred artifacts, whose very nature often defied rational judgment, is making to other tribes. In some cases, the restoration of the presence of mystery is an end in itself. Elsewhere, objects have become tools for the explicit revival of culture and a foundation for rediscovered identity. The Navajos and some other tribes have made a policy of allowing medicine men to borrow repatriated religious paraphernalia, some of it fragile and of great antiquity, for use in ceremonies. "These things breathe by going outside," Harry Walters, director of the Navajo Tribal Museum, maintains. "They have to be used in order to renew their power." When the Sacred Pole, the simple cottonwood rod that was the central symbol of identity of the Omahas, was returned to the tribe and displayed for the first time in more than a century on the powwow grounds at Macy, hundreds lined up to touch it. Many wept openly. A few turned their backs, afraid to lay eyes on a thing so powerful. Wynema Morris, the tribe's business manager, was a member of the tribal delegation that drove to Omaha to pick up the Sacred Pole at Eppley Airport. A practicing Catholic, Morris is also one of the best-educated and most thoughtful members of the tribal government. This is what she remembers:

"At first I thought, it's just an artifact. Why not leave it in the museum? Why bring it back? I thought, well, because he is an Omaha, because he belongs here. Then when I saw him at the Omaha airport, suddenly a real loving feeling came over me. I totally broke down. I felt finally I was coming in touch with my past. I thought, for the first time, that my people really had a meaningful past. I cried. It was like a thunderbolt hit me. I felt that the person who wanted to leave him in the museum no longer existed now. I felt *Waxthe'xe* loving and speaking directly to me. It was miraculous. In spite of all the ills, as ragtag and pitiful as we are, our culture eroding so quickly, I think there will always be Omahas. It gives me hope that in 150 years I could come back here and there would still be Omahas. The pole says to me: 'It's all right, it's okay. Don't pine for the past. It's okay, daughter.' "

The bluffs of Nebraska seem remote, at first, in the stark fluorescent light of Doug Owsley's laboratory on the fifth floor of the Museum of Natural History in Washington, D.C. Yet one has a haunting sense of history branching off tantalizingly in countless directions, like the tributaries of some only barely explored river, here among the crates of bones that fill the floor-to-ceiling racks along the walls: there are Revolutionary War soldiers from the Yorktown battle-field, Confederates who died at Glorietta Pass in New Mexico, colonists from an eighteenth-century Maryland graveyard, a pro-miscuously integrated collection of black and white skeletons from a disused New Orleans cemetery of the 1840s. Other, recent re-mains lie scattered on plastic trays. "This one's a homicide from Florida," remarks Owsley, who is sometimes called upon to per-form identifications for the FBI. "It looks like a couple of guys hanged him."

The bones of the Omahas are spread on brown plastic cafeteria trays on four metal tables. There are pelvises, ulnae, femura, verte-brae, knuckles, clavicles, humeri, tibiae and scapulae, fibulae and patellae. Some are stained red from the seeping effect of the sacred cinnabar that was applied to the flesh after death, others metallic green from copper ornaments that long ago rotted away, others orange or patchy with the blackening effect of fungus in the soil. The skull of the child with otitis media peers from a steadying ring of foam, with Gothic effect: pitted maxillas look like fantastic cathedrals in miniature, teeth like crocketed pinnacles, the roof of the mouth like yellowish catacombs, full of ragged holes, the me-mentos of infection.

The bones, with the tribe's somewhat grudging approval, are on temporary loan to Owsley, one of the preeminent forensic anthro-pologists in the United States, who will add data gleaned from them to an ambitious attempt to document the evolution of Plains cul-tures across the past two millennia. Knowledge that the Omahas' bones would soon be returned to the earth lent urgency to Owsley's work. Museums in almost all the Plains states were abandoning their collections. The Nebraska State Historical Society had given four hundred remains back to the Pawnees. North Dakota had turned over its holdings in 1986, and South Dakota a few years later. More collections had been handed back in Kansas and Iowa. Pressured by federal legislation, the Smithsonian itself had recently relinquished over one thousand remains.

Owsley labeled each often fragmentary Omaha skeleton with a numerical code based on the site where it was found; "the merchant" thus became 15-DK-10, and the child with otitis media 25-DK-10, and so on. Every bone was then subjected to anywhere from a few hours to several days of extraordinarily meticulous study. Photographs were made, X rays taken, the density of every bone measured, every tooth inventoried for cavities and periodontal disease. Different codes were assigned for every type of bone disease and fracture, and for every infection and whether it was still active at the time of the individual's death, and then logged into the laboratory's computers, where they were tabulated and dovetailed with statistical profiles of native populations from Texas to Montana.

The Omahas were especially important to Owsley in documenting the arrival of European disease. While the ludicrous claims of nineteenth-century phrenology long ago fell into disrepute, bones can in fact communicate with much greater subtlety than Samuel Morton and his colleagues ever dreamed. Even the density of bones, Owsley explains with the flat drawl of his native Wyoming, can be remarkably expressive. Human bones, which are essentially simple tubes, have a normal thickness of about five millimeters. During the earliest period of contact with Europeans, the thickness of Indian bones grew, reflecting the introduction of new tools that made hunting and cultivation easier and made Indians, in turn, wealthier and healthier; but as contact progressed, bone thickness sharply decreased, encoding with infinite precision the human implications of Manifest Destiny.

Owsley places X rays of a child's ulna onto a backlighted screen. It is an extraordinary sensation, this peering into the pith of a child who might have gaped at Lewis and Clark, or witnessed, terror-struck, the plunder of Blackbird's tomb; at first there is the embarrassment of intrusion but then an unexpected sense of connection.

The images are hauntingly beautiful, and terrible. Owsley, who is accustomed to such intimacies, is clinical. "This child's bone is just four millimeters thick. What that means is that he's growing thinner. You know he's not eating any more. He is, in effect, devouring his own bones. He's dying."

Basing his work wholly on the study of human remains, Owsley has added layers of unimagined complexity to the Indian history of the Plains, making clear that the coming of the Europeans, cataclysmic though it was, was but the latest in a succession of transformations that reshaped Indian lives in unexpected ways. "Whether it was 2,000, 1,500, or 500 years ago, Plains demography was always dynamic. Patterns of mortality might change within any given generation, and across the centuries they changed many times over. Between 1200 A.D. and 1400 A.D., for instance, you find a large loss of both infants and older people. Then, after the shift from hunting and gathering to systematic horticulture, it becomes clear that cultures that depended on corn, beans, squash had even higher infant mortality. Meanwhile, warfare was as true of prehistory as it became during the contact period. You had native groups moving into the northern Plains, displacing other groups, producing territorial disputes, constantly shifting." Owsley has simultaneously, and permanently, shattered the notion that Indians were ever the time-frozen folk of the white man's romantic ideal: they were in constant motion of every variety, moving from foot to horse, and from a diet of meat to one of corn and beans, moving physically from the sea to the forests, from mountains to the flatlands, exploring new lands, fusing with other tribes, endlessly adapting and readapting, withering and being reborn as new peoples.

Science, Owsley quietly reminds, is a stumbling process, and breakthroughs are often a matter of chance. A minimum of thirty to thirty-five skeletons of any given type is necessary to attempt any kind of comparative study; to compare different age groups within the same community, thirty to thirty-five samples of each of the subgroups are required. Several hundred may thus be the bare minimum needed to carry out complex analysis. "We are constantly going back over our research and notes, and devising new tests. This checking and rechecking is really the way science goes. If you close that off, you close off one of the great avenues of scientific advancement."

Compared to the passion, and apparent anguish, of Indian demands for repatriation, scientists' concerns tend to sound mundane. Ironically, however, the very science that so many Native Americans find suspect has enabled the Indian dead to speak with astonishing clarity, literally from beyond the grave, both of the ravages that were wrought by contact with Old World disease and of the homely details of their long-ago lives. Ways of learning from bones will continue to grow as computer technology and new microscopic and chemical techniques open up fresh ways of asking questions about the Indian past. The extraction of antibodies from bones will soon enable researchers to study the antiquity of diseases and how far they spread, to learn finally, for example, how many Omahas really died from smallpox and other epidemics that took place beyond the perimeter of European sight. Even more far-reaching, techniques for the extraction of DNA will make it possible to track the routes of ancient migrations and the evolution of tribes through time, and eventually to link them one day to the Old World populations from which they originally sprang. Because Indians kept no written records, their precontact history is still, in large part, a terra incognita that invites precisely the kind of facile mythologizing that distorts Native realities in the eyes of white Americans. In their haste to undo historical wrongs, Indian tribes, abetted by well-meaning legislatures, may perhaps be sacrificing the best source of truth about their own past.

"The era of building collections is over," Owsley says, natural reticence shrinking beneath the intensity of regret. "But it's really the next generation that will suffer. What my research can tell us now may pale by comparison to what some Omaha tribal scholar twenty years from now could learn from these bones, if he could see them. But scientists who come after me won't be able to check my work, or revise it. After we've reburied these bones, those scholars will be stuck with what I've said. This is the end."

Research on the bones had now gone on almost a year longer than originally planned, and the Omahas were growing impatient. There was an atmosphere of desperation in Macy. Plans for an ethanol plant that was supposed to create jobs had just fallen through. There was desultory talk of opening a casino. People who stopped for gas at the Pronto station near the site of Tonwantonga said they could hear the weeping of the unburied dead. The tribe was now insisting that the bones go back into the ground by October, and Dennis Hastings was showing the strain.

"The tribe put its head on the slab," he is saying with palpable annoyance. "The Pawnees and the other tribes, they believe in complete burial. They think we're crazy to do this. We're trying to tell other tribes, this is one way to survive in the future, by letting science tell us about our own past. We decided to give the scientists a chance. Science is helping those guys speak to us. But my situation here is precarious. If Reinhard doesn't wrap it up now, it could destroy me. The tribe won't listen to me any more. People would say that I'm not a real Indian, just an advocate for the white man."

The remark has a special edge here on the bottomland below the bluffs, where cottonwoods clump densely along the Missouri's broad trough. Before the Corps of Engineers stabilized its flow, the river treacherously shifted its course as often as twice a year; three foundered riverboats, Hastings says, are still buried somewhere beneath the tilled fields. Near here, in the 1870s, the Omahas built a village of cabins where they first tried to imitate the white way of life. Omaha cynics of the time called it "Village of the Make-Believe White Men."

"Science hasn't been accountable to anyone," Hastings says. "All those years, when science had the bones, they did nothing with them. It didn't care about us at all. Academics get out of control, you know. They start thinking that everything belongs to them. It's that old frontier attitude. When it comes to natives, non-Indians feel they can do anything they want. Reinhard has had our people long enough. Indian philosophy always held that everything belongs to everybody. But American society believes in strength. We're just learning the lesson that you only get what you need if you stand up and fight for it. Even so, if I had the money myself, I'd buy a permanent vault for those bones so that scientists could study them in the future. But I'm walking a tightwire. I know what science could do in the future. But I've got to please the tribe. People want those bones to be buried."

There is a man lying in a ditch by the side of the road, his arms flung wide. The image takes a moment to register; by then, Hastings has driven a hundred yards past. He turns and drives back, peering through his window at the crumpled body.

"I know him. He's an old wino."

Hastings watches him a while longer. "His head's moving. I

thought he was dead. Probably he got ornery, and someone tossed him out of their car."

It is a balmy night in Lincoln. Crickets saw monotonously in the cottonwoods; in the shadows of dorms, young lovers stand with their loins pressed together. Inside the concrete tower of Nebraska Hall, there is a melancholy bustle. Karl Reinhard, wearing a wrinkled oxford shirt and faded shorts, is perched on a table amid jaws and skulls, staring at the cranium of the child with otitis media; silhouetted in the dim light, beard jutting, he resembles a suppliant in an Assyrian frieze. The child's skull with its tragic, infected bone sits on a piece of black felt. A graduate student is photographing it from different angles with a Canon fixed on a tripod. "He is a very sick kid," Reinhard says meditatively. "I never noticed that there were so many lesions. There was still a lot to learn from this baby."

Teams of graduate students pull plastic bags from long spools, snip them with shears, slip in an assortment of vertebrae, teeth, or a handful of corroded ribs, then seal them shut with heat, to protect the bones from the damp. Two or three packets are placed in each cardboard storage box. There is a faint hope that some future solution will one day enable scientists to conduct further tests. "You've got the wrong mandible," someone is saying; and someone else, "Is this a loose jaw I've got?"

New revelations have continued to be made almost to the last minute. Tom Myers discovered that shell wampum buried with some of the skeletons had been made as far away as New York or New Jersey. Then, just last night, Reinhard realized that one of the skulls belonged to a white woman. "There was no skeleton along with it, so I hadn't paid it much attention before. Then when I pulled it out it just didn't look right. It was something about the shape of the cranium. Who was she? How did she get here? We'll never know."

An ever-expanding panorama of research has abruptly shrunk to the vanishing point. The analyses of burial rituals and activity patterns, the dental castings and pigment tests, the nutritional studies, the genetic studies, the pathological studies will never be completed now. And then there is the mystery of the poisonous lead, which like some malignant force infiltrated and sapped the already frail bodies of the Omahas, killing them as invisibly as microbes and as surely as the shafts of Sioux arrows. Reinhard had puzzled over the mystery for months. Surely there was an answer, a final truth encased in the bones spread out before him. For months, a suspicion had been growing in him, not yet a certainty, but at least a probability that could eventually be tested, studied, proved. The lead could have come to the Omahas in cookware and wine casks traded by whites; infants could have teethed on the bright scraps of it left over from the making of musket balls. It could well have happened that way. But now he will never be sure.

The facial reconstructions were the hardest thing of all to let go; Reinhard craved to see the people who had lived again in his mind and his life. "You become attached to the bones as individuals," he is saying. "It will be devastating when these things are put in a box and lost." He tries to picture them now, the enfeebled men and women, and the afflicted children, tended by brothers and sisters made old ahead of their time, straining at being families in the camp of the dying and dead.

But looking at the child's melted bones, he sees something else, too. The boy had lived for years with his terrible infection. He survived because he had been cared for, proof of a family's, perhaps a whole dying people's, desperate commitment to its young. Reinhard could see it, too, in the young woman's fused knee. The fall had happened in childhood, and her bones had taken years to heal. All that time, someone had fed her, helped her to walk again. The Omahas had endured their suffering even in the midst of the tribe's collapse, had kept them alive against overwhelming odds, had loved them.

The archer is ready to be boxed now. His skull sits on the Formica table, the teeth and mandible forming a tentative, enigmatic smile. Reinhard looks at it, with the print of wampum across its brow. It is a head with character, Reinhard thinks. "This is a man I'd have enjoyed meeting." How did that guy get here? he wonders. But he will never know that, either.

By now, the child's ravaged skull and his few handfuls of ribs and paltry vertebrae have been bagged and sealed. Reinhard takes a final look at them.

"The kid's ready to go."

Torrential rain has turned the earth into red gumbo. Four-by-fours filled with reporters fishtail over the slick bluffs, squirting muck. The air is dense and strange. Scraps of undulant hills burst through thick mist, green and gold, ripe and intense, and then suddenly disappear. Tribal officials and functionaries, anthropologists from as far away as Vancouver and Bloomington, and Karl Reinhard and an entourage of graduate assistants are clumped at the edge of the grave. TV men from Lincoln and Omaha prowl the trench with cameras wrapped in plastic and their hair-dos melting in the rain.

Reinhard seems stunned. He has only now realized that the true interment, the sacred moment, occurred the day before, and that he missed it. Soaking in a tweed jacket and scarlet tie, he stares down at the plastic tarp that someone has thrown over the missile crate, as if through it, at the dead. Their funeral is also the funeral for his project.

Dennis Hastings has been transformed. Anxiety has drained from his broad face, softening it, leaving gregarious good humor. When a jet streaks overhead he draws a laugh, joking, "That must be the tribal air force come to pay respects." Then, expansively: "I feel like twenty pounds has been lifted off my shoulders." Next morning, he will meet with a team of volunteer architects he has rounded up, who will present plans for a tribal museum.

"Today we're putting our family to rest," he tells a newsman. "Maybe one of them was even a relative of mine. Today they're back home with us. It was good that the scientists studied and found out what kind of sickness there was in our tribe, how we existed, how we were destroyed. But I felt kind of hurt with them down there in Lincoln. I feel happy now that they're back where they belong."

He walks up to Reinhard and offers his hand. People who know them watch uneasily from the corners of their eyes.

"I guess we did about the best we could," Hastings says with a smile, with genuine warmth.

Reinhard lets his hand be taken.

"It's not what I expected," he says vaguely. "I can feel the loss, but I really can't see the gain."

Later a reporter asks him his feelings. It seems a struggle for him to speak.

"We are burying some very remarkable people. They lived their biological lives 150 years ago, in a very tumultuous time in history, and now they live a kind of second life through our work. One thing we all realize is that these don't cease to be people just because all we've got left of them is bones. Humanity still remains in them. Humanity is what this whole thing is about. Scientists want to express it by studying them. These folks here want to express it by giving them a home." It may only be the rain. But it seems, for a moment, that Reinhard is starting to weep. "I can't believe they are all going back. I can see their faces. Those were noble, magnificent faces. It's hard to say good-bye to them."

An elder, Clifford Wolfe, Sr., has moved to the head of the trench. He mumbles, "These people here," and then breaks off. For several minutes it appears that he doesn't know what to say. Then it is obvious that he, too, is close to tears. "These people, they met Lewis and Clark when they came around. People stole their white buffalo robe and stole the Sacred Pole. Now we've brought them home." He pauses again for a long time, oblivious of the soaking rain, and then, with some effort, goes on. "This is our land. We call it Omaha land. We're going to be here forever."

Finally, the backhoe swarms up through the red slime, abruptly wheels, and without ceremony begins shoving earth into the trench. The nameless Omahas disappear beneath the soil at last, the archer, the merchant, the crippled woman, and all the rest, all loved with a strange intensity even in death. Soundmen in soaked jeans and nylon jackets rush to kneel in the red mud, mikes extended to catch sound bites of the falling earth.

6

Predators, Victims, and Mother Earth

DEAN JAMES P. MORTON'S VOICE reaches through Gothic gloom of St. John the Divine, inviting the more than five thousand New Yorkers who have gathered for this service of thanksgiving to enter into the primeval sacred realm of the Indian. "This is really a special event," the dean declares as he calls upon his listeners to share with humility and admiration what he meaningfully calls "the native gifts." His voice resonates through the ribbed vaults of the great cathedral on Manhattan's Upper West Side. "We go back to the beginning, to learn how we were, what one is, why one is, what really is holy, what the four-legged are, what the two-legged are, brought back to the beginning, to the beginning of things."

Figures in starburst headdresses and fringed buckskins pose hieratically in front of the altar. Above their heads, a globe made of some synthetic material and set within a large feathered hoop dangles in a dim bluish light. Drums thunder; volunteers fan the smoke of sweetgrass and cedar. Bundles of cornmeal, juniper, cedar, and pollen are handed out for "clearing and cleansing," a pious voice intones over the public address system, "as a way of recalling what is of value to each of you this evening." Overhead the globe darkens and brightens portentously, revealing the map of the world.

"Mother Earth . . . Mother Earth," the voice murmurs. "Gaia . . . All things are connected."

There are several speakers. The tone is fervent. A Gwich'in woman from Alaska speaks of the calving grounds of the Arctic caribou, which, she says, are threatened by oilfield development. A Taina Indian from Puerto Rico says, "We have struggled long and hard to maintain the wisdom of our ancestors, in caves, underground. Only the prophecy of love has sustained us." Steven T. Plummer, the Episcopal bishop of Navajoland, tells the audience that Christian missionaries were sent among the Indian people "to take away their religion, take away their Mother Earth and their Father Sky—but it didn't succeed."

Pride of place, however, is given to a seventy-year-old Apache grandmother from Tucson named Ola Cassadore Davis. Picked out by a spotlight, her bulky frame seems larger than life in the cavernous silence. "There is a mountain in Arizona," she begins. "The University of Arizona and the Vatican have decided there must be telescopes atop that mountain. It's really sad. It's a very difficult struggle for Apaches because this is their sacred place."

Mount Graham is the highest peak in the jagged massif known as the Pinaleno Mountains, which rise abruptly to heights of more than ten thousand feet from the desert floor, one hundred miles southeast of Phoenix. For nearly a decade, environmentalists and more recently nearby Apaches have fought to block the building of a complex of ultramodern telescopes there by a consortium that includes the University of Arizona, Germany's Max Planck Institute of Radioastronomy, the Arcetri Astrophysical Observatory of Florence, Italy, and the Vatican Observatory, which are seeking locations far from Europe's polluted skies. Davis and other members of the group she nominally heads, the Apache Survival Coalition, maintain that any disturbance of the mountain constitutes a form of sacrilege.

She is self-conscious and plaintive as a speaker, casting herself as a lonely crusader in a world of unfeeling powers and institutions. Her message is passionate, and garbled facts seem somehow beside the point. "We Native Americans suffered these four hundred years since whites came to America," she declares, her rasping voice at first shaky, but then steadily gathering force. "White men said they came here to show us the way. Indians say, 'We know our way, we know who we are.' Whites say, if you don't follow our way we'll slaughter you. They don't respond to us, they don't respect us. Now we're a target of that telescope. There was no road construction, no nothing up there. This is our Apache sacred mountain. Us Native American Indians, we have no building, we pray outside on a mountain. This is the way we are. We have not one door—we have open doors all around us. Mount Graham is just as sacred as this church. If I try to destruct this church I know something terrible will happen to me. That's exactly how my Apache tribe feels about Mount Graham. Hear my voice: we don't want this telescope atop Mount Graham! They need to move it somewhere else. I need your help, you religious people. I put out my voice: please don't build the telescope atop Mount Graham! Help me—pray for him!"

Applause thunders through the sweet blue haze, cannonades from the ribbed vaults. From somewhere behind the altar, ethereal voices rise in breathless song: "I've been given eyes to see by the eagle . . . My spirit makes me free."

The next evening, Davis addresses a much smaller gathering at the American Indian Community House, a converted loft near the fashionable gallery district of SoHo. Apart from a handful of Shinnecocks from Long Island and a few tribal people from upstate and the Plains, the majority are again white; before Davis arrives they banter mostly about sweat lodging, Buddhist retreats, and the Tao.

Again and again Davis returns to the pathetic theme: the Apaches are "still government slaves," who don't know which way to turn for help. "We don't have no right to be heard in public," she says. "I tried to talk to the White House, but they don't respond to me. It kind of hurts my people. It's really sad, being Indian."

In this more intimate setting, Davis is very appealing. Large plastic-rimmed glasses add a humorous touch to the broad, wrinkled, rather severe face. There is reassurance in the rugged features and sagging flesh. Her struggle to speak coherent English comes across as a straining to articulate painful truths; indeed, her very clumsiness, her crippled grammar seem a kind of cachet, proof of authenticity and innocence.

Opponents of the observatory commonly describe the mountain as "the historical base of Apache religion" and liken it to Sinai, Olympus, and Ararat. Yet there is scant mention of Mount Graham in anthropological writings and almost no reference to it in historical literature. Somewhat disjointedly, Davis attempts to explain that Mount Graham is the home of the Ga'an, the benevolent deities who were traditionally believed to protect the Apaches from harm. "It's where they lived from the beginning," she says. "The mountain spirit, he come around like a whirlwind—he come to teach the Apache how to be a medicine man, a spiritual teacher. You go up there, the spirit touches you, comes out of nowhere—the tears come to you, you start crying. The spirit touches you, it's just there. We don't want no telescope up there."

A pale, expensively dressed white woman interrupts in an apparent effort to clarify. This is Ann Roberts, founder of the Fund for the Four Directions, a private organization interested in Indian spiritual issues, which has paid for Davis's trip to New York. "To Native Americans, the Earth is a living spirit," Roberts says. In contrast to the earthy Davis, she is firm and sure of herself, but remote. "It is as if you had a room in your house where you could meditate and be at peace, and someone came in and rearranged the furniture. This is far worse, as if someone said, 'I don't like the way the Creator has set up your body. I'm going to move this arm, this leg, and so on.' This land is very sacred because of the energy there, because Indians are able to communicate multidimensionally."

"Very true," Davis says, nodding, although it is by no means clear that she, or anyone else, understands exactly what Roberts is talking about. She goes on, "What the Apaches say is, they're using some iron things, punching through the mountain spirit's skull. They're hurting it."

"The Earth has its own nature, and it's being hurt," Roberts breaks in. "We've forgotten that the Earth is living. It's our lack of understanding that causes pollution, causes cancer, causes so many sicknesses that we are suffering from."

Like a great many Apaches, Davis was raised as a Lutheran on the San Carlos reservation, which lies about an hour north of Mount Graham. However, her father is widely remembered as a man knowledgeable in the ways of the old tribal religion; a brother, now also dead, is credited with reestablishing the traditional puberty rite for young women. Davis herself dropped out of school after the ninth grade and moved to Dallas, Texas, where she worked in a factory. She later moved to Tucson, where for many years she held unskilled jobs in hospitals and rest homes, and where she eventually retired to keep house for her husband, a Choctaw Indian from Mississippi.

"When I was seventeen years old, we came out at the foot of

Mount Graham to collect food to eat," Davis is saying. "My father said, 'Mount Graham, he's a person. You need help, you come to him. There are sacred things inside Mount Graham—he'll always help you.' "

Davis pauses unexpectedly. With visible effort, she abruptly begins to describe the remarkable dreams that are her inspiration. Her voice quivers. For her, the dreams are clearly freighted with awesome power. They began one night in 1989. In the first dream she found herself on top of Mount Graham. "I looked down. I saw the people—children, old men—they were crawling up the mountain, saying, 'Help me! Help me!' I wondered why they were crying. There were so many of them, crawling all the way around the mountain." The next night she dreamed again. "A real bright light shone over me. People were coming up the east side of the mountain. I had a drum and I was singing a song. Then the people all started singing." The third night she dreamed that the mountain had become transparent, like glass, and that spirits were dancing toward it from the four directions.

The dreams left Davis troubled and confused. On the advice of a friend, she traveled up to the reservation to see Franklin Stanley, Sr., a high school janitor and onetime Mormon elder who had embraced traditional Apache beliefs and who had some following around the town of Bylas. When Davis had recounted her dreams, Stanley told her that she had seen the spirits of the mountain and that they were trying to tell her that they were suffering. Davis says, "He told me, 'You seen it all. The Creator, he's telling you the true things, the way it is.' "

Environmentalists were already protesting the observatory that was planned for the mountain, asserting that it would destroy the habitat of a rare squirrel. Injunctions under the Endangered Species Act repeatedly stalled construction. Although court-mandated research determined that the project would have little impact on the squirrels, which were found to be five times more numerous than anyone imagined, a spokesman for the Maricopa Audubon Society told the press that the squirrel was "on the threshold of extinction." On the mountain, an equipment-filled trailer was set afire. Scientists observed strangers in camouflage gear videotaping them as they worked. Volunteers chained themselves to road graders and climbed trees that were about to be felled. Threats were made to destroy the telescopes' multimillion-dollar mirrors. When all else failed, the activists asked Davis for her help.

Davis wondered if in her dreams she had seen the future, whether it was the telescopes that were to be the source of the mountain's pain. The message of her dreams, Davis understood with Stanley's help, was this: that the observatory would torment the earth, that unless it was forestalled it would leave the earth impotent and the spirits dispersed, perhaps forever. Not long after that Davis dreamed again. In this dream Davis's father came toward her and stood beside her bed. "Do you really want to do this work?" he asked. "Yes, I do," she replied. The dreamed father said, "Then go ahead."

"Astronomy, that's not a connection with our prayers," Davis is telling the Buddhists and Shinnecocks, and stray Onondagas and Sioux. "Apache religion don't go for astronomy. The metal they're going to put up there, it's going to spoil our religion. We're not supposed to interfere with the sky or the stars—we're supposed to leave them be, just enjoy them, not bother them. Those telescopes will bother them. We're not supposed to mess with the earth and water."

Davis's portrayal of herself as an isolated crusader is somewhat disingenuous. The observatory has for several years been the focus of a vociferous protest campaign that has involved the Audubon Society, the National Council of Churches, numerous Hollywood personalities, the Association on American Indian Affairs, and other national organizations and has also received a fair amount of attention in the press. Indian leaders have publicly denounced it as a form of "spiritual termination" and as "an insult to all Native Americans." More than a dozen tribes petitioned the U.S. Forest Service to stop the observatory in the name of religious freedom. The Morningstar Foundation, a Washington lobbying organization, extravagantly accused the University of Arizona of "sheering the top off Mount Graham," while the Boulder-based Native American Rights Fund charged that the observatory posed a direct threat to basic religious freedom and to the United States Constitution. Several members of Congress demanded a halt to the project. Brock Evans, the executive director of the National Audubon Society, declared, "It's like the massacre at Wounded Knee. This is the most blatant violation of religious freedom I have ever seen. It's basically a case of might claiming to be right."

Mount Graham touched a raw national nerve. As Ola Davis presented it, the university's behavior appeared all too obviously to recapitulate the long, dishonorable history of war, removals, and double-dealing that was by now familiar to every American. The campaign to force the astronomers off the mountain soon became a staple in the gathering nationwide effort by tribes to regain control of many kinds of land lost through treaties or by brute annexation. Perhaps more than any other aspect of Indians' struggle to redefine their place in American society, this effort seeks to extend the principle of sovereignty into the less well defined realm of the spirit. The moral mandate that Ola Davis and others claim draws upon a web of mysticism and self-righteousness, quietism and defiance that deeply entangles Indian feelings about the American earth. It demands that other Americans rethink their own relationship to the earth and consider new kinds of claims beyond those admitted by law and custom. It also suggests that extreme traditionalists, with the help of those who believe that Indians share a unique spiritual bond with the soil, may increasingly assert the right, indeed even the religious duty, to challenge the activities of other Americans far beyond the boundaries of reservations.

As the original environmentalists, so a certain type of popular thinking goes, Indians everywhere have always lived in a state of unchanging and profound communion with nature. Similar qualities are attributed to living Indians, as well, as a matter of course. "Native Americans tend to consider themselves inseparable from the natural elements of their land," as a story on Indian ecologists in the Sierra Club's magazine self-confidently put it not long ago. It is a view, an ideology really, that is based on an assortment of intertwined misconceptions that have been wittily encapsulated by the anthropologist James A. Clifton in his book *The Invented Indian:* that all Indian tribes perceived their land as sacred territory from which they never moved for thousands of years, and which they worshipfully personified as Mother Earth, and upon which they lived in profound harmony; that to the Indian all creatures, all things, all thoughts, and all natural phenomena were pervasively infused with the sacred; and that, in defiance of the laws that govern cultural change everywhere else in the world, the beliefs of primeval Indians remain indelibly and irreversibly imprinted in the souls of their present-day descendants, having been passed down for endless generations unaltered by contact with the outside world, as if Native Americans alone among all the world's peoples existed utterly outside the flow of history.

Beneath such fuzzy sentiments typically lurks the conviction that industrial society has left humankind corroded by inner emptiness that cannot be filled without a spiritual renaissance and that spiritually superior native peoples are uniquely fitted to lead the bewildered and the tormented back onto a path of "balance" and "harmony." As the philosopher Theodore Roszak, who has admiringly described "re-earthing" ceremonies in which Californians adopt names like "Dead Leaf" and "Mountain" and sing made-up "native" chants to the beat of drums, has written, "Images of noble savagery haunt the modern Western world, a healthy sign of self-doubt." It is scarcely a new idea. Ever since Montaigne celebrated the Indian as an ideal being whose "original simplicity was governed by the laws of nature," Western man has periodically been prone, in a sort of cyclical historical neurosis, to hold the native up as a living reproach to the complexities of civilized life. Today such thinking is more popular than ever. In *The Conquest of Paradise*, Kirkpatrick Sale, a leading ecologist and cofounder of the New York Green Party, condemned the "ecocide" that he believes was perpetrated by Europeans upon the Western Hemisphere, declaring, "There is only one way to live in America, and there can only be one way, and that is as Americans—the original Americans—for that is what the earth of America demands. We have tried for five centuries to resist that simple truth. We resist it further only at the risk of the imperilment—worse, the likely destruction—of the earth." Similarly, in the film *Dances With Wolves*, which is a virtual compendium of currently popular attitudes about Indians, Euro-Americans are portrayed almost without exception as sadists, thugs, or lost souls. Encountering the carcasses of bison skinned and left to rot on the prairie, Kevin Costner's disillusioned cavalryman wonders, "Who would do such a thing? It must be a people without values, without soul." He is, of course, talking about whites. By contrast, among the Sioux, "Every day ends with a miracle." The message is clear: to act Indian is to transcend oneself, to be reborn. It suggests as well that being Indian is not merely an ethnic or a physical fact but, in essence, a spiritual condition.

There is no certainty that native tribes even possessed the idea of nature as a whole. There are also many proofs of the devastation of nature by Indians. Like Euro-Americans, not to mention the rest of humanity, Indians used the means at their command to bend nature to their use, and within the limits of their technology, they were no less inherently exploitative of it. Even in the thinly settled parts of North America, tribes often exhausted the resources of their area and were obliged to move on. The Iroquois broke off entire tops of trees to harvest cherries and, even before the white man's arrival, probably overhunted deer, beaver, and other animals. In heavily populated Mexico, ancient farming practices in some places caused staggeringly high rates of soil erosion that were unsurpassed after the arrival of the conquistadors. Archaeological excavations at numerous sites on the Great Plains have shown that long before the arrival of the white man, Indians commonly slaughtered buffalo wholesale, often taking only the most delectable parts—humps and tongues—and leaving the rest unused. The painter George Catlin recorded in 1832 that a Sioux hunting party, having left the carcasses of the animals to rot on the Dakota prairie, "came into the Fort with 1,400 fresh buffalo tongues, which were thrown down in a mass, and for which they required but a few gallons of whiskey, which was soon demolished, indulging them in a little, and harmless carouse."

Those who romanticize Indians as the ultimate ecologists fail to comprehend the vast diversity of genuinely traditional native religions, and that the majority of modern Indians are in fact Christians. According to a 1990 survey of high school seniors nationwide, nearly 70 percent of Indian youths identified themselves as Christian, of every possible variety, 15 percent said they had no religion, while only 6 percent belonged to "other," presumably traditionalist, faiths. (Nine percent declined to answer.) Romanticizers fail to see that the apparently flattering image of the Indian as selfless caretaker of the earth is, in essence, little different from the ugly exploitation of caricatured Indians as school mascots, for both are equally rooted in the assumption that Indians and their beliefs (real or imagined) are icons free for the taking, to be appropriated for any white man's cause. Not surprisingly, moreover, such preconceptions are easily abetted by Indian spokesmen who specialize in manipulating the guilt of sentimental whites. Indeed, so conventional has the belief become that Indians possess rare spiritual knowledge denied to everyone else that otherwise intelligent Americans willingly suspend disbelief and accept even the dimmest sort of platitudes as wisdom.

In an interview that was widely shown on the Public Broadcasting System, for instance, Bill Moyers allowed Oren Lyons, a chief of the Onondagas, of upstate New York, and a tireless advocate for ideas of Indian superiority, to assert without even a hint of challenge that the ancient Iroquois had foreseen present-day air and water pollution, and that all the problems of American society could be traced to its failure to combine church and state. "That's where you went wrong," Lyons, a former commercial artist, told the visibly awed Moyers. Lyons then went on to say:

> We have these wellsprings of knowledge about place that only aboriginal people would know, because they've lived there—they have an intimate knowledge of what's there. They've seen the sun come up in the same place many hundreds, thousands of years, so we have a familiarity with the earth itself, the elements and what we know about them, and we know what it is to enjoy that. And so the ceremonies that are as ancient as we are carry forward this respect. Our people were always spiritual people, religious people.

At a time when such ideas lend an impression of spiritual gravity to the political goals of modern ecologists, the plight of Mount Graham seems no less than a metaphor for the helpless earth itself in a predatory human world. "Mount Graham is more than a mountain in Arizona," the *National Catholic Reporter* editorialized, alongside a news story strongly sympathetic to Ola Davis and her supporters. "It is a symbol of the ecological web the world is wrapped in. Wherever history touches it, the whole web vibrates— Warsaw, Moscow, Tiananmen Square; a mountain, a forest, an eight-ounce squirrel."

The impact of all this upon the observatory has not been insignificant. Several American sponsors, including Ohio State University, Harvard University, and the Smithsonian Institution have withdrawn from the project. After Davis and several of her allies traveled to Europe in 1992, their fares paid for by non-Indian supporters, city councils in Rome and Florence called upon the Italian government and the Vatican to renounce their parts in the observatory and demanded that the United States "guarantee to the Native American peoples the freedom of religious practice." Twenty members of the German Bundestag demanded an official inquiry into the

Max Planck Institute's involvement, as did Green members of the European Parliament. Lawsuits have caused years of delay in construction and forced the University of Arizona and its associates to cut back the original plan for seventeen telescopes on sixty acres of land to seven telescopes squeezed onto six and a half acres. Although the courts have consistently granted the university's right to continue with the project, scientists have been forced onto the defensive. "We imagined there would be little or no opposition," says Peter Strittmatter, the embattled director of the University of Arizona's Steward Observatory, which is managing the Mount Graham project. "In that we were obviously wrong."

Eight thousand feet below the summit of Mount Graham, beneath the lichenous crags and the scrub oak and mesquite, the Arizona desert spreads vastly away toward the distant peaks of the Dragoon range, where Ola Davis's ancestors made their last stand against the U.S. Cavalry in the 1860s. For Jaap Baars, the spectacular panorama is much less interesting than the faint waves of radiation that course invisibly toward the earth from the most ancient reaches of space. For most of a decade, the rangy, ginger-haired physicist has overseen the development of a telescope jointly owned by the Max Planck Institute for Radioastronomy and the University of Arizona, and he is understandably proud of it. He is walking, loping really, through the telescope's iron shell, talking about shims and concrete and then, abruptly, about the primordial explosion that sent hydrogen flooding through space to coalesce over billions of years into atoms, molecules, stars, and galaxies. "What we are now asking is, how were stars born?" he says, in a voice inflected with the flat consonants of his native Holland. "How were galaxies created? When, where were the life-supporting elements produced? How did life come to exist on this planet? Are there living organisms elsewhere in the universe?"

If Davis fails in her crusade, at least three and perhaps as many as seven telescopes will eventually poke up through the ponderosas and spruce. They represent the latest phase in the struggle that began with Galileo to achieve an ever clearer and less ambiguous view of the heavens. Baars's Submillimeter Telescope, as it is called, will be one of the most refined instruments on earth, capable of detecting the submillimeter frequencies between radio and infrared waves, the only emissions of energy from the dark, cold regions of interstellar space. The dark emptiness between the stars is an illusion, Baars explains. "Space" is actually dense with clouds of cold gas and dust; inside them, by infinitesimal degrees, stars are born, recapitulating the unseen process of creation that has taken place since the beginning of celestial time. "If we want to look at the early stage of stars and planets, that is where we look. In the optical range, these clouds just look like black blots. But in the submillimeter range, we can see right into them and through them. By examining the radiation that is emitted, we can find out what is the physical state of material from which stars are formed and what complex molecules exist that might help generate life later."

Across the cramped worksite, Jesuits in hardhats and jeans are directing the construction of the Vatican's telescope, which is designed to operate in the optic and infrared zones of the electromagnetic spectrum. Much of what they will see is still uncharted territory. "Serendipity is a wonderful aspect of our science," Baars is saying, gesturing gregariously with wide hands. "We listen for a certain signal that we want to hear, but we hear something unexpected instead, and then we try to figure out what it means." It is well known that clouds are pulled together by the force of their own gravity; while the Submillimeter Telescope maps a cloud's density, temperature, and velocity, Vatican astronomers may examine the warmer material at its core, where stars have formed and where the density of hydrogen finally becomes great enough to produce fusion. "At that point you may say that the light has turned on, that you have got a star," says Baars. "Up to now, this has never been observed. There are lots of theories but no answers." The search for answers is, of course, rooted in science's conviction that the universe is intelligible, that its origin can be known, and that humankind will benefit from learning it. "Ultimately, everything we do leads back to how it all came into being. The only way we know how to do it is to observe the facts."

Mount Graham was chosen for the observatory in the early 1980s because of its exceptionally dry air and clear skies. Many other sites were considered. Political instability precluded several locations in the Middle East and Africa. Nighttime light pollution from Las Vegas excluded a peak in Nevada, and turbulent air another in California. Still others were protected wilderness areas or difficult of access. Contrary to what Ola Davis tells audiences, Mount Graham was not pristine wilderness. Timber companies had

lumbered the peaks for nearly a century. Scores of summer cabins
dotted the lower slopes. For decades, a commercial dairy had produced milk for Phoenix and Tucson. There was a summertime Bible
camp, an eleven-acre recreational lake, and a permanent work
camp built by the U.S. Forest Service, which manages the mountain
as part of Coronado National Forest. A paved highway built in the
1930s was bringing a quarter-million campers and sportsmen to the
mountain annually, a figure that the state estimated could double
by the end of the century.

In 1985, the University of Arizona wrote to the eighteen Indian
tribes in Arizona and New Mexico, inviting them to comment on
the environmental impact statement it had prepared. None replied
except the Zunis, whose ancestors had occupied the area many
centuries before. At the university's suggestion, the Zunis sent a
delegation to the mountain. They found three long-abandoned
shrines, which the university segregated from the worksite. Compared to the Zunis, the Apaches were newcomers, having arrived in
present-day Arizona from the far north only a few generations before the Spaniards appeared in the 1500s. The Apaches ranged
across the Southwest and far into Mexico, earning a deserved reputation for courage, brutality, and battlefield brilliance, until they
were finally hemmed in by white settlement. The San Carlos reservation was founded in 1872, to consolidate a diverse and sometimes mutually hostile assortment of bands for the Army's convenience. It was a bleak place, without grass or game, and the only
water was brackish and malarial. Although they did not prosper,
the Apaches did survive, converting in large numbers to Christianity, struggling to farm the unyielding desert soil, and taking up
what wage work they could find on railroads and ranches. Until
1990, the five thousand Apaches who lived at San Carlos showed
little interest of any kind in the fate of Mount Graham.

In that year, startled astronomers learned to their consternation
that the tribal council had passed a resolution proclaiming its "firm
and total opposition" to the observatory. Ola Davis, having decided to collaborate with white environmentalists, had gathered the
support of several spiritual leaders and had lobbied the council
hard. The resolution stated that the "proposed destruction" of
Mount Graham would contribute directly to the degradation of
fundamental aspects of the traditional and spiritual life of the
Apaches: "Any permanent modification of the present form of this

mountain constitutes a display of profound disrespect for a cherished feature of the Apaches' traditional homeland as well as a serious violation of Apache traditional religious beliefs." One of the resolution's sponsors, a young artist named Ernest Victor, Jr., declared, "Traditional people had never been to school, but they already knew astronomy, and they didn't destroy nothing. Why do they need those telescopes up there? What do they want to see up there—the stairway to heaven?"

There were a few Apaches who wondered aloud whether Mount Graham was the Crown Dancers' home at all and ventured to suggest that Indians might benefit more from studying astronomy than from frustrating it. Ola Davis attacked them harshly. "How could poor Indians become astronomers?" she retorted. "They can't even do anything for themselves. They are very uneducated. Looking at the stars is something very bad for the traditional Apache. They are not allowed to look at the stars through those telescopes because the Apache believe that God made those things for us to enjoy as they are. If they really believe the telescopes should be built, they are a lost tribe within their own culture."

Attacks in the press increased. Campus protests mounted. Astronomers were accused of bigotry and racism. Scientists such as Baars were stunned. "Part of the beauty of astronomy is that you only observe, that you are not interfering with the process of things," he says, sounding bewildered, even hurt, at the protesters' failure to appreciate the passive quietude of astronomers' work. "We can't do any harm—it's just impossible."

When Ola Davis and Franklin Stanley are asked to explain precisely what it is about Mount Graham that is sacred, they are maddeningly vague. "Because our traditional knowledge is passed from one generation to the next orally, there are no records of much that is known," Stanley stated in a deposition submitted to the federal district court in Phoenix. "Ordinarily, these matters are not spoken about at all. It is very likely that there are only a few Apache who know what is sacred about Mount Graham, and that if they did and were asked, a truly traditional Apache might very well not answer or admit to knowing." He went on to say, with dizzying circularity, "In order to understand why there cannot be any telescopes on Mount Graham you would have to understand our religion, language and culture, and you would have to know how to show respect. Why should we try to explain why the telescopes are a terrible thing to do to the mountain, if you will use what is said disrespectfully? The heavens is something you want to own and control through their [sic] science and without respect for the Indian people. But the heavens belong to God."

At a meeting with University of Arizona faculty in March of 1992, Keith Basso, one of the most distinguished anthropologists who has worked among the Apaches, lent his support to the former Mormon bishop, declaring, "It is apparent to me, beyond a shadow of a doubt, that Mount Graham, or *dzil nchaa si an,* occupies a place of enormous importance in Apache religious belief and practice." For many Apaches, Basso said, talking candidly about religious knowledge was a sacrilegious act, while silence was a form of piety. Even to ask Apaches to explain what they believed was an intrusion upon their spiritual privacy. "Deferential avoidance in word and deed" was, Basso said, a central ingredient in the preservation of "productive relationships with all forms of life and their sacred powers."

In effect, Stanley and Basso were presenting silence as the ultimate argument. Denial of the mountain's significance—or seeming ignorance of it—was to be understood as evidence that Mount Graham was in fact sacred. To say nothing was to say everything; to appear to know nothing was to know all. It was a stunning argument. In lieu of fact, they offered mystery and a blank slate upon which anything at all might be written by the willing imagination.

To many of the Indian leaders who gathered in Albuquerque, New Mexico, for the American Indian Religious Rights Summit in 1991, it seemed that Mount Graham was part of a larger pattern of assault against Indian beliefs of all types. "Whether we like it or not, we are engaged in a spiritual termination, and we cannot allow it," Henrietta Mann, a Cheyenne-Arapaho who then headed the Religious Freedom Coalition Project, declared. "Corporate America and the federal government are seeking to destroy our sacred sites. Telescopes, roads, oil and gas, and continued energy exploitation are a direct threat to our spirituality, rooted in the earth."

The mood of the conference was one of almost unrelieved anxiety and defiance. "They tried to de-Indianize this continent through termination, assimilation, and education," Raymond Apodaca, a Pueblo speaking on behalf of the National Congress of American Indians, told the several hundred Indian politicians, activists, and spiritual leaders gathered in a mauve meeting room at the Albuquerque Conference Center. "But up to now they"—Indians do not need to be told that, in polemics of this sort, "they" can only mean white Americans—"have never been able to touch our soul. Now they are trying to do that. Without our communication with our Creator through our ceremonies we are nothing, we are lost." Walter Echo Hawk of the Native American Rights Fund asserted, "Ever since Columbus set foot on the New World, religious discrimination has been one of the basics of relations between Europeans and Native Americans, right up to the present day. Everybody has religious freedom in America except for native people. The question is, can our religion survive into the twenty-first century without legal protection?"

It cannot be surprising that history has cursed Indians with an instinctive sense of imminent doom. Idealists such as Senator Dawes who saw Indians' salvation in the destruction of the reservation were equally committed to the extinction of what they universally referred to as "superstition." Well into the twentieth century, Bureau of Indian Affairs regulations stipulated that any Indian found guilty of participating in the sun dance or any other "so-called religious ceremonies" could be punished "by withholding from him his rations for a period of not exceeding ten days; and if found guilty of any subsequent offense under this rule, shall be punished by withholding his rations for a period not less than fifteen days nor more than thirty days, or by incarceration in the agency prison for a period not exceeding thirty days." Anyone attempting to serve as a medicine man was to be imprisoned for no less than ten days "or until such time as he shall produce evidence satisfactory to the court, and approved by the agent, that he will forever abandon all practices styled Indian offenses under this rule."

Repression was formally ended by the Indian Reorganization Act of 1934. In 1978, Congress explicitly repudiated past abuses with the American Indian Religious Freedom Act, which Indians commonly refer to by its acronym, AIRFA. Like much Indian policy, it was a well-meaning measure but it ultimately failed to take into account either the growing popularity or the ambiguities of Indian spiritual practices. The act recognized traditional religions as an "irreplaceable part" of Indian life and acknowledged that insensitive and inflexible enforcement of federal laws had "often resulted in the abridgement of religious freedom for traditional American Indians." Declaring that it was now federal policy to protect Indians' "right to believe," it required government agencies to consult with tribal religious figures to ensure access to sacred sites, unimpeded use of sacred objects, and freedom to worship in traditional rites. However, the act included no enforcement provisions, a fatal flaw in Indian eyes, and it proved largely ineffectual when it came into conflict with other federal and state laws.

To the dismay of members of the Native American Church, the Supreme Court ruled that taking the hallucinogen peyote as a religious sacrament was not protected by the First Amendment. In several states, authorities prosecuted Indians for the possession of eagle parts, which federal law protects as an endangered species but which many Indians covet for inclusion in ritual fans and other objects. Elsewhere, prison officials declined to allow Indian inmates to build sweat lodges, or to grow their hair long as a ritual act, or to see medicine men as other inmates would a minister or priest. However, nothing provoked greater Indian resentment than the refusal of courts to protect off-reservation lands that traditionalists held to be sacred. Courts generally agreed to prohibit development only when Indians could prove that a site was indispensable to a tribe's spiritual life and that change would not merely harm but virtually destroy a religious practice or belief.

Indian leaders estimate that, in all, somewhere between fifty and one hundred sites around the country are endangered. There is no typical sacred site, any more than there is a generic Indian or tribe. A few approximate European ideas of the sacred: it is not difficult to understand the Navajos' hostility to tourist development around Rainbow Bridge, where they believe their ancestors entered upon the earth, or efforts to stop U.S. Park Service plans for a tourist center at Medicine Wheel, an ancient stone ceremonial circle in the Big Horn Mountains of Wyoming that is still used by members of several Plains tribes. Some sites are as finite as a waterfall, or a burial ground, or a clifftop where a revered visionary once dreamed. Others are confusingly ill-defined; during a campaign to prevent oil drilling in the vast Lewis and Clark National Forest, a Blackfeet healer named Molly Kicking Woman asserted, "All of the mountains and not just the area where we pick plants and roots are important to our religion." Many sites now lie on private or federal property, and their return to Indian control would pose complex problems for non-Indians who live and do business there. Lummi Indians in the State of Washington, for instance, are protesting the logging of privately owned land that they say is a favored place for the collection of ceremonial materials and herbs, while Bannocks oppose the expansion of a Boise, Idaho, suburb that they say will destroy hot springs that were once used for spiritual healing.

In 1988, the Supreme Court attempted to define the nature of the claim that sacred Indian land may have on the nation's conscience and failed. The Court ultimately rejected an appeal by members of three small tribes who wished to halt construction of a six-mile road through Six Rivers National Forest in northern California, where medicine men and herb gatherers carried out rites that they maintained were essential to the tribes' welfare. Testimony indicated that while few Indians actually visited the most potent sites, many apparently believed that the stability of the world hinged on the ceremonies performed there. Traditionalists argued that their rituals would lose their power if the area's natural state was disturbed. Turning down the Indians' appeal, Justice Sandra Day O'Connor wrote that although the road might have "devastating effects" on traditional religious practices, "government simply could not operate if it were required to satisfy every citizen's religious needs and desires . . . The First Amendment must apply to all citizens alike, and it can give to none of them a veto over public programs that do not prohibit the free exercise of religion." O'Connor concluded, "Whatever rights the Indians may have to the use of the area, however, those rights do not divest the Government of its right to use what is, after all, its land."

In a dissent written by Justice William Brennan, three liberal justices attacked the majority's "astonishing conclusions" that "stripped respondents and all other Native Americans of any constitutional protection against perhaps the most serious threat to their age-old religious practices, and indeed to their entire way of life." Brennan added scathingly that he found it difficult

> to imagine conduct more insensitive to religious needs than the Government's determination to build a marginally useful road in the face of uncontradicted evidence that the road will render the practice of respondents' religion impossible. Nor do I believe that the respondents will derive any solace from the knowledge that although the practice of their religion will become "more difficult" as a result of the Government's actions, they remain free to maintain their religious beliefs.

Given today's ruling, that freedom amounts to nothing more than the
right to believe that their religion will be destroyed.

No native land claim has remained longer without resolution, been
fought with greater tenacity, or spawned more bitterness than the
Sioux claim to the Black Hills. They are the ultimate terra irridenta
in the landscape of native North America. And nowhere have Indians challenged the white man's ownership of the land more compel-
lingly and with more potential consequence for its non-Indian occupants. "For Indians all over the United States, the Lakota have
made these mountains the most visible and significant, as they are
physically the largest, battleground in the struggle for land possession between the races on this continent," the historian Donald
Worster has written. In contrast to Mount Graham, whose ambiguous holiness is asserted by only a comparatively small number of
Apaches, the "sacredness" of the Black Hills is an article of faith
that is virtually unchallenged throughout the Sioux country. In a
typical statement, a Pine Ridge tribal councilman by the name of
Gerald Big Crow told the United Nations Working Group on Indigenous Populations, which in 1991 was considering a resolution
condemning the U.S. government's "confiscation" of the Hills in
the 1870s: "The taking of the sacred Black Hills was the same as
taking our spiritual altar. It would have the same impact if all
churches and synagogues were closed."

On a prosaic plane, the Black Hills are a central pillar of South
Dakota's economy. Taken altogether, commercial activities in the
Hills provide the state with $600 million in revenue annually, one
of its largest sources of income. The vast strip-mined vistas around
the town of Lead may be prototypes of environmental rape, but
they are also evidence of the fabulous wealth that has been extracted from the Hills since the discovery of gold there by an expedition headed by General George Armstrong Custer in 1874; by the
mid-1990s, the Homestake Mine, the richest single mine in the
United States, had alone produced nearly $18 billion in gold ore.
Every year, millions of tourists, campers, and hikers come to enjoy
the thousands of acres of federally managed parkland and to visit
the presidential shrine at Mount Rushmore and the old frontier
town of Deadwood, whose long economic decline was recently reversed when the state legislature legalized casino gambling there.
Elsewhere, highways through the Hills sport lurid, interminable

garlands of wax museums, miniature golf courses, reptile gardens, waterslides, dude ranches, and ersatz frontier towns as well as more singular tourist traps such as the "Home of the Talking Woodcarvings" and the "Flintstones' Bedrock City" ("Yabba Dabba Do!" ubiquitous billboards crow).

There is, at the same time, in spite of the trashy development and the scarred slopes, something undeniably enigmatic about the Hills. Perhaps it is something in the way in which they seem to someone driving westward on Interstate 90 to erupt so unexpectedly from the otherwise featureless, coppery-green plain, or perhaps something in their interior topography of concealment and surprise: in the weird forests of unearthly landforms, the secluded pastures, the steep wooded vales made mysterious by the chiaroscuro of hard prairie light. Whatever its origins, it is a quality that lends itself to dreams and mythmaking and to notions of the transcendental, to the idea that somewhere here humankind might truly, on some primeval afternoon, have sprung full-blown from its bowels.

In the eyes of Lakota fundamentalists, the Black Hills are less a landscape than a complex spiritual phenomenon: they are Wamaka Og'naka I'Cante, "the Heart of Everything That Is," the birthplace of the Sioux and thus, in Lakota minds, of mankind. "The spiritual integrity of the Lakota people requires contact with the Black Hills and the ability to carry out ceremonies there," Gerald Clifford is saying, picking his words carefully to avoid divulging the intimacies of ritual. "Ceremony makes that relationship real, and the integrity of ceremonial life requires visiting the sacred places." Clifford, a one-time Roman Catholic monk, is the coordinator of the Black Hills Steering Committee, which represents the policy of the Sioux tribal governments in their collective effort to recover the Hills. He speaks often of integrity; it is a word that resonates significantly on the Pine Ridge reservation, where he makes his home, and where unemployment, epidemic alcoholism, and political instability have undermined both civil society and economic development.

The compact cedarwood house where Clifford lives with his wife and teenage son lies in a secluded fold of white clay hills outside the hamlet of Manderson, ninety miles east of the Black Hills. The disarray of books and files, the sport jacket, the corduroys, the backswept silvering hair all suggest a man of professorial habits. But in the thin smile and cool eyes there is also the appraising wariness of the Lakota, in whom friendliness can snap in an instant into scathing contempt.

Clifford is well aware that the weight of scholarly opinion holds that the Sioux originated in the northern Midwest, and reached the Black Hills only in the 1770s. Scholars similarly believe that the story of the emergence of the Pte from the earth is a portable myth that the Sioux brought with them from the East and that originally it never applied to the Black Hills at all. Says William K. Powers of Rutgers University, one of the foremost authorities on Lakota belief, "The fact is, the Lakotas came from present-day Minnesota; their creation stories have to do with places and events that relate to a time when they were living around the Great Lakes. Over time, they have assigned these things to the Black Hills." In his book *Oglala Religion,* a scholarly survey of the central Lakota cosmology and ritual, there is no mention of the Black Hills at all.

"Personally, I reject the nonsense written in history books," Clifford says with cutting vehemence. "The people who wrote them were just justifying the rape and pillage of Indian land. They were never told what was sacred to the Sioux." Like many Lakotas, Clifford prefers to believe that the ancestors of the Sioux originated from within the caves that honeycomb the Black Hills. He maintains that Lakotas have occupied the Hills for ten thousand years and that Lakota existence is so deeply intertwined with the Hills that any modern claim to them is dwarfed by comparison. "We have always been here, spread out. We have been to both coasts. In fact we had an obligation to do that, tradition says, to make sure the earth lived and survived. We traveled in each direction to see that it was so."

Few people who knew Clifford as a boy could have imagined that he would become a sun dancer or, for that matter, that he would ever come back to Pine Ridge. He was raised a Christian, the son of a coach at Holy Rosary Mission, which since the 1880s has been the center of Catholic evangelism at Pine Ridge. As a boy, Gerald knew nothing about what was then generally dismissed as the "old-time religion." He recalls, "When we heard drums down below the school the nuns told us it was 'devil worship.' " It was an education in tune with the assimilationist philosophy that had driven Indian schooling since the nineteenth century. For generations after Senator Dawes's stirring oration at Mount Mohonk, reforming whites had taught Indians to disdain tribal culture as primitive and that they would have to be stripped of it if they were ever to take their place as American citizens.

Clifford was a brilliant student. His mother wanted him to become a priest. Instead, he studied engineering at the South Dakota School of Mines in Rapid City; in 1959, at the age of nineteen, he became its youngest graduate ever. Like many ambitious young Lakotas, then and now, he headed West to California, where he found a job with North American Aviation in San Jose, working on the B-70 bomber; later, in Los Angeles, he designed fuel cones for Polaris missiles. Although his career was assured, Clifford became disenchanted with life in middle-class America. In 1962, he became a novice with the Camaldolese, an order of contemplative monks, and went to live in their monastery at Big Sur; five years later, he moved to the order's headquarters in Rome. He might well have remained there permanently, immersed in his studies of the Russian mystics and the stylite hermits of Syria. But at that point his life took another abrupt turn.

"Mom died, the home burned down and I had family responsibilities, and I came back," Clifford says. He returned to Pine Ridge in time to witness the worst calamity to befall the Lakotas since the Seventh Cavalry shot down hundreds of Ghost Dancers and their helpless families at Wounded Knee in 1890. In 1973, in an effort to capitalize on the publicity they had garnered during the previous year's seizure of the Bureau of Indian Affairs in Washington, activists belonging to the American Indian Movement and scores of their non-Indian supporters occupied the site of the Wounded Knee massacre, a few miles outside Pine Ridge village. The armed warfare that ensued between AIM and adherents of the tribal government left dozens of dead on both sides, set back reservation development by a generation, and left vengeful rivalries that remain up to the present day. It was a bewildering atmosphere for Clifford, who had not lived on the reservation for more than a decade. "For a while I thought, you're going to be either a Lakota person or a white person." But he had already tried to be white, and it hadn't worked. "So then I spent a lot of time asking, what does it mean to be an American Indian?"

A pivotal experience for Clifford, as it was for many Indians of his generation, was his discovery of the visionary mysticism of Nick Black Elk, whom the Nebraska poet John Neihardt had introduced to the world in his 1932 book *Black Elk Speaks*. Neihardt's book has become one of the religious classics of the twentieth century, read by millions of people who may know nothing else about the Lakotas beyond what they find between its covers. More than any other single book, it has shaped white Americans' idea of Indian religion, and for young Indian traditionalists, it has become what Vine Deloria, Jr., has called "a North American bible of all tribes," a ubiquitous sourcebook for spiritual guidance, sociological identity, and political insight.

Black Elk's extraordinary life began in the 1860s, when the Sioux ranged freely over the northern Plains, and ended only in 1950. He was present at several of the most historic events of the late nineteenth century. As a boy, he scalped a soldier at the Battle of the Little Big Horn; later he traveled to England as a rider in Buffalo Bill's Wild West Show, and he was also a witness to the Wounded Knee massacre. Neihardt's account centers on the apocalyptic vision that was vouchsafed to Black Elk when he was nine years old. Over a period of twelve days, during which time he appeared delirious to his family, Black Elk encountered the multitudinous spirits of the old Lakota pantheon, who showed him the terrible suffering that his tribe was to undergo in the future and its ultimate redemption. As he stood, in the vision, upon Harney Peak in the Black Hills, the spirits bestowed upon him the power to destroy and to give life, and called upon him to lead the Lakotas onto the "good red road" of unity and health and to "bring the people back into the nation's hoop." It was a vision of tremendous power, vividly rendered by Neihardt; it eventually led Black Elk to become a healer and ultimately, around the turn of the century, to his formal rejection of traditional spiritual practices and to a wholehearted embrace of Catholicism. Apparently, Black Elk saw his conversion as a way of broadening his lifelong mission to bring a message of spiritual renewal to the Sioux. When Neihardt met him, Black Elk had already served for more than thirty years as a Catholic catechist, or lay preacher, and had personally converted some hundreds of Lakotas to the Roman faith. On a trip to the East, he even visited prisons such as Sing Sing, in New York, where he lectured inmates on the Christian life. (It is significant to note that nowhere does Black Elk refer to the Black Hills as the sacred land of the Lakotas, even though the youthful vision that inspired him throughout his life occurred on their highest promontory; indeed, he pointedly told Neihardt, "Anywhere is the center of the world.")

Neihardt, curiously enough, chose not even to mention Black Elk's well-known Catholicism and his years of ardent missionary work, choosing instead to see him as an "old man waiting for yesterday," a feeble vestige of a golden age that had passed beyond recall, and a symbol of traditional Indian values withering in modern America. By doing so, Neihardt consciously rejected the bulk of Black Elk's life as well as what the catechist may have regarded as his most important spiritual work, for yet another version, however eloquently rendered, of the Vanishing American. Black Elk was, in fact, very much a man of his time, a complex and modern man, who was concerned with helping his fellow Lakotas meet the demands of twentieth-century reservation life. In the 1970s, Black Elk's daughter Lucy Looks Twice told the anthropologist Michael Steltenkamp that her father resented Neihardt's censoring out of his life as a Christian: "My father wanted it known that after he quit his medicine practice, he became a catechist. But this man [Lucy pointed to a picture of John Neihardt] really believed in the Indian religion." However, it is the pre-Christian Black Elk—Neihardt's Black Elk—who has become the patron saint of the modern traditionalist revival.

Like many other Lakota fundamentalists, Gerald Clifford believes that Black Elk abandoned Catholicism before his death and returned to the religion of his childhood. In Black Elk's mysticism, Clifford found some support for his own distaste for modern materialism. "White society is based on what you can own and sell, on the bottom line," he says with unconcealed contempt. "The tendency to look at land as an object, as a resource to be exploited— that kind of greed and selfishness—is something that Indians have derived from the white man." He began purifying himself in sweat lodges, questing for visions, and, finally, submitting himself to the ultimate mortification of the sun dance, historically a central rite of northern Plains tribes that has grown in popularity in recent years after decades of suppression by federal authorities appalled at the participants' ritual piercing of their flesh. He came to believe that God had placed the Lakotas around the Black Hills for a purpose and that the recovery of what he regarded as the living center of the tribe's spiritual universe—the Black Hills—was an inescapable part of his own spiritual journey.

Lakotas widely regard the Fort Laramie Treaty of 1868 as the cynosure against which all subsequent history must be measured.

Although there was no specific mention of the Black Hills in the treaty, it did recognize Sioux ownership of the entire western half of the Dakota Territory and parts of present-day Nebraska, Wyoming, and Montana. The treaty ignored the competing claims of other tribes to the same land and accepted Lakota domination as a fait accompli. Donald Worster writes:

> The whites created, in their own cultural terms and backed up by their own legal institutions, a set of native user rights. How, before the coming of the whites, did the Lakota acquire those acres? Quite simply, by force of arms—by naked conquest. They entered and they pushed aside whoever was there. . . . Now for the Lakota the whites offered a new, enhanced measure of security in their land tenure—at the price of their accepting the white man's ideas of law and property.

In return for the guarantee of their borders against both white settlers and other Indians, the Lakotas agreed to settle down on family homesteads of 320 acres and to apply for citizenship in the United States. They would receive free plows, seed, and oxen for thirty years, along with yearly allotments of clothing and cash.

Modern Lakota nationalism holds, as an article of faith, that true Lakotas could not even consider selling the Black Hills. "Only someone with no Lakota heart beating within them would consider taking money in lieu of the land," Gregg J. Bourland, the chairman of the Cheyenne River Sioux Tribe, declared in a public television report devoted to the question of the Black Hills in 1992. The historical record tells a somewhat different story. Although mid-nineteenth-century Lakotas recognized that the Hills held a wealth of food and construction material that was crucial to the tribe's well-being, not a single tribal leader of the period referred to the Hills as sacred or holy. On the contrary, although some Lakotas, including Crazy Horse, refused to relinquish the Hills on any terms, when American negotiators pressed the Indians to either lease mining rights or sell the Hills outright, the leading chiefs offered to give them up for $70 million.

Indeed, their words give the lie to modern notions that traditional Indians understood neither money nor the concept of real estate; the Lakotas knew perfectly well what it meant to sell land, and they sought to drive the best bargain they could. "The Black Hills are the house of Gold for our Indians," Little Bear declared. "If a man owns anything, of course he wants to make something out of it to get rich on." Red Cloud, who had led the Lakotas in their successful war against the U.S. Army in the 1860s, said: "You can see it plain enough that God Almighty placed those hills there for my wealth, but now you want to take them from me and make me poor, so I ask so much that I won't be poor." Added Spotted Tail, "I want to live on the interest of my money. The amount must be so large as to support us."

The whites offered $6 million. The Indians balked at what they considered a paltry sum. Soon miners and settlers began pouring into the Black Hills. Clashes with the Indians steadily increased and finally flared into full-scale war. The annihilation of Custer's command by a combined force of Sioux, Cheyennes, and Arapahos under Sitting Bull in the summer of 1876 allowed the Indians briefly to imagine that they might reconquer the Hills by force. But within months, the threat of starvation had driven the Indian bands to surrender. Congress presented them with a draconian ultimatum that reflected popular revulsion at the massacre of Custer and his men: no funds would be appropriated for their subsistence until the Sioux agreed to cede the Black Hills. Washington ignored existing treaties that required the signatures of a majority of Sioux males for any cession of land; when only a handful agreed to sign away the Hills, Congress annexed them anyway. Today, Lakotas refer to the agreement of 1877 bitterly as the "sign-or-starve" treaty.

The subsequent story of the Black Hills land claim suggests the sisyphean difficulty of evaluating Indian demands in a political climate that is layered with ever-changing philosophies about where Indians fit in the United States and about what they are owed by other Americans. During the allotment era, courts not surprisingly took a hands-off approach to the federal appropriation of Indian land. It was not until 1920 that tribes were finally allowed to claim compensation for lands that might have been illegally appropriated by the federal government. Three years later, the first of many versions of the Black Hills claim began to make its tortuous way through the U.S. courts. Lawyers for the Indians argued the United States had illegally annexed the Hills by failing to obtain a sufficient number of signatures for the Treaty of 1877 and that the terms of the 1868 treaty were therefore still valid. Different versions of the claim demanded reparations ranging from $150 million to more than $750 million. Considering the spiritual importance that is now universally attributed to the Black Hills, it is interesting that until the 1980s the Lakotas never argued their claim in terms of religion. "Forty or fifty years ago, you didn't hear people assert a spiritual connection to the Hills," recalls William K. Powers, who began working among the Lakotas as an anthropologist in the 1940s. "You heard people talk about various vision quest sites as sacred, but not the Black Hills. Monetary compensation was clearly what people wanted."

In 1942, the U.S. Court of Claims dismissed the Black Hills suit with apparent finality. The court ruled that Congress had, in effect, already compensated the Indians for the Hills by providing them with more than $45 million worth of food and other necessities over the preceding seventy years. The tribe's lawyers continued to press the claim, but with little practical effect at a time when Washington was hostile to anything that could compromise the prevailing philosophy of Indian assimilation. By the 1970s, however, allotment and assimilation were less likely to be seen as idealistic endeavors than as forms of cultural imperialism, and the annihilation of Custer less as a heroic victory for civilization than as a well-deserved defeat by the underdogs in an Indian war of "national liberation." New life was breathed into the Black Hills claim in 1974, when a Congress eager to redress wrongs done to the Indians amended the charter of the Indian Claims Commission to specify that "expenditures for food, rations, or provisions shall not be deemed payments" on any claims. Five years later, the United States Court of Claims awarded the Sioux $17.5 million, which was judged to be the market value of the Black Hills in 1876, plus $450,000 in damages and 5 percent interest on the value of the land, for a total of $106 million. In 1980, the Supreme Court upheld the award, asserting, in a decision penned by Justice Harry Blackmun, that a "more ripe and rank case of dishonorable dealing will never, in all probability, be found in our history."

Then something happened that no one, at least in Washington, ever expected. The Sioux refused to accept the money that they had sought so tenaciously for nearly sixty years. Just days after the award was announced, in July 1980, the Black Hills Sioux Nation Council repudiated it. (The tribes did not exactly reject the money either: the federal government banked it in interest-bearing accounts in the name of "The Sioux Nation," where it remains untouched, and by 1995, the total had reached more than $350 million.) Some Lakotas found themselves in a moral and ideological dilemma. "If they voted to use the Black Hills money," Edward Lazarus, the most exhaustive historian of the Sioux claim, wrote, "they faced certain accusation of having repudiated their heritage and having accepted as justly resolved the tribe's grievances against the United States that for a century had served to explain and excuse four generations of shattered lives." Others wanted a much larger payment, which reflected the value of all the ore that had been extracted from the Hills since the nineteenth century. The Oglala Sioux Tribe soon sued the federal government, demanding the return of the Hills and an additional $11 billion in "damages" that had allegedly resulted from the years of white occupation. But something more profound than simple political strategy was also at work. The Black Hills themselves had profoundly changed.

The religious revival that was sweeping the Sioux country had now infused the land claim with a mystical dimension that it had conspicuously lacked before. The Hills were not ordinary land, Lakota leaders argued, but sacred space that had been profaned by the white man's "exploitation." Chief Frank Fools Crow, a revered Lakota elder, proclaimed in 1981, with what many Lakotas regarded as unimpeachable authority, that the Hills were "the foundation of Indian religion." New theological tracts appeared identifying Wind Cave with the place where the Lakotas were said to have emerged onto the earth, the lowlands just outside the Hills as the "racetrack" where legend said that the animals had once held a race to determine the fate of humankind, and Devil's Tower as the place where the sacred pipe was first given to the Lakotas. "Star charts" purported to show that the Lakotas had associated areas of the Hills with certain heavenly bodies since time immemorial. Cloaking the land claim in myth lent an aura of antiquity to what could also be seen as an increasingly dogmatic assertion of political sovereignty. Instead of money, the Sioux now demanded the return of the Black Hills themselves.

In 1983, Gerald Clifford was appointed to lead the Sioux tribes' joint lobbying effort in Congress. It was a logical choice. Clifford was one of the best-educated Lakotas at Pine Ridge, and he was untainted by political self-interest. He had some experience in the ways of Washington, having worked with a national coalition to win greater tribal control over Indian education, and he had earned a reputation as an astute diplomat for reorganizing the highly politicized Pine Ridge tribal police after the chaos of the 1970s.

Clifford convinced New Jersey Senator Bill Bradley, who had visited Pine Ridge as a professional basketball player with the New York Knicks, to sponsor legislation that would, in effect, have restored control of the Black Hills to the Sioux.

Taking the religious assertions of the fundamentalists at face value, the Bradley bill of 1985 described the Hills as "the sacred center of aboriginal territory of the Sioux Nation" and conveyed to the Sioux tribes all federal lands in the western part of South Dakota, except Mount Rushmore, along with all federal mineral and water rights and timber leases. Non-Indians would retain their property rights, but they would be excluded from all religious sites and from any lands that the Sioux designated as a "wildlife and wilderness sanctuary for living things which have a special sacred relationship to the Sioux." The tribes would also have unrestricted criminal jurisdiction over non-Indians. The Sioux would get to keep their claim money with accrued interest as "damages" for lost use of the land. (No one, Indian or otherwise, suggested that the Sioux might pay compensation to the Crows, Kiowas, Pawnees, Mandans, Omahas, and other tribes whose lands they had seized in the eighteenth and nineteenth centuries.)

White residents of the Black Hills were virtually apoplectic at the prospect of coming under tribal authority. They realized that if the bill became law, most of the state's income from the Hills would go to the Sioux tribes. Governor Mickelson, one of the calmer voices, called the Bradley bill "a giant step backward" at a time when the existing claim money could be spent to improve health care, education, and job opportunities on the reservations, adding that the proposal's plan to reserve federal land for ceremonial use compromised the separation of religion and the state. Even South Dakotans who were generally sympathetic to the Sioux regarded the bill as naive and flawed. "Star charts, petroglyphs and pictographs notwithstanding, there is abundant evidence to indicate that those tribes identified in the Bradley bill came fairly recently to the Black Hills region," charged David Miller, a professor of history at Black Hills State College in Spearfish. "At what point in time does an historic seizure of land without just compensation become a moot point?"

Lacking sufficient support in Congress, the Bradley bill died before reaching the floor of the Senate. Bradley reintroduced the bill in 1987, but almost immediately the Black Hills Sioux Nation

Council and the Gray Eagle Society, an organization of influential elders, publicly declared their opposition to it. In the mid-1990s, the most doctrinaire Indian leaders continue to call for the establishment of an independent Sioux Nation based on the boundaries of the Fort Laramie Treaty of 1868. "We own it all, and we should control it all," says Gregg Bourland, who believes that the Black Hills ought to be preserved as a religious sanctuary. "There will never be another way. To give up the Hills, that would be like an American saying to hell with the flag and the Constitution. We are the Sioux Nation. Anyone who says we should sell the Hills is not a Lakota and should be cast out."

A steady procession of Lakota spokesmen has sought to bring the question of the Black Hills before the United Nations and the International Court of Justice at The Hague, so far to little effect. Although some Indians, Gerald Clifford among them, remain committed to the legislative process, the members of South Dakota's congressional delegation continue to oppose any proposal that involves a transfer of land to Indian control. Other factions would like to bypass Congress entirely by asserting the Sioux tribes' supposed status as a unitary sovereign state. "They do not represent the Sioux Nation," Mario Gonzalez, a Lakota lawyer who represents the Gray Eagle Society, provocatively asserted in 1992. "The Lakota people hold dual citizenship status, one as members of the state, the other as members of the Sioux Nation. The South Dakota congressional delegation does not represent the Sioux people in their relationship with the federal government." Precisely what the majority of the Sioux would like remains as mysterious as the shadowy fastnesses of the Black Hills, for the tribal governments have never put the question to a popular vote.

In the chalky hills outside Manderson, Gerald Clifford continues to wait, confident that powers beyond earthly history and law will one day redeem the Hills. "Viewed from the white perspective, maybe there's not a hope in hell that legislation will be passed. But who expected the Berlin Wall to come down? We are not naive. We know that we have to be patient. If the Lakotas return to the spiritual ways, then they will get their Black Hills back, and no little white men are going to stand in their way. We are going to have spiritual possession of them. Time is not important." He pauses, intense, and then surprising. "Maybe it was necessary to have them taken away from us so that we could bring about this revival, begin to bring all this knowledge back, and renew our integrity."

American society did its utmost to eradicate Sioux religion and language in the nineteenth century; by the middle of the twentieth, collectors had carried away most of what remained of material culture, as well. "Where the old ways are alive," the British historian Eric Hobsbawm has observed, "traditions need be neither revived nor invented." It is hardly strange that many Sioux are ransacking both the real and the imagined past for values and practices that will give meaning to modern Indian life. Thus the Sioux campaign to reclaim the Black Hills has already succeeded in a quite unexpected way, transforming them from a shaming reminder of all that has been lost into a modern symbol of collective salvation. "Although the Hills may not have been sacred in the past, that doesn't mean that they are not sacred to the Lakotas now," says Powers. "There is no doubt that the Black Hills are extremely important to Lakotas today and that they are the source of a whole lot of spirituality. Religious attitudes can legitimize a place as sacred almost overnight. It is a natural evolution; Hindu immigrants, for instance, build shrines all over the world and they become sacred instantly. The antiquity of a particular belief doesn't matter. What does matter is the relationship between the human beings and the shrine."

That the alienation of the Black Hills is felt by traditionalist Lakotas in a highly personal and painful way there can be no doubt. Although Indians are of course free to use public land like anyone else, it is a common complaint that it is difficult, and even humiliating, to attempt to hold ceremonies in the Hills. "You can't build a purification lodge over there because there's too much red tape," says John Around Him, a respected religious leader at Pine Ridge, who attributes his recovery from alcoholism to his embrace of Lakota spiritual disciplines. "If I want to pray, I've got to be careful because I might trespass on somebody's land. Somebody tells you, 'You just take your sacred lodge and get the hell off here.' Someone is always around you."

Just as politics and religion have now fused together in the Black Hills claim, so any permanent solution that would satisfy the Sioux is inseparable from the problem of tribal sovereignty. A reasonable compromise might involve turning over limited tracts of the Custer National Forest and other federal land in the Hills to the Sioux tribes, to be managed as religious enclaves, where Indians would be able to carry out ceremonies and vision quests undisturbed. But questions abound: Who exactly would be permitted to enter these enclaves? Would admittance be based on race? Would Anglo practitioners of Indian rites, or Christian Indians, or members of other tribes be excluded? Despite disclaimers by tribal officials, once sovereign tribal authority is granted, there is little to stop tribes from simply exploiting the land for their own commercial gain. Moreover, surrender to tribal demands would instantly transform sacredness into a property right that might well inspire Americans of all sorts—New Age cultists, radical environmentalists, or anyone at all—to discover transformational spiritual power in land over which they would like to exert control.

Polemically, at least, the debate over the Mount Graham observatory came to a head in a public assembly at the University of Arizona in April 1992. Roger Angel, one of the most highly regarded astronomers in the United States, tried to explain to the mostly hostile audience that the observatory would be "at the cutting edge of astronomy." Franklin Stanley, Sr., the former Mormon bishop, retorted, "If you put that telescope on Mount Graham, it will be like cutting an arm and a leg off the Apache. Why don't you just exterminate all of us and get it over with?" Charles Babbit, president of the Maricopa Audubon Society, accused the university of behaving like a land developer. "If you are aggressive enough, if you are well-financed enough and have enough political connections, you can get your project done, environmental laws of this country notwithstanding." Students read aloud from the teachings of Buddha and hurled catcalls at the bewildered astronomers.

Then, to everyone's astonishment, a San Carlos woman by the name of Karen Long rose and declared, "To say that our livelihood depends on Mount Graham and to say that any permanent modification of the mountain might jeopardize our prayers, songs, and ceremonies is an outright lie." Norma Jean Kinney, the granddaughter of the most important twentieth-century Apache religious figure, declared that he had never mentioned Mount Graham as a holy place. A former tribal chairman, Buck Kitcheyan, said, "I can safely say that there is absolutely no religious or sacred significance to Mount Graham."

Among the small group of Apaches who had driven down from

San Carlos to voice support for the observatory, there was a soft-spoken, thirtyish man with shoulder-length hair by the name of William Belvado. Barely a decade earlier, Belvado's life seemed likely to follow the same futile trajectory as that of many young Apaches. He had dropped out of school at the age of nine. Later, at home on the reservation, he recalls, "Getting drunk, getting high was my everyday life." He credits his present sobriety to the determination of his wife, Vera, most of whose immediate family had died from cirrhosis of the liver.

Although twentieth-century medicine has tempered the once-fatal malarial atmosphere of San Carlos, it is still a hard, poor land of scrawny cottonwoods, infrequent rain, and gravel-laden winds, which sometimes sweep the dusty plain, denuding it of every vestige of vegetation. Efforts to instigate farming long ago came to naught. However, the land has never failed to yield a rich harvest of rodents, scorpions, and other vermin. Six years ago, the Belvados pooled their savings and borrowed money to start an extermination company. It was only the second privately owned business to be established on the San Carlos reservation, after a general store.

The Belvados' white brick ranch house, one of several in a small suburban loop down the road from the tribal baseball diamond, would be unremarkable in any middle-class American community; but here, like the Chevy Brahma in the driveway, it is a symbol of rare success. Belvado's muscular frame, hip hairstyle, purple T-shirt, and sweatpants suggest a style of the streets, but they belie a serious and self-effacing nature. "There's a feeling here, on the part of the tribe, that an Indian can't do as good a job as the white man from Globe," he is saying with resentment, which his soft voice tries but fails to conceal, at the disdain of many Apaches for those who, like himself, have struck out on their own. "People here just sit at home. They are never taught how to go out and make a living."

Belvado considers Ola Davis to be little more than a tourist, who was rarely seen on the reservation until she began asking tribal politicians to base policy on her dreams. "Some of these people are still trapped in the 1960s, where they think all white people are out to get them from around every corner. But not all of us believe in that 'Oh, us poor Indians, no one treats us fair' mentality. It really bothers us, these people going around making those claims that Mount Graham is sacred." It is possible, even probable, Belvado allows, that some Apaches around Bylas have very strong feelings for the mountain. "They say the Crown Dancers come from Mount Graham. Well, we believe the Crown Dancers come from another area, from the Superstition Mountains. We've all got different ways of treating the land. We're not all the same."

The road to Norma Jean Kinney's goes through the town of San Carlos, which preserves a vestige of its military past in the functional grid of its streets, its glaring absence of commerce, and the stolid old fieldstone agency buildings, which have now been taken over by the tribal government. The road also passes flimsy plywood shacks and gutted automobiles where some of the most impoverished Apaches live. "Some of them are alcoholics, but others are just ordinary people," Belvado is saying, pointing with his chin out the window of the Brahma. "People with political connections get their homes renovated by the tribe every year, while other people who are in need can't even get a floor put in. When Washington demands an accounting of where all the housing funds went to, the tribe says, 'That's tribal sovereignty—it's none of your business.' " To the south, shaggy clouds cling to distant peaks, promising rain.

Kinney, a large, amiable woman, lives in a beige ranch house near Noline's Country Store. Her grandfather Silas John founded what Apaches call the Holy Ground religion, which blended old tribal customs such as snake handling, curing rites, and the conjuring of rain with some aspects of Catholic ritual and evangelical preachments against drinking, gambling, and stealing. John's numerous followers attributed to him the supernatural powers of Monster Slayer, the son of the sun in old Apache mythology, to whom they also referred, to the chagrin of Christian missionaries, as the Son of God.

"I've lived here all my life and I've never heard anyone say that Mount Graham was sacred, until Franklin Stanley began saying it two or three years ago," Kinney says with a mixture of annoyance and perplexity. "We're still trying to figure out exactly what he believes. What he says, it may be true for him, but he doesn't speak for anyone else."

"One mountain just isn't that important," says Belvado. "The observatory isn't going to destroy our culture. We know it will bring lots of tourists to the area, but that will be good for the tribe. We have maybe 80 percent unemployment, and it will mean jobs. We shouldn't reject everything—we should try to accept what is going to benefit us as a whole people. We want our kids to learn from the stars. When Indians attack the university, it's like saying that education itself is not an Indian value, that it's un-Indian to learn. We should be working on education, the economy, programs for the elderly. Instead, the tribal council spends all its time going on about something that's not taking us anywhere."

That Ola Davis and her supporters have succeeded in retarding one of the most important scientific projects in North America may owe less to her fierce single-mindedness than to the power of myth to sway the hearts of Americans who continue to see relations between Indians and whites as an unending morality play of predators and victims, of evil and innocence despoiled. Without the aid of well-meaning whites, it is doubtful that her voice would have been heard beyond Tucson and San Carlos. In a typical attack on the Mount Graham observatory and the presumed abuse of other sites, the *Denver Post* editorialized, "At stake is the very survival of American Indian cultures. If these sacred sites are destroyed, then the rituals unique to those places no longer will be performed and many tribes simply may cease to exist as distinct peoples." Such logic implies that only Native Americans who profess to live like pre-Columbians are true Indians and that others must therefore fall short. It leaves scant room for William Belvado, Silas John, or Nick Black Elk (before John Neihardt's bowdlerizing), or indeed for entire peoples like the Cherokees, who in their distinct ways seized the unexpected opportunities presented by life in the modern, more complicated world.

"When I hear non-Indians going on about how this is going to destroy our culture," says Belvado, "I think, what are they talking about? If they really want to help, let them bring $10 million onto the reservation to build youth centers and schools and to fence in our real sacred sites and make them worthy. There are plenty of holy places on our own land that have been looted because no one bothered to protect them. And if these environmentalists are so concerned about us, why not help us with our water supply, our garbage dumps, and sewerage? Why don't they provide funding for these things, instead of spending money to send people to Europe who don't represent us?"

The rain, which has been hanging fire over the mountains, finally breaks loose. "It seems like those environmentalists just have some idea of their own about what Indians are supposed to be," says

Kinney, ignoring the hard droplets that come pelting down now in violent, spasmodic bursts. "I don't know what it's got to do with us."

Nothing clouds the almost perpetually sunny view from the top of Mount Graham. In the crystalline light of an early autumn morning, Mexican workmen are welding iron sheets for the Vatican telescope, under the direction of a diminutive Englishman from Dorsetshire by the name of Christopher Corbelly. A Jesuit by vocation and an astronomer and engineer by training, Corbelly is responsible for seeing the telescope's construction carried through to completion. Although it is hard to put a finger on it, there is something about him, a certain air of remoteness, perhaps born from years of similar introspection, or from professional preoccupation with the sacred, that recalls Gerald Clifford.

"For us," Corbelly says, "this project is concerned with God's action in the world. We understand the Creator by understanding what he created. Although the word of God is clear in the Bible, it is filled out by understanding the process of the universe. By putting astronomy before us like a filter, as it were, we see an enhancement of God's action in the world."

7

"A Scene Most Resembling Hell"

INSIDE THE SWEAT LODGE, the men are mere shadows in the darkness, more felt than seen, shut off completely from the icy light of a New Mexican winter's afternoon. They sit cross-legged and bent forward toward the rocks' red glow. "It's pretty hard to learn to help ourselves, but this is how we learn," Robbie Daniels is saying. "We're going to bless ourselves in the four directions, to where we'll be in balance, so we'll have some possession of ourself. There are Holy People in here. They see us, and hear us, and come down and touch our mind. If you purify yourself, they're going to be able to help you. When the flap is opened they return to the heavens, carrying our prayers." To the rocks, to the roiling steam, to the air dense with the mingled aromas of cedarwood and sage, and to the spirits who reside in them, Daniels says, "Your grandchildren are going to try to help themselves now."

He takes a pinch of sweetgrass from a Ziploc bag and sprinkles it on the rocks. Then he wraps a wad of tobacco in a piece of cornstalk. He blows smoke into his palm and brushes it over his scalp, his chest, his thighs. "Maybe we done something wrong. Maybe we're carrying some kind of pain today." Daniels's flat drawl is tentative and deferential, addressing itself to the spirits that inhabit the darkness as much as to Burt, Jack, and Leslie. "This smoke is a medicine, a way to take a load off ourselves." One man after another takes the tobacco and follows Daniels's example. Then, dipping a branch of sage into a plastic bucket, Daniels flicks water onto the stones. A moment later, a surf of heat rolls suffocatingly through the sweat lodge. As he shifts into Navajo and begins to sing, Daniels's cowboy inflections become plaintive, pleading for a subtler kind of relief.

Each man has brought his own private agony into the sweat lodge. Leslie has been out of jail five days. "I'm suffering," he says fragilely. "I want to be whole again. I know I've got a lot to learn." Jack is drawn back in defensive silence, imagining himself protected, perhaps, by the tattooed serpents that swarm, invisibly now, in the dark, across his huge torso. He says noncommittally, "I got a little sobriety now. I hope I can keep it." Burt, their counselor at the treatment center down the hill, is also a veteran of Gallup's bars and jails, and he prays with the urgency of a man who feels that he may hold the weight of the others' sobriety, if not their lives, on his own shoulders. All three have lived, and have come close to dying, on the streets of the city that lies but a short walk across the desert and whose bars remain every day's alluring alternative to the prayers and heat.

Robbie Daniels is the director for substance abuse at the Indian Health Service hospital in Gallup, and every Sunday he leads the "sweat," as he says, on this scrubby hillside east of town. He is also a refugee from Gallup's mean streets and carries into the spirit-filled darkness his own ineradicable memories of the years when home was a discarded mattress next to the Shop 'N Save, and dinner was something filched from garbage cans, and when his life's highest goal was a bottle of Sweet Georgia Red or Kachina tokay, or a gallon jug of mixed hair spray and water.

New Mexicans who don't like Gallup call it "drunk city." It grew up (stretched out, really) first along the tracks of the Santa Fe Railroad and then along Route 66, which bisect Gallup from east to west. In past times, Gallup prospered from the mining of coal and uranium and from the movie companies that filmed countless Westerns against the spectacular desert landscapes nearby. It is still a center of the Southwestern turquoise trade. More than anything else, however, it is alcohol that puts Gallup on the map. A bottle sold over the counter in Gallup increases four times in value by the time it reaches the Navajo reservation, a short drive to the north, in the back of a bootlegger's truck. There, on the most populous Indian reservation in the United States, where prohibition remains in force, public intoxication carries a $50 fine and possession of alcohol can bring a sentence of up to six months in jail. Gallup has a permanent population of 22,000. On weekends, that number swells several times over with Navajos, and in lesser numbers with Zunis, who have come to shop, to take in films, and, with an often deadly determination, to drink.

In McKinley County, which includes Gallup, the rate of death from alcoholism is six times the national average. For years, the county has led the nation in alcohol-related motor-vehicle deaths. In 1990, according to Gallup police chief Frank Gonzalez, Gallup also endured 1 murder, 15 rapes, 26 robberies, 365 burglaries, 115 car thefts, and 1,350 assaults due to alcohol. In another recent year, Gonzalez's department made 33,000 arrests for drunkenness, more than the entire state of Illinois. It is no secret that levels of consumption that spell disaster for Indians provide Gallup with a thriving economy. "If it wasn't for them coming in, this city wouldn't be as well off as it is," says Gonzalez. "You've got to take the bad with the good. That's the way it is."

Americans who imagine Indian life to be an unrelieved social disaster might see a mythic dimension in Officer Nick Begay's workaday world. Gallup's nighttime streets present a stunning panorama of failure and chaos that suggests a world beyond hope of redemption, the ultimate doomsday rendering of Indian fate in modern America. The female voice that crackles over the radio in Begay's prowl car is neutral and precise. "I've got a Five-Five, Code Three behind the Corner Pocket. He's still breathing." Begay guns the Chevy Caprice past pawnshops and warehouses, cramped stucco cottages, and flophouse motels. It is November and there is an icy edge to the air. If it freezes, drunks passed out in the tamarack along the Rio Puerco will die. Fifty or more of them freeze to death every winter. The streetcorner bottle gangs call them Popsicles.

Begay is a Navajo. He grew up on the reservation and served with the tribal police force before joining the Gallup police, whose salaries are significantly higher. Despite his bulk and height, which is well over six feet, Begay fairly radiates efficiency and self-control. Nearly everything he does on the job involves alcoholism and its aftermath, but he soon makes it clear that he dislikes talking about

Indians and alcohol, that he dislikes the fact that nearly every drunk of the night will be Navajo, and that he does not much enjoy questions about it. "I don't think nothing can be done about it," he says, businesslike and abrupt. "To stop it, you'd have to shut down every bar in town."

The Corner Pocket is a pool hall popular with Indians. The interior is dim and feral, packed with truculent young Navajos who have had too much to drink. In a vacant lot alongside the building, the Code Three is crumpled up in a mess of mud and broken bottles. Blood is pouring from his eyes and nose. There is a large bloody rock next to his head.

"Hey! Talk to me!" Begay shouts into the bloody, filthy ear. "Hey! What happened to you? Open your eyes!"

He fishes in the man's pockets, finally comes up with a scrap of paper with a name: "Alvin."

"What happened to you, Alvin?"

Amazingly, the crushed face stirs. "I got jumped."

"How old are you?"

"Twenty-three."

"Where are you from, Alvin?"

"I don't know."

Dark figures wearing billed caps and denims rise unsteadily from the scrubby grass and linger in the shadows, swapping comments in slurred voices. The smell of alcohol and sour breath is everywhere. A fat young man with smashed teeth and an enormous, pendulous belly keeps asking, monotonously, "Is he dead, or what?" The destroyed face, the imminence of death—they are the night's entertainment.

Begay radios for an ambulance. By the time it arrives, Alvin has gone silent again, this time perhaps for good.

Later, Begay is driving east on Route 66. A crimson Mustang is angled crazily across the sidewalk, jammed into a utility pole just past the Super 8 Motel. The young Navajo woman at the wheel is laughing hilariously, asking if she is in Window Rock yet, twenty-five miles away.

"I was driving and they went in front of me," she says without much conviction, as if it were an explanation.

Accidents are so common in Gallup that passing cars don't even bother to slow. In 1990, Begay and his colleagues investigated 1,800 accidents, an average of almost five each night, nearly all of them involving alcohol. In typical years, they also make between 800 and 1,000 arrests for drunken driving.

Getting out of the patrol car and leaning into the Mustang, Begay informs the woman that she is going to be taken into custody. Meanwhile, another young Navajo named Jimmy Yazzie is careening eastward in a white Pontiac Grand Prix. He must see the patrol car parked directly in front of him, with its dome light flashing. Nevertheless, traveling at perhaps fifty miles an hour, Yazzie slams into Begay's Chevy in a cloud of steam and gushing oil smoke, jolting it forward, barely missing Begay.

Though he has escaped death, or at least serious injury, by only a few feet, Begay remains impassive as he learns that Yazzie has no driver's license, and indeed has never had one, and then finds and confiscates the half-empty quart of Budweiser hidden on Yazzie's seat. Yazzie will now join the driver of the Mustang and the hundred or so other Navajos who will be picked up in the course of the night in what used to be known as the drunk tank but is now more euphemistically called "protective custody," or "pc."

Within the hour, Begay has exchanged the damaged Chevy for a fresh car. The reports of disintegrating lives continue to crackle over the radio throughout the night. Someone is throwing beer bottles at the Red Rock Inn. A boy stoned on drugs has been caught stealing license plates in the parking lot at the Cactus Motel. Two bodies slumped against the wall of Car Quest Auto Parts have been found to be merely drunk and have been taken into protective custody. Several underage drinkers have been arrested. A woman has been found in a drainage ditch, stabbed in the chest.

Gallup reformers are talking about building a "crisis center" where drunks would detoxify for three days as a more humane alternative to spending a night in the drunk tank at the jail. Drunkenness would be decriminalized, treated more like an illness. Begay says, "They're trying to 'rehabilitate' them, I guess, but I don't know if that can be done." The jail's "pc" unit would be closed. The center would have one hundred beds. "We pick up 150 on weekend nights," Begay is saying ruminatively. "What are we supposed to do with the other fifty? Just leave them on the street, I guess."

At 1:20 A.M. there is a disturbance at the Lariat Motel, a flophouse on Route 66. "A family dispute," the dispatcher's bland voice announces.

A toddler dressed only in underpants is wandering on the wet pavement in the parking lot in front of the motel, coughing uncontrollably. The temperature is forty-five degrees and dropping. A teenage girl in jeans is standing unsteadily in the parking lot, swearing at a young man named Raymond, who is standing in the doorway of room 30.

Raymond, who is haphazardly dressed in sweatpants and a T-shirt, looks frightened and confused. He cannot be more than twenty years old. The child wandering in the parking lot is his son. So is a second, wary boy behind him in the room.

Inside, there are plastic bags of dirty laundry, a few pieces of flimsy furniture, broken toys in a plastic box. On a table, there are blocks of wood and some half-carved kachinas. Another young woman is sitting cross-legged on an unmade bed. A tipsy man in a baseball cap is swaying blearily in the corner.

"She left the kids with no warning," Raymond says defensively. "She left!"

The woman in jeans shrieks, "Don't lie, Raymond!"

Begay tells her to shut up.

From Raymond, Begay elicits a murky tale. The children's mother has gone "partying," the universal euphemism in Indian country for a serious spree. A sister-in-law, the woman in the parking lot apparently, was supposed to pick up the children but showed up drunk. Raymond, meanwhile, has shacked up in the motel with a girlfriend. No one even attempts to explain the drunk in the baseball cap.

Both children are sneezing uncontrollably. They have pneumonia, Raymond explains matter-of-factly.

"How tall are you?" Begay asks the sister-in-law, testing for sobriety.

"I dunno."

"How much do you weigh?"

"I dunno."

"Where do you work?"

"I don't work."

"How come your eyes are bloodshot?"

"I dunno."

"She always charges me with beating them up," Raymond is whining. "They're all against me."

"Don't listen to him," the woman shrieks. "He's a minor. He's a drunk."

"Shut up!" shouts Begay.

Turning to the sister-in-law, Begay says, "You're obviously intoxicated. I can't give the children to you."

"She don't take care of these kids for me," Raymond says vaguely. It's unclear whether he is talking about the wife, or the sister-in-law, or possibly the woman on the bed. "She don't even feed them in a day. I even have to get up sometimes and make a bottle for them."

"I don't smell liquor on your breath," Begay says to Raymond with palpable disgust. "I got to give the children to you."

Begay looks from father to sister-in-law, to the children, to the drunk in the corner, to the blowsy woman on the bed. It is obvious that he can barely contain himself. His craggy face is swollen with rage. He looks ready to scream.

Illness, as Susan Sontag has written, is not a metaphor: "The most truthful way of regarding illness—and the healthiest way of being ill—is one most purified of, most resistent to, metaphoric thinking." Like cancer and tuberculosis (and, increasingly, AIDS), alcoholism has long sustained a rich and obfuscating mythology that incorporates any number of puritanical variants on "the rake's progress" as well as equally persistent and romantic correlations between alcohol and art. Within its pantheon of myths and metaphors, none has been more enduring than the crude caricature of the "drunken Indian." Although perhaps less openly acknowledged than it once was in this era of politically correct skittishness, it is an image of the Indian that is as deeply entrenched in the popular psyche as that of the Noble Red Man and encapsulates within it a widespread perception of modern Native Americans as fundamentally pathetic and helpless figures, defeated by a white man's world with which they cannot be expected to cope. That said, it is impossible to evade the fact that even in the midst of vigorous political and cultural revival the grim reality of native alcoholism remains a common denominator of poverty, ill-health, and social pathology, continuing to wreak a degree of human devastation upon Indian communities that can only be compared to the ravages of smallpox in centuries past.

In 1855, the Commissioner of Indian Affairs, George Manypenny, lamented,

> The appetite of the Indian for ardent spirits seems to be entirely uncontrollable, and at all periods of our intercourse with him the evil effects and injurious consequences arising from the indulgence of the habit are unmistakably seen. It has been the greatest barrier to his improvement in the past, and will continue to be in the future, if some means cannot be adopted to inhibit its use.

Almost a century and a half later, alcoholism still presents a landscape of epidemic, seemingly intractable addiction that ravages the personal health of Indians, undermines the stability of entire communities, and frustrates tribal development. In 1977, the American Indian Policy Review Commission declared alcohol abuse to be "the most severe and widespread health problem among Indians today." Eight years later, a comprehensive study by the Indian Health Service reported that "after a century and a half of prohibition, few Indians have used alcohol in any context except that of rapid consumption, or 'drinking to get drunk.' Social drinking practices may eventually become a possibility for many Indians, but few have used alcohol in this manner up to the present."

Rates of alcoholism are not easy to measure in a field where there is little consensus on either methods of study or the true nature of alcoholism itself. According to the National Council on Alcoholism and Drug Dependence, 67 percent of the general American adult population drinks, while about 9 percent may be considered alcoholic. Estimates of the extent of alcoholism among Indian tribes vary widely. For example, a study by the Oklahoma Department of Mental Health found that the rates of alcohol-related deaths on eleven of the state's tribes ranged from a low of 6 per 100,000 for the Cherokees to a high of 294 per 100,000 for the Cheyenne-Arapahos. Alcoholism counselors who work mainly with Indians commonly suppose that alcoholics may make up anywhere from 50 percent to 80 percent of reservation populations. Less subjectively, a comparative study reported in the *Journal of Social Biology* estimated that among the Utes 80 percent drank and 26 percent were "heavy drinkers," in contrast to 84 percent and 42 percent respectively for the Ojibwas. A report by the Omaha Tribe acknowledged that as much as 85 percent of its members may be actively alcoholic. Research done at the United States Public Health Service Hospital in Phoenix put the rate of "heavy drinking" among members of Southwestern tribes generally at 52.5 percent for men and

24.4 percent for women; the lowest figure for a particular tribe, the Hopis, was still a substantial 21 percent. A survey carried out by four small tribes in the State of Washington reported that about one-third of males "usually consumed enough to pass out when they drank," but inexplicably classified only 8 percent as "chronic drinkers."

Probably the most comprehensive analysis of drinking in a single tribe was carried out by James O. Whittaker of Pennsylvania State University, who in 1960 and again in 1980 studied the Standing Rock Sioux reservation, which borders Cheyenne River on the north and extends into North Dakota. In 1980, he found that 58 percent of the population over the age of twelve drank alcohol, including about one-third who drank heavily and on a regular basis. However, significantly larger numbers reported suffering classic symptoms of alcoholism: 62 percent of drinkers experienced blackouts, 70 percent an inability to stop drinking once they started, and 87 percent changing drinking patterns to control their drinking.

The cumulative effect of alcoholism on Indians is staggering. According to the Indian Health Service, Indians are three and a half times more likely than other Americans to die from cirrhosis of the liver, a benchmark of addiction. They are also four times more likely to die from accidents, and three times more likely to die from homicide and suicide, in all of which alcohol is usually present. Between 5 percent and 25 percent of Indian babies may be born mentally and physically damaged by fetal alcohol syndrome, compared to less than one-fifth of 1 percent in the general population. Alcohol is also at least a contributing factor in many, perhaps most, Indian deaths from pneumonia, heart disease, cerebrovascular disease, diabetes, and cancer, and it ultimately accounts for perhaps as much as 70 percent of all the treatment provided by the Indian Health Service's hospitals and clinics. Indians are twelve times more likely than other Americans to be arrested for alcohol-related offenses, and most Indians who are in prison are there because of a crime committed under the influence of alcohol. Alcohol also takes an immeasurable toll in chronic disability, lost earning capacity, unemployment, emotional pain, family disruption, and child abuse; one treatment program that works with Indian children has estimated that as many as 95 percent of girls and 33 percent of boys raised in alcoholic homes may have been sexually molested by the age of nine.

At least some Indian communities have begun to define alcoholism forthrightly as one of the most critical hurdles to the fulfillment of their political and cultural aspirations. No tribe has addressed it more vigorously than the Cheyenne River Sioux Tribe. In 1987, the tribal council proclaimed a "war" on alcoholism and promised, rather overoptimistically, to eliminate it from the reservation by the year 2000. In 1991, Gregg Bourland's newly elected tribal administration declared that "the disease of alcoholism now constitutes an epidemic on the reservation" and acknowledged alcoholism to be the tribe's foremost health, socioeconomic, and legal problem. An official manifesto proclaimed that "the effects of this disease have been devastating, widespread and pervasive and have very nearly destroyed the basic structure of the family as a viable unit of tribal society," and that "it has become evident with the passage of time and futility of effort that no meaningful, lasting progress can ever be realized by the Tribe until this disease is brought under some degree of control."

In his cluttered office at the tribal alcoholism treatment center in Eagle Butte, Greg Ducheneaux, its director, is talking about the recent dead. There was Jack Red Bear, a solitary drinker who hanged himself from a bridge on Bear Creek Road, leaving behind five small daughters. "A damn nice guy. He just kind of gave up on life." There was Boston Garreau, who once owned a hundred head of cattle and then drank them away, along with his land, and his family, and eventually his pickup, and wound up panhandling on the street until he died from cirrhosis. "Booze just got to him." And there was Barbara Jewett, who lived alone in the woods behind the high school and died on a playground bench at the age of twenty-five. "She just overdrank. You always knew she was going to die like that."

Ducheneaux has compiled a list of everyone who has died on the reservation from the effects of alcoholism since the late 1950s. "There are between eighteen and thirty every year. Their average age is thirty-four." Alongside the names there are the dates and causes of death. It is a depressing litany: "homicide/gunshot to head" . . . "exposure" . . . "cirrhosis" . . . "knife wound" . . . "suicide" . . . "suicide" . . . "dysentery" . . . "car accident" . . . "drowning/suffocation" . . . "stab wound" . . . "cirrhosis." There are entire families on the list, three or four generations spanning the decades, one after another dying young and cruelly.

Ducheneaux estimates that since the federal government legalized the sale of alcohol to Indians in 1953, drinking has caused the deaths of between five hundred and six hundred members of the tribe, in a population that today numbers just under six thousand. "We accept these deaths as normal. Suffering is normal. Violent death is normal. They just shrug it off. It's our way of life."

Officially, the tribe affirms that more than half of its members are active alcoholics, roughly average for much of Indian Country. Ducheneaux believes the number is actually much higher. "It's very difficult to get accurate figures. There's a lot of privacy, a lot of denial, a lot of resistance, not only from individuals but from the tribal government." Alcohol, he says, affects everything—the schools, churches, businesses, the functions of government. "We even vote dysfunctionally: we grab for this, grab for that, and come up with nothing. Politicians know that if they try to change things too much, they'll be thrown out of office."

Ducheneaux's job and the effects of his own drinking years have left his pale, finely boned face scored with anxiety; he radiates impatience, sitting still for only minutes at a time, then bounding up, prowling the office for charts, news clips, statistics. "Ninety-five percent of our law-and-order problems are related to alcohol or drug addiction. Eighty-five or 90 percent of court cases are the result of alcoholism. Poor folks sell whatever they have to buy liquor. The children of elderly tribal members often extort money to buy alcohol, or steal their commodities and sell them for alcohol. Alcohol abuse exacerbates unemployment because it results in tardiness, absenteeism, and poor work. Most of the divorce cases are connected to alcoholism. Most of the adoptions are kids from alcoholic homes. Children go to bed at night seeing shouting and fighting, and drinking, and sex going on. Then they go to school and try to absorb education, but they can't because of what they saw last night at home."

Ducheneaux was born in 1944 into one of the reservation's great mixed-blood clans, the descendants of French fur traders who settled and intermarried; his father and an older brother both served as tribal chairman, while another brother was for many years the chief aide to the chairman of the Senate Subcommittee on Indian Affairs. " 'Breeds,' " he says, favoring the old, coarse shorthand for "half-breed," "had the Indian whipped out of them. We were raised to be whites. We'd go to the movies as kids and we'd sit there and root for the white folks to be saved from the damn dirty Indians."

His family connections ensured that Ducheneaux could usually find a job somewhere in the tribal administration. In the meantime, he went through three marriages, lost six children as a result of divorces, and lived a life that he now describes ironically as one long party. "Drinking, fighting, and women was my sole concern." The party ended in 1986, when he came out of a blackout to discover that he had forced a girl into his car, tried to rape her on the road, and then beat her senseless when he failed. Charges of kidnapping and attempted rape were ultimately plea-bargained down to assault. "I was sent to the pen for doing something I had no memory of. It woke me up. I made up my mind I had to quit." When he left jail, sober, Ducheneaux was determined that someday he would run the tribe's alcoholism program.

Ducheneaux is a crusader in a culture where crusades have usually come from outside, from whites, and have spelled trouble. "We need some kind of firm action. Some people say, give everybody a job and everything will be okay. The fact is, give them jobs without getting them sober and it will still be chaos. People will only become interested in the future when the disease is arrested. Right now life has no meaning for them. Their overriding concern is the disease and its constant demand to be fed."

The clinic's eight counselors treat about four hundred clients, many of them remanded by the tribal courts. The results are discouraging. Nearly nine out of ten relapse into active drinking. "They're just not strong enough to stay sober on their own, and we're sending them back into a dysfunctional community. If we had only ten or twenty alcoholics here, then, fine, we could just wait for them to hit bottom. But when the whole people is alcoholic, you've got to take strong measures. We've got to get to the whole family. We need to commit them to enforced treatment where you hope something might sink in."

In spite of its ravages, alcoholism still remains, to most Indians, an ambiguous phenomenon. "Some people think Indians have a genetic predisposition to alcoholism," Gregg Bourland says, venturing a possibility that inspires uneasiness in most Indian leaders. "I guess that's possible. But we also have 60 percent or 70 percent unemployment on the reservation and no relief in sight. A poor economy leads to alcoholism, and alcoholism leads to a poor economy. It's self-esteem, too. Lakota men used to be warriors and providers. Once that was stripped away from them and they were educated to accept annuities and commodities from the government, alcoholism became prevalent." Pausing for a while with characteristic thoughtfulness, he pursues another avenue of possibility. "Then, too, alcohol was only recently introduced into Indian culture. We had nothing in our culture like that, that affected us that way. There was always a mystique about it."

Definitions of alcoholism are protean and unsatisfying. In *The Natural History of Alcohol,* the most comprehensive study to date on the nature of alcoholism, Dr. George E. Vaillant asserts that "alcoholism becomes a disease when loss of voluntary control over alcohol consumption becomes a necessary and sufficient cause for much of an individual's social, psychological, and physical morbidity." The National Council on Alcoholism and Drug Dependence defines it as "a chronic and progressive disease characterized by a loss of control over the use of alcohol, with subsequent social, legal, psychological and physical consequences." Alcoholics Anonymous, which has achieved considerable success in arresting alcoholism among non-Indians, eschews complex definitions, describing alcoholism simply as a mental, physical, and spiritual illness. Dr. Donald W. Goodwin, the chairman of the Department of Psychiatry at the University of Kansas Medical Center, one of the nation's leading authorities on alcoholism, has tersely written: "A tree is known by its fruits; alcoholism by its problems. An alcoholic is a person who drinks, has problems from drinking, but goes on drinking. This may be the best definition of alcoholism that exists."

Beginning in the late 1970s, Goodwin undertook a six-year study that he hoped would determine conclusively whether alcoholism was shaped by biology or by the effects of environment and upbringing. He reckoned that he could do so by tracing the fate of adoptees. He set himself two goals: first, to determine whether the sons of alcoholics were more likely to have problems with alcohol even when they were raised apart from their biological parents, and, second, to find out whether sons raised by their own alcoholic parents were more likely to develop alcoholism than were their brothers who were raised by nonalcoholic foster parents. Goodwin carried out his study in Denmark, where adoption records were unusually detailed and more open to scholarly research than in the United States. From a pool of five thousand cases, he selected men with at least one biological parent who had been hospitalized for alcoholism and from whom they had been separated in early infancy. As a control, he selected another group of adoptees, none of whom had a biological parent who had been treated for alcoholism.

Goodwin found that the sons of alcoholics were four times more likely to become alcoholics themselves than were the children of nonalcoholics, even if they were never exposed to their alcoholic parent after birth. Almost without exception, the alcoholic group had more drinking problems than the controls, including blackouts, hallucinations, loss of control, morning drinking, seizures, and hospitalizations for alcoholism. They also registered far more marital trouble, job problems, encounters with the police, and arrests for drunken driving. Meanwhile, Goodwin found that sons who had been raised at home with their alcoholic biological parents were no more likely to become alcoholic than those who had been separated from them at birth. In a related study that bolstered his findings, Goodwin observed that the children of nonalcoholics showed low rates of alcoholism even when they were reared by alcoholic foster parents. Clearly, he reasoned, exposure to the alcoholic parent did nothing to increase the chances of acquiring the disease.

Goodwin's research was the first convincing evidence that alcoholism might, at least in part, be a hereditary illness. "It is interesting how little environment appeared to contribute to the development of alcoholism among the sons of alcoholics in this sample," Goodwin wrote. "Our findings tend to contradict the oft-repeated assertion that alcoholism results from the interaction of multiple causes—social, psychological, biological." He added, "The 'father's sins' may be visited on the sons even in the father's absence." In essence, Goodwin's conclusions strongly argued that most alcoholics did not drink because they were emotionally ill or socially disadvantaged, but because they were alcoholics.

More recent biochemical research also suggests that hereditary factors predispose many individuals to alcoholism. In a series of ongoing experiments, Dr. Marc A. Schukit, a psychiatrist at the University of California School of Medicine in San Diego, found that the college-age sons of alcoholics consistently showed less consciousness of intoxication, less initial change in motor performance, and less alteration in hormones that are known to be altered by alcohol than did the sons of nonalcoholics, and that they were much more likely to become alcoholics themselves later on. Other studies undertaken in the 1980s found that identical twins, who have the same genetic makeup as their siblings, were significantly more likely to experience similar histories of alcoholism than were fraternal twins, who share only half as much of each other's genetic material.

More rarefied studies have further implied that there may be genetic structural differences in the enzymes that control the metabolism of alcohol in various ethnic groups. But no study has yet identified specific genetic "markers" that would prove beyond a doubt that alcoholism is wholly rooted in the genes. The closest that anyone has come was in 1990, when Kenneth Blum, a pharmacologist at the University of Texas at San Antonio, and Ernest Noble, an alcoholism researcher at the University of California, Los Angeles, were examining a gene that manufactures a protein on the surface of nerve cells. Because it attaches itself to a chemical called dopamine that carries electrical impulses between nerve cells, the protein is termed a dopamine receptor. Earlier research had suggested that alcoholism might be caused by an inability of certain nerve cells to receive adequate amounts of dopamine. Blum and Noble found that one of the several possible couplings of the protein and the receptor, which they termed the A1 version, occurred far more frequently in the brain cells of deceased alcoholics than in others. They speculated that the A1 version was, in effect, a defective coupling and required the artificial stimulation of alcohol or drugs in order to give a person a normal reaction of pleasure.

Most Indian advocates reject even the suggestion that biological factors play an important role in alcoholism or that Indians suffer disproportionately from an illness that in some quarters is still regarded as a moral failing. In 1991, Dr. Terrance Sloan of the Aberdeen, South Dakota, area office of the Indian Health Service reassured a Sioux audience, "The Lakota are not a diseased people, nor is alcoholism a genetic disease." Others, who fear the labeling of Indians as metabolic cripples, argue that the very notion of Indian alcoholism is if not racist, then at best a fiction in the eye of the biased beholder. "There is nothing in Native Americans that makes them live up to the 'drunken Indian' stereotype," Carol Lujan, a Ph.D. in sociology who heads the BIA's Office of Alcohol and Substance Abuse Prevention, asserted in tribal court during the Cheyenne River Sioux Tribe's campaign to tax white-owned bars. "They suffer instead from a drinking style that throws the dysfunctional effects of binge drinking into high relief and reinforces long-standing stereotypes." Specialists in Indian alcoholism point out, correctly, that there still is no absolute proof that Indians are physically affected by alcohol any differently from other people. Some suggest that drunkenness among Indians is something fundamentally different from alcoholism among non-Indians and, indeed, that it sometimes even embodies positive traits, a spirit of camaraderie rooted in tribal tradition or an assertion of "Indianness" in the face of a hostile white world. They tend, somewhat facilely, to see destructive drinking mainly as a learned habit or even a form of social protest. A 1989 report by researchers at the State University of New York at Buffalo, for instance, blamed Indian alcoholism largely on such things as "a history of discriminatory government policies," the "unclear legal and social status of Indians," and Native Americans' lack of awareness of their rights.

"Tribe after tribe learned not only to drink but how to drink from Europeans whose bad manners, determination to get drunk, and lack of restraint were notorious, and eventually this 'trapper style' of liquor consumption became incorporated into some Indian communities," Michael Dorris writes in his study of fetal alcohol syndrome, *The Broken Cord*. Drinking in "unacceptable" ways, he suggests, became one of the few possible forms of protest and ethnic self-expression open to Indians during generations of cultural repression. "It was a means of refusing colonization, of affirming group identity and of refusing compliance with intolerable laws. It was also a means of oblivion, a quest for an illusion of power, an escape from frustration and failure in an age when the customs, spiritual beliefs and social conventions honed over thousands of years had suddenly become useless or illegal."

Such theories, intentionally or not, shift responsibility for Indian drinking problems into the past and onto whites; they also suggest that otherwise intelligent and adaptive Indians were simply unwilling to change their behavior even when it became obvious that excessive drinking was wreaking havoc in their lives and communities. The effects of alcoholism were in fact manifest among Indians long before binge drinking became common among whites after the American Revolution and well before native cultures crumbled under the pressure of colonization, when tribes were still a political and military presence to be reckoned with. Dorris suggests that what he pointedly calls the "supposed phenomenon" of Indian alcoholism was merely "as good an excuse as any to impose restrictions and prohibitions . . . on people who were culturally different and, more to the point, in the way." In reality, it was most often Indians themselves who demanded that white Americans control their access to liquor.

There is an eerily contemporary ring to the words of the Delaware chief who, in 1698, struggled to explain his people's ambivalence toward alcohol to a group of New Jersey colonists. "We know it to be hurtful to us to drink it. We know it, but if people will sell it to us, we so love it that we cannot refuse it. But when we drink it, it makes us mad; we do not know what we are doing; we abuse one another; we throw one another in fire. Through drinking, seven score of our people have been killed."

Intoxicants were not wholly unknown to the pre-Columbian peoples of the Americas. The Tohono O'Odhams and Apaches of present-day Arizona drank corn beer on ceremonial occasions, while some tribes on the Atlantic coast may have made a kind of wine from fermented persimmons. European colonists usually introduced distilled spirits—rum in the English colonies, brandy in the French, and gin in the Dutch—to local Indians as a gift and as a toast during the formalities that preceded trading or negotiation. But Indian demand soon transformed it into a staple, and in many regions the mainstay, of frontier trade. At least at first, some tribes seem to have regarded drunkenness as a kind of hallucinatory possession that produced wisdom and insight. Tellingly, the Lakotas named alcohol *mni wakan,* which may be rendered two ways: as "magic water" or as "the water that makes men foolish."

But, from the start, there was clearly an irrational and catastrophic element to the way in which Indians were drawn to alcohol. Indians seemed compelled to drink to the point of total intoxication and beyond and to consume all the alcohol that was available at a single sitting. Entire villages were known to disintegrate in drunken brawls. Violence and promiscuity became epidemic. French missionaries reported that alcohol set the Hurons to fighting and killing each other, biting off ears and noses, firing guns, flashing knives, setting fire to their own lodges, violating women, killing their own domestic animals, occasionally stabbing their own wives and children and hurling them into roaring fires. At a bacchanalia that followed an otherwise placid intertribal council at Carlisle, Pennsylvania, in 1753, Benjamin Franklin was dismayed to find the same tribal emissaries with whom he had conferred only hours before now drunk; the sight of them "running after and beating one another with Firebrands, accompanied by their horrid Yellings, forms a scene the most resembling our Ideas of Hell that could well be imagined." In 1796, the agent to the Six Nations of the Iroquois reported matter-of-factly that "they have recd their payments and immediately expended it for liquor & in the course of a frollick have killed one or two."

Such descriptions might be dismissed as biased, except that Indian observers reported much the same thing. Handsome Lake, who was inspired by his own recovery from alcoholism to lead a spiritual revival among the Senecas, described the horrific aftermath of a trading expedition in which he had participated in 1798:

> Now that the party is home the men revel in strong drink and are very quarrelsome. Because of this the families become frightened and move away for safety. So from many places in the bushlands camp fires send up their smoke.
>
> Now the drunken men run yelling through the village and there is no one there except the drunken men. Now they are beastlike and run about without clothing and all have weapons to injure those whom they meet.
>
> Now there are no doors in the houses for they have all been kicked off. So, also, there are no fires in the village and have not been for many days.

White traders well knew that a drunk Indian was easier to exploit than a sober one, and many an Indian was tricked out of the fruits of his hunt when he was offered "a free dram" before bargaining began. At the turn of the nineteenth century, William Henry Harrison, the governor of Indiana Territory, and later president, reported that Indian trappers were commonly plied with liquor and then "made drunk and cheated of their peltries." A few years later, the sympathetic Henry Schoolcraft, who served as Indian agent at Sault Ste. Marie and who is widely regarded as a forerunner of modern anthropology, sadly observed, "Little does the spirit of commerce care how many Indians die inebriates, if it can be assured of beaver skins." Increasingly, the demand for alcohol and manufactures drove Indians to hunt not for food, but for hides and other commodities with which to barter. Weakened by alcohol, Indians more readily fell prey to smallpox, tuberculosis, influenza, and other illnesses. Hunters debilitated by alcohol had increasing difficulty providing for their families, making Indians steadily more dependent on whites for their subsistence.

More than a few treaties and land cessions were signed only after Indian participants had been made more pliable with drink. Secretary of War Lewis Cass remembered how an elderly chief of the Potawatomis, during negotiations at the Treaty of Chicago, in 1821, begged the commissioners to give his people alcohol, saying, "Father, we care not for the money, nor the land, nor the goods. We want the whiskey. Give us the whiskey." Indian leaders continually pleaded with Washington to use troops to prevent peddlers from coming to their villages. In 1822, James Madison finally ordered that the trading licenses of any merchants found to be carrying alcohol into Indian Country be canceled and all their goods confiscated. When this failed to stem the flow, Congress imposed the first prohibition law in United States history, declaring in 1832: "No ardent spirits shall be hereafter introduced, under any pretence, into the Indian country."

Unfortunately, this law, too, proved impossible to enforce on the frontier, where government manpower was already stretched thin, Indian demand remained unslaked, and natives mingled increasingly with white settlers as they colonized the West. Unlicensed traders operated with virtual impunity, introducing such words as "bootlegger," "whiskey-runner," and "hooch" into the national argot. The commandant of Fort Gibson, in what is now Oklahoma, complained that "the Indians are furnished with whiskey by almost every Steam-Boat of any description which passes up the Arkansas," while an estimated eight thousand gallons of illicit whiskey traveled up the Missouri each season, bound for the tribes of the northern Plains.

The cruel stereotype of the "drunken Indian" became a ubiquitous symbol of Indian helplessness as tribe after tribe succumbed to disease, military defeat, and removal. The readers of Mark Twain's *Roughing It,* his 1872 account of a journey in the Far West, were quite prepared to find his description of the Goshutes of Nevada hilarious because it fit assumptions that were already firmly entrenched. The Goshutes were, Twain wrote, "treacherous, filthy, and repulsive" creatures, their faces and hands bearing dirt which they had been hoarding and accumulating for months, years, and even generations, according to the age of the proprietor; a silent, sneaking, treacherous-looking race; taking note of everything, covertly, like all the other "Noble Red Men" that we [do not] read about, and betraying no sign in their countenances; indolent, everlastingly patient and tireless, like all other Indians; prideless beggars—for if the beggar instinct were left out of the Indian he would not "go," any more than a clock without a pendulum . . . savages who, when asked if they have the common Indian belief in a Great Spirit, show a something which almost amounts to emotion, thinking whiskey is referred to.

By the late nineteenth century, Indians were no longer enemies to be taken seriously; they had become impotent, irrelevant, and pitiable. It was easy to shrug off the legal claims of peoples who could be dismissed, collectively, as drunks.

With the repeal of national prohibition in 1933 and the discrediting of the temperance movement in general, the continued ban against alcohol in Indian Country was increasingly perceived as a form of racial discrimination. It became even less tenable after World War II, when thousands of Indian veterans returned home to their reservations to find that they were still not allowed to buy drinks that they had enjoyed without inhibition in Europe and the Far East, not to mention around military bases everywhere in the United States. In 1949, Congress voted to permit the use of alcohol on privately owned land within reservation boundaries. Four years later, Congress repealed Indian prohibition entirely, leaving it up to individual tribes to decide whether they wished to legalize drinking on tribal land. The great majority chose not to. In the early 1990s, the sale of alcohol was legal on only 91 of the 293 reservations in the lower forty-eight states.

Greg Ducheneaux remembers the thrill that swept the Cheyenne River reservation in 1953, when the tribal council voted to legalize drinking. "The men were so happy! They felt, now they could really be men!" Before then, it was unusual to see someone drunk. "Now the sober ones are the minority."

Late in 1991, Ducheneaux unveiled a draconian program of compulsory treatment that would effectively convert entire communities into collective treatment centers and, ultimately, he hoped, into showcases of sobriety. He told the tribal council, "It is no longer sufficient, and in many cases even futile, to treat the alcoholic on an individual basis." He added emphatically that "the family unit must be the major focus of our efforts."

Ducheneaux proposed the wholesale segregation of alcoholics from nondrinkers. To create an enclave of sobriety, the tribe would use its power of eminent domain to compel drinking families to exchange their homes for ones that belonged to abstinent families. "It would be illegal to enter that section under the influence of alcohol or other drugs on foot or in an automobile, with them in one's possession, or to use them while inside the boundaries," Ducheneaux suggested. "The people residing therein would be asked and encouraged to report immediately any violations, regardless of their relationship to the violator."

Some drinking families would soon recognize the improved quality of life in the dry areas and apply for permission to move into them. They would be required to "prove themselves" by undergoing family treatment for up to six months, until they demonstrated that they could remain abstinent. They would then be assigned a home in the dry area where they would become part of "one large sobriety support group."

In the meantime, the incomes of chronic alcoholics would be confiscated by the tribe and doled out on their behalf by counselors and social workers. An appointed committee of representatives from the tribe's social, legal, and mental health agencies would then select problem families for rehabilitation. If the families refused, the tribe would petition the courts for their involuntary commitment as family groups to a tribal treatment facility. Ideally, they, too, would eventually be returned to dry sections in their original communities to serve as sober family role models.

Ducheneaux recognized that the tribe could not guarantee that everyone who underwent treatment would manage to stay sober permanently. "Certainly there will be family heads that will relapse. When this occurs, these families will be visited immediately by the counselor and a concerted effort be made with the other residents to return this family to sobriety. If this is not possible after a reasonable effort is made, they must remove from the dry section." By such means, the sober areas would be protected and gradually expanded until entire communities could be declared dry, and the few remaining drinking families moved elsewhere. Within five years, Ducheneaux predicted, a significant proportion of the reservation's communities could be made sober and stable.

To Bourland, the totalitarian aspects of Ducheneaux's plan were obvious. To those who objected to it on moral grounds, Ducheneaux replied, "We're fighting a war here. Our people are dying. We need the weapons to fight for them."

However, without the support of the tribal council and Gregg Bourland, Ducheneaux's plan stood little chance of passage. Apart from its frontal assault upon basic civil rights, it was also much too radical for an electorate that would, after all, be on the plan's receiving end. Who would sit on the committee? Bourland wondered. Who would appoint it? If only one member of a family had a relapse, was the entire family to be banished from the dry section? What would be the social impact of displacing and relocating such a large number of families?

In early 1992, he expressed more of his reservations in a letter to Ducheneaux:

> What happens to the family who refuses to comply with this new system of order? Where will the funding for such dry sections come from? Who will determine which areas are to be dry and which will not be dry? What happens if there is a private home in a dry section [privately owned] which is inhabited by a family who is alcoholic? Do we force them out of their home or under eminent domain take their home from them? What happens to the family who is taken from a dry section, but refuses to move where they are told to?

Bourland had already considered prohibition and rejected it, in light of the considerable evidence that prohibition leads to more drunken driving, bootlegging, and corruption of tribal officials as well as to a general disrespect for the law. He instinctively sought a more measured approach, and one that could be achieved politically.

At Bourland's urging, the tribal council passed laws banning the cashing of welfare checks in liquor stores, the sale of alcohol to anyone who appears drunk, and, in an effort to reduce drunken driving, the sale of liquor through drive-up windows. Reservation bars were required to post signs warning of the danger of fetal alcohol syndrome, while women were made liable to civil prosecution in the tribal court if they drank during pregnancy; moreover, a woman found to have harmed her fetus by drinking could be compelled by the tribe to accept involuntary treatment. Most far-reaching in national terms was legislation that levied taxes on bars, like

Micki Hutchinson's, which were located on land owned by non-Indians.

While Bourland's program promised no speedy end to the ravages of alcoholism, unlike Ducheneaux's it carried little risk of a backlash from reservation voters. From a purely political point of view, it had the additional virtue of focusing attention on the sellers of alcohol rather than on the drinkers, at the same time as it extended tribal authority over the mainly non-Indian towns within the reservation's boundaries. Bourland pledged to dedicate what he hoped will be annual revenues of $75,000 in taxes to the construction of new treatment facilities. He says, "The solution is education and treatment."

To Ducheneaux, Bourland's belief that alcoholism can be brought under control by regulation and taxation is too little and too late. "Closing a few bars is not going to have any effect on tribal alcoholism," he drawls with the irritable weariness of a man who feels he has had to make an all-too-obvious argument too many times. "It's not just in the bars. It's in the kids. It's in the elderly. It's in the homes."

There is an almost unnerving intensity to Ducheneaux, a tendency to see things in apocalyptic terms, born, perhaps, from having squandered too many years in his own addiction, or from the relentless proximity of death and wrecked lives in a community where everyone is related by bonds of blood or shared experience. "The measures I have urged are stringent, but they have to be," he says. "We're dealing with an epidemic, not a head cold. It's so bad, we've lost the ability to say what is right and wrong for us. Civil rights are secondary. What the hell do questions of legal jurisdiction mean when our kids are stoned on inhalants? If this were an epidemic of influenza, we'd take special measures to stamp it out. Extraordinary measures must be taken. We are at a fucking bottom, and we are dying. Are we supposed to just sit back, and wait, and hope?"

When James O. Whittaker compared the results of his research on the Standing Rock Sioux reservation in 1980 with those from 1960, he found that among men the percentage of heavy drinkers had doubled, while drinking among both women and young people had also increased significantly. "Perhaps the most startling change of all, however," he reported, "is the number of people who identify themselves as either alcoholics or recovered alcoholics." In 1980, he found that 42 percent of the people he interviewed totally abstained from alcohol, 11 percent more than in 1960, and that fully 50 percent of the abstainers described themselves as "recovered alcoholics." Similar figures have been recorded on a number of other reservations. For instance, a study of drinking on the Warm Springs reservation in Oregon found that more than 40 percent of adults did not drink at all, while a survey of the Navajo reservation by the University of New Mexico found that 42 percent were abstainers; two-thirds of the Navajos interviewed believed, moreover, that it was wrong to take even one drink.

It is an unpleasant fact that among non-Indian alcoholics only a small percentage, perhaps as low as 10 percent, ever achieve stable sobriety. That would seem to suggest that even with massively expanded treatment, Indian communities may remain crippled by the effects of pervasive alcoholism. However, American history offers a precedent for dramatic and rapid reduction in both liquor consumption and alcoholism. Alcohol use reached its historical peak between 1800 and 1830, an era of considerable social upheaval, when Americans consumed an average of 9.5 gallons of alcohol per capita, roughly four times as much as they do today. Commentators at the time described the ravages of alcohol in terms not a great deal different from how observers of addiction in Indian communities do now. The temperance movement that arose in grassroots response to the seemingly unbridled alcoholism of the time achieved remarkable success by incorporating individual spiritual revival with appeals to patriotism and social responsibility, and the ongoing support of fellowships of recovered alcoholics. With virtually no resort to legislation, the movement succeeded in reducing liquor consumption by almost two-thirds by 1845 and to just 1.8 gallons per capita by 1900; the institution of national prohibition in 1919 was, in fact, mere anticlimax and failed to reduce consumption significantly at all.

However virulent alcoholism may be among Indians, it is not inherently any more resistant to treatment than it is for other Americans. Alcoholics Anonymous has helped many Indians to sobriety, including Robbie Daniels, although its potential is hampered by the widespread perception that it is, as some Indians disparagingly put it, "a white man's thing." The Native American Church, which bases its ritual on the vision-inducing use of peyote, has also had some success in inspiring sobriety among its members, as have the Mormons and other abstaining Christian sects that have been active in missionary work among Indians. Alcoholism is almost unknown, for instance, among the Alabama-Coushattas of East Texas, who, like their non-Indian neighbors, are hard-shell Baptists who forswear drinking as an article of faith.

Perhaps most promising, however, is the current proliferation of treatment techniques that combine modern psychotherapy with traditional or reinvented spiritual practices. The "Talking Circle," a device widely used in tribal treatment facilities in the West, is essentially conventional group therapy that deemphasizes confrontation and incorporates the use of an eagle feather, which is passed from hand to hand as participants speak. "The main thing is, it's ours," says Greg Ducheneaux. "You're all Indian in there, and you all need help. Just the fact that, by being there, by passing an eagle feather, you're saying, 'I'm an Indian, I'm desperate, I need help, and we're all going to deal with it as Indian people.' You daren't lie. The feather pulls the truth out of you. The feather needs you to be well."

Similarly, sweat lodges have become almost universal as therapeutic tools throughout Indian Country. "Something touched my mind in there," Robbie Daniels says of his first experience in a sweat lodge. He had been compelled by court order to enter a rehabilitation clinic, although he had no intention at the time of getting sober. But in the darkness and the physical agony of the roiling heat, he seemed to hear a voice speaking from within him. He remembers it saying, " 'You were born and raised a Navajo. You are part of the Red People.' " A series of recognitions followed. "I realized that the Great Spirit was telling me that I didn't have to pretend to act like I was one of the white people any more, and that spirituality was a God-given talent that had been given to me, too, and that there was a place of balance between God's spirit, myself, and the earth, and that I could find it." As a therapist, Daniels sees his role as essentially a passive one, as a conduit, like the sage and sweetgrass, for the passage of sacred spirit. "I leave it all to the Great Spirit. He touches my heart and mind. I only know that if it works for me, I try to share it with somebody else. I just try to do what seems right."

The many varied and increasingly forthright efforts to confront native alcoholism surely represent one of the most hopeful and important trends among Indians today. Taken together, they have much in common with the broader phenomenon of cultural and spiritual renewal that incorporates revived ceremonialism, demands for repatriation and for the recovery of sacred lands, and the like. More subtly, however, they also represent a translation of the fundamental concept of sovereignty from the political plane into the most intimate personal terms. If they cannot promise an ultimate solution to all the pathologies that flourish wherever alcoholism thrives, they at least offer an opening, an escape route from the trap of fatalism and demeaning metaphor into a wider world of individual possibility.

Sprawled amid the welter of sleeping bags, gym wear, boots, and melons where he has flung himself down, Gene Thin Elk strains to focus, partly from exhaustion and partly, perhaps, from a reluctance to be drawn back to pedestrian concerns. Most of the time, Thin Elk is an assistant professor of education at the University of South Dakota, in Vermillion. For the past three days, here on this rolling brow of South Dakota prairie, he has led thirty recovering alcoholics, their bodies toughened by fasting and ritual sweats, through the grueling rite of the sun dance. All day they have danced, though the plainness of the word fails to convey either the drama or the solemn intimacy of a stern rite whose mere description by outsiders is regarded as a moral offense by Thin Elk and others.

The ritual is done, having climaxed in its epiphany of pain, communion, and hope. The atmosphere is almost festive now; all around him, the dancers are collecting their gear and getting dressed, pulling on jeans and sweatshirts over their bloody rosettes, and cracking jokes about steaks and pizza. Thin Elk speaks haltingly, between gulps of Gatorade. "By the time we were three or four years old we were already dealing with abuse and illness. These are our seminal experiences, things you cannot change. It's all inside us." He is a handsome, amiable man, with the muscular physique of the basketball champion that he was in his youth; in spite of fatigue, he projects a kind of placid grace, the poise of a man in tune with himself.

"Suppose this is alcohol," he says, holding up the bottle of Gatorade. "Suppose I need this to ease my pain, that I can't live without it. I take this bottle, and my mind and my body follow.

Spiritually, now I am tied to a hollow bottle. Somehow I've got to call myself back from there. We've got to replace it with something of greater value." The shame of the past can be overcome, he insists in the soft cadences of a voice that is accustomed to speaking to the frightened and hopeless. "Any second, any minute, we can begin to change. All those relatives there will help prepare the ground for us and clear the air for us," he says, pointing with a broad hand toward the pines, toward the prairie, toward the fading orange light and the naked white buttes of the Badlands, meaning it literally.

Thin Elk shies from describing his impoverished reservation childhood or his own drinking in much detail. "I saw dehumanizing, aggressive things. I had a couple of cars run over me." Speaking of an attempted suicide, he is elliptical. "I wanted to ask the Creator to take me out of this life and put me in another." Against the odds, he survived. "I read the Bible, the Book of Mormon, Zen, Hindu, Buddhist, Catholic, Seventh-Day Adventist. I compared them all. In the end, it led me back to my own traditions." He had his last drink in 1979. After that, he trained professionally to counsel other Indian alcoholics.

"There is a lot of emotional retardation," he says. "There is a lot of anger." Bitterness at childhood abuse and neglect, lonely years in federal boarding schools, and the memory of historical aggression tended to fuse into an intractable, volatile mass of pain. "We stuff, stuff, stuff, until it all comes out and explodes." He also recognized that addiction warped what he regarded as a traditional respect for a life of simplicity into the self-destructive idea that there was virtue in poverty and failure. "For example, we have the idea that money is no good, that it belongs to the white man's world."

It seemed obvious to Thin Elk that, for Indian alcoholics, traditional disciplines like sweat lodging and the sun dance possessed great therapeutic and spiritual potential. The key to recovery, he came to believe, lay in pursuing what he terms the "seventh sacred direction," meaning, more or less, a merciful embrace of the inner self. "At the center is the Wakan, the sacred, the source, the Grandfathers, or, as Christians say, the image of the Creator. Everything we seek is already inside us. The things that can make us happy are already there. It means starting from the heart, where the understanding of sacredness is."

The recovery model that he developed, known as the Native American alcoholism program, and more familiarly as the Red

Road Approach, has been widely adopted by treatment centers that serve an Indian clientele in many parts of the United States and Canada. Unlike more conventional traditionalists, Thin Elk recognized that psychotherapy provided strategies of self-renewal that tradition did not. In one of several videotapes that he has prepared for use in counseling, he says:

> Some of us have been in very, very hard lives, in an environment where there is alcoholism, sex abuse, violence, death, so much death that you can almost smell it on people. We think it's these events that are holding us back. But we can't change those events. They happened. We have to look not just at events, but at the feelings that are attached to those events, and then take responsibility for them, and then let them out.

He later adds, "We can have the greatest government, the greatest funding, but it won't bring us back to health and productivity if we don't look inside ourselves and change ourselves in a good way." While such ideas may sound unoriginal to most late-twentieth-century Americans, they represent a radical departure for Native Americans, who were largely bypassed by the Freudian revolution.

"What part of our culture do we use?" Thin Elk asks with the gravity of a man for whom such questions have wrenching personal implications. "What parts of other cultures do we use?" They are questions that have bedeviled Native Americans ever since Columbus set foot in the Western Hemisphere. Fundamental to Thin Elk's answer is the conviction that the Indian world has been irrevocably changed by contact with Western culture and that Indians must find what is of value in it and reject what is unhealthy. "There's nothing wrong with money," he says. "The more you have, the more you can share, the more you can give." Also implicit in his answer is the belief that native tradition is not just a refuge for the defeated and frightened, but that it can be made to work for Indians who are destined to live their lives in the modern world. It is entirely possible, he asserts, for traditionalists to live a healthy existence among non-Indians and for "bicultural Indians" to understand and honor their native heritage.

"We have to have a redefinition of ourselves as individual people and a redefinition of Lakota culture," he says. "We have to broaden our horizons to include the entire world—look at all cultures and see the uniqueness of ours, see how our sacred ceremonies apply today, how they are relevant and timeless, and how we can be a part of them today to heal ourselves, and to see that we actually have the power to heal ourselves with our own minds. We can come to the point where we say that poverty is no longer a concept in our existence, that people don't have the power to make us second-class citizens, that we deserve the best the world has to offer, that we are not better than anybody, but that we have an equal right to the universe."

With the clump of sage, Robbie Daniels splashes water onto the glowing rocks. More and more stones have been added to the pile, until there are now more than twenty. Waves of searing heat roll through the sweat lodge. The flesh fairly aches from it. "You're going to feel pain," Daniels says. "They say a man can't feel the pain of your mom when she gives birth. But this is what it's supposed to be like inside her, dark like this. The pain we feel is like her pain as you begin to grow inside her." The cramped space has become dense with the mingled smells of sage, cedar, and sweetgrass, and claustrophobic. It is difficult to breathe. The spirit beings have entered, Daniels says, filling every empty space, listening.

Prayers spring from invisible mouths. Muffled voices blur together, crying for faith, connection, the strength to stay away from a drink.

"God help me to stay sober!" Leslie is crying in palpable anguish. "Take me in your hand!"

From somewhere, there is Burt's nasal basso. "I pray, God, to help all of us who are suffering today, who are struggling to be sober one day at a time and who are struggling to be honest with themselves."

"O Grandfathers!" Daniels is calling. "Come into my life, O Grandfathers!"

Sweat courses over chests, legs, thighs, faces, as if shame, fear, and despair could truly turn to water and soak away into the earth, to be claimed there and embraced.

"O God, I suffer!" Burt is crying. "Oh, thank you for my suffering! Thank you for my life!"

When it is over, the men crawl out into the startling sunlight, gasping at the touch of ice-edged air. From the outside, the sweat lodge suddenly seems insignificant, just a hump of black canvas in the sagebrush. Snow crusts the piñons and picks out the spectacular crags and cliffs in the distance, beyond Interstate 40. Burt quietly begins shoveling dirt onto the cooling rocks. Leslie and Jack shamble away together, unreadable, downhill toward the rehab. Robbie Daniels repacks his tools in silence, stowing the sage, cedar, and cornmeal that he has not used back in their toolbox. Then he climbs into his pickup and drives away through the sagebrush, toward the suburbs of Gallup.

8

"The Hollowness of a Person Needs to Be Filled"

HENRY REAL BIRD is hurtling at eighty miles an hour across the Montana prairie, clutching the steering wheel of his dust-streaked Dodge like a pulpit, swearing prodigiously. "There are a lot of demented fucking Indians here! All the boys got big bellies and don't want to do anything for themselves anymore. Government handouts! Got tribal jobs, living in HUD houses, living on tribal money. They put 'em on energy assistance. Don't even chop their own wood any more! There are no more human rights, no more treaty rights. Everything's twisted! They have no culture! All they've got left is the fucking pavement between the farms and the fields."

Real Bird's conversation bucks wildly along three or four tracks at a time, from the best place to shoot buffalo, to poetry, to myth, to a grandfather who, he says, was once taught a song by a bull. Cottonwoods, orange and yellow, flicker by, then silvery wastes of sagebrush, then fields of sugar beets and corn, then herds of Black Angus foraging across the silvery green prairie. Like much in Indian Country, the emptiness of the prairie is an illusion. Beneath the grid of twentieth-century agriculture, there is another land, hidden in the chiaroscuro of low, pinched hills, intricately webbed with tradition and memory. There are places, people say, that still remember the steps of Old Man Coyote, who made the earth, and of his wife, who stained the soil red with her blood. There are buffalo jumps and slaughtering grounds and the fields of tribal battles that were never recorded in books. Other places still fairly quiver with intimations of the divine: the red cliffs where for centuries the Crows have quested for visions, and the medicine wheels, the rings of stone that lie everywhere out of sight in the yellowing buffalo grass, mementos of sacred communions without number.

Real Bird is a cowpuncher and a poet, whose loping verse travels a landscape of bad drunks, foreclosed herds, and northbound freights. He also recruits students for Little Big Horn College, one of the most original, and arguably one of the most effective, institutions of higher learning in the United States. Real Bird and his colleagues are, in their way, like Gene Thin Elk and Robbie Daniels, like Dennis Hastings and Gregg Bourland, revolutionaries who have carried the concept of self-determination beyond politics and into the lives of ordinary men and women. Largely on their own, and on a budget that would not support even a department at a mainstream college of the same size, they have undertaken the regeneration of an entire people: the transformation of drunks, dropouts, welfare moms, the chronically unemployed, and the survivors of a commercial depression so pervasive and intractable that it can hardly even be called an economy, into modern men and women.

Real Bird ranges as the spirit moves him over the Crow reservation, whose rolling prairie and abrupt peaks cover an area larger than Rhode Island. He has an instinct for the failures, the washouts. "It's like rawhiding. When you move a herd out, there are the cows that hang back in the streams and hills and valleys. I go in and get them out. I hang around the welfare office and write down the names of the ones I see, and then I go to work on them. I'm like a used car salesman. I say, 'The most ignorant person in the world is the one who doesn't even have a dream, and I'm here to give you one!' I hang around the trash dump and talk to the people who scavenge the garbage. I go to a guy in jail and tell him, 'Remember your grandfather and how he prayed all those years for you to get an education?' Or take a lady who's just been divorced. She wants a ray of hope. I say, 'Get into business and become a secretary so you don't need that guy any more.' I know, because I've been there, how a guy feels when he stands on the street with a black eye, without having changed his clothes for a couple of days. So when I see people who've been in fights and feel bad, I say, 'Hey, we've got

psychology classes where you can find out something about yourself.' The hollowness of a person needs to be filled."

Fields of mown hay flicker by, then arabesques of tilled furrows,
then colossal Rube Goldberg contraptions that suck sugar beets up
into towering bins. "All the cattle, all the wheat—white people's,
all of it." Waving, Real Bird yelps a greeting to a white man baling
hay alongside the road. "He's out there enjoying the land our fathers bled for. When they didn't steal it, they married us out of it."
Real Bird grabs his crotch in a vast fist and shakes it hard. "The
good old catfish credit card."

Crows, in contrast to neighboring Plains tribes, were long and
fast allies of the United States. "The First Maker blessed us with the
best earth he created, but he tested our courage when he surrounded us with the most militant tribes in North America," Real
Bird is saying. In the 1870s, Crows fought alongside the U.S. Cavalry against the encroachments of the imperial Sioux; they scouted
for Custer during his ill-fated last campaign, which ended on a
gentle ridge a few miles east of Crow Agency. The Crows were
rewarded for their service with a generous reservation of 37 million
acres. Today, 8 million acres remain; the rest was whittled away by
treaties and obscure cessions that historians have still not wholly
unraveled.

This land should have brought wealth to the Crows. There is
timber, oil, good pastureland, and one of the largest unexploited
coal seams in the United States. But the impression of rupture is
everywhere, the sense of a people cramped and splintered by lost
opportunity. Although federal law prohibits non-Indians from
owning more than two thousand acres of reservation land, some
white ranchers have accumulated much more than that (allegedly
up to fifty thousand acres in one case). As much as half the land that
appears on maps as Crow has probably passed out of Indian hands.
Real Bird talks of illicit land transactions, of vast tracts ceded to
white homesteaders, of Crows who sold their allotments for ten
cents an acre, of white ranchers who feed corporate cattle for
twelve dollars per head on land rented from the Crows at three
dollars an acre. Then he laughs, waving his wide, flat hands like
paddles. "But there just ain't no sense being angry. You've just got
to live around all the chrome-plated plastic insanity."

The prairie peters out at Crow Agency, amid the monuments to
bad politics and broken dreams. There is the mill where carpets

were briefly made, the hulk that was an electronics plant, the abandoned feed mill, the looted and overgrown motel, the shuttered gambling hall—"Res-a-Vegas." Ghetto blasters bleat pop music from a congeries of battered trailer homes and flimsy government-built split-levels, across yards strewn with gutted cars and spilled household trash and an occasional dogged lawn.

The girl is perhaps twenty or so, pretty, and togged in fuchsia trousers and a pink T-shirt. She clings warily to the door frame, shrinking behind it, exhausted eyes hinting at some kind of unspoken problem, perhaps drugs or a brush with the law. Real Bird's barroom cockiness evaporates. He offers a college catalog. "We've got English, science, and math. You could become a social worker, a teacher, whatever. There are all kinds of opportunities. No money down."

As in many Indian conversations, there is more silence than speech. After a while, Real Bird asks, "What do you want to do?"

Finally, shyly, she replies, half hidden behind the door frame, "Be a secretary."

"Where?"

There is another long silence.

"City."

With a wide smile and palpable sincerity, Real Bird tells her, "We need you."

He leaves her shrugging feebly in the doorway, worn out and opaque.

"Our students are so timid and fragile." He claps his hands together loudly, with a wild laugh. "It's like running cattle across a river. You've got to push 'em in. The more you push, the more that get across. Most of them are going to come through alive."

Like most junior colleges, Little Big Horn offers two-year degrees in conventional subjects such as business administration, data processing, mathematics, psychology, science, nursing, industrial arts, home economics, and "office systems." Uniquely, however, it also requires that students, nearly all of whom are members of the Crow Tribe, take courses in Crow language, oral literature, tribal history, "Indian Identity," Indian philosophy and law, and "American Indian political science," among others. The college's mission statement promises:

1. To develop Crow and American Indian adults in paraprofessional and professional areas that reflect Crow Indian reservation personnel needs and career development.

2. To assist Crow and American Indian adult academic and personal development, for self-empowerment, workplace preparation or transfer to a senior institution; centering on respect for Crow and American Indian scholarship and bilingual capacities, across the disciplines.

3. To build the Crow Indian family, community and tribe, through understanding and knowledge pertinent to local issues, promoting and participating in community building activities.

4. To actively strive for Crow Indian cultural preservation and protection, vitalizing Crow Indian scholarship across all disciplines; to recognize that tribal tradition separates Crow and American Indians from mainstream American society; to appreciate culture and tradition as the foundation of strength and wellbeing for the Crow and the American Indian community; and to strengthen the unique, self-governing Crow Tribe of Indians.

The jargon belies a shift of tectonic proportions that is taking place in the way that education is increasingly shaping Indians' sense of place in American society. The vast federal system of Indian education that Theodore Roosevelt once ferociously termed "a colossal, pulverizing engine" was designed explicitly to destroy tribal loyalty and to force Indians into mainstream American life. Increasingly, Indian educators such as Little Big Horn's president, Janine Pease-Windy Boy, perceive education as a tool, indeed perhaps the only tool capable of reviving tribal identity and of simultaneously molding a new kind of Indian able to make his way in the modern world. They also bluntly challenge the traditional American belief that one of the primary duties of education in the United States is to assimilate every child to a common history and sense of place in the larger national culture.

In a number of respects, schools like Little Big Horn and the twenty-three other tribal colleges around the country represent the most hopeful single development in Indian Country today. They symbolize the extension of tribal sovereignty beyond politics to encompass the Indian mind and its shaping; while their primary mission is education, they also preserve language, artistic traditions, and oral history, devise training programs for local industries and development plans for the tribes themselves. The largest of the schools, Navajo Community College, serves two thousand students, half of them more than thirty-five years old, and offers a comparatively sophisticated curriculum with degrees in computer science, earth and life sciences, preengineering, administration of justice, business, social work, liberal arts, and Navajo studies. "Our object is to provide the student with choices and to temper those choices with his living, breathing culture," says Don McCabe, the dean of Finance and Administration. "We believe that Navajos have a body of knowledge that is as important to preserve and impart as Western philosophy. We want to create Navajo biologists who will have respect for animals, birds, and plants, and engineers who, if they build a road, will approach the mountains with prayer and respect, who will seek out consultants from among the medicine men, and who will consider where the medicinal herbs grow and the vegetation people use to graze their sheep."

Given their paucity of resources, the achievements of the tribal colleges are all the more remarkable. Indian students who transfer from tribal colleges to four-year universities are forty times more likely to succeed there than those who go directly from high school, according to a 1989 study by the Carnegie Foundation for the Advancement of Teaching. Tribal college graduates have a similarly improved likelihood of finding jobs. Standing Rock College, in North Dakota, found that fewer than 5 percent of its mostly Sioux and Blackfeet graduates were unemployed or not pursuing further education, on a reservation with an unemployment rate of 80 percent. Eighty-three percent of the graduates of Dull Knife Memorial College on the Northern Cheyenne reservation in Montana were working or had gone on to further study. Turtle Mountain Community College in North Dakota found that 28 percent of its vocational education graduates transferred to a four-year college and that, overall, more than 70 percent found jobs immediately after graduation. Of the 113 associate of arts graduates from Sisseton-Wahpeton Community College in South Dakota, 91 percent were attending a four-year institution; in addition, three had earned a master's degree and one a Ph.D. In 1995, a Carnegie Foundation survey of tribal college students throughout the United States found that 80 percent of them planned to go on to four-year schools.

While their enrollment, sixteen thousand students nationwide, is modest by national standards, tribal colleges have an impact far beyond their size on small, often isolated communities. On the Pine Ridge reservation, the number of Indian teachers has increased from one to nearly one hundred since the establishment of Oglala Lakota Community College. Salish Kootenai College, which serves the Flatheads of northwestern Montana, has over five hundred students registered on a reservation of just over three thousand people, while Little Hoop Community College has enrolled 10 percent of the three thousand Sioux and Assiniboines who live on the Fort Totten reservation in North Dakota. In contrast to historically black colleges, which perceived their mission as assisting their graduates' assimilation, Indian schools are primarily interested in teaching skills that will enable their students to live productive lives on the reservation. "While we want to give our graduates the ability to go anywhere they want, we need them all desperately here on the reservation," says Pease-Windy Boy. "Our first goal is to train young people to serve their own community: we need engineers, data processors, dental technicians, specialists in animal husbandry, premed, everything."

Pease-Windy Boy has been the college's guiding spirit since its inception. Over the last decade, she has nursed it from an adult ed program lodged in two used trailers to its present position as a national model in Indian education. She disarms at first encounter. The brownish-black hair pulled back from the moon of her face, the stiff burgundy suit, the self-containment reflect the plain style of the prairie hamlets where she has spent most of her adult life. Her cramped office in the former gymnasium that now houses the college is adorned, if that is the word, with a photo of Desmond Tutu, a bronze statuette of Chief Plenty Coups at the gallop, and a plastic plaque behind her desk that reads: "We have done so much for so long, with so little, we are now qualified to do anything with nothing." There is also an architect's drawing of the modern campus that Pease-Windy Boy has fairly begged the tribal government to build for the college; there is anticipation in the air, for the council is scheduled to vote this week on allocating the $5 million to build it.

"We are trying to prove that education can happen anywhere, and for anyone. We start with people who have never known success and expect to fail at anything they try. Until now, few of them even had access to higher education, and few of the ones who did ever finished college. Nearly all our students are drop-outs. Most are on welfare, probably most of them have been divorced, and nearly all of them have children to support. They are people who worry about having enough money to eat lunch, and in the winter a lot of them double up two or three families to a house because they can't afford heating fuel." The soft voice sounds misleadingly vulnerable; beneath it, there is sudden blunt toughness. "Indians are quite capable of helping themselves. No one here is suffering from the missionary, let's-help-the-poor-Indians syndrome. This place isn't about pity."

The atmosphere inside the old gym is brisk and businesslike, in startling contrast to the sleepy seediness that characterizes most of Crow Agency. Hortatory signs proclaim "Crow students are good in math" and the like. Jeff Hooker, who teaches basic science in a lab that was formerly a shower room, says, "You see students go in two years from learning fractions, to doing calculus, to designing their own experiments." In a new computer lab, accounting students lean over ranks of word processors, puzzling out software. Across the hall, in a class on "Indian Identity," Barney Old Coyote is lecturing on the German painter Karl Bodmer, whose luminous canvases provided the first Western image of Crows: "The clothes and the backgrounds were always different, but no matter what tribe Bodmer was painting his Indians all had the same face." Down the hall, Joe Medicine Crow, a historian who holds a Ph.D. from the University of Southern California, is unfurling a map that shows the original nineteenth-century boundaries of the Great Plains reservations: "I wanted you to see this and know it, because this is the basis of Crow country as we know it today." Magazines such as *The New Yorker, Kiplinger's,* and half a dozen computer publications may be found in the new library, which the school's construction class recently built to replace a corrugated steel shed. "There's a track record of failure here, and we're flying in the face of it," says the college librarian, Tim Bernardis, with a passion typical of the school's staff. Barnardis has often risen before dawn to be the first in line at book sales in Billings, ninety miles away across the prairie. "If we don't succeed, it'll be over my dead body."

Tribal scholars sponsored by the college are compiling oral histories of the Indian in Roosevelt's New Deal and of Crow service in the United States armed forces. (There are wonderful continuities— Barney Old Coyote's grandfather rode as a scout for Crook's cavalry against the Sioux, while his grandson launched Tomahawk missiles against the Iraqis in Desert Storm; Old Coyote himself flew B-17s during World War II.) In a cinder-block cubicle across the road, the college recently established a tribal archive, making public to ordinary Crows for the first time the treaties, genealogies, census records, reports of mineral exploration, and minutes of tribal council meetings that created the present-day Crow world.

Pease-Windy Boy is passionately proud of it. "Information is power. Until now, we've always had to rely on white folks because they had the data and could come in here and lead us around with it. Now we can say to Crows, 'If you want to know the history of a coal agreement, or what happened at a council meeting last year, come on, here it is, it's yours.' "

She can recite a litany of impressive statistics. Annual enrollment has grown to 250, and since 1983, more than one-quarter of the 8,500 members of the Crow tribe have taken at least one course at the college. Fifty-three percent of those who graduate find jobs immediately, mostly as teaching assistants, nurses, clerks in tribal, county, or BIA offices. Admittedly, these are modest careers, but in a community with a per capita income of $3,000 per year and 85 percent of its members on welfare, any job at all represents a radical transformation. In 1992, another 25 percent of each graduating class transferred to four-year colleges. Twenty graduates of the college were working to earn bachelor's degrees at mainstream universities; twelve had already earned full university degrees in the hard sciences, ten more than in the previous eighty years. To Pease-Windy Boy, this is all rooted in a cultural revolution: "If our graduates are doing well, and they are, it is because they come out of here knowing what it is to be Crow. We tell them, you must study and become literate in the Crow language, because it is through language that the philosophy, religion, and ideals of our culture are transmitted, but you must also pass college algebra."

"Baakuhutacwaaalakode."
Dale Old Horn, a rancher who holds a degree in linguistics from MIT, is talking about sacred powers.

"Heavens," he says, translating the tongue-twister for a class of half a dozen young Crows. Then, with a felt marker, he writes: "wind—*Huche,*" then "fire—*bilee,*" then "animals—*baaaxuaw-ishe.*"

"This word is sometimes used to mean animals that are fur-bearing, but it can in fact mean insects, reptiles, fish, all creatures that are animate."

Old Horn perches on the back of a small chair, his feet on its seat and lanky knees jutting. He is, in class, amiable and engaging. At forty-six, gray streaks his swept-back, shoulder-length hair; the face is broad, thoughtful. He is dressed, in the cowboy-style that Plains Indians favor, in a blue shirt with faux pearl buttons that snap over the pockets and new, tight blue jeans.

"These powers are not gods. They are what He created. Let me remind you, by the way, that we say 'He' for God because when we speak in English we're bound to Eurocentric language, which identifies God as male."

Later, in the spartan cubicle that serves as his office, Old Horn is brittle and easily provoked, uneasy with questions. Like many Indian intellectuals, his view of history is unforgiving and rooted in a sense of permanent crisis. At times, he hints at notions of racial purity that most of American society has abandoned.

"The dominant society attributes Indian poverty to native culture. They link our failure to the fact of our being Crow, and they tell us the only alternative is assimilation. They say, for instance, that the only way to succeed in America is to speak English; it's really an ultimatum. We're talking about the very existence of the Indian race. The culture of a people only survives if people practice it. If they don't, those people will die and be forgotten. When the white man came, we were first subjected to three kinds of death: germ warfare, starvation by government policy, and death by bullets. Then missionaries told the Indian that his religion was 'devil worship.' Then white education displaced native knowledge. Then assimilation took the Indian out of his own territory and put him among whites, where his sense of self-esteem and identity was diminished."

He points to a *National Geographic* map of North American tribes tacked to the wall behind him. His broad index finger moves slowly across the continent.

"Mohicans . . . Narragansetts . . . Chesapeakes . . . Karankawas, on and on and on. They're all already on the lost list. Crows are now on the endangered species list. There were ten thousand of us when the white man came. By 1900, there were only two thousand of us left. Today we are eight thousand, but we are still an infinitesimal number of people. We have to think of our culture in terms of survivability." He smiles with deceptive amiability and then, pausing pregnantly between words, deliberately accuses: "Lest . . . we . . . become . . . dead.

"If economic success were the only important thing, we could all leave the reservation, go off and look for jobs in Los Angeles and New York. But culturally we'd join the Mohicans and Karankawas. If I am amalgamated, my dark features will disappear, and I'll look like a white man, or an Oriental, or a black man. My own disappearance becomes a symbol of the defeat of the nation. But biological type is not as important as what resides in the life of the mind."

Indians have been the subjects of the longest and the most ambitious succession of educational experiments in the history of American education. Indian children were among the first students at the school established by the East India Company at Jamestown in 1621. Fifteen years later, Harvard College listed among its goals "the Education of the English and Indian youth of this country in knowledge and Goodness." In the next century, the pious Eleazer Wheelock, the founder of Dartmouth College, declared it his intention to "cure the Natives of their Savage Temper" and to "purge all the Indian out" of his mostly Iroquois students. Wheelock added, with evident frustration, "Few conceive aright of the Difficulty of Educating an Indian and turning him into an Englishman but those who undertake the Trial of it." Such difficulty was no deterrent to those who were determined to transform the Indian in spite of himself. Education was seen by well-intentioned Americans both as a moral imperative and as a practical gateway to modern civilization. However, their optimism was often rooted in the naive conviction that Indians were but blank slates waiting to be inscribed with the vigorous script of American civilization.

Although Indian leaders have been among those demanding the benefits of education, through the years they have recognized its hurts and incongruities, as well. Having listened to Benjamin Franklin expound the benefits of learning, an eighteenth-century chief politely replied:

> But you, who are wise, must know that different nations have different Conceptions of things; and you will therefore not take it amiss, if our ideas of this education happen not to be the same with yours. We have had some Experience of it; Several of our young people were formerly brought up at the College of the Northern Provinces; they were in-

structed in all your sciences; but, when they came back to us, they were bad Runners, ignorant of every means of living in the Woods, unable to bear either Cold or Hunger, knew neither how to build a Cabin, take a Deer, or kill an Enemy, spoke our Language imperfectly, were therefore neither fit for Hunters, Warriors, nor Counselors, they were totally good for nothing.

Enlightened by education, it was expected that the Indian would willingly relinquish his bow for the plow and abandon the tribe for the security of private property. But within this logic, there often lurked an ultimatum. "In the present state of our country one of two things seems to be necessary," the House Committee on Appropriations declared in 1819, as it allocated a $10,000 "Civilization Fund" for the education of Indians. "Either that those sons of the forest should be moralized or exterminated." Through the first half of the nineteenth century, the education of Indians was haphazard at best and took place mainly in the homes of missionaries who, like the Reverend Samuel Worcester, shared the hardships of their charges when they were uprooted from their homes; the Cherokees, in an ironic turn of events, were removed to the West just as they were creating their own syllabary and system of public education. After the Civil War, treaties often included a provision for a classroom for every 30 children, although they did not promise a full education through high school and college, as some twentieth-century apologists have inferred. It was not until after 1871, when Congress declared that tribes were no longer to be treated as sovereign but rather as dependent peoples, that government shouldered full responsibility for Indians in all aspects of their lives, taking on the task of establishing permanent reservation boundaries, of ensuring food, clothing, and shelter for displaced persons, defusing rebellion, protecting Indians from settlers and settlers from Indians—of creating, in short, a Pax Americana.

For the first time since contact was made with white newcomers in the 1500s and 1600s, there was peace in Indian Country. Peace meant that soon, for the first time on record, the nation's Indian population would begin to increase, as it continues to do today. It meant a chance for children to be born and grow up in safety. Peace also meant new and forceful work for former military officers. Indeed, it was a military man fresh from the Indian wars who systematized Indian education with the establishment of the Carlisle

Industrial Indian School, at a former military barracks in Pennsylvania, in 1879. Its founder, Captain Richard Henry Pratt, became an ardent supporter of Indian assimilation after serving with Cherokee scouts against the hostile tribes of the southern Plains. Pratt epitomized the liberal dilemma: he was deeply sympathetic to Indians but regarded reservation life as a morally repugnant form of segregation little different from that which he had fought against during the Civil War. Convinced that physical separation was responsible for the Indians' failure to become more like white Americans, Pratt relentlessly condemned what he called "this whole reservating and segregating process"; he once suggested, apparently seriously, that the country's quarter million Indians be spread, nine to a county, among the nation's 2,700 counties. His unflagging insistence that the complete isolation of Indian children from tribal life could remake them within a single generation shaped the national idea of Indian education well into the twentieth century. Egalitarian in the style of his time, Pratt declared that the Indian "is born a blank, like all the rest of us. There is no resistless clog placed upon us by birth. We are not born with language, nor are we born with ideas of either civilization or savagery." Vigorously democratic though his vision was in aspiration, it was authoritarian in execution. In 1892, after more than a decade as the nation's foremost educator of Indians, he wrote: "A great general has said that the only good Indian is a dead one, and that high sanction of his destruction has been an enormous factor in promoting Indian massacres. In a sense, I agree with the sentiment, but only in this: that all the Indian there is in the race should be dead. Kill the Indian in him and save the man."

Pratt's system was copied widely. When the Haskell Institute opened in September 1884 in the former abolitionist stronghold of Lawrence, Kansas, Chancellor Lippincott of the University of Kansas declared at the dedication: "When one Indian boy or girl leaves this school with an education, the 'Indian problem' will forever be solved for him and his children." Almost as soon as they arrived, they were given new names. Howling-from-Above became Paul Rodney, Go-He-Ah-Sah became Alice Walker, Wahkakuekusha became Mary Lane. Inspired by Carlisle, Haskell and other federal boarding schools adopted a self-consciously military style. Students slept in "quarters," ate in a "mess," and were allowed "annual leave" rather than vacation; at Haskell, they were mustered to class in double lines to the beat of Sousa marches. Each day was split equally between school and work. Children fresh from the Dakota prairie or the wastes of Nevada learned English by reading *Peter Rabbit, The Three Bears,* and *Mother Goose.* Boys would be taught carpentry, blacksmithing, shoemaking, tailoring, printing, painting, baking, and agriculture; and girls, a knowledge of sewing, cooking, and house- and laundry work.

There is a photograph in the Watkins Community Museum, in Lawrence, that shows Haskell students mustered for dress parade on a Sunday in February of 1921. There are dozens of tribes represented—Blackfeet from Montana, Mdewakanton Sioux from Minnesota, Osages from Oklahoma, Oneidas from New York—but they are, of course, indistinguishable. The girls wear identical black frocks, and their hair is identically cropped and bobbed. The boys wear uniforms modeled on those of World War I, replete with jodhpurs and peaked caps. The boys stand ramrod-straight, the girls tilted oddly forward at the shoulders, perhaps having been taught that this odd posture indicates modesty or submissiveness. There is a palpable air of expectancy. The children are waiting for something to happen, perhaps a homily from the school superintendent, who is invisible somewhere on the dais behind the camera. The image is quite literally captivating, an image of Indians as other Americans wished to have them: under control, orderly, tamed. If ever there was a picture that epitomized the end of the frontier, it is this.

The transformation of the Indian through education became a staple of the popular press, with such headlines as "Noble Red Man Is at Last Willing to Sit at the Feet of His White Conqueror and Listen to the Words of Teachers." Even a century later, these stories are often painful to read. In 1890, in one entitled "Waifs of the Forest," a journalist for the *Topeka Daily Capital* reported after a visit to Haskell:

A thorough training in one of these institutions cuts the cord which binds the Indian to a pagan life, and substitutes civilization in place of superstition, morality in place of vice, cleanliness in place of filth, industry in place of idleness, self-respect in place of servility, an elevated humanity in place of abject degradation. As long as the Indian wears the blanket, wears moccasins and eats roast dog he is worthless, but time has shown that the education which he has received at the training school makes him an industrious workman, and not the lazy, worthless savage that his father was.

Children younger than ten were sent (sometimes having been removed from their parents by force) hundreds of miles to Haskell and other schools, to Gothic fortresses that must have seemed grotesquely forbidding to children accustomed to the open prairie and camp. Thomas J. Morgan, the Commissioner of Indian Affairs from 1889 to 1893, bluntly denied that Indians

> who, for the most part, speak no English, live in squalor and degradation, make little progress from year to year, who are a perpetual source of expense to the Government and a constant menace to thousands of their white neighbors, a hindrance to civilization and a clog on our progress—have any right to forcibly keep their children out of school to grow up like themselves, a race of barbarians and semi-savages. We owe it to those children to prevent, forcibly if need be, so great a calamity from befalling them.

Chauncey Yellow Robe, a Lakota, writing in 1925, remembered traveling east to Carlisle at the age of fifteen, in feathers, blanket, painted face, and long hair, knowing not a word of English, nor ever having seen a school or a book before. Upon arrival:

> I was stripped of my native costume. They cut my long hair and put me in a bathtub of warm water with plenty of soap, and thus began my first process in civilization. I was dressed in a new suit of civilized clothes, which was as uncomfortable to my physical nature as the new and strange environment was in breaking my spirit. Never had I experienced such homesickness as I did then. How many times have I watched the western sky and cried within my broken heart, wishing to see my father and mother again and be free on the Plains.

Although modern critics tend to look back on federal boarding schools almost exclusively as a form of cultural aggression, they were often understood by both whites and Indians of the time as a special opportunity. (Earlier in the century, American workers had even rallied for the privilege of "twenty-four-hour" schools on the grounds that only boarding schools could provide equality of education with the elite.) Large off-reservation boarding schools became the single most powerful unifying force in shaping a collective sense of being "Indian" over and above parochial loyalty to tribe. Students were recruited from many tribes. Graduates went on to work together, especially as administrators in the federal Indian service, which for many years was dominated by Haskell graduates. They also married fellow students from widely separated native communities, which over the years brought Indian people together across tribal and reservation lines. Yellow Robe, it might be noted, penned his poignant memoir of boarding school while serving as the popular and respected boys' advisor at the Rapid City Indian School, where he spent much of his professional life.

Although basic assumptions of Indian education remained rooted in a democratic view of man and his place in society, they also continued to demand, well into the twentieth century, that Indians totally deny their heritage in order to become full-fledged Americans. At Haskell, as late as the 1950s, any evidence of attachment by students to their own cultures was treated as an act of defiance. Punishment was sometimes brutal. Reuben Snake, a Nebraska Winnebago, remembered being tied to a stairpost and flogged with a strop for performing a forbidden Indian dance. Ella Irving, a Lakota who attended Haskell in the 1920s, recalls what occurred when students attempted to organize a strike over the quality of food. "The girls were all packed in the halls. The principal came walking down the hall with a big club, swinging from side to side, knocking the girls down one after another. They said the ringleader was an Iroquois girl from New York. First they completely cut all her hair off. Then she was sent to the dungeon, which was full of rats. That was in September. We didn't see her again until March. For a long time after, I had nightmares, I'd wake up yelling, thinking I was still at Haskell."

As times changed, government schools failed to change with them. Bureaucrats focused more on simply getting children into school (not an easy task, given the remoteness of many reservations —not until the late 1940s were there schools for all the children of school age on the vast Navajo reservation) than on what actually went on in them once the children had gotten there. But the fundamental flaw that increasingly characterized federal Indian education might best be understood as a failure of spirit. There was little trace of awareness of education as a door to the life of the mind. Indeed, it was not at all clear to many white educators that there was such a thing as an Indian mind. Curricula remained puerile and static. John Collier, whose long reign over Indian policy in the 1930s and 1940s might have made a great difference, did little to improve matters. Even as he reinvented moribund tribes by means of the Indian Reorganization Act, he failed utterly at creating modern schools that could produce the educated citizenry necessary to make the new tribal governments work. Stern discipline coupled to an unresponsive and paternalistic system that was increasingly out of touch with the dreams of students, and disconnected from the ongoing, changing "real world" of which Indians were inevitably a part, ultimately bred fatalism and inadequacy. "Indian folks are real nervous about their ability to be competent and efficient," says Marvin Buzzard, a Cherokee from Oklahoma who taught in various BIA schools in the Midwest before he became dean of students at Haskell. "There is a sense that our children are lost in a maze and can't find their way out. Not long ago, a kid came to me and said he wanted to drop out of school. I asked him why. He said, 'Because that's what Indians do.' "

The year is 1983. Picture Janine Pease-Windy Boy, slim and precise, picking her way through the scum of broken bottles, crumbled insulation, and horseshit that carpets the abandoned gymnasium. The ruin is a donation to the college from the Bureau of Indian Affairs. Weeds and trees grow through gaps in the cinderblocks. Windows are broken, and the heating fixtures have been stolen. Melting snow seeps through holes in the roof, and when the wind rises, the entire ceiling lifts inches off its broken moorings. Pease-Windy Boy's mood is almost evangelical.

"I knew that there was no shortage of Crows who had the ability to be successful, but they didn't even know it. They had to be taught how to see their own talent. The problem was, where would the money come from to turn that mess into something? If we waited for someone to come and build us a college, I knew we'd be waiting until hell froze over. Then I thought, if our ancestors could learn sitting under a tree or around the campfire, why can't we learn in a falling-down gym?"

She recruits volunteers, and together they unplug toilets, scrub walls, put in new windows. They collect rocks from the Little Big Horn River to hold down the roof, beg for secondhand furniture from the BIA, and scour the tribal garbage dump for thrown-away desks and shelves. They cobble together tables and benches, repair the boiler, and wire a new phone system. Fifty-nine students come in the first year. They are abandoned wives, embittered veterans, ex-cons, orphans from alcoholic homes, mothers with half a dozen children to care for, people from families that have been on welfare for two or three generations. Two-thirds are women. Some have never earned a wage in their lives. They are me, Pease-Windy Boy thinks, remembering a time when she also had to make the last four cans of pork last for two weeks. Sometimes rats and mice scurry across the floor, devouring computer printouts and library books. Sometimes pipes burst and flood the floor. "We'd put the files up on stilts and get down to business, and hold our class. The students would sit with us in the middle of the water. The thing of it was, people really wanted to learn."

Pease-Windy Boy was raised more in the white world than the Indian, by a Crow father and a mother of Cornish immigrant stock, itinerant teachers who moved around the timber country of eastern Washington. She spent summers at Crow, camping in the Big Horns, hunting antelope and chokecherries, learning the ways of horses and prairie folk from a grandfather who knew the intricately braided genealogies of everyone for a hundred miles around the reservation. It is a happily remembered childhood. "Until I was eight or nine I thought everyone had a tribe. Then I realized that the people who lived around us were white, and I discovered that they didn't care about us very much."

An awful story comes now, in fragments. She completes college in Washington and trains as a teacher. Then marriage takes her to the Rocky Boy reservation, remote in northern Montana. There is a failure of some kind, a breakdown; the husband, a tribal official, is suddenly unemployed. She finds herself left alone with two infants at the onset of winter. She is thirty-five miles from the nearest town and without a car. The telephone is cut off when she can no longer pay her bill. She goes onto public assistance, struggles to survive on $130 a month. She watches her heating fuel diminish week by week, her food supplies dwindle. People die of exposure every winter here, where the temperature drops to forty below zero.

But this story is not about pain or fear. When she is in need, food appears at her door. Neighbors turn up with a pheasant or a duck, or a bucket of berries, a quarter of an elk. They understand her desperation; it is part of the coarse, everyday fabric of reservation life. They share what they can. Pease-Windy Boy knows that they will not let her die. In time, she teaches herself to bead moccasins; tourists buy enough to enable her to travel to Billings for job inter-

views. Finally Eastern Montana College hires her to recruit Indian
students. Even there, the neighbors keep appearing, with sacks of
canned beans, instant potatoes, coffee. When a delegation of Crows
invites her to become president of their embryonic college, her answer comes easily.

The story has a homespun moral, the discovery that a sense of
shared responsibility has survived in spite of the destruction of the
old Indian way of life, the isolation, the joblessness, the listlessness
of people cut off from the opportunities of twentieth-century America. The desperation of the poor and frightened can be put to use,
transformed, made the glue of collective renewal. "What I learned
is that every individual holds an equal responsibility for the community. No one holds more than he is worth, and no one is expendable. People are not interchangeable. Everyone has something to
contribute."

The college had a building now. But it was only the beginning.
Larger, subtler problems loomed. If the white man's education
wasn't good enough, the Crows would have to educate themselves.
That was clear. But what was that education to be? What must the
Crows know? Who were they to become? What was their place in
the world? They were questions that Indians everywhere were attempting to answer.

Picture Pease-Windy Boy and half a dozen of the college's faculty
on a hilltop above Fort Smith, in sight of the jagged peaks of the
Wolf range and the gorge of the Little Big Horn, where it plummets
through the rock from the Yellowtail Dam. "In the high places is
where your direction comes, where your mind can be clear, your
heart open, where you listen. We wanted to be as close to the
mountains as we could get." They have come together here in a
kind of collective vision quest, an evocation of the old-time warrior's rite of passage that would guide him through life. It is a
groping for the cachet of tradition, a struggle to make old ways
work.

"We prayed first, asking for guidance so that our hearts and
minds might be kind to each other, that we be aware of our grandchildren, be aware of the wisdom of our grandparents, and choose
our words carefully. The idea was to bring the spiritual together
with the practical. We started out looking at the jobs that were
available in the area, and then we tried to figure out what training
was necessary for them."

She would remember Minnie Fritzler from the Indian Health Service arguing for more doctors and nurses "who will care for us the way Crows care for each other, not just in a traditional sense but in a scientific sense, too." The tribal chairman, David Stewart, urged banking, finance, and accounting courses. Pease-Windy Boy remembered his words: "We're trying to manage a tribe with people who have no education. We have plenty of bright people, but they have no training." Joe Medicine Crow, whose grandfather rode with Custer, spoke for history. She remembered what he said, too: "People need to have a sense of the past, a factual sense, not something pumped up, not a we-and-they thing. If we are to be full, whole human beings, and not fragmented ones, we must know about art, music and history, but we can learn about them in the context of Crow studies." Pease-Windy Boy herself believed that science, math, and business should be the college's first priority. "I also felt that Crow studies had to be the backbone of everything else. But whatever we did, I thought, we had to do it well."

To an extent, "Crow education" is a matter of inflection, of accommodating Crow habits. "For example, in Indian culture it is not a sign of respect to look someone in the eye, while in white culture a teacher typically thinks that if you avert your eyes you've got something to hide. Likewise, we respect silence as being as important as expressing an opinion. To an Indian, silence may mean reflection or understanding, not just that a student doesn't know the answer to a question." Similarly, math problems are tailored to tribal life; for instance: "The Left Hand family wants to attend a powwow on their vacation. A rental car from Rent-A-Rez has a daily rate of $39.75 plus 25 cents per mile. Their daily car rental budget is $80.00 per day for three days. Determine the mileages that will allow them to stay within their budget."

More substantively, the college relies heavily on the tribal ethic of mutual support. Groups of cousins are recruited together and encouraged to take the same classes, to do their homework side by side, and to make sure that no one is lagging behind. Competition is deemphasized in favor of cooperation. Pease-Windy Boy likes to tell the paradigmatic story of a class that petitioned to have its graduation postponed until one member had given birth to her baby and they had helped her make up her incompletes. The point is in the punch line: "Our millennial inheritance is one of cooperative tasks. You can never fail here. You may not pass a course, but that doesn't mean that you have failed; it simply means that you take the class again until you understand everything that is taught in it. You don't get penalized for taking a long time. Time packages are a very white thing. There is nothing in our culture that says if you don't accomplish something in three months, you're 'dumb.' With us, you struggle, you take your time, you try again, eventually you succeed. Forgiveness is a basic Crow trait."

"Mary"—she prefers to keep her real name out of print—pertly looks the student part, in two-tone oxfords and purple socks, with a nylon backpack slung over the navy blazer, and much younger than her thirty-seven years. A smile comes only warily and uncertainly; behind it there is a glimmer of the shame that lies, often well concealed, beneath the surface of very many Indian lives. She was one of the ones who weren't supposed to fail. She graduated near the top of her high school class, edited the school yearbook. She was the first in her family to go to college, to Eastern Montana, in Billings. "Mom and Dad really put me up on a pedestal." But that was nearly twenty years ago. Cruel discoveries came quickly. "I wasn't used to eye-to-eye contact or to expressing myself to an instructor." While she was a high achiever among reservation students, she in fact read only at seventh-grade level. Sometimes she spoke backward, instinctively following Crow word order instead of the English. Every assignment was a struggle. "I already felt degraded and hurt, but I was raised to keep my feelings to myself. I got up courage and went to my advisor, and I said I needed help. He said, 'I do not tutor Indians—they just do not want to learn.' "

It is difficult to imagine this conversation, to take it as a literal report. But of course it is the remembered words that matter, and the effect. "I thought, what's the use? I was angry at everything. I needed help and they wouldn't give it to me." Afterward there is the shamed walk across campus, beneath the red bluffs of Billings, and then a nervous collapse, resignation from school, and finally the terrible drive home to the reservation. She had been in the university for only three weeks.

"When I came back, I was kind of like in a gutter." The details are held back. But the gutter is not a kind place in Crow Agency, and it often ends sprawled next to a bottle under Two Leggins bridge, or walking into an eastbound freight outside of Hardin. "It was years before I felt that I was worth anything." In time, she accumulates a marriage and a divorce, three children. Finally there is a small victory, a clerk's job with the tribal police, a salary. In the office there are computers; they catch her eye, symbols perhaps of an alien world, a place where things are always new, where things work, the white people's world.

This is where Henry Real Bird enters. She remembers it this way: "He kept badgering me, 'Why not go to school?' I'd say, 'Me?' He'd say, 'Yeah, you!' I always thought, if it's an Indian school, it can't be any good. But one day I said, 'You got computers over at that college?' He said, 'I got a whole lot of them!' " Almost grudgingly, she takes the leap.

"It was hard for me to come, at first. I was thirty-six years old, older than everyone else, and I felt ashamed. But from the first day, it was a new experience. I didn't have to look anyone in the eye or give up my language. The computer teacher always took time to say that if I needed help, come and ask. When I got poor grades I felt low, but gradually I began to feel that I could do better the next time." After the first quarter she surprises herself by earning As and Bs. "What I have learned here is how to be self-disciplined, how to be a self-starter, how to complete what I set out to do. I've learned how to compete in a white man's world. I've learned how to make myself equal." The prosaic words are dramatic in a human landscape where even the most able expect defeat as a matter of course.

After graduation from Little Big Horn, she plans to continue on to a four-year college and to someday serve as a computer specialist for the Crow tribe. "My roots are here. I could never be happy living anywhere else. If I don't see my brothers and sisters for a day, I worry about them." The achievement is modest, the future narrow and within the tribe's embrace. But there is something deeply bracing in the story, repeated again and again among the college's students, of small, steady victories, of attainable ambitions and a success that is measured less in money than by the intimacy of family and place.

Pease-Windy Boy is eloquent on the subject of wealth. "Having a lot of money is not an important goal. There isn't even a true Crow word for money. We say *buhla,* which derives from the English word 'dollar.' We know that wealth doesn't bring quality of life. We see whites live alone and die alone, and it seems that an excess of money may only bring loneliness. We pity the shyster businessmen, the chiseling coal developers, the rip-off land developers who have no people with them. We feel real sorry for them. What is important to Crows is relationships and respect. To us, excess is of no purpose. If you have some extra money, you probably use it to support your brothers and sisters, or cousins. People here only ask a decent life—a roof, a decent car, an education for their children, good water, to be near their relatives, and near the mountains and the land."

Little Big Horn College, however, cannot operate without *buhla*. Like many Indian institutions, the college stands uneasily in the midst of overlapping jurisdictions. While Little Big Horn is chartered by the Crow tribe, tribal politicians resentful of its independence have generally denied it financial support and have declined to provide $5 million for a new campus from a recent $37-million windfall in rebated state taxes. Like the other tribal colleges, however, Little Big Horn also comes under the nominal authority of the Bureau of Indian Affairs, even though it is wholly managed by the Crows. Yet the federal government has provided only the most halfhearted support for schools that may offer the best chance to prepare young Indians for the challenges of life in modern America. In 1978, Congress mandated that up to $5,200 per student be given annually to tribal colleges, but it has in fact never allocated more than $3,200 in any given year and has sometimes voted as little as $1,900. In 1994, tribal colleges received an average of just $2,991 per student; by contrast, historically black colleges received about $17,000 per student, and community colleges as a whole a little under $7,000.

That Little Big Horn has survived at all is due, in no small part, to the self-sacrifice of its faculty. The college can afford to spend approximately $3,000 annually to educate each of its students, only about half as much as community colleges in non-Indian towns. Students pay a modest tuition of $20 per credit. The school offers no loans. "We don't believe in them," says Pease-Windy Boy. "Besides, people as impoverished as our students don't have the means to pay them back." Initially, Pease-Windy Boy's salary and the salaries of the faculty and clerical staff were all set at the same level, about $12,000 a year to start. To save money, menial jobs were shared among the faculty, and for most of the school's first decade, Pease-Windy Boy's was swabbing the toilets. Although remuneration has improved, teachers still work an average of sixty hours per week for about two-thirds the salary of faculty at non-Indian colleges in the area. They must also choose between health insurance or a pension; the college can't afford both.

In 1985, with one of the stunningly shortsighted decisions for which it has become famous, the Bureau of Indian Affairs announced that welfare recipients would no longer be permitted to attend school. It meant not only that twenty-five of Little Big Horn's hundred students suddenly had to withdraw, but also a loss of $75,000 in federal money, only a fraction of which could be made up from cash reserves.

A meeting is called. Pease-Windy Boy, Old Horn, Medicine Crow, a dozen others sit uneasily in dim evening light on the old gym bleachers and an assortment of broken chairs. Everyone knows that the great experiment may be at an end, that the gym is on the brink of becoming another monument to Crow failure, like the hulks on Agency's outskirts, the carpet mill, the motel, Rez-a-Vegas. Pease-Windy Boy speaks.

"We have met with disaster. Our students have left us. Somehow $60,000 will have to be cut, or Little Big Horn College will have to close."

Worried voices suggest abandoning the courses with the smallest enrollment or firing the teachers with the least seniority. These are the logical choices. Pease-Windy Boy is scared. She looks at the faces around her. Who could they let go? If they give up Dale Old Horn, Crow students will lose their language. If they fire Barney Old Coyote, how will young people learn the tribe's history? If they relinquish any of the math or science teachers, then students' access to technology will be diminished or lost altogether. She speaks again.

"We can abolish some of our courses or fire some teachers. But if we do, our catalog will become a lie. When we wrote it we made a contract with our students: this is what we offer you, come hell or high water. We made a commitment to each other to survive as a whole."

Without dissent, the faculty decides to accept a 10 percent cut in their already modest salaries and to forgo pay entirely during the summer months. The college stops buying paper and pens. Students are told to bring their own toilet paper and to use writing paper on both sides. Pease-Windy Boy takes a part-time job as a secretary at an attorney's office in the nearby town of Hardin. Instead of store-bought food, she feeds her family dried antelope and elk, and she bathes in the river that runs near her home to save on the cost of water. She abandons all but the most urgent travel on the college's behalf and stays overnight only with relatives and friends, "shirttail cousins," as the Crows say.

Two years later, in 1987, the BIA belatedly reversed itself and permitted welfare recipients to return to school. But by then it was almost beside the point. The college had crossed a watershed. It had learned to survive on its own. Survival, the Crows are fond of saying, is an Indian art form, but there was something new in this determination at all costs to keep faith with a people ingrained with an intense, perhaps even defining, sense of betrayal by not just the outer, white society but by tribal institutions, as well. Pease-Windy Boy and her colleagues had called for sacrifice not in the name of the tribal past—that often self-serving staple of Indian rhetoric—but on behalf of a new kind of collective future, in which self-reliance and public integrity would be the benchmarks of modern Indian life. The college was becoming the first truly independent institution on the Crow reservation, an achievement that reached beyond issues of tribal sovereignty, toward a more fundamental kind of freedom, the right to autonomy beyond the control of the tribal government.

For a decade, the college has served as the only island of stability in a community that has suffered for as long as anyone cares to remember from chaotic and at times stunningly corrupt tribal politics. Since 1948, no tribal chairman has served three two-year terms in succession. One chairman was impeached for corruption in the 1970s, and for most of the 1980s, the tribe's finances were in receivership as a result of fiscal incompetence. By 1990, rival factions had completely paralyzed the tribal government, until federal agents finally seized the tribe's records and indicted virtually the entire regime on criminal charges. The tribal chairman and eight other officials were sentenced to prison for bank fraud, conspiracy, and embezzlement.

"As far as freedom of speech goes, we were a wasteland," Pease-Windy Boy says. "Free speech is not a tradition on reservations, and academic freedom never existed here before we established it. The majority, whoever it is, has never been respectful of the rights of the minority. Ordinary people did not really know how to talk freely, to speak out, to solve problems together. Until now, there was no place here where people could even learn to do that. In a place where it's so cold that for half the year it's impossible to meet outdoors, it was easy to suppress dissent simply by denying your opponents a place to meet." As a matter of course, Crow officials obtained tribal court injunctions to forestall meetings of their political opposition, while churches denied meeting space to groups that failed to conform to their practices. "This school is now that place that never existed, an island of safety. Our facilities are open to anyone. We don't care what they meet about, whether they're bird-watchers or political reformers."

Nevertheless, it was "desperately hard," in Pease-Windy Boy's words, to keep the college out of tribal politics. "Politics corrupted everything it touched, and we knew that it would destroy us, too, if we let it. Just because we were independent, the tribal government kept looking for ways to get control over us." In 1984, after the college permitted opposition politicians to rent space for a forum on government, goons sent by the chairman cut the locks and forcibly took over the gym for their own rally. A few years later, a tribal government dominated by fundamentalist Christians attempted to prevent the college from allowing the peyote-using Native American Church to meet there. When still another government attempted to seize administrative control over the school in January of 1991, it was forestalled only by the first student demonstrations that Crow country had ever seen.

The anxiety shows on Pease-Windy Boy's face on a Saturday afternoon nine months later. The tribal council is about to vote on the $5-million grant that the college has long sought for a new campus. She has enemies in the room, and strange, abrupt things can happen in council; constitutionally, it can do anything it wishes on the spot—vote to remove her from office, for instance, or impose tribal hacks on the school's board of directors. She sits hunched forward, long-legged, self-contained, watching through the fog of cigarette smoke the tribal leaders alongside the dark, rotund figure of Chairman Clara Nomee, lined up at the Formica table in the center of the council's old chinked-log octagon. Teenagers scout the milling crowd, hawking tacos to stout women in pressed Sunday-go-to-meeting double-knits and Stetsoned men in check shirts and crisp jeans; kids hop up and down the bleachers with toy tanks and jeeps, shrieking "Beep! Beep!"

Hours slip past in discussions of budgets, a proposed tribal meatpacking plant, and another that would generate power from coal-bed methane, until the college's resolution reaches the floor. In accordance with tribal law, if it is defeated today, it may not be brought up again for a year. Pease-Windy Boy thinks of the architect's vision, the drawing on her office wall. There would be classrooms for twice as many students, offices for every teacher, enough toilets, space for more computers, and more labs.

An elderly man in braids, swaying from side to side, intones more than speaks. Occasional English words break through the Crow, like rocks in a flood of sibilants and gutturals: "scholarship" . . . "electrical engineer" . . . "board of trustees," and then, finally, in a sudden spate of the white man's tongue, "Those young kids deserve an education. To go off and compete with the white guy you have to educate yourself, show them out there you're not just another bum Indian."

Next comes a young tribal trucker, a graduate of the college, who speaks with the smack of political ambition: "I challenge you to come up with the $5 million. You have to invest in education. You say we can't afford it. But can we afford not to? If we don't take it from the $37 million that the state has given back to us, when will we ever find it? Show you're willing to invest in education!"

The chairman's chief of staff, Kale Howe, is at the microphone in an instant, squat, snide, and fuming. "You come up here and try to discredit everything the tribe does for you." He turns theatrically to the bleachers. "The tribe hired him, the tribe gave him a job! And now he criticizes us!"

Nomee herself needles Pease-Windy Boy now, almost plaintively. "I am for the children, for the kids who are going to the college, but the leader of the college got to work with us, but she don't want to. I'm kind of hurt. I asked Janine for an audit of the college, but I never got it."

Howe bellows into the microphone that there was a "discrepancy" of $83,000 in the expenditures of the Head Start program that was headquartered in the college. It is a tangled issue, rooted in expenses disallowed by the federal government rather than theft. The imputation is a clever weapon. But the college never administered Head Start at all. The accusation is a smear. In fact, the college has a B-plus loan rating with Dun and Bradstreet; the tribal government, after years in federal receivership, has no rating at all.

"We sure don't want to give up $5 million if there was a discrepancy," Howe is shouting. "I'm not going to give $5 million, and then in five years they'll come back and say they don't know what happened to it."

Pease-Windy Boy strides to the microphone, waits for Howe's voice to roll on to its conclusion. Then she leans forward into the mike, speaking precisely. "I will stand up to this administration as I have to every other one. The records show that we never managed Head Start. Our budget has been submitted to federal audit every year. If you're really concerned, you can access every one of those budgets."

Joe Medicine Crow is there, and Dale Old Horn, and old Mrs. Real Bird, Henry's mother, in the knee-high moccasins that scarcely anyone wears any more. But the school's supporters, perhaps sensing defeat, are unexpectedly thin on the bleachers. For weeks, the college's enemies have lobbied quietly. Only this morning, scandal sheets appeared around Crow Agency, lying that Pease-Windy Boy had given away $100,000 of the college's money to the last, discredited tribal administration.

Howe is back at the microphone, moving abruptly to table, seconded by the chairman.

"They're going to kill it," says Old Horn. "We haven't got the votes."

Voices are called in favor of the resolution to table. The sound is raucous and deafening, and it is suddenly over. As she slips out into the sudden bright light of the afternoon, Pease-Windy Boy is angry and quiet, the figure of an extraordinarily patient woman who is undeterred by defeat.

The lost opportunity to integrate culturally intact Indians into American society may have been the greatest failure of public education in American history. It is a failure that strongly suggests that Indians, like most other people, will only grudgingly submit to schooling that they perceive as hostile to their own values. In an era when an ever-more complex world market is creating new kinds of opportunities for the educated, young Indians might theoretically be better off learning German and Japanese than the tongues of their ancestors. However, it cannot be surprising that Indians feel urgently compelled to reclaim what remains of their cultural heritage before they embrace a wider world.

Perhaps predictably, the historical tyranny of conventional Indian education has bred reaction and, in the extreme, an ethnic fundamentalism that tends to portray Indians as the source of all civilization and to denigrate the wider American culture in which, like it or not, Indians must learn to survive. An editorial in the *Lakota Times,* a nationally distributed Indian weekly, asserted without qualification that "Indian people have contributed, among other things, three-fifths of the kinds of foods consumed globally, democratic theory of government and a spiritual philosophy that 'can keep the earth sweet and alive.' " Indians are now commonly taught to believe that American democracy is based on the Iroquois Confederation, a curious notion that relies on a handful of rhetorical remarks by Benjamin Franklin. A fund-raising letter sent out by the Native American Rights Fund during the Columbus quincentenary declared: "We greeted the European newcomers with open-handed generosity. They treated us with cruelty unsurpassed in the subjugation of people throughout history." Similarly, but more astonishingly, a newsletter published by the Smithsonian Institution that is directed mainly toward Indians, asserted in a recent article on Christopher Columbus that "At most, his voyage increased the circumference of one world and the diversity of world views." In a similar vein, Wayne Ducheneaux, the president of the National Congress of American Indians, assured a standing-room-only Native American Day crowd at the Black Hills Stock Show, in 1991, that the pre-Columbian inhabitants of the Americas "were far superior to what Columbus brought. They were superior religiously, socially, and politically." Even Haskell, now a junior college, has thoroughly jettisoned the convictions of its founders; indicatively, the course description for Western Civilization I promises to "immediately undermine the ethnocentrism (essentially Eurocentrism) of the so-called Western intellectual tradition."

One of the most influential purveyors of such thinking was Reuben Snake, a former leader of the American Indian Movement who later became an elder of the Native American Church. On a raw October day in 1992, Snake, a man of ponderous size whose harsh polemics belied his gentleness of manner, was already showing the strain of the diabetes that would kill him in less than a year. "Indian people used to be able to speak to nature, to birds, to the trees. It was the Garden of Eden. We were so in harmony with the Creator that when we called our grandfather spirits for rain, it came to us. We were not savages wandering aimlessly on earth. When we migrated, we were moved by the spirit of God. Intuitive, cyclical thinking makes you seek your place in the universe, to be in harmony with it." His home, before his move to New Mexico, was a small government-issue split-level on the Winnebago reservation in the northeastern corner of Nebraska; as he spoke, he would turn away abruptly from time to time to catch up on the Geraldo Rivera show on the TV. "But beginning in 1492, we were thrown into the Euro-centered, rational, linear-thinking mind-set, and we see what that's doing to mankind. To be blunt, we're fucking up the world. The ozone layer is disappearing, the air is unbreathable, and the water is undrinkable. The Greek, Judeo-Christian philosophy changed us all. It's Greek philosophy that screwed us up. That Greek word *politeia,* it means 'control,' the ability to control things. European thinking teaches that God gave man dominion over the earth. All this time they have been trying desperately to do that."

With its emphasis on science and higher education beyond the reservation, Little Big Horn College has made some attempt to buffer its students against cultural solipsism. Even so, one of its talented graduates can still exclaim, "Why should we adapt to 'them'—the Eurocentrics? Why don't they conform to us?" Reminded that Crows number but 8,000 in a nation of 260 million, she responds, "I don't accept that I am a minority at all. There is no majority. Everyone belongs to a minority." Has it even occurred to her that she lives, however reluctantly, in a nation that will never conform to the customs of the Crows? She replies, as if it were an answer, "They've committed genocide . . . oppressed us, crushed our culture."

There is danger in this; doctrinaire rage and the mystique of race are cul-de-sacs, too. "We spend too much time telling kids that Indians all lived in harmony, and then all of a sudden white people came and destroyed it," says Marvin Buzzard, who sees only a dead end in the ideology of bitterness. "What we need to be talking about is the concept of individual responsibility, about commitment to self and to the community. We've got to look at ourselves and where we are now in a way that seeks less to assign blame and more to focus on ways of guiding ourselves toward the future. But it is very difficult to do that without being branded an apologist for mainstream culture. We have convinced ourselves that there is a tremendous tension between white and Indian values. We've been sold the notion, not just by the larger society, but by ourselves, that

Indians are noncompetitive, that they don't care about money, that if they don't own anything, that is an expression of their 'Indianness.' This sort of thing is both racist and romantic, and it abets a lot of the self-destructive behavior that is out there. It tells us, in effect, that we have to decide between 'being Indian' and being able to provide for our families, that unless you're suffering, you're not really an Indian. I doubt that Crazy Horse rode around in rags. And what's more competitive than counting coup? Sitting Bull said, when you go down the road you pick up whatever you can use. There's nothing wrong with borrowing something of value from white culture. Any notion that we can, or should, live in isolation from contact with whites is absurd. The most important thing education can do is give kids a choice about how to live their lives. Think of it as providing the weapons of survival for the modern warrior."

This is not a new debate. It has been taking place in one form or another as long as Indians have been forced to figure out where they stood in white America. Since the earliest years of contact, Indian character has been shaped by the competing, sometimes fatal, tug of self-righteous rage, the shame of betrayal and defeat, and the lure of the new. But for the first time, the dialectic of that struggle is increasingly being argued by Indians themselves, by people such as Janine Pease-Windy Boy, Dale Old Horn, and Marvin Buzzard. While its outcome is uncertain and may never become completely clear, it is redefining modern Indians as products both of their own tribal history and of American society, as men and women genuinely of two worlds, no longer lost like the forlorn mixed bloods at the distant and empty horizon of Henry Real Bird's poem, "Where the sky and ground are one, and there is nothing all around."

Out beyond Pryor, the land crumples into steep bluffs and damp bottomland studded with elms and cottonwoods. Henry Real Bird is talking about how he punched cows here when he was a boy. But his mind is on other things. He is picking his way on foot through a trash of machinery, the shards of rusted-out harvesters, searching for the traces of stone rings where tepees stood long ago. This is one of the hidden places, invisible to the untutored eye but indelibly printed in Crow memory. Here, "in 1859 or 1860, by white people's count," Real Bird is saying, the Crow people almost met its end. The Sioux were expanding aggressively across the northern

Plains; they had pushed the Crows across the Yellowstone, then across the Powder, then across the Little Big Horn. Many of the Crow warriors were away in the Missouri Country; the thousand or so Crows who remained were outnumbered at least several times over by the Sioux and their Cheyenne and Arapaho allies. "When we saw them coming, we dug holes in the ground inside our tepees and put the women and children into them. Then, to frighten the Sioux, we turned our tepees inside out, so that they showed nothing but black soot from cook fires." But the Sioux continued to come on, up Pryor Creek and over the sage-covered breaks, seemingly unstoppable. Then something strange and awesome occurred. "A rider on a paint horse who no one ever saw before came down that western ridge, bowled right through the creek and right into the Sioux, where he made a big commotion. He'd go back and do it again and again, and it made the Crows inebriated with courage. Our warriors rallied, and we pushed the Sioux back across the Pryors, all the way to the Wolf Mountains." The warrior was a spirit rider, simultaneously vision and event, the spirit of the Crow earth fused with the spirit of the Crow people itself.

Real Bird, in the common way of Indians, speaks of the transcendental matter-of-factly, as whites will of money and sex. "Our people were spared here because we were kind to the spirit of the ground. Today when we bring them into school, they bring with them the same spirit that saved them here. That spirit may not sound exactly the same. Right now the spirit wants computer classes, and math and science. But you've got to be nice to that spirit. You've got to help those people, or else that spirit will just flow away again into the ground, and we'll be begging to get it back."

9

"Our Lives Have Been Transmuted, Changed Forever"

PHILADELPHIA, MISSISSIPPI, is the kind of place that seemed to survive more from habit than reason after the timber economy that was its mainstay petered out in the 1950s. Mills closed, people drifted away, but the town somehow hung on. There is a scruffy, frayed-at-the-edges look to the empty shopfronts and the discount stores where more vibrant businesses used to be, but by the standards of rural Mississippi, Philadelphia counts itself lucky. The mayor, an amiable former postman by the name of Harlan Majors, is not above boasting. "Kosciusko and Louisville, they have to wait to buy a tractor or, sometimes, even to meet their payrolls. And they don't have a fire department worth a hoot. I have sixteen full-time firemen." Philadelphia's trump, the thing that other towns will never have, is Indians. "Our best industry by far is the Choctaw Nation," Majors says. "They're our expansion and upkeep. They employ not only their own people but ours, too. It has never been as good as it is now for the last forty years. Our economy depends on them. If the tribe went bankrupt, we'd go into a depression."

Until a generation ago, the Choctaws virtually defined the futility of reservation life. Over the last quarter century, however, they have defied even their own modest expectations by transforming themselves from a welfare culture into one of the largest employers in the state. Today, Choctaw factories assemble wire harnesses for Xerox and Navistar, telephones for AT&T, and audio speakers for Chrysler, Harley-Davidson, and Boeing. The tribal greeting card plant hand-finishes 83 million cards each year. Since 1992, the tribe has operated the largest printing plant for direct-mail advertising east of the Mississippi River. By 1995, sales from the tribe's industries as a whole had increased to more than $100 million annually from less than $1 million in 1979. As recently as fifteen years ago, 80 percent of the tribe was unemployed; now, having achieved full employment for its own members, nearly half the tribe's employees are white and black Mississippians. Says William Richardson, the tribe's director of economic development, "We're running out of Indians."

The quality of life for the great majority of Choctaws has measurably improved. The average income of a family of four is now about $22,000 per year, a sevenfold increase since 1980. Brick ranch houses have largely supplanted the wood-frame huts and sagging government-built bungalows amid the jungle of kudzu-shrouded oaks and pines that forms the heart of the seventeen-thousand-acre reservation in east-central Mississippi. The new Choctaw Health Center is among the best hospitals in Mississippi, while teachers' salaries at the new tribal elementary school are 25 percent higher than at public schools in neighboring, non-Indian towns. "They're willing to buy the best," says a non-Indian teacher who formerly taught in Philadelphia. "I never heard of anyone being fired in the public schools. Here, they fire Indians and non-Indians alike in a heartbeat, if they don't do their job." The tribal television station, the primary local channel for the region, broadcasts an eclectic daily menu of shows that includes thrice-daily newscasts, Choctaw-language public service shows on home financing and microwave cooking, and, on one recent day, reruns of *The Cisco Kid,* a British film with Dirk Bogarde, and Choctaw-produced commercials for local clothing and food stores and for a quilting display sponsored by the Daughters of the American Revolution.

The Choctaws are also a national leader in transferring the administration of federal programs from the Bureau of Indian Affairs to the tribes. Virtually everything once carried out by the bureau— law enforcement, schooling, health care, social services, forestry, credit, and finance—is now performed by Choctaw tribal bureau-

crats. "We're pretty well gone," says Robert Benn, a courtly Choctaw who is the BIA's local superintendent and whose sepulchral
office is one of the last still occupied in the bureau's red-brick
headquarters in Philadelphia. "We've seen our heyday. The tribe is
doing an exemplary job. They're a more professional outfit than we
ever were."

Some Choctaws hold that their forebears arose pristine from the
earth at Nanih Waiya, in present-day Winston County. "After coming forth from the mound, the freshly made Choctaws were very
wet and moist, and the Great Spirit stacked them along the ram-
part, as on a clothesline, so that the sun could dry them," as one
story has it. Others say that they came from the West, carrying huge
sacks filled with their ancestors' bones. Throughout historical
times, the Choctaws were mainly an agricultural people, raising
corn, beans, pumpkins, and melons in little plots by their cabins.
However, exhibiting an instinct for business that was probably far
more prevalent among Native Americans than those who think of
Indians only as innocent children of nature wish to believe, they
raised more corn and beans than they needed for their own use and
sold the surplus to their neighbors. During most of the eighteenth
century, the Choctaws were prominent allies of the French in their
wars for influence over the tribes of the Southeast. Although they,
like their neighbors the Cherokees, were adapting rapidly to a modern way of life, the relentless pressure of settlement steadily whittled
away at their lands until, in 1830, in the rather poignantly named
Treaty of Dancing Rabbit Creek, they relinquished what remained
of their land in the East and agreed to remove themselves to the
Indian Territory, where their descendants still inhabit the Choctaw
Nation of eastern Oklahoma.

There were, however, a few Choctaws who remained behind,
scattered through the familiar forests of oak and pine. Many more
eventually drifted back from the West, disillusioned by the anarchy
of tribal politics and the difficulties of life on the distant frontier.
Ironically, the tripartite racial segregation that deepened as the century progressed only strengthened the Choctaws in their traditions,
language, and determination to be Indian in a part of America
where, for all intents and purposes, Indians had simply ceased to
exist. Rather than send their children to schools with blacks, the
Choctaws refused to send them to school at all. By the time the
federal government winkled enough land from private owners to

establish the present-day Choctaw reservation in the 1920s, nearly 90 percent of the tribe were still full-bloods and most spoke no English at all.

Today it would be difficult to find a community anywhere in the United States that makes the case for tribal self-determination better than the Mississippi Band of Choctaws. There is, in their story, no underlying irony, no tragic catch, no corrosive seed of failure. It is a success story, pure and simple, not by any means the only one in Indian Country, or even the most dramatic, but nonetheless one of the most important of all just because it was so improbable, so much against the odds. It is a story that also suggests that tribal sovereignty, far from being a universal threat to neighboring non-Indian communities, has the capacity to become an engine for rural revitalization. Says Mayor Harlan Majors, "All the little towns up and down the state look at me and say, 'How do you do it?' I say, 'Get yourself an Indian chief like Phillip Martin.' "

The story of the Choctaw revival is inseparable from that of Phillip Martin, the remarkable chief who has guided the tribe's development for most of the past thirty years. Martin is a physically unimposing man, short and thick-bodied, with small opaque eyes and thinning hair that he likes to wear slick and combed over his forehead. Beneath the grits-and-eggs plainness, he combines acute political instincts with unflagging tenacity of purpose and a devotion to the destiny of his people that is capable of disarming even his enemies. "He's like a bulldog at the postman, he just won't go away," says Lester Dalme, a former General Motors executive who has managed the tribe's flagship plant since 1979. "At the same time, he'll give you the shirt off his back whether you appreciate it or not. He truly loves his people. He can't stand even one of his enemies to be without a job." At 9:30 P.M., Martin is still at work in his office, reading and signing documents from the alp of folders stacked on his desk. "Folks elected me," he says, "and they expect me to do my job."

By all rights, Martin's fate should have been as gloomy as that of any Choctaw born in the Mississippi of 1926. "Everybody was poor in those days. The Choctaws were a bit worse," he recalls. As a boy, he cut pulpwood, herded cows, and chopped cotton for fifty cents per hundred pounds. In those days, Choctaw homes had no windows, electricity, or running water. Alcoholism and tuberculosis were endemic. The Choctaws' cultural isolation was intense.

Few had traveled outside Neshoba County, and many had never even been to Philadelphia, only seven miles away. The etiquette of racial segregation was finely modulated. Although Choctaws were not expected to address whites as "sir" or to step off the sidewalk when whites passed, they were required to sit with blacks in movie houses and restaurants. "But we never had enough money to eat in a restaurant anyway," Martin says in his porridge-thick drawl.

Martin, rare among Choctaws of that time, earned a high school diploma at the BIA boarding school in Cherokee, North Carolina. His first experience of the larger world came in the Air Force at the end of World War II. Arriving in Europe in 1946, he was stunned by the sight of starving French and Germans foraging in garbage cans for food. White people, he realized for the first time, could be as helpless as Indians. At the same time, he was profoundly impressed by their refusal to behave like defeated people and by their determination to rebuild their lives and nations from the wreckage of war. He wondered, if Europeans could lift themselves back up out of poverty, why couldn't the Choctaws? After the war, he returned to Mississippi, but he soon learned that no one was willing to hire an Indian. Even on the reservation, the only jobs open to Indians were as maintenance workers for the BIA, and they were already filled. Martin recalls, "I saw that whoever had the jobs had the control, and I thought, if we want jobs here we're going to have to create them ourselves."

He eventually found work as a clerk at the Naval Air Station in Meridian. He began to take an interest in tribal affairs, and in 1962 he became chairman at a salary of $2.50 per hour. Although the tribe had elected its own nominal government since 1934, the tribal council had no offices, no budget, and little authority over anything. In keeping with the paternalistic style of the era, the BIA superintendent presided over the council's meetings. He also decided when tribal officials would travel to Washington and chaperoned their visits there, as Indian agents had since the early nineteenth century. Says Martin, "I finally said to myself, 'I've been all over the world. I guess I know how to go to Washington and back. From now on, we don't need the superintendent.' So after that we just up and went." Martin became a fixture in the Interior Department and the Halls of Congress, buttonholing agency heads and begging for money to replace obsolescent schools and decrepit homes and to pave the reservation's corrugated, red-dirt roads.

The tribe's first experience managing money came during the War on Poverty in the late 1960s, when the Office of Economic Opportunity allowed the Choctaws to supervise a unit of the Neighborhood Youth Corps that was assigned to build new homes on the reservation; soon afterward, the tribe obtained one of the first Community Action grants in Mississippi, for $15,000. "That $15,000 was the key to all the changes that came afterward," says Martin. "We used it to plan a management structure so that we could go after other federal agency programs. I felt that if we were going to handle money, we had to have a system of accountability and control, so we developed a finance office, and property and supply. Then we won another grant that enabled us to hire accountants, bookkeepers, personnel managers, and planners."

The Choctaws remained calculatedly aloof from both the Civil Rights Movement of the 1960s and the Indian radicalism of the 1970s. Martin says, "We didn't want to shake things up. Where does it get you to attack the system? It don't get the dollars rolling —it just gets you on welfare. Instead, I thought, we've got to find out how this system works." Eighty percent of the tribe's members were then on public assistance and receiving their food from government commodity lines. "It was just pathetic. By now we had all these federal programs, but that wasn't going to hold us together forever. I knew that we had better start looking for a more permanent source of income." It would have to be conjured from thin air: the reservation was devoid of valuable natural resources, and casino gambling was an option that lay far in the future.

In key respects, Martin's plan resembled the approach of East Asian states that recognized, at a time when most of the third world was embracing socialism as the wave of the future, that corporate investment could serve as the driving force of economic development. Martin understood that corporations wanted cheap and reliable labor, low taxes, and honest and cooperative government. He was convinced that if the tribe constructed a modern industrial park, the Choctaws could join the international competition for low-skill manufacturing work. Says Martin, "We know who our competitors are: Taipei, Seoul, Singapore, Ciudad Juárez." In 1973, the tribe obtained $150,000 from the federal Economic Development Agency to install water, electricity, and sewer lines in a twenty-acre plot cut from the scrub just off Route 7. "It will attract somebody," Martin promised. For once he was dead wrong. The site sat vacant for five years.

With his characteristic tenacity, Martin began writing to manufacturers from one end of the United States to the other. He kept on writing, to 150 companies in all, until one, Packard Electric, a division of General Motors, offered to train Choctaws to assemble wired parts for its cars and trucks; Packard would sell the materials to Chahta Enterprises, as the tribe called its new company, and buy them back once they had been assembled. On the basis of Packard's commitment, the tribe obtained a $346,000 grant from the Economic Development Administration, and then used a Bureau of Indian Affairs loan guarantee to obtain $1 million from the Bank of Philadelphia.

It seemed, briefly, as if the Choctaws' problems had been solved. Within a year, however, Chahta Enterprises had a debt of $1 million and was near bankruptcy. Production was plagued by the kinds of problems that undermine tribal enterprises almost everywhere. Many of them were rooted in the basic fact that for most of the tribe, employment was an alien concept. Workers would abruptly take a day off for a family function, and not show up for a week. Some spoke no English. Others drank on the job. Many were unmarried women with small children, no one else to take care of them, and no reliable way to get to work. The tribe's accountants had already recommended selling everything off for ten cents on the dollar. But Martin knew that if the plant was sold, the tribe would never get a loan again.

The man to whom Martin turned was Lester Dalme, who was then a plant manager for GM and who had been raised in rural Louisiana with a virtually evangelical attitude toward work. "My mom taught us that God gave you life and that what you're supposed to do is give Him back your success," says Dalme, now a trim man of about fifty, whose office at Chahta Enterprises is as plain as his ethics. "If you don't, He's going to be very unhappy with you." Martin promised Dalme freedom from political interference and full control in the plant; there would be no pressure to hire relatives or to keep people who wouldn't work, problems that were well known to be common on other reservations. Dalme remembers facing the plant's demoralized workers. "They had no idea how a business was run, that loans had to be paid. None of them, none of their fathers, and none of their grandfathers had ever worked in a factory before. They had no idea what quality control or on-time delivery meant. They thought there was a big funnel up there somewhere that money came down. They thought profit meant some kind of plunder, something someone was stealing." Dalme told them, "Profit isn't a dirty word. The only way you stay in business and create jobs is to make a profit. Profit is what will finance your future."

Dalme cut back on waste, abolished the manager's golf club fee, and put supervisors to work on the assembly line. Baby-sitters were hired for workers with small children, and a pair of old diesel buses organized to pick up those without cars. Dalme told employees that he would tolerate no alcohol or hangovers in the plant. Anyone late or absent two times in the first ninety days would receive a warning; the third time would mean probation, the fourth extended probation, and the fifth immediate dismissal. He kept an average of three of every ten people he hired, but those who survived were dependable workers. Thirty days after Dalme took over, Chahta Enterprises turned its first profit.

Dalme saw people who had been totally destitute begin to show up in new shoes and clothes without holes, and then in a car. After six or seven months, he saw them begin to become hopeful and then self-confident. Workers speak with an almost redemptive thrill of meeting deadlines for the first time. Wayne Gibson, a Choctaw in his mid-thirties who worked the assembly line for several years and is now in management training, recalls, "Factory work taught us the meaning of dependability and punctuality. You clock in, you clock out. It also instilled a consciousness of quality in people. You're proud of what you do. When I was on the production line and I had rejects, it really bothered me. I had to explain it the next day. We're proud of coming in here and getting that '100 percent zero defects' rating."

Chahta Enterprises grew steadily from fifty-seven employees in 1979 to more than nine hundred in the mid-1990s. Once the tribe had established a track record with lenders, financing for several more assembly plants and for a modern shopping center followed. In 1994, the Choctaws inaugurated Mississippi's first inland casino as part of a resort complex that also included a golf course, conference center, and 314-room hotel. "Now we're more into profit centers," says William Richardson, a former oilman from Jackson who was hired by Martin to function as a sort of resident deal-maker for the tribe. "Our philosophy is, if it's good business, if it's legitimate, if it makes a profit, there ain't nothing wrong with it. That's what we're about. We're as aggressive as hell and we take risks." By the mid-1990s, the jobs that the tribe had to offer its members were increasingly technical and intellectual, as engineers, business managers, teachers, and statisticians: it was, in short, ready to create a middle class.

In the 1980s, the Reagan administration hailed the Choctaws as a model of entrepreneurship and self-reliance. It was a mantle that Martin accepted with considerable unease. "Some of the current administration's representatives are now touting us as an example of the kind of success that all tribal governments should be able to achieve, which is fine," he said in a speech to the Association on American Indian Affairs. "But it begs the question of how we got to the point of even being able to think of success in the first place. Though we are proud we have received considerable attention from the administration, we are somewhat uncomfortable with it." He criticized what he called the administration's "Horatio Alger view" of reservation development and went on to emphasize that the foundation of the tribe's economic progress—"a stable tribal government, efficiently managed and with centralized administration systems"—lay upon federal programs that originated during the Great Society era of the 1960s. "Without the Office of Economic Opportunity and the philosophy of local control of policy by low-income people, we would never have had the chance to develop tribal governmental institutions to a point of sophistication at which the representatives of some of America's largest corporations would think of speaking with us." He might have added that the tribe's willingness to hire professional managers unencumbered by ties to tribal politics was also a contributing factor to its success.

Martin continues to call for unflagging federal investment in Indian tribes, the kind of commitment that is today increasingly out of fashion among Americans embittered at the perceived ineffectiveness of government and swollen budgets, not to mention the seemingly inexhaustible demands of aggrieved minorities. "We don't want anything more than what the U.S. gives the state governments," he says. "But you cannot bring people out of poverty with minimum wages and minimum budgets. When people control their own lives, you'll see better results. We are able to manage our own programs. Control by others kills initiative. Give tribes the responsibility for development and management and how they live their lives. If we screw up, let us deal with it."

The onus of history is inescapable wherever Indians have conspicuously disappeared from the American landscape. It is no great wonder that many Americans have for so long been reluctant to face the magnitude, or the moral implications, of the catastrophe that befell Indians during the settlement of the nation. The mind shrinks from the full impact of the deaths of so many men, women, and children from centuries of rampant disease, the damage done to so many cultures, the acts of deliberate genocide, the repeated removals, and the revolving-door policies that attempted, no matter what the human cost, to reinvent the Indian with each succeeding generation. Collectively, by anyone's measure, it is a history that constitutes one of the great long-lasting tragedies in human existence. It is as impossible to deny, should anyone wish to, the effects that such a history continues to exert on the hearts, minds, and politics of modern Indians, as it is painful to contemplate history's many missed opportunities, the many New Echotas that a more farsighted nation might have encouraged to rise on the American landscape.

Nevertheless, historical guilt, like romanticism or mindless pity, is a narrow and cloudy lens through which to view present-day realities, including that of Native Americans. It makes no more sense to hold white Americans forever guilty for the settling of the continent than it does to blame Muslims for conquering the Middle East, the Mongols for spreading the Black Plague to Europe, the British for colonizing Ireland, or, for that matter, the Sioux for overrunning the Great Plains. "If the Sioux keep demanding an apology from the U.S. government for what it did to them, we're going to demand one from the Sioux for what they did to us," the Omaha historian Dennis Hastings says with palpable bitterness.

It is also important to realize, without minimizing the degree of trauma that was suffered by virtually every Indian tribe in North America, that American history cannot be measured solely, or even mainly, by the plunder and cruelty that was committed against native peoples. More consistently than any other in the nation's history, Indian policy has embodied the nation's unending struggle to apply moral standards to the conduct of public policy. Whatever the limitations of federal Indian schools, they represented a genuine commitment on the part of Americans to open up isolated and vulnerable native communities to a larger world. Allotment was originally conceived as a plan to make Indians free and independent participants in American society. And while many Indian land cessions were negotiated under pressure, and to Indians' disadvantage, it is also true that, by the estimate of Felix Cohen, a profoundly sympathetic advocate for Indian interests as solicitor of the Bureau of Indian Affairs in the 1930s and 1940s, the United States paid more than $800 million for the lands it purchased from tribes since 1790. Asked if that was an honest price, Cohen replied: "The only fair answer to that question is that except in a very few cases where military duress was present, the price paid was one that satisfied the Indians. Whether the Indians should have been satisfied and what the land would be worth now if it had never been sold are questions that lead us to ethereal realms of speculation." Since the establishment of the Indian Claims Commission in 1946, an additional $818 million has been awarded to a number of tribes as reparation for "grossly inadequate and unconscionable" payment for lands that were ceded in the nineteenth century. The federal government has continued to provide substantial sums to ensure the survival of Indian communities; in the last twenty-five years alone it has appropriated roughly $50 billion for the nation's tribes, quite apart from land claims settlements. It is a record that, though flawed, is unequaled by any other nation in its dealings with aboriginal peoples.

Charles Wilkinson, whose writings on Indian law are among the most trenchant since those of Cohen a half century ago, has pointed out that the recurring theme during the modern era is whether and to what extent old promises should be honored today. The essential promise made to tribes primarily in the nineteenth-century treaties was that they would be guaranteed a measured separatism on their reservation homelands, free to rule their affairs outside of state compulsion but subject to an overriding federal power and duty of protection. Although that promise has often been honored more in the breach than in the observance, it has never been abandoned. "For all its many flaws, the policy of the United States toward its native people is one of the most progressive of any nation," writes Wilkinson. He adds:

> The United States never disavowed its relationship with native tribes, has never abrogated its treaty commitments, nor withdrawn its recognition of Indians as distinct peoples with cultures, lands of their own.

From even the earliest colonial times, settlers felt obliged to purchase Indian lands, and to make some kind of provision for displaced tribes. These facts set the United States above other nations in its treatment of native people, and provide a moral and legal setting from which a forward-looking policy of Federal-Indian relations must progress.

Seen in its most positive light, the deepening national commitment to tribal sovereignty thus reflects the latest phase in an ongoing, and today largely unchallenged, effort to accommodate what are perceived to be unique Indian rights and cultural values. "There is no reason for me or for any of you not to support the permanency of tribal sovereignty any more than we would be reluctant to support the permanency of federal or state sovereignty," Ada Deer, a veteran Menominee activist from Wisconsin, and the first woman to head the Bureau of Indian Affairs, told the Senate Select Committee on Indian Affairs at her confirmation hearing in 1993, adding, "The role of the federal government should be to support and to implement tribally inspired solutions to tribally defined problems. The days of federal paternalism are over."

On one plane, tribal sovereignty is simply a form of government decentralization, a pragmatic alternative to the federal micromanagement and failed social engineering of earlier generations. When Indian leaders speak of "sovereignty," they are sometimes only claiming rights and powers that other American communities have always taken for granted. Even as many tribes seem to struggle to set themselves apart from the rest of the United States in the name of sovereign autonomy, in practice they do not usually behave much differently from ordinary county or state governments. Beleaguered in her café on the South Dakota prairie, Micki Hutchinson plaintively wonders aloud, "Why can't they just be more like us?" In fact, for the most part, they are. What the Cherokees began at New Echota a century and a half ago has largely become the Native American norm. Indeed, when Indians speak of "national sovereignty," they are, after all, espousing a European concept of the nation-state that never existed in pre-Columbian America and a modern government whose practical authority is expressed mainly by means of zoning, tax codes, and the American legal system. It is hard to refute Ivan Makil, the chairman of the Salt River Pima-Maricopa Tribe, when he says, "Washington tells us that we can develop our land, establish businesses, govern our community, and make laws, but that we can't enforce them on one group of people. Why is it that when we go to Phoenix or Scottsdale, we're subject to their laws, but when they come here, they're not subject to ours? It is basically a racist point of view."

But the sovereignty movement also has other, more disturbing implications. While it is giving much-needed flexibility to tribes, it is also creating a hodgepodge of economically, and perhaps politically, unviable states whose role in the United States is glaringly undefined in the U.S. Constitution. Even more troubling, the ideology of separatism is partly rooted in the questionable premise that Indians will be better off if they are protected from contact with mainstream America. While it is probably true that tribal governments funded by federal tax dollars will serve the self-interest of their bureaucracies quite well indeed when they are protected from accountability by the principle of "sovereign immunity," there is little evidence at all that sovereignty serves the rights of Indians as individuals. Tribal sovereignty, unfortunately, is not synonymous with democracy. Indeed, the continuing expansion of tribal powers has the potential to create governments that are, in effect, impervious to federal oversight, and where it may be possible to institutionalize discrimination and the abuse of civil rights against both Indians and others and to elevate racial separatism into an ideology of government.

" 'Sovereignty' is often just a mask for individuals who rob people of their rights as U.S. citizens," says Ramon Roubideaux, a member of the Rosebud Sioux Tribe, who has probably litigated more civil rights cases than any other lawyer in South Dakota over the last half century. Round-faced and owl-eyed, he speaks with ferocious intensity. "Tribes are able to deny fundamental rights in tribal court and then hide behind the principle of sovereignty. They have the power to do anything they want to do. Many tribal court decisions have nothing to do with fairness. Without the separation of executive, legislative, and judicial powers that exists everywhere else in the United States, we have no way to enforce justice on the reservation if the tribal council says no, irrespective of the lip service that may be paid to tribal and appellate courts. Otherwise, you will see a worsening of every aspect of life on the reservation, because there is no place we can go to get an appeal on a decision. We've got to live within the legal framework of the U.S. whether we like it or not. We've got to develop along those lines because at least it has the goal of honesty and fair dealing."

No single event more vividly revealed the inherent weakness that characterizes many tribal governments than the crisis which led, in 1989, to the downfall of Peter MacDonald, the chairman of the Navajo Nation. The story of what some have called the "Navajo Watergate" is preserved on rolls of microfilm that may be found in the archives of the tribal government at Window Rock, its capital, in the ruddy desert of eastern Arizona. In contrast to most reservation towns, Window Rock truly feels like a seat of government, with signs pointing officiously to the "Supreme Court," "Tribal Computer Center," "Legal Aid," and the like, and the stolid field-stone office buildings clumped beneath the dramatic, punctured sandstone scarp that gives the place its name. Thanks to the policy of open government instituted by MacDonald's successor, Peterson Zah, the microfilmed transcripts are available to anyone who asks for them and will be handed over by young women whose cheerful efficiency typifies the professionalism of Navajo administration. Within the whirring spools lies a tale of revolution.

Now picture the scene. It is a frigid day in February of 1989. MacDonald sits on the chairman's raised dais, facing the epic murals of the sacred sandpainters and women grinding the maize that was the traditional Navajo staff of life. His craggy, thickening features are inscrutable. He wears the mantle of authority as naturally as his expensive Italian suits. As chairman of the Navajo Nation, MacDonald is the most powerful leader in Indian Country, presiding over a reservation larger than West Virginia, with a population of 125,000 and a budget of nearly $100 million per year. He surveys the tribal council that he has dominated for nearly a quarter of a century. What does he feel? Calm self-assurance? Imperious disdain? Well-concealed terror? Perhaps a little of each. Scores of councilmen are clamoring to be recognized. MacDonald knows by now that his fate hangs on the impending vote.

There is a tragic dimension to what is about to happen. There has always been something larger than life about MacDonald. He was born on the open range in the midst of a sheep drive; he enlisted in the Marines at the age of fifteen; having earned a degree in electrical engineering after World War II, he served on the team that designed the guidance system for the Polaris nuclear submarine for Hughes Aircraft. He had, in many ways, been a brilliant tribal chairman.

He had successfully renegotiated mineral leases worth millions of dollars annually to the tribe. He founded the first tribal college in the United States as well as one of the first tribal forestry programs and was among the first chairmen in the country to assert the sovereign rights of tribes.

As time went on, however, MacDonald's style of governing had become increasingly imperial. He told a local journalist, Bill Donovan, in 1982, "As long as you allow committees to run government, you'll have five different opinions, and nothing will happen. You need someone to be very strong to be in power, to accomplish what he believes needs to be accomplished." Navajo government, like that of many other tribes, was a mostly ad hoc arrangement in which political power went to the most aggressive bidder. There was a structural vagueness, an indefinition of powers that fairly invited strong-arm rule. There was no tribal constitution and no statutory separation of powers. The chairman controlled who was allowed to speak from the council floor, what items could be listed for debate, and the length of time members were allowed to speak. Critics increasingly compared MacDonald to Manuel Noriega and Ferdinand Marcos.

There had been rumors for years of bribes and payoffs. Finally, in 1988, a U.S. Senate investigation prompted by revelations in the *Arizona Republic* (based mainly upon the work of a young Shoshone-Bannock reporter named Mark Trahant) revealed an appalling pattern of corruption. MacDonald had accepted hundreds of thousands of dollars in kickbacks from contractors, along with Christmas shopping expenses, money for his wife's birthday party, all-expenses-paid trips to Hawaii and Las Vegas, and more than $20,000 for a private jet trip to the Orange Bowl. He had also managed to spend $650,000 to renovate his private office; Navajos called it "the palace." MacDonald maintained power in the tribal council by spreading around the largesse, often in the form of loans that wound up as gifts, and by awarding "consulting" contracts to his supporters on the council. In the process, he had virtually bankrupted the tribal treasury.

"Big Bo" was the last straw. In the autumn of 1988, MacDonald had used his power as chairman to suppress debate over the purchase of the half-million-acre Big Boquillas ranch from an oil and gas company for $33.4 million. Earlier the same day, the oil company had bought the same property from a cattle company for only

$26.2 million. Both the president of the gas company and the broker for the sale were longtime friends of MacDonald. In essence, MacDonald had helped them flip the ranch for an instant profit of $7.2 million. According to the Senate investigators, his share was to be $850,000 and a BMW.

MacDonald admitted taking the money but asserted, astonishingly enough, that his various benefactors were simply "showing appreciation" for his friendship and assistance. Accepting such gifts was a Navajo "tradition," he cynically claimed, a form of politeness. He hadn't wanted to insult anyone by saying no. But with "Big Bo" he had finally overstepped the bounds that even the traditionally passive Navajo electorate could accept. Fewer and fewer Navajos believed him. Now, in February, the reservation was in political chaos, fueling fears that the tribe was headed for collapse. A petition drive calling for MacDonald's removal had obtained more than forty thousand signatures. For the first time ever, Navajo demonstrators had taken to the streets. Protesters crowded outside the council chamber, demanding the chairman's resignation. MacDonald's supporters retorted with shouted warnings that his defeat would lead to a takeover of the tribe by the BIA.

Inside, MacDonald repeatedly accused his opponents of trying to destroy tribal government, of overthrowing sovereignty, of playing into the hands of their "enemies." He blamed his troubles on the Senate, the FBI, and the Bureau of Indian Affairs. The tribal government would come to a standstill, he warned. "No one will want to do business with this tribe ever again without having weekly reports on the chairman's popularity."

You can still hear, in the transcripts of the debate, the sour Nixonian blend of self-flattery and pain, the disbelief of a man who had accustomed himself to imperial power, who amazingly believed that it was he who was the real victim. He told the council, "Ronald Reagan had the Iran-Contra Affair, Jimmy Carter the hostage crisis, Lyndon Johnson the Vietnam situation."

Never before had a Navajo council attempted to remove a sitting official. Many wondered whether they even had the right to try. Councilman Gilbert Roger, speaking in Navajo, said, "It hurts my heart very deeply. Are we in fact doing the right thing? Are we going in the right direction? Are we just throwing out our laws? What will the Navajo people say now? Will they say that we change the laws as we go along?"

Councilman Leo Begay turned to James Stevens, the area director of the BIA, whom he humbly referred to as "our trustee," a revealing locution that suggested how difficult it is to break ingrained habits of paternalism and deference. Begay asked plaintively, "Are we doing right? Are we having this meeting legally?"

Stevens replied, "The Supreme Court has pretty well ruled that the Bureau of Indian Affairs has no part in these types of deliberations. In the Martinez case, they very carefully told us that we have no business there. I appreciate your consideration of my expertise, but there you are."

Eloquently expressing the sentiment of the majority, Councilman Morris Johnson said:

> Our government is like a young, new concept that is developing, is struggling to grow, and I think that we should all be aware that it is a growing nation, and that there are still a lot of things that need to be changed about our government, making it so it's more responsive and receptive to the people in this nation of ours. I see this only as one stage of growth, maybe what one might refer to as a growing pain, because that's what we're going through. But I think it's essential, because we all talk about the need to develop a government that will be standing for the future of our kids, and I think this is only one step in that direction.

In the end, the council voted to strip MacDonald of all executive and legislative power and to place him on leave. It did not end the crisis, however. Just days after MacDonald grudgingly stepped down, his supporters forcibly reoccupied the tribal offices. MacDonald, emboldened, then signed an executive order creating his own judges, one of whom immediately reinstated him as tribal chairman. Soon there were two courts, two chiefs of police, and two governments. At one point, there were even two different chairmen, one representing MacDonald and the other the tribal council, who sat side by side on the dais, each with his own gavel.

The three-member Navajo supreme court was faced with the most difficult decision in its history. Without a constitution or laws to guide it, the court had to determine whether the tribal council in fact had the authority to remove the tribal chairman. Intense political pressure was brought upon the members of the court to find in favor of MacDonald. MacDonald argued demogogically that his power came directly from the people and that since there was no established balance of powers, the legislature had no authority to remove him or to appoint a successor. In the end, seeking precedent, the court ruled that ultimate power must lie with the tribal council, because it had appointed the tribe's first modern chairman in the 1930s.

In 1990, MacDonald was found guilty on forty-two counts of accepting fraud, bribes, conspiracy, and the violation of Navajo ethics. Two years later, he was convicted on sixteen federal charges of taking bribes and kickbacks. In February 1993, he was sentenced in federal court to fourteen and a half years in prison for conspiracy and burglary, stemming from a riot in 1989, along with a concurrent sentence of seven years for extortion, bribery, and fraud.

In subsequent months, profound structural reforms were undertaken. The tribal chairman was stripped of the power to preside over the council and to appoint committees, and legislative and executive powers were formally separated. The position of tribal chairman was replaced by that of a president with the authority to veto legislation, which the council could override by a two-thirds vote. Peterson Zah, a prominent reformer, was elected to fill the new office. In the course of the campaign to unseat MacDonald, a different, equally encouraging kind of transformation had also taken place: Navajos had discovered their own political voice. "It was a political awakening for a vast number of Navajos," says John Chapela, a Navajo civil rights lawyer who organized the petition drive for MacDonald's recall. "There was a real change in the way that Navajo people looked at their government. The recall drive, for the first time, gave them the idea that they didn't have to be servile to an individual or to a group of politicians any more. They realized that they had a right to be told why a politician had acted the way he did. They began to feel that government was answerable to them."

The "Navajo Watergate" demonstrated that with political will tribal institutions can be made to work successfully and democratically, and, perhaps most important, that even tribes with a legacy of corruption and passive voter involvement are capable of reforming their governments without federal help. It presented a new model for the expression of popular democracy as well as setting a new standard for judicial activism and probity; for the first time ever, tribal courts had resolved a constitutional crisis without resorting to the power of the BIA. However, the far-reaching influence that, in a more perfect world, MacDonald's ouster might have had was hampered by the isolation and diversity of the nation's tribes, for many of whom the Navajo revolution seemed as remote as if it had occurred on the other side of the world.

Even as Navajo democrats were struggling to reform the organs of their own government, all-too-typical reports of official corruption continued to seep out of Indian Country. In 1990, the former casino manager of the White Earth Band of Chippewas, in Minnesota, was found to have forged enough absentee ballots to throw the tribal election. In 1992, the chairman of the Rosebud Sioux Tribe was forced to resign when it was proved that he had pocketed reimbursements for his trips to Washington, D.C. The same year, a BIA investigation revealed the looting of expense accounts by the chairman of the Crow Creek Sioux Tribe. In 1993, the police chief of the Pyramid Lake Paiute Tribe was fired for arresting two powerful members of the tribal council for drunken driving. When Tribal Chairman Elwood Lowery resigned in protest, one of the arrested councilmen was elected chairman in his place and appointed an unemployed mechanic as police chief; within days, the new chief himself was arrested for drunken driving and violation of probation. To be fair, a certain amount of official wrongdoing only reflected the sort of petty graft to which underpaid officials are vulnerable anyplace where public money lies easily to hand and where the power of the investigative press is weak or nonexistent. Elsewhere, however, it bore troublingly on rights that other Americans take for granted.

"On the reservation, you don't have any rights at all," says Robin Powell, who attempted to bring modern journalism to the reservation of the Turtle Mountain Band of Chippewas in North Dakota. "They can just be violated at any time. It's in the atmosphere. How can you fight it?"

In 1993, Powell was working on a master's degree in journalism at the University of North Dakota when she received an offer from the tribal chairman, Richard L. "Jiggers" LaFramboise, to become the editor of a new tribal newspaper. "It was my dream," she recalls. In numerous ways, Powell was the epitome of the new Indian that educators like Janine Pease-Windy Boy have struggled to shape. She was independent and ambitious, well schooled in her tribal culture and language in classes at Turtle Mountain Community College, experienced in the ways of the outer world, and committed to her own community. "I felt lucky," she says. "I thought, 'Things are really changing.'"

There were warnings. Friends told her, "You won't last long. You don't think that you're going to be able to report the news, do you?" Nevertheless, Powell was filled with anticipation as she put out the first issue of the *Turtle Mountain Times*. "It was like going into a no-man's-land," she says. "We were brand-new. No one knew the rules." Typical stories reported on the appointment of a new manager for the tribal casino, the tribe's effort to obtain payments from the federal government under an old treaty, and a sixth-grade class's collection of pennies for a leukemia fund; there were traditional animal stories for small children and regular installments of Norwegian folk tales for the descendants of immigrants who had settled in the area.

Some difficulties were ones she had anticipated, in a community where work styles reflected the habits of the ranch more than those of a newsroom. Sometimes reporters simply failed to show up for work; when they failed to get a story, they were often too shy to call in. The real problems began when Powell ventured to publish a story about several local murders. She learned that one of the victims, a housewife, had gone to the tribal court and told the judge that her husband had threatened to kill her. "The judge laughed at her and sent her home," Powell recalls. Soon afterward, the husband murdered not only the wife but her sister and an uncle, as well. When she tried to dig deeper, she discovered an impenetrable layer of fear. "Everyone knew who did it, but no one was ever prosecuted for it. People were afraid to stand up and speak out. There was so much fear—fear of the authorities, fear of speaking the truth. I began to realize that's just the way people live there."

Increasingly, she began to feel that the tribal government itself was part of the problem. "Reservation politics was very corrupt. It's dog eat dog. It was outrageous." There were allegations that one councilman had built a commercial gym for himself with tribal funds so that he would have something to fall back on if he was defeated for reelection and that certain officials were able to walk into the tribal casino at any time and demand money. "There was no accountability. Everyone got money. It was a way of life."

Like many tribal governments, the government of the Turtle Mountain Band had operated in virtual secrecy for as long as anyone could remember. When Powell sought statistics on drunken driving, both the police and courts simply refused. "I was told, 'Where is it written that you have a right to anything?' " Then she began requesting, and eventually demanding, copies of the minutes of council meetings. The council refused, without explanation. In an effort to force the council's hand, Powell began printing a blank gray box in each issue of the paper: "Day 126," it read, for instance, on March 21, 1994. "This space is still reserved for the tribal minutes."

After only eight months on the job, Powell was fired, in April 1994, allegedly because of personality differences with members of her staff. "It's not really a firing," a spokesman for the tribe declared. "It's a reduction in force." In a letter to Powell confirming her dismissal, Chairman LaFramboise stated, "It is very disturbing to find people who are thinking they are professional and only have hidden agendas including manifestations of political grandeur."

"The issue here is not the fact that the Turtle Mountain tribal council fired Ms. Powell; they have that right as an employer, in accordance with established personnel policies," Elmer Savilla, a former director of the National Tribal Chairman's Association, wrote in *Indian Country Today*. "The overriding issue is the responsibility of any tribal government to its people to inform them of its activities. Otherwise the democratic government perishes and is replaced by an autocracy, or worse, a dictatorship."

"In a city, they wouldn't have been allowed to get away with this," says Powell, who returned, if anything emboldened by her experiences at Turtle Mountain, to her graduate studies at the state university. "Too many people there are aware of their rights. A paper is supposed to contain news, to find out what people want to know and give them a voice, give them a sense of empowerment. But the council didn't understand that. They thought it would just write good news about them." Somewhat facilely perhaps, she blames the failure of tribal government on the way in which Indians "were taught to copy white government, in all its corrupt, devious systems." But in her determination there lies a kind of hope whose power cannot be underestimated. "People have been hurt so many times, they can't trust any more. Every time a promise was made, it wasn't kept. We live not as our ancestors had planned, but as their worst nightmare, a nation of bureaucrats of the worst kind. We have become so imbalanced in our world that the chances of getting punished for doing a good job are higher than for doing a bad job.

If each one should speak out, we could begin to trust each other once again and respect each other for having the courage to try and change."

Superficially, the May 1994 Albuquerque "Listening Conference," as it was rather self-consciously billed by its sponsors, the Departments of Justice and the Interior, provided a spectacle of enlightened official concern. Three members of the President's cabinet—Attorney General Janet Reno, Secretary of the Interior Bruce Babbitt, and Secretary of Housing and Urban Development Henry Cisneros—along with Commissioner of Indian Affairs Ada Deer sat side by side in a stylishly appointed meeting room at the Albuquerque Conference Center, cocking the ear of government both literally and symbolically to the oratory of a hundred or so assembled tribal leaders who had been invited to express their concerns. The conference differed from similar periodic gatherings that take place mostly in Washington only in the lofty credentials of the satraps on the dais, who were determined to show the depth of the new Democratic administration's interest in Indian problems.

For two days, the procession of tribal leaders recited the incantatory formulas of the sovereignty movement. "Sovereignty is a nonnegotiable item," Wendell Chino of the Mescalero Apaches, the longest-serving tribal chairman in the country, declared. He then demanded that President Clinton issue an executive order "so that the whole U.S. knows that we are governments." A spokesman for the Sisseton-Wahpeton Sioux called for Indian affairs to be transferred to the State Department because "the Department of the Interior deals with wildlife, and State deals with governments." Appropriations to tribes, it was asserted by others, should be treated as foreign aid. State and federal courts were called upon to recognize Indian "national" courts for the "extradition" of convicted criminals. The establishment of gambling casinos was described repeatedly as "a fundamental sovereign right," while several speakers called upon the federal government to create an official Indians-only game of chance that would give tribes a permanent competitive edge in the gambling industry. Others demanded the complete ouster of state governments from regulatory oversight and all other aspects of tribal affairs. "Since tribes are governments," Joanne Jones of the Wisconsin Winnebago Tribe said with breathtaking logic, "their activities are thus self-regulating."

There was a monotony to all this after a while, as the dialogue took on the strange, stylized quality that it always does at such affairs, as if Indians and officials had been forever frozen like figures in a Babylonian frieze, facing each other in postures of complaint and defensiveness, rage and guilt, as if it were impossible to consider Indians as anything but beleaguered victims and government as anything but the culpable heir to an unbroken history of deceit and repression. Not a soul spoke about the need to protect the civil rights of individual Indians from their own governments or those of non-Indian residents of "sovereign" reservations. No one spoke of the need to ensure a free press, free speech, and separation of powers. No one spoke of the futility of attracting investment to remote reservations without resources, trained workers, transportation, or nearby markets, or asked how Indian tribes might fit into the larger national and world economies. No one spoke of the bloated and expanding tribal bureaucracies or the inherent contradiction in proclaiming "national sovereignty" while relying on federal and state appropriations or about the urgency of finding common cause between tribes and their non-Indian neighbors. No one mentioned the catastrophic effects of alcoholism on Indian economies, governments, and families, or showed even the slightest grasp of the social consequences that may ensue from widespread tribally run gambling. Nor did anyone even hint at the long-term political implications that may one day result from the fact that, by any traditional measurement of ethnicity, Native Americans are rapidly becoming less "Indian" by the decade.

Behind the boilerplate rhetoric of tribal sovereignty, modern Indians are still as difficult to see clearly as the Wiyots of Indian Island were for the nervous townsfolk of Eureka. For the most part, their concerns still come to us like distant voices distorted by the lingering effects of guilt, arrogance, and wishful thinking. For much of American history, the national discourse about Indians has seemed like a kind of intellectual solipsism, a closed dialogue among popular fantasies about a people who are simultaneously "savage," "noble," and "pathetic" and who are forever said to be on the brink of vanishing from the earth. As a result, even the best-intentioned efforts to create a place for Indians in American society have sometimes proved disastrous to the very people they were intended to help.

In an age when guilt and romantic fantasy masquerade as politics, tribal sovereignty seems like a panacea for the wounds of the past. However, like so many other hopeful policies that have gone before, along with the obvious benefits it brings tribes, the drive toward sovereign autonomy is freighted with the seeds of potential disaster. Profound questions that bear upon the very nature of the United States itself hovered glaringly unasked in the mauve conference room at Albuquerque: What are the limits of federal powers? How can tribalism be squared with the legal and moral dictates of equal protection under the law? What is the role of the states in Indian Country and of the tribes in the constitutional democracy? What is the scope of tribal regulatory powers? What is the civil jurisdiction of tribal courts? How can the United States support tribal regimes that reject fundamental aspects of American democracy? What does it mean to be a citizen of a state and yet to be immune from its laws? What is the basis for asserting that reservation Indians shall have representation in state government but without taxation? On the other hand, what is the basis for asserting that non-Indian residents of Indian Country shall not be represented in tribal government yet be subject to tribal law, courts, and taxation? How can we, as Americans, tolerate double standards?

There is nothing abstract about such concerns in Glencross, South Dakota. Once, 150 people lived there. There was a railroad station, two schools, three lumberyards, two feed companies. Trucks used to line up twenty deep alongside the grain elevators. "The elevators were right over here, but they're gone now," Steve Aberle is saying in his softly modulated, lawyerly voice. His compact frame and pale, finely boned features accentuate the impression of a man who values efficiency and control; in his business suit and tie, he seems almost spectral amid the desolation. "There was a real nice Catholic church. It's abandoned now. All around here there were dozens of houses. Over there"—pointing to a squat peak-roofed building—"that was a school. And here was the café. They sold up and moved to Texas." Aberle's clapboard house is one of the last three still occupied in Glencross. He likes the emptiness; in his spare time, he plants trees. "It's a good place for my kids. They can raise their own livestock. They get to see how things grow."

It is also an eerie place. Buffalo grass has reconquered the unpaved streets. Perfectly aligned tree belts mark the boundaries of farms that no longer exist. The decaying buildings seem too recent, too familiar to be ruins; there is an unsettling sense of witnessing the end of one's own world. How fast it all happened! In the span of a single lifetime a town was born, flourished, shriveled, and died, a monument to the demise, or at least to the ambiguous transformation, of the American West. Nothing breaks the silence, not even the B-1 bomber that streaks soundlessly high over the coppery green prairie toward some destination in another world.

Glencross suffered no special, violent fate. The Great Plains are filled with failed communities like this, which seem to drift like derelict ships upon the rolling hills, sinking before your eyes. Trail City has shrunk from a population of 350 to 30, Firesteel to a single general store; Landeau has disappeared completely. The entire region is hemorrhaging jobs and people. In Dewey County, the only labor market that is expanding is the bureaucracy of the Cheyenne River Sioux Tribe. Six of the neighboring counties have lost half their population since 1930. Fifty of Nebraska's fifty-two Plains counties have lost population, thirty-eight of North Dakota's forty-one, twenty-two of Oklahoma's twenty-three. Entire towns have lost their doctors, banks, and schools. Dreamers speak seriously of returning vast tracts to the buffalo. From a certain angle of vision, Sioux demands for the restoration of the reservation to its original nineteenth-century limits are simply an anticlimax.

Every morning, Aberle drives to the storefront office that he shares with his father across the street from Pepsi's Café in Timber Lake, nine miles west of Glencross. The glory days when Indians pledged their allegiance here, as if Timber Lake were some capital city of the prairie, are long past. But there is nonetheless a certain suggestion of steadiness in the cottonwood-lined streets of frame cottages, Quonset huts, and trailers. Timber Lake is one of the lucky places: the presence of the Dewey County offices will keep it alive, along with the jobs at the rural electric co-op, the central school, the cheese factory. Even so, one hundred of the six hundred people who lived here a decade ago have moved away to places with better prospects and more hope.

The people of Timber Lake—the mechanics, the teachers, the co-op clerks, the men who work at the grain elevator, the retired farmers—are the human fruit of allotment, the flesh-and-blood culmination of the cultural blending that Senator Henry L. Dawes so idealistically envisioned a century ago. "Everyone here has got some relatives who are Indian, or a brother or a sister married to an

Indian," says Aberle. There is the white nurse who just married a Sioux, and a few houses down from her the quarter-Indian school aide who married a white man; down the block lives Timber Lake's former mayor, who is married to a one-eighth Indian, and beyond him a farmer married to another one-eighth Indian.

Aberle is one of the offspring of the Senator's dream, too. His paternal grandparents were ethnic Germans who fled Russia eighty years ago, family tradition holds, to escape some kind of now only vaguely remembered persecution. His father married a Ducheneaux, the descendant of a prominent clan of French trappers and traders who had intermarried with the Sioux and become powers in the tribe. Steve Aberle, who was born in 1960, is thus one-eighth Sioux; he is a voting member of the tribe and served for two and a half years as chairman of the tribal police commission. "Probably I associate myself more with the Indian quantum because people make more of it. But I don't deny that I'm Russian-German or that I'm part French."

There is little support in Timber Lake for the kind of blanket sovereignty that the tribal leaders in Eagle Butte now claim. Although Aberle is himself a tribe member, he shares the resentment of non-Indians who feel themselves slipping toward a kind of second-class citizenship within reservation boundaries. "It would be better to be in a situation where everybody works together and deals with people as people, but it's hard to do that when people know they pay taxes but are excluded from benefits and services. My grandparents were outcasts in Russia. The United States government told them that they would be full citizens if they moved out here. Now I see people being told that they can't even take part in a government that wants to regulate them. Something is inherently wrong when you can't be a citizen where you live because of your race. It just doesn't fit with the traditional notion of being a U.S. citizen. At some point, there has to be a collision between the notion of tribal sovereignty and the notion of being United States citizens. The people who settled here never had any idea that they would be living on an Indian reservation. The land was given to them fair and square by the government. These people have been here almost one hundred years themselves now. Then the rules were changed in midstream. Anytime you have a group not represented in the political process, they will be discriminated against. It's going to hurt these communities. People start looking for jobs elsewhere.

You lose a business here, a business there. There's going to be more and more friction. People don't want to see their kids growing up feeling victimized by the Indians."

In 1994, the Supreme Court rejected the bar owners' last appeal against the Cheyenne River Sioux Tribe. By the following summer, the tribe was earning between $15,000 and $17,000 a month in taxes on the sale of alcohol. "Every penny goes to our halfway house and our alcoholism treatment centers," says Gregg Bourland. There were vague though unsubstantiated rumors of Ku Klux Klan activity among disgruntled whites. "The rednecks haven't backed off completely, but they have to follow the law," Bourland says. "Basically, they don't have much choice. They're fully under our regulation."

The Lakotas were the victims of nineteenth-century social engineering that decimated their reservation. But the adventurous emigrants from Oslo and Odessa were also the victims of a terrible historical prank, the trick of the disappearing and now magically reappearing reservation. Their grandchildren are today discovering themselves in a strange new political world that was not of their making, hungry for protection and obliged to learn the new and difficult language of tribal power. It is a rhetoric that, reasonably enough, demands for tribes a degree of self-government that is taken for granted by other Americans; it also asks non-Indians to live under tribal taxation, police, and courts of sometimes dubious reliability. Moreover, the achievement of a sovereignty that drives away taxpayers, consumers, and enterprise may be at best but a pyrrhic victory over withered communities that beg for cooperation and innovation if they are to survive at all.

On a deeper plane, the ideology of sovereignty seems to presume that racial separateness is a positive good, as if Indian bloodlines, economies, and histories were not already inextricably enmeshed with those of white, Hispanic, black, and Asian Americans; it seems to presuppose that cultural purity ought to, or even can, be preserved. With little debate outside the parochial circles of Indian affairs, a generation of policymaking has jettisoned the long-standing American ideal of racial unity as a positive good and replaced it with a doctrine that, seen from a more critical angle, seems disturbingly like an idealized form of segregation, a fact apparently invisible in an era that has made a secular religion of passionate ethnicity. As Arthur Schlesinger has written in *The Disuniting of America*:

> Instead of a transformative nation with an identity all its own, America increasingly sees itself in this new light as a preservative of diverse alien identities. Instead of a nation composed of individuals making their own unhampered choices, America increasingly sees itself as composed of groups more or less ineradicable in their ethnic character.

The belief that Indians are somehow fundamentally different from other Americans, however romantically the idea may be expressed in terms of native "tradition" or magical notions of affinity for the earth, implies a failure of basic American values, for it leads inexorably toward moral acceptance of political entities defined on the basis of racial exclusion. Although the concept of tribal sovereignty has parallels in other ideologies of racial and ethnic separatism, it is potentially far more subversive, for Indian tribes, unlike the nation's other minorities, possess both land and governments of their own and have at least the potential to transform not only their hopes and creativity but also their biases into political power in a way that others never can. It should, moreover, be obvious to anyone that legitimizing segregation for Indians will set a precedent for its potential imposition upon black, Asian, and Hispanic Americans.

Such critical concerns will surely be further exacerbated in the years to come as Indian identity becomes increasingly ambiguous. Virtually all Indians, whether they acknowledge it or not, are moving along a continuum of biological fusion with other American populations. "A point will be reached—perhaps not too far in the future—when it will no longer make sense to define American Indians in generic terms, only as tribal members or as people of Indian ancestry or ethnicity," Russell Thornton, a Cherokee anthropologist based at the University of California at Berkeley and a specialist in native demographics, has written. Statistically, according to Thornton, Indians are marrying outside their ethnic group at a faster rate than any other Americans. Most Indians are already married to non-Indians, and by the late twenty-first century only a minuscule percentage of Native Americans will have one-half or more Indian blood. It is plain that the principle, or the pretense, that blood should be a central defining fact of being Indian will soon become untenable.

How much blending can occur before Indians finally cease to be Indians? Unfortunately, the implications of this dramatic demographic trend remain virtually unexamined. The question is sure to loom ever larger in the coming generations, as the United States increasingly finds itself in "government-to-government" relationships with "Indian tribes" that are, in fact, becoming less ethnically Indian by the decade. Within two or three generations, the nation will possess hundreds of semi-independent "tribes" whose native heritage consists mainly of autonomous governments and special privileges that are denied to other Americans.

In the meantime, relations between Indian tribes and both the federal and state governments are likely to become more complicated. Increasing control over their sources of revenue will enable more and more tribes—primarily those with marketable natural resources, well-run tribal industries, and proximity to big cities—to achieve some degree of practical autonomy. However, without enlightened leadership and an educated and self-confident electorate, not to mention the collaboration of the federal government, political sovereignty is only a pipe dream. "There's no such thing as being half sovereign any more than there is being half pregnant," says Ramon Roubideaux. "We are only sovereign insofar as the U.S. allows us to be. Sovereignty can only be preserved as long as you have the force to protect it, not just brute force, but political force, too. So unless you have an army, you'd better get used to that. Indians who think differently are just kidding themselves."

The scene on the factory floor of the Choctaw Manufacturing Enterprise, just outside Carthage, Mississippi, is prosaic enough at first glance. Although the building itself is architecturally undistinguished, just a low, white-painted rectangle hard against the cow pastures and pine woods, it is modern and spacious, and well ventilated against the withering summer heat. Inside, workers perch at long worktables, weaving wires onto color-coded boards that will become part of Xerox photocopiers. It is slow work; as many as three hundred wires must go into some of the harnesses and be attached to up to fifty-seven different terminals. Painstakingly, in deft and efficient hands, the brown and green wires are made to join and bifurcate, recombine and intertwine again in runic combinations that to the untutored eye seem as intricate and mysterious as the interwoven clans of the Lumbees. As they work, the long rows, mostly of women, listen like factory hands in similar plants most anywhere in America to the thumping beat of piped-in radio, and swap gossip, and news of children, and of planned trips to Jackson, and menus for dinner. Across the floor, at other similar tables, more women and men are weaving harnesses, assembling telephones, putting together circuit boards for computers, audio speakers, and motors for windshield wipers.

In another sense entirely, the factory floor is remarkable and profound. The faces bent over the wires and phones and speakers record a transformation that no one in Mississippi could have envisioned forty years ago, when Phillip Martin came home from Europe looking for some kind of job. The faces are mostly Choctaw, but among them are white and black faces, too, scores of them, all side by side in what was once one of the poorest backwaters of a state that was second to none in its determination to keep races and classes apart.

In 1989, there were four Choctaws in the plant's management; now there are twenty-five. "The next generation will be able to manage their own businesses," says Sam Schisler, the plant manager, a freckled Ohioan in mauve trousers and a navy-blue polo shirt who joined the Choctaws after running plants for Packard Electric. "I'm happy to manage myself out of a job." There is also something more. The audio speakers whose parts have been imported from Thailand and the circuit boards that have come from Shreveport are not glamorous, but they are symbolic: the children of the sharecroppers for whom a visit to Philadelphia, Mississippi, was a major undertaking have begun to become part of the larger world. "We'll be building these ourselves at some point," Schisler says.

The plant, the humid pastures, and the pine woods lack the drama of the rolling prairie and the sagebrush desert that are the more familiar landscape of Indian Country. But the red clay of Neshoba County has endured the same trials as the soil of Pine Ridge, the Truckee basin, and the Little Big Horn. It has been equally warred over, and equally as stained with racism, ineradicably one might have said, until less than a generation ago. It is also a land of redemption; not the exotic redemption of evangelical traditionalists who would lead Indians in search of an ephemeral Golden Age that never was, but a more prosaic and sustainable redemption of a particularly American kind, which comes with the opportunity to work a decent job and know that one's children will be educated and that the future will, all things being equal, probably be better than the past. It is one culmination of a natural and perhaps inevitable human process of adaptation that Indians have been choosing to undertake ever since the arrival of Columbus.

History was, after all, not only a story of wars, removals, and death but also one of calculated compromises and deliberately chosen risks and of both Indian communities and individuals continually remaking themselves in order to survive. To see change as failure, as some kind of cultural corruption, is to condemn Indians to solitary confinement in a prison of myth that whites invented for them in the first place. In the course of the past five centuries, Indian life has been utterly transformed by the impact of European horses and firearms, by imported diseases and modern medicine, by missionary zeal and Christian morality, by iron cookware, sheepherding, pickup trucks, rodeos and schools, by rum and welfare offices, and by elections, alphabets, and Jeffersonian idealism as well as by MTV, *Dallas,* and *The Simpsons* and by the rich mingling of native bloodlines with those of Europe, Africa, and the Hispanic Southwest. In many ways, the Indian revolution of the 1990s is itself a form of adaptation, as Indians, freed from the lockstep stewardship of Washington, search out new ways to live in the modern world.

"Our lives have been transmuted, changed forever," Rayna Green, who is of mixed Cherokee extraction and director of the Native American Program at the Museum of American History, said in a speech at the New York Public Library in 1993. "We live in a world where everything is mutable and fragile. But we are here, and we are not going to go away. Indians look around at the malls and stores of America, and say, 'None of this is ever going to be ours.' But none of it is going to go away either. This is still our home. We are all here willy-nilly together. Somehow we must face the consequences of history and live with it. We don't need only to remember the tragedy, but to also remember the gift, to live in this place, to know it gave us birth, to feel the responsibility we have for it. We have to sit down and figure out how to not hurt each other any more."

Self-determination gives Indian tribes the ability to manage the speed and style of integration, but not the power to stop it, at least for long. Integration may well mean the eventual diminishing of conventional notions of "tribal identity," but it must also bring many new individual opportunities along with membership in the larger human community. Those tribes that succumb to the impulse to exclude and to segregate, to build walls against the outside world, are likely to pay a high price. "People and their cultures perish in isolation, but they are born or reborn in contact with other men and women, with man and woman of another culture, another creed, another race," the Mexican author Carlos Fuentes has written. Indians will continue to survive as people, although they will surely be much less recognizable as the white man's idea of "Indians" as time goes on. Tribes, too, will survive, if anything as stronger and more problematic entities than they have been for many generations. The question is whether they will attempt to survive as islands isolated from the American mainstream or as vital communities that recognize a commonality of interest and destiny with other Americans.

"I don't like what this country did to the Indians: it was all ignorance based on more ignorance based on greed," Phillip Martin is saying in his meditative drawl. It is now past 11:00 P.M. The night shift has begun at the plants down the hill from the tribal offices. Outside, in the humid moonlight of east Mississippi, the red earth is a landscape of shadows and the kudzu an eerie shroud over the pines. "But I don't believe that you have to do what others did to you. Ignorance is what kept us apart. But we'd never have accomplished what we did if we'd taken the same attitude. We only have a short time to live on this earth. Everybody has got to get along somehow. We live here surrounded by non-Indians. We have to live with our neighbors and with our community. I don't condemn anyone by race. What kept us down was our own lack of education, economy, health care—we had no way of making a living. At first, I never thought that Choctaws could fit into the larger society and remain Choctaw. But, in fact, we don't have to give up our language, our culture, or our traditions. I believe that if we're going to fit in this country, we'd better try our best to do it on our own terms. If we can help local non-Indian communities in the process, we do it. And when we do it, we build up a lot of political and social support. We all have a common cause here: the lack of jobs and opportunities has kept everyone poor and ignorant. The future is going to bring a lot of change for everyone. It's going to be very difficult for a tribe to isolate itself and develop its own economy. We all depend on one another, whether we realize it or not."

Epilogue

B Y EARLY 1995, life in Salamanca, New York, had
for the most part settled back into its accustomed
groove. Under the terms of its new lease, Salamanca was now officially part of the Seneca Nation. The city's annual lease payment to
the Senecas had increased to $712,000, about twelve times what it
had been at the start of the decade. The rage of a few years past had
not disappeared, but it had noticeably diminished. The majority of
the city's non-Indian residents were resigned. "The lease isn't perfect, but it has been ratified by Congress and it's the law," Salamanca's new mayor, Rosalyn Hoag, an engaging woman gifted
with an unusually soothing manner, was telling people. "We're
going to live with it. We're going to go forward."

Hoag was an inspired choice. Her husband, Robert, who died in
1989, was a Seneca who had served in a variety of tribal offices,
including president, during the 1970s and 1980s. Her twin sons are
strikingly Indian in appearance—"You'd never know I had anything to do with it"—but since the Senecas recognize only matrilin-
eal descent, they can never become members of the tribe. "People in
Salamanca look at them like Indians, and on the reservation they're
considered white," she says with amused irony. Another grown
daughter, who is adopted, is an ethnic Crow.

There were signs that business might be picking up. An appliance store had taken over a vacant storefront on Broad Street; a travel agency had opened, and a sporting goods shop. Seneca entrepreneurs had opened two crafts galleries and three or four places that sold tax-free cigarettes and gas.

In 1994, the city had begun negotiating with the tribe to collaborate on the development of a ski resort and on the renovation of the handsome old Erie Railroad depot for offices or shops. Some Senecas were talking about bringing in casino gambling, and there were whites who were listening with interest. Other Salamancans were beginning to point out that federal loan guarantees reserved for Indian tribes could help develop the city. People were starting to remind themselves that Senecas and Salamancans used to live together without friction. "We were beginning to get some rapport," says Nancy Milligan, the head of the local community development agency.

Then hell broke loose on the Senecas' sister reservation at Cattaraugus, twenty-five miles west of Salamanca. In accordance with Seneca law, the tribe is governed by a council of sixteen members, eight of them elected from each of the two reservations. In November, the newly elected tribal chairman, Dennis J. Bowen, Sr., asserted that two councilmen had been illegally appointed by his predecessor and ordered them locked out of the tribal administration building. Opponents began charging that Bowen, who had lived for twenty-five years on the Navajo reservation, didn't "think like a Seneca any more," that he had "become Navajo." In reaction, a majority of the council, including the two dismissed members, voted to impeach Bowen and to appoint Councilwoman Karen Bucktooth president in his stead.

In spite of a federal court ruling in Bowen's favor, Bucktooth refused to back down. In February, two Bowen men were beaten and a third shot before a meeting of Bucktooth supporters. Then, in March, three of Bucktooth's men were shot dead in the middle of the night during a confrontation at the tribal building. Bucktooth claimed that the men were dragged into the administration building "and finished off." Said Bowen, "They had been drinking day and night. They had alcohol amnesia. They were so drunk they shot their own guy."

Salamancans watched uneasily as the Seneca Nation slid toward chaos. The talks over the ski center and the old station came to an abrupt halt. The sense that an opening had been created, the hint of possibility, faded. The future again became cloudy and uncertain. "We're part of the Seneca Nation now, and I guess whatever the nation does, we'll have to adjust to it," Mayor Hoag says. "It's heartbreaking for me. I just keep hoping that someone comes up on the horizon who wants to cooperate with us. If Salamanca and the nation could work together, the opportunities would be limitless. Economy, industry, tourism—there'd be no stopping it. But they're all tied up down there with tribal politics."

"We are entering an era unlike any since the European arrival, when choices made by Indian tribes will determine the future," Douglas Endreson, a nationally prominent Indian lawyer, ringingly proclaimed in 1992 to a conference of tribal leaders in Washington, D.C. "From the time that the Europeans arrived, tribes were forced to defend themselves, their rights and their people. At stake was their sovereign right to govern themselves and to make their own choices. Tribal powers are now well established in federal law. The battle for the recognition of sovereignty has been won. The new battles will center on the exercise of sovereignty as tribes struggle to achieve economic, political, social, and religious objectives. The Indian future now depends not on the federal government, but on the choices that tribes make in the exercise of their sovereignty. Tribes are no longer on the defensive—they are on the offensive."

In its broadest sense, the sovereignty movement carries within it the hope of regeneration not just for tribes as political entities but also for many thousands of men and women whose lives have been diminished by the lack of opportunity and by social pathologies that have resisted the best efforts of mainstream institutions. On the cultural plane, it represents the struggle of peoples who have been flattened out into cliché and myth to regain dimension and to shape an identity that is simultaneously more traditional and more modern, more conscious of history and less dominated by it, and, ultimately, both more Indian and more American. Furthermore, it offers tribes the most promising opportunity in generations to cope in their own way with the effects of the centuries-long collision with European civilization and to restore both the viability and the dignity of economically crippled communities. It means the revitalization of tribal languages, faiths, and traditions and, at least potentially, a foundation for the birth of a more vigorous tribal citizenship.

Like the Pte, the mythical ancestors of the Lakotas, non-Indians now find themselves in a new country, obliged to learn a new language and unable to return to the simpler if darker past. In the years to come, scores of once virtually forgotten peoples are certain to become skillful and assertive political players on the national scene. Revived tribes, with their casinos and newly established control over watersheds and timberlands, will have a direct and unpredictable impact on many communities, and not only in the lightly populated West. Tribal efforts to resuscitate moribund land and resource rights challenge conventional American beliefs about private property and the writ of law. The stunning revival of Indian traditional beliefs demands that Americans expand their idea of what constitutes religion, while campaigns to protect sacred lands challenge other Americans to think more profoundly about the nature of the earth and the consequences of our actions upon it. When Indians demand, as a right, the return of human remains from anthropologists' laboratories, they are questioning what most other Americans consider the fundamental freedom of intellectual inquiry. And when they insist on the return of a carved idol or medicine pouch, they are calling into question the right of other Americans even to see as art an object that Indians believe partakes of God.

Without a clear, nationally agreed-upon idea of what tribal sovereignty is really supposed to be, we may find ourselves, a generation or two hence, living in a land that has little in common with the goals of today's good intentions. Imagine a multitude of politically unstable, tax-supported Lebanons, Macedonias, and Tajikistans in the American heartland. Imagine a future in which Americans need passports to cross Indian-ruled parts of South Dakota, Montana, and Arizona. Imagine tribally run gambling casinos in every major city, as part of a racially based industry protected from competition by federal law. Imagine the planning of towns and cities permanently hobbled by claims that development constitutes aggression against the sacred soil of Mother Earth. Imagine whole tracts of the U.S. where civil rights do not apply. Imagine dozens of "tribes" of Americans who are distinguishable from their fellow U.S. citizens only by the special rights that were bestowed upon their Indian ancestors. These are, of course, improbable scenarios. What is certain is that without more examination and public debate than it has so far received, tribal sovereignty will continue to transform Indian Country in ways that are impossible to predict.

We are still haunted by John Marshall's brilliant, evasive compromise, whose definition of Indian tribes as "domestic dependent nations" bequeathed a contradiction in terms that continues to confuse our thinking about Native Americans up to the present day. As the landscape of Indian Country becomes steadily more complex and ever more reflective of the vast diversity of tribes that always existed beneath the conforming grid of federal policy, it is increasingly essential to disentangle the contradictions with which the principle of "sovereignty" has become freighted. To do so with enough finality to accommodate the rights of tribes as well as those of individual Indians and of other Americans deserves, and may well require, an amendment to the United States Constitution. Such a measure might, for instance, clearly define Indian tribes as self-governing entities subject in every respect to the laws of the United States but not to those of the states in which their reservations lie. If it is to guarantee democratic freedoms to all, it should prohibit discrimination by tribes based on race, religion, or tribal origin; guarantee the civil rights of tribe members and other residents of reservations, perhaps by the establishment of a board of appeal along the lines of the British Privy Council within the Justice Department; assure both Indian traditional religions and other faiths equal protection under the law, including the protection of authentic sacred sites; require tribal constitutions to enforce the separation of governmental powers; explicitly make tribal officials accountable to federal laws; ensure freedom of the press; require free, fair, and open elections subject to federal scrutiny; and guarantee permanent residents of reservations who are not enrolled members of tribes some form of representation in tribal forums.

Since political autonomy must ultimately be contingent upon economic self-sufficiency, true tribal sovereignty has to mean cutting not only the apron strings of the federal government but its purse strings as well. William Richardson, the senior business official of the Mississippi Choctaws, who also served as a deputy to the Under Secretary of the Interior for Indian Affairs during the Bush administration, has suggested the creation of a "Native American Five Year Plan," a voluntary program that would require tribes to submit a comprehensive blueprint showing how they would become self-sustaining within five years. For the first four years, tribes would receive a block grant that they would be free to allocate in any way they wished. Then in the fifth year, they would become entirely self-funding. But before tribes received any money under the program, they would be required to meet strict accounting standards, to segregate the operation of their businesses from tribal politics, and to operate their governments with constitutions and separate legislative, judicial, and executive branches.

Real sovereignty would also carry grave risks. As self-supporting states, tribes would have to accept responsibility for their own economic failures and social problems and face the possibility that bad investment or mismanagement could even lead to the liquidation of the tribes themselves. But the fact is, although tribal leaders complain loudly and incessantly about federal interference in their affairs, very few are willing to consider relinquishing the safety net of public services and federal protection of tribal assets, or to jeopardize in any fundamental way a relationship that provides them, collectively, with $3 billion per year in taxpayers' money, including free schools, health care, and technical assistance.

Tribes that have been blessed with valuable natural resources or proximity to big cities may well achieve real economic self-sufficiency in the fairly near future. Many more, such as the Pyramid Lake Paiutes, some of the Pueblos of the Southwest, and the Senecas of Western New York, among others, may have a bright future in conjunction with larger regional economies if they are able to solve their internal problems and come to terms with their non-Indian neighbors. While Indian "gaming" is widely regarded as the ultimate economic panacea, most analysts of the gambling industry predict that the boom is already nearing its peak. In January of 1994, Timothy Wapato, the executive director of the National Indian Gaming Association, acknowledged that while, at present, "gaming is probably the most viable economic development for Indian tribes," it would probably taper off as an important source of tribal income by the end of the decade, as states continue to legalize more forms of gambling and the proliferation of competing ventures leads to market saturation. "Realistically," Wapato said, "we know Indian tribes have a relatively short window of opportunity to generate that cash flow so other economic opportunities can be explored, so a broader base for their economy can be set up." By the turn of the century, abandoned casinos may well join the disused factories and empty motels that already blight the landscape around many reservation towns.

Unfortunately, there is an irreducible conflict between the aspirations of many tribes for a self-sufficient homeland and their need for imported capital and industry in order to create even a minimum number of jobs. A federal study carried out in the 1980s discovered—no secret to anyone who has attempted to generate profit-making enterprise in Indian Country—that private investment is discouraged by jurisdictional disputes between tribal and state governments, by the frequent turnover of tribal regimes and their ineptness at business management, by unskilled and unreliable Indian labor forces, and by the cumbersome regulations of the BIA. It can scarcely be surprising that communities far from airports, interstate highways, and cities, populated by ill-trained workers, and governed, in some cases, by politicians who do not abide by the most basic democratic rules are not prime locations for large-scale investment. Moreover, without permanent outside aid, the land base of arid and isolated reservations will never be able to support more than a fraction of the population that already lives there, much less sustain future increases. Although it borders on heresy to say so in the current political climate, some tribes might serve the interests of their members best by helping them relocate to urban areas where they might find decent employment. "Let's get down to reality—sooner or later, we're going to have to push people out into the world," says Ken Smith, the longtime CEO of the Confederated Tribes of Warm Springs. "That's when government can play a role. Face it, we can't all stay at home. We need to go where the jobs are. Maybe we've got to train and educate people to move off the reservation." Smith has proposed that tribes set up their own employment and job-counseling offices in cities, perhaps in conjunction with community colleges or local corporations.

At the same time, it is no longer possible to ignore the religious needs of peoples who are striving to revitalize a heritage that the United States sought for almost a century to destroy. But if public policy is somehow to be made from the tangle of inventions and aspirations that have endowed the Black Hills and Mount Graham and similar places with sacred power for Indians, other Americans must undertake a painful separation of history from wishful myth and of true political obligation from romantic attachment to idealized notions of the Indian. Not only whites but Indians as well will somehow have to overcome the false polarity that calls upon us to see the relationship between whites and Indians as one of irreconcilable conflict between conqueror and victim, corruption and innocence, Euro-American "materialism" and native "spirituality."

In the 1990s, there is no single "Indian Question," as the nineteenth century liked to phrase it, just as there is no single Indian future. Nor is there any simple formula for Indian policy that is equally applicable to tribes as varied as the Campos and the Navajos, the Senecas and the Cherokees, the Pequots and the Crows, not to mention ambiguous groups such as the Lumbees. With the maturing of tribal governments, the very concept of a single "national" Indian policy must increasingly be regarded as an anachronism, as what used to be called "Indian policy" steadily becomes "tribal" policy and reflects what Indians have decided for themselves rather than what Washington has decided for them. It is patently untrue, as many self-serving tribal politicians would have it, that treaties committed the United States to providing food and shelter to Indians until the end of time. Nevertheless, Washington's role in Indian affairs will never wholly disappear, as much as some Indians and many other Americans might wish that it would, if only because there is no alternative to federal power to ensure that the multitude of small and poorly endowed tribes that lack the resources, staff, and political will fully to manage their own affairs receive the services that all American citizens have come to expect.

While the Bureau of Indian Affairs epitomizes for virtually all reservation-dwelling Indians the bureaucratic inefficiency and petty-mindedness of the federal government, few tribal leaders wish to see it abolished. However, the BIA's role is likely to change considerably as tribes increasingly take over the functions that it once performed. For some time to come, it will probably remain the best source of technical support for smaller tribes that have neither the population base nor the funds to develop sophisticated administrations of their own. As it sheds its colonial habits as the administrator of one-size-fits-all federal programs, it could be reshaped as the tribes' principal advocate within the federal government, consolidating proposals based on the needs of regional groupings of tribes and serving as their representative to Congress and the White House. At the same time, the BIA might also serve as a mechanism to continue to monitor how public money is spent on Indian reservations, a function that will become more critical as more programs are taken over by tribal governments with little accountability either to Washington or to the people who elect them. The BIA's efficiency would be much improved by eliminating "Indian preference," which represents the most glaring example of hiring by racial criteria in the United States, and by replacing it with a system based on merit and talent.

The Choctaw experience has made clear that even the least well endowed tribes, with able and determined tribal leadership, a pragmatic willingness to cooperate with non-Indians, federal support, and the ability to raise capital, can at least in theory remake themselves into viable communities able to compete in the modern American economy. Since on most reservations there is no such thing as a middle class, and therefore little or no private capital, tribal governments are likely to remain the only source of investment capital for some time to come. A number of federal financial tools already exist that can help tribes create a more attractive climate for private investment, and they deserve a much larger national commitment: expanding federal loan and insurance guarantee programs to include Indian tribes, creating more community development banks, establishing enterprise zones, and providing more investment and employment tax credits for businesses willing to locate on tribal lands.

Tribal economies will also benefit from more aggressive federal protection of tribal water, grazing, mining, and land-use rights as well as the systematic reduction of "checkerboarding" through the purchase of property now in private hands, enabling tribes to make efficient use of their land. The recent effort of the Cheyenne River Sioux and several other tribes to develop commercial buffalo herds is an innovative attempt to transform the nostalgic impulse to recapture a bygone way of life into one of the very few even marginally viable economic enterprises possible on the Great Plains, a region for the most part so ill-suited to modern development that the descendants of the settlers who muscled the Indians off in the nineteenth century have largely abandoned it themselves. Tribes would also be well served by a far greater national investment in their human capital, most particularly through the network of tribal colleges, which have proven themselves to be the most effective single tool for moving Indians into the ranks of the skilled working class and beyond, while preserving what has been salvaged from tribal traditions that were once universally expected to vanish.

That Indians survived at all ranks among history's greatest miracles, a resounding retort to the centuries that were convinced, for good or ill, that native peoples were doomed to wither and disappear "like the leaves of the forest swept away by the autumn winds." Yet nowhere in the United States is there a monument that even attempts to express the meaning of the vast centuries-long catastrophe that has so irrevocably shaped the history of the Indian. Perhaps we have collectively shied away from the very difficulty, and implications, of the task. How, after all, could any single work of man hope to symbolize the numbers of dead beyond reckoning who succumbed to war, disease, removal, and poverty over the past five hundred years?

Thomas W. Killion, a senior historian at the National Museum of Natural History, who has presided over the Smithsonian's effort to repatriate the thousands of Native American bones in its collections, has suggested the creation of a Tomb of the Unknown Indian: "It could be the final resting place for one of the nameless Indians whose bones can never be repatriated, because we will never know what tribe he originally came from. Let one stand for all the rest." Located in Washington, near the new Museum of the American Indian, such a memorial would be a public acknowledgment that the history of the Indian lies at the center of our national story, a reminder of the power of the past, and a national testament not only to shared grief and to Indians' remarkable survival but also to their ongoing transformation into modern Americans.

The Indian story does not, of course, end with an intellectual accommodation with the past or even a moral coming to terms. Indeed, the story does not end at all. Until now, each age has imagined its own Indian: untamable savage, child of Nature, steward of the earth, the white man's ultimate victim. Imagining that we see the Indian, we have often seen little more than a warped reflection of ourselves; when Indians have stepped from the roles to which we have assigned them, we have often seen nothing at all. There will be no end to history, but an end may be put to the invention of distorting myth. With that may come a recognition that Indians are not, at last, poignant vestiges of a lost age, but men and women of our own time, struggling to solve twentieth-century problems with the tools of our shared civilization. To see Indians as they are is to see not only a far richer tapestry of life than our fantasies ever allowed but also the limitations of futile attempts to remake one another by force. Stripped of myth, the relationship between Indians and other Americans may yet remain an uncertain one, an embrace that permits neither consummation nor release, but that is, nonetheless, full of hope.

Notes

Introduction

p. 9 I spent several days: The story of the leasing controversy is based partly on interviews with Patrick Callahan, who represented Salamanca in negotiations with the Senecas; David Franz, corporation counsel for the city of Salamanca; Antonio Carbone, Salamanca's mayor; Joseph Fluent, president of the Coalition of United Taxpayers; Carl Lundberg, director of the Beautiful River Development Corporation; Bob Maas, Merle Watt, Jack O'Brien, and Emma and Lloyd St. Clair; Salamanca, New York, July 1991.

p. 9 sharp-dealing speculators: *Survey of Conditions of Indians in the United States* (U.S. Senate report, 1930), 4934–5004.

p. 10 "The Indians are": Interview with Lloyd St. Clair.

p. 10 "When they negotiated": Quoted in "Indians Bill New York Town as Its 99-year Leases Expire," *New York Times,* June 11, 1990.

p. 12 new third sphere of sovereignty: Charles F. Wilkinson, *American Indians, Time, and the Law,* 61–63.

p. 12 "letting France make laws": Quoted in "Leadership Determines Future," *Lakota Times,* December 31, 1991.

p. 12 "by Indian acts": *Special Message on Indian Affairs,* Richard Nixon to Congress, July 8, 1970.

p. 13 "Nothing, or next to nothing": Interview with Phillip Martin, Choctaw reservation, June 1992.

p. 13 accounting for 70 percent: Sharon O'Brien, *American Indian Tribal Governments,* 228.

p. 13 whose legendary mismanagement: Mark N. Trahant et al., "Fraud in Indian Country" (special series), *Arizona Republic,* October 4–11, 1987; "Inquiry

Says Indian Agency Lost Track of $95 million," *New York Times,* January 12, 1991; "BIA Mismanagement Blasted," *Lakota Times,* April 8, 1992.

p. 13 a Lakota woman: Interview with Ella Irving, Pine Ridge, May 1991.

p. 15 Shannon County, which included: Peter L. Kilborn, "Sad Distinction for the Sioux," *New York Times,* September 20, 1992.

p. 16 In terms of statistics: *Trends in Indian Health,* Indian Health Service, 1991.

p. 16 In spite of: Ernest L. Boyer, *Tribal Colleges* (1989 report by the Carnegie Foundation for the Advancement of Teaching), 59.

p. 16 "a tangle of squabbling nationalities": Arthur M. Schlesinger, Jr., *The Disuniting of America,* 137.

1. "The Very Dregs, Garbage and Spanne of Earth"

Interviews: Ron Nichols, Little Big Horn Battlefield, Montana, June 1991; Jack Norton, Eureka, California, October 1992; R. Bruce Ross, Tahlequah, Oklahoma, June 1991.

p. 25 "There's just too much": Interview with Bill Wells, Little Big Horn Battlefield, June 1991.

p. 26 a sense of gloom: Description of the controversy surrounding the battlefield is based partly on interviews with Joseph Medicine Crow, professor of history at Little Big Horn College; Kitty Belle Deernose, battlefield curator; Ron Nichols; Jim Court, former battlefield director for the National Park Service; Douglas McChristian, senior battlefield historian; Little Big Horn Battlefield, June 1991.

p. 27 mythology of Manifest Destiny: An excellent discussion of the mythology of Custer's Last Stand will be found in Richard Slotkin, *The Fatal Environment,* 373–476.

p. 28 We, the Indigenous Peoples [extract]: *Statement of Vision Toward the Next 500 Years from the Gathering of Native Writers, Artists and Wisdom Keepers at Taos* (press release), Morningstar Foundation, Washington, D.C., December 10, 1992.

p. 29 To them, Custer has become: *Indian Country Today,* June 23, 1993.

p. 31 The whites landed: Jack Norton, *Genocide in Northern California,* 81–85; also Kathleen Albano, *Various Accounts of the Gunther Island Massacre* (unpublished paper), Eureka-Humboldt Library collection.

p. 31 "A scream went up": Undated speech by Robert Gunther to the Old Sequoia Yacht Club, Eureka-Humboldt Library collection.

p. 32 "Here was a mother": Quoted in Albano, op. cit.

p. 32 The immediate reason: Norton, op. cit., 85–88.

p. 32 "after a strict examination": Quoted in Norton, op. cit., 85.

p. 33 "white man's Indian": Robert F. Berkhofer, Jr., *The White Man's Indian,* 3–4.

p. 33 "very gentle and": Quoted in Kirkpatrick Sale, *The Conquest of Paradise,* 100.

p. 33 "living in that golden world": Ibid., 198–99.

p. 34 "so pure and simple": John Florio, trans., *The Essayes of Montaigne,* 164.

p. 34 "In the beginning": Quoted by Berkhofer, op. cit., 22.

p. 34 "In proportion as": Jean-Jacques Rousseau, *Discourse on Inequality*, 177.

p. 34 "If I consider him": Ibid., 172.

p. 34 His imagination paints [extract]: Ibid., 181.

p. 35 darker archetypal vision: Robert H. Fuson, trans., *The Log of Christopher Columbus*, 172.

p. 35 "Rooted in Evill": Quoted in Berkhofer, op. cit., 20.

p. 35 "spetiall instrument": Ibid., 83.

p. 35 The degree of violence: The savagery of early colonial warfare is vividly described in Francis Jennings, *The Invasion of America*, 147–70; for examples of the dehumanizing patterns of colonial imagery of the Indian, see Berkhofer, op. cit., 20–21, 83–85.

p. 36 Boast not proud English [extract]: Berkhofer, op. cit., 53.

p. 36 invention of scalping: A discussion of the scalping question will be found in James Axtell, *The European and the Indian*, 16–35; see also Georg Friederici et al., *Scalping and Torture*, 1–34.

p. 37 Although many modern polemicists: The context of Knox's policies is discussed in Francis Prucha, *American Indian Policy in the Formative Years*, 39ff.

p. 37 "unjustifiable conduct": Report by Henry Knox to the Continental Congress, July 1788, in Francis Prucha, ed., *Documents of United States Indian Policy*, 11.

p. 37 "If any citizen": Quoted in Prucha, *American Indian Policy in the Formative Years*, 149.

p. 37 "Unless such crimes": Ibid., 150.

p. 37 "No people will sit": Ibid., 143.

p. 38 The Seneca Nation [extract]: Quoted in Lois Barton, *A Quaker Promise Kept*, 1.

p. 38 "We shall with great pleasure": Ibid., 214ff.

p. 38 National leaders struggled: Quoted in Prucha, *American Indian Policy in the Formative Years*, 216.

p. 38 "miserably to waste away": Quoted in Brian W. Dippie, *The Vanishing American*, 53.

p. 39 "Those who come": Quoted in Bernard W. Sheehan, *Seeds of Extinction*, 127.

p. 40 self-consciously redefined their nature: Grace S. Woodward, *The Cherokees*, 122ff.

p. 40 according to Boudinot: Theda Perdue, ed., *Cherokee Editor*, 72.

p. 41 "A spirit pervades": Letter from "Rev. Mr. Steiner" to a Moravian colleague, *Philadelphia Recorder*, March 18, 1826.

p. 41 "We, the Representatives": *Constitution of the Cherok Nation*, as adopted in 1827.

p. 41 At the urging of: Perdue, op. cit., 7–9.

p. 42 "It needs not": "Address to the Whites," speech by Elias Boudinot at the First Presbyterian Church of Philadelphia, May 26, 1826.

p. 42 "What are the prospects": Ibid.

p. 43 In times of peace [extract]: Ibid.

p. 43 "If the Cherokee Nation": Ibid.

p. 43 a fateful deal: Woodward, op. cit., 130–31.

p. 43 Indian removal originated: Prucha, *American Indian Policy in the Formative Years*, 226.

p. 44 "the hunter or savage": Quoted in ibid., 228.

p. 44 "There is no alternative": *Acts of the General Assembly of the State of Georgia*, 1827, 249–50.

p. 44 "ample district": Message by Andrew Jackson to Congress, December 8, 1829, in Prucha, *Documents of United States Indian Policy*, 48.

p. 44 "an interesting commonwealth": Ibid.

p. 44 null and void: For an outline of this legislation, see Woodward, op. cit., 158–59.

p. 44 "in digging for gold": Quoted in John Ehle, *Trail of Tears*, 225.

p. 44 "A few thousand": Speech by Wilson Lumpkin to the Georgia House of Representatives, December 2, 1831.

p. 45 "as human beings": Francis Prucha, ed., *Cherokee Removal*, 282.

p. 45 *Cherokee Nation v. Georgia*: Prucha, *American Indian Policy in the Formative Years*, 227–49. The continuing legal implications of the Marshall court's trilogy of Indian rulings are discussed at length in Charles F. Wilkinson, *American Indians, Time and the Law*.

p. 45 "a distinct political society": *Cherokee Nation v. Georgia*, in Prucha, *Documents of United States Indian Policy*, 58.

p. 46 "You asked us": Quoted in Ehle, op. cit., 254.

p. 46 "a distinct community": *Worcester v. Georgia*, in Prucha, *Documents of United States Indian Policy*, 61.

p. 47 "the decision of": Quoted in Prucha, *The Great Father*, 77.

p. 47 "John Marshall has": Quoted in Ehle, op. cit., 255.

p. 47 "their only hope": Ibid.

p. 47 Another four thousand Cherokees: A detailed discussion of possible Cherokee losses is contained in Russell Thornton, *American Indian Holocaust and Survival*, 114–18.

p. 48 "graceful and unrestrained": James Fenimore Cooper, *The Last of the Mohicans*, 47.

p. 48 "some precious relic": Ibid., 48.

p. 48 "It is melancholy": Quoted in Dippie, op. cit., 15.

p. 49 "snow before the vernal influence": Ibid., 13.

p. 49 "the leaves of": Ibid.

p. 49 "So alien to himself": Quoted in Berkhofer, op. cit., 95.

p. 49 "Their arts, wars": Quoted in Michael Paul Rogin, *Fathers and Children*, 116.

p. 49 The goldseekers were: Theodora Kroeber, *Ishi in Two Worlds*, 44–45. For patterns of violence in general, see Kroeber, 56–87; also James J. Rawls, *Indians of California*, 171–86.

p. 50 the federal government reimbursed: Norton, op. cit., 76.

p. 50 "after a meeting": Quoted in ibid., 68.

p. 50 "The whitemen built": Ibid., 54–58.

p. 50 "Cold-blooded Indian killing": Ibid., 96.

p. 50 "two or three times": Quoted in Thornton, op. cit., 204.

p. 50 "Indians, or persons": Quoted in Rawls, op. cit., 87.

p. 50 Professional slave hunters: Norton, op. cit., 41–49; also Rawls, op. cit., 91–105.

p. 50 "Some of the agents": Quoted in Norton, op. cit., 42.

p. 50 Indians were heard: Interview with Jack Norton.

p. 51 the Indian population: Norton, *Genocide in Northern California*, 171; also Thornton, op. cit., 49.

p. 51 "The Indians are": *Humboldt Times*, December 22, 1860.

p. 51 "men of intelligence": Gunther speech, op. cit.

p. 51 "errors of nature": Quoted in Berkhofer, op. cit., 20.

p. 51 "more brutish than": Ibid., 21.

p. 52 No one really knows: Douglas H. Ubelaker, "North American Indian Population Size, A.D. 1500 to 1985," *American Journal of Physical Anthropology* 77 (1988): 289–94; also Thornton, op. cit., 15–41.

p. 54 United States census: Dirk Johnson, "Census Finds Many Claiming New Identity: Indian," *New York Times*, March 5, 1991.

p. 56 The Cherokee Nation: Details are based partly on interviews with Dan Agent, Tommy Thompson, and C. Clinton Fixin, Tahlequah, Oklahoma, June 1991.

p. 57 "Sometimes I really feel": Speech by Wilma Mankiller to the National Tribal Leaders Forum, Washington, D.C., May 12, 1992.

2. "We Ain't Got Feathers and Beads"

Interviews: Cynthia L. Hunt, Ruth Locklear, Claude Lowry, Reverend Weldon Lowry, and Linda Oxendine, Pembroke, North Carolina, March and June 1991; Jack Campisi, Charlotte, North Carolina, March 1991; Holly Reckord, Washington, D.C., April, 1992; James H. Merrell, Poughkeepsie, New York, June 1992.

p. 61 forced the Ku Klux Klan: Karen I. Blu, *The Lumbee Problem*, 88–89, 124–26.

p. 63 a guesswork story: Ibid., 36–44.

p. 63 "Indians running": Quoted in *The Lumbee Petition*, 13.

p. 63 "a mixt Crew": Ibid., 14.

p. 63 "a mob railously assembled": Ibid., 16.

p. 63 described in censuses: Ibid., 38.

p. 64 sought official federal recognition: Ibid.; the history of their lobbying is recounted on 52–77.

p. 64 sent a Harvard anthropologist: Ibid., 85–87.

p. 64 "Border line case": Letter from Carl Seltzer to the Commissioner of Indian Affairs, July 30, 1936.

p. 65 "Diagnoses were based": Ibid.

p. 65 "Nothing in this Act": Quoted in *The Lumbee Petition*, 96–97.

p. 65 "lords of the forest": Catlin, *Letters and Notes on the Manners, Customs and Conditions of North American Indians*, 2.

p. 66 "honest, industrious": Quoted in Russell Thornton, *American Indian Holocaust and Survival*, 189.

p. 66 "Indians only in": Ibid.

p. 67 "An Indian is one": Interview with Henry Real Bird, Crow Agency, Montana, October 1991.

p. 67 "An Indian is someone": Momaday is cited in "View from the Shore," *Northeast Indian Quarterly*, Fall 1990, 7.

p. 67 But Ross Swimmer: Testimony before the U.S. Senate Select Committee on Indian Affairs, August 12, 1988.

p. 67 A 1991 federal law: *Indian Trader*, August 1991.

p. 68 "I don't know": Quoted in ibid.

p. 68 "Make no mistake": "Banished Seneca Sue Tribe over Treason," *Indian Country Today*, January 7, 1993.

p. 68 Recently, one group: Interview with Holly Reckord.

p. 68 "As I use it": Court transcript quoted by Jack Campisi in *The Mashpee Indians*, 32.

p. 69 "any Indian or": *25 Code of Federal Regulations*, Chapter 1, 1995.

p. 69 the Catawba "nation": James Merrell, *The Indians' New World*, 18–26, 47–48.

p. 70 The North Carolina Band of Cherokees: Interview with Thomas Killion, Washington, D.C., July 1992.

p. 70 "The Secretary": *National Museum of the American Indian Act*, 1989.

p. 71 "shattering, aggressive drive": John Collier, *From Every Zenith*, 93.

p. 71 "this Red Atlantis": Cited in Robert F. Berkhofer, Jr., *The White Man's Indian*, 178.

p. 71 "a magical habitation": Collier, op. cit., 125.

p. 71 "They had what": John Collier, *Indians of the Americas*, 7.

p. 72 "Collier assumed that": Brian W. Dippie, *The Vanishing American*, 312.

p. 72 "awakening the racial spirit": Francis Prucha, *The Indians in American Society*, 67.

p. 72 The United States Supreme Court has affirmed: *Santa Clara Pueblo v. Martinez*, 1978.

p. 72 criteria for membership: This subject is discussed in Thornton, op. cit., 190–200; many examples will also be found in Sharon O'Brien, *American Indian Tribal Governments*, 200.

p. 73 "in effect, cause the tribe": "Tribe Wins Appeal in Fight for Custody of Indian Girl," *Los Angeles Times* (Orange County edition), August 4, 1992.

p. 73 Since abolishing: *Indian Country Today*, January 7, 1993.

p. 73 "full-blood for the purpose": Interview with tribal spokeswoman Terry Bell, Ledyard, Connecticut, May 1991.

p. 74 each Pequot is guaranteed: Kirk Johnson, "Tribe's Promised Land Is Rich but Uneasy," *New York Times*, February 20, 1995.

p. 74 the Lumbees assert: *The Lumbee Petition*, generally, 4–18.

p. 74 the enfeebled remnants: This process is lucidly described by James Merrell in "Some Thoughts on Identifying Indian Tribes in Early America," a paper presented to a conference on the federal recognition of tribes, Peace Studies Program, Wellesley College, November 9, 1990.

p. 74 white, mulatto, and black: The early mingling of the races and the evolution of racism is discussed by James Merrell in "The Racial Education of the Catawba Indians," *Journal of Southern History*, August 1984.

p. 75 "free negro": *The Lumbee Petition,* 24.

p. 78 the biological future: Thornton, op. cit., 236–37.

p. 81 "The Lumbee tribe has": *The Lumbee Petition,* 2.

p. 82 "If Congress creates": Resolution by the Southern Pueblos Governors Council, October 14, 1988.

p. 82 "There is no": Interview with Philip Martin, Choctaw reservation, Mississippi, June 1992.

p. 82 "extensive inter-marriage with": Testimony by Jonathan L. Taylor before the House Interior and Insular Affairs Committee, September 26, 1989.

p. 82 an estimated $90 million: Testimony by Ross Swimmer before the Senate Select Committee on Indian Affairs, August 12, 1988.

p. 83 "Both as a matter": *Special Message on Indian Affairs,* Richard Nixon to Congress, July 8, 1970.

p. 84 authorizing the preferential hiring: Bureau of Indian Affairs personnel management letter no. 72-12, 1972.

p. 84 "Indian people will never": *Indian Self-Determination and Education Assistance Act,* January 4, 1975.

p. 84 "the relationship of": *Final Report of the American Indian Policy Review Commission,* May 17, 1977.

p. 85 1. that Indian tribes [extract]: Ibid.

p. 85 "to convert a": Ibid.

p. 85 the assertion of inherent [extract]: Speech by Lloyd Meeds to White House conference on Indian education, quoted in *Lakota Times,* January 28, 1992.

p. 86 Ostensibly at issue: A concise discussion of Martinez will be found in Charles Wilkinson, *American Indians, Time and the Law,* 113–16.

p. 87 Much has been written [extract]: *The Indian Civil Rights Act* (report by U.S. Commission on Civil Rights), 16.

p. 87 "culturally and politically distinct": *Santa Clara Pueblo v. Martinez,* 1978.

p. 87 "providing in wholesale fashion": Ibid.

p. 87 Given Congress' concern [extract]: Ibid.

p. 87 the case of Tom Shortbull: Details are drawn from *Shortbull v. Looking Elk,* 677 F.2nd 645, 650 (8th Cir., 1982); also interview with Ramon Roubideaux, who represented Shortbull, Rapid City, South Dakota, July 1992.

p. 89 "The system is weak": "Salway Charges Corruption Kept Him from Success," *Lakota Times,* January 21, 1992.

p. 89 some 280 complaints: *The Indian Civil Rights Act,* op. cit., 19.

p. 90 "No effort has been made": Ibid., 20.

p. 90 "Not one Federal dollar": Ibid., 77.

3. The Reinvention of Indian Country

Interviews: Ivan Makil, Richard Wilks, and Martha Whitman, Salt River Pima–Maricopa reservation, Arizona, November 1991; Gregg J. Bourland, Wayne Ducheneaux, and Marvin LeCompte, Eagle Butte, South Dakota, July 1992; Micki Hutchinson, Isabel, South Dakota, July 1992; Steve Aberle, Timber Lake, South Dakota, July 1992; George Mickleson, Pierre, South Dakota, July 1992; Terry Bell and Kevin McBride, Mashantucket Pequot reservation, Connecticut, May 1991.

p. 93 A few minutes: The story of Biscuit Brown's murder and its aftermath is based on interviews with Martha Whitman, Ivan Makil, Richard Wilks, and Tribal Police Chief Edward Reina, Jr.

p. 97 People said later: The narrative of events at Isabel is based on interviews with Micki Hutchinson, Marvin LeCompte, and Gregg J. Bourland, and on news reports in the *Rapid City Journal*, March 28, 29, and 30, 1991.

p. 98 "have the benefit": *General Allotment Act*, February 8, 1887, *U.S. Statutes at Large*, 24:388–91; and *Subdivision of the Sioux Indian Reservation*, March 2, 1889, 25 Stat., 888.

p. 98 the 1908 law: *Public Law No. 158*, 60th Congress, 1st Sess., Chap. 218, 1908.

p. 101 "that the 160 acres": Wallace Stegner, *Where the Bluebird Sings to the Lemonade Springs*, 62.

p. 101 lay three deep underfoot: Richard Critchfield, *Trees, Why Do You Wait?* 57.

p. 103 Many Sioux hold: The story of the emergence is told in William K. Powers, *Oglala Religion*, 79–81.

p. 104 Anthropologists believe: George E. Hyde, *Red Cloud's Folk*, 3–19. The date the Sioux reached the Black Hills, a point of great political importance, is discussed on 20–42; also Edward Lazarus, *Black Hills—White Justice*, 3–8.

p. 104 a profoundly enthnocentric people: Royal B. Hassrick, *The Sioux*, 61ff.

p. 106 Increasingly, Indian leaders: Speech by Rudolph C. Ryser to symposium on Indian self-governance at Evergreen State College in Olympia, Washington, October 15, 1988.

p. 107 "We, the members": Confederated Tribes of the Warm Springs Reservation of Oregon, *Declaration of Sovereignty*, 1992.

p. 107 "Our sovereignty is based": Ibid.

p. 107 Tribal "gaming": An excellent discussion of tribal gaming, its profitability, and the conflicts that it engenders with the states will be found in Robert Goodman, *Legalized Gambling as a Strategy for Economic Development;* see also "The Face of Indian Gaming" (a special report), *Reno Gazette-Journal*, April 11, 1993.

p. 108 "What happens within a state": Quoted in Goodman, op. cit., 162.

p. 108 Governor Lowell P. Weicker, Jr.: "Slot Machines Are Delayed; Weicker's Deal Is Hailed," *New York Times,* January 16, 1993.

p. 108 $6-billion industry: Goodman, op. cit., 150.

p. 108 "Gaming is all": Statement by Gaiashkibos before the House Interior and Insular Affairs Committee on Gaming on Reservations, January 9, 1991.

p. 109 By far the most profitable: Peter Passell, "Foxwoods, a Casino Success Story," *New York Times*, August 8, 1994.

p. 109 grossing about $800 million: Kirk Johnson, "Tribe's Promised Land Is Rich but Uneasy," *New York Times*, February 20, 1995.

p. 110 a disturbing illustration: For a critical Indian view of the modern Pequot tribe, see "Tribal Power Plays Weaken Sovereignty Stance for All," *Indian Country Today*, July 27, 1995.

p. 110 The Pequots, once powerful: A full account of the Pequot War and its legacy is given in Richard Drinnon, *Facing West*, 36–61; see also Laurence M. Hauptman and James D. Wherry, *The Pequots in Southern New England*, 69–95.

p. 111 "Pequod, you will no doubt": Herman Melville, *Moby Dick*, 100.

p. 111 the tribe had shrunk: Hauptman and Wherry, op. cit., 134; the reemergence of the tribe is discussed at length on 117–40.

p. 111 "The sovereignty issue": "Tribes 'Will Not Stand' for Further Gaming Restrictions," *International Gaming and Wagering Business*, January 5, 1994.

p. 112 "quasi-sovereign domestic dependent nations": Policy statement by President Bush, June 14, 1991.

p. 112 "still possess those aspects": *United States v. Wheeler*, 435 U.S. Reports (1978), 322–28, 332.

p. 112 "sovereign power": *Merrion v. Jicarilla Apache Tribe*, 455 U.S. Reports (1982), 130.

p. 112 "when that conduct": *Montana v. United States*, 450 U.S. Reports (1981), 544, 566. For more examples, see Charles F. Wilkinson, *American Indians, Time and the Law*, 135.

p. 112 "Without land, 'sovereignty' becomes": Speech by Georgia C. George at the National Tribal Leaders Forum, Washington, D.C., April 15, 1991.

p. 112 In 1948, Congress decreed: 18 U.S.C. (1948), 1151; see discussion of the concept of "Indian Country" in Wilkinson, op. cit., 87–93.

p. 113 subject to tribal judicial processes: Kirk Johnson, "An Indian Tribe's Wealth Leads to the Expansion of Tribal Law," *New York Times*, May 22, 1994.

p. 114 "The legal rights": Quoted in ibid.

p. 115 his impoverished childhood: Dawes's early years are described by Fred H. Nicklason in *The Early Career of Henry L. Dawes, 1816–1871* (unpublished doctoral dissertation), Yale University, 1967.

p. 115 "from the night": Herbert Welsh of the Indian Rights Association, quoted by Francis Prucha, *The Great Father*, 204.

p. 115 "absolute conformity": Speech by Merrill E. Gates, in *Proceedings of the Eighteenth Annual Meeting of the Lake Mohonk Conference of the Friends of the Indian*, 1900.

p. 115 "uniformity of action": Ibid.

p. 115 "tribal mass": Ibid.

p. 115 "American ideals, American schools": Ibid.

p. 116 "all the Lands and Territories": Francis Prucha, *American Indian Policy in the Formative Years*, 13.

p. 116 "set apart for": Quoted in Don C. Clowser, *Dakota Indian Treaties*, 135.

p. 116 "shall ever be": Ibid.

p. 116 No sooner had the treaty: Ibid., 73ff.

p. 117 "of spoliation, of wars": Quoted in *Fifteenth Annual Report of the Board of Indian Commissioners*, 1883, 69–70.

p. 117 "as an individual": Ibid.

p. 117 He estimated that: Ibid.

p. 117 "devoid of appearance": Quoted in Lazarus, op. cit., 105.

p. 117 "wool shoddy apparently": Ibid.

p. 117 "They promised to": Ibid., 104.

p. 117 "in darkness, heathenism": *Proceedings of the Fifth Annual Meeting of the Lake Mohonk Conference of the Friends of the Indian,* 1887.

p. 117 28,000 Indians occupied: *Proceedings of the Fourth Annual Meeting of the Lake Mohonk Conference of the Friends of the Indian,* 1886.

p. 118 "a squirrel's jump": Ibid.

p. 118 "When the Indian begins": Francis Prucha, ed., *Americanizing the American Indians,* 29.

p. 118 none of the selfishness: *Proceedings of the Fifth Annual Meeting of the Lake Mohonk Conference of the Friends of the Indian.*

p. 118 He wondered how: Ibid.

p. 119 "disappear like an April cloud": *Proceedings of the Fourth Annual Meeting of the Lake Mohonk Conference of the Friends of the Indian.*

p. 119 "It is perfectly plain": *Annual Report of the Commissioner of Indian Affairs,* September 28, 1886.

p. 119 "a theory utterly repugnant": Ibid.

p. 119 "To me": Ibid.

p. 120 "If you will prepare": Ibid.

p. 120 "by the collar": Ibid.

p. 120 "We need great patience": Ibid.

p. 121 Our work must [extract]: Ibid.

p. 121 "I have more": Ibid.

p. 121 "two milch cows": 50th Congress, 2nd Sess., 25 Stat., 888, Chap. 405, March 2, 1889.

p. 121 "for the promotion": Ibid.

p. 122 On the Papago reservation: Janet A. McDonnell, *The Dispossession of the American Indian 1887–1934,* 19.

p. 123 "Forasmuch as the": Quoted in ibid., 95. (Such scenes are vividly evoked in Charles Fergus's interesting novel about McLaughlin's tour of the reservations, *Shadow Catcher.*)

p. 123 "Grafting has become": Quoted in McDonnell, op. cit., 93.

p. 123 Within a few years: Ibid., 93, 100.

p. 123 In 1931, the average monthly income: Lazarus, op. cit., 165.

p. 124 Doran Morris, Sr., then chairman: Interview with Doran Morris, October 1991.

p. 124 "the greatest single": McDonnell, op. cit., 24.

p. 125 House of Representatives closed the void: "Sovereignty Prevails: Duro Case Overturned," *Lakota Times,* November 6, 1991.

p. 126 "This is a great victory": Navajo tribal press release, November 1, 1991.

4. The Shadow of Chief Seattle

Interviews: Ralph Goff, Campo reservation, California, October 1992; Elwood Lowery, Mervyn Wright, Glorene Guerrero, and Paul Wagner, Pyramid Lake Paiute reservation, August 1992; Joe Ely, Phoenix, Arizona, August 1992; Robert Pelcyger, Boulder, Colorado, June 1991, and Nixon, Nevada, August 1992; John McIntyre, Sparks, Nevada, August 1992; Lyman F. McConnell and Ted deBraga,

Fallon, Nevada, August 1992; David Lester, Denver, Colorado, June 1991; Ken Smith and Louis Pitt, Warm Springs reservation, Oregon, September 1991.

p. 129 The single resource: Details of the plan are contained in *The Campo Model: The Search for Solutions* (tribal study), May 13, 1991.

p. 130 Geologists hired by: Letter from Ted Smith, a professional geologist, to Ronald Jaeger, area director of the Bureau of Indian Affairs, San Diego, April 25, 1992.

p. 130 "How can you": Interview with Donna Tisdale, October 1992.

p. 131 "The idea is": Excerpts are from "Chief Seattle Speaks," frontispiece for a Greenpeace report by Bradley Angel, *The Toxic Threat to Indian Lands,* 1993.

p. 132 "Perhaps in these pockets": Speech by Oren R. Lyons, "on behalf of the indigenous nations and peoples," to the preparatory committee for the United Nations Conference on Environment and Development, March 18, 1991.

p. 133 "one of the most moving": Al Gore, *Earth in the Balance,* 259.

p. 133 In 1993, Greenpeace: Angel, op. cit.

p. 133 If Seattle's musings: Christian F. Feest, in James A. Clifton, *The Invented Indian,* 316–17; also "Chief's 1854 Lament Linked to Ecological Script of 1971," *New York Times,* April 21, 1992.

p. 133 "Basically, I don't know": Ibid.

p. 134 At least 50 percent: Sharon O'Brien, *American Indian Tribal Governments,* 227.

p. 134 Until quite recently: Many examples will be found in Mark N. Trahant et al., "Fraud in Indian Country" (special series), *Arizona Republic,* October 4–11, 1987.

p. 134 "You must discourage": Quoted in Martha Knack and Omer C. Stewart, *As Long as the River Shall Run,* 310.

p. 135 "transition from Federal": *Indian Self-Determination and Education Assistance Act,* January 4, 1975, *U.S. Statutes at Large,* 88:2203–14.

p. 135 their own resource policies: For examples, see O'Brien, op. cit., 227–28.

p. 136 "It's the whole ecosystem": Statement by Sarah James before the House Subcommittee on Fisheries and Wildlife Conservation and the Environment, August 7, 1991.

p. 136 "No one should": Interview with Brenda Itta-Lee, Washington, D.C., April 1991.

p. 137 still-unexploited Indian water: Charles Wilkinson, *The Eagle Bird,* 51.

p. 137 Without the Truckee: The dependence of the region on the Truckee is described in detail in a special series on the watershed in the *Reno Gazette-Journal,* August 21–25, 1988.

p. 138 Francis Griffith Newlands: Personal details are based on a telephone interview with William Rowley of the History Department of the University of Nevada, Reno, May 1994. For Newlands and the development of federal reclamation policy generally, see Marc Reisner, *Cadillac Desert,* 115–18; Knack and Stewart, op. cit., 269; Donald Worster, *Rivers of Empire,* 166–69; and M. F. Hudson, *Senator Francis G. Newlands.*

p. 139 "Nevada was born": Quoted by William Rowley.

p. 139 "the vast speculative": Wallace Stegner, *Where the Bluebird Sings to the Lemonade Springs,* xix.

p. 139 "I tell you gentlemen": Quoted in Stegner, *Beyond the Hundredth Meridian,* 342–43.

p. 139 "The aim [of irrigation]": *Congressional Record,* 56th Cong., 2nd sess., January 30, 1901, 1701.

p. 139 "nationalize the works": Quoted in Marc Reisner, op. cit., 117.

p. 140 The Paiutes' early history: Knack and Stewart, op. cit., 1ff.

p. 141 The Kuyuidokados' story: Sarah Winnemucca Hopkins, *Life Among the Paiutes,* 6–7.

p. 141 "A number of": Quoted in Knack and Stewart, op. cit., 33–35.

p. 142 "After a few volleys": Ibid., 35.

p. 142 "The money will not": Ibid., 113.

p. 142 "only to satisfy": Ibid., 272.

p. 142 the effects were catastrophic: Ibid., 271–72.

p. 143 Farmers discovered: Reisner, op. cit., 118–21.

p. 144 Although the Supreme Court had declared: *Winters v. United States,* 207 U.S. Reports (1908), 564.

p. 144 "The Indians have": Quoted in Knack and Stewart, op. cit., 293.

p. 144 In 1944, the Department of Justice: *Orr Ditch Decree,* described in "Orr Ditch Was 1st Suit in Truckee Legal Flood," *Reno Gazette-Journal,* August 21, 1988.

p. 145 With some difficulty: Richard Drinnon, *Keeper of the Concentration Camps,* 284–85.

p. 145 "We intend to": Quoted in ibid., 286.

p. 145 By midcentury, it seemed: The story of the recovery of the cui-ui is based on the *Cui-ui Recovery Plan (Second Revision),* 1992; "Truckee River/The Legal Battle," *Reno Gazette-Journal,* August 21, 1988; "Rare Pyramid Fish Complicate Water Dilemma," *Reno Gazette-Journal,* August 23, 1988; also interviews with Paul Wagner, tribal fisheries biologist, and Tom Strekel, aquatic biologist, BIA, Reno, Nevada, August 1992.

p. 146 district court ruled: *Pyramid Lake Paiute Tribe of Indians v. Morton,* 354 F.Supp. 252, 4 ERC 1714 (1973).

p. 146 Next, a federal court: *Carson-Truckee Water Conservation District v. Watt,* 549 F.Supp. 704 (1982).

p. 146 "an old-fashioned showdown": Patricia Limerick, *The Legacy of Conquest,* 136.

p. 146 The Paiutes wanted: The account of the negotiations is based partly on interviews with Sue Oldham, Robert Pelcyger, and Joe Ely.

p. 147 wholly unforeseen collaboration: *Preliminary Settlement Agreement Between the Pyramid Lake Paiute Tribe and the Sierra Pacific Power Company,* May 23, 1989.

p. 148 "When we talk": Testimony of Joe Ely before the Senate Subcommittee on Water and Power, February 6, 1990.

p. 150 By conservative estimate: "Where the Truckee River's Water Goes," *Reno Gazette-Journal,* August 22, 1988.

p. 151 water flow to Newlands: Interview with Lyman F. McConnell.

p. 151 simply "the settlement": *Fallon Paiute Shoshone Indian Tribes Water*

Rights Settlement Act of 1990, in *Sacrificing Dreams, Building Reality: Fighting over the Truckee,* 191–216.

p. 152 "new ethic of place": Wilkinson, op. cit., 138.

p. 153 It is a sultry Friday: The account of the water committee meeting is based on the author's notes.

p. 153 the worst drought in generations: "Water: The Facts of Life," *Reno Gazette-Journal,* August 2, 1992; and "River Drying a Slow Death," *Reno Gazette-Journal,* August 11, 1992.

p. 153 "Maybe a few": "If We Keep Ignoring Realities, We'll Turn Drought into Disaster" (editorial), *Reno Gazette-Journal,* October 13, 1992.

p. 154 Almost alone on: "Prosser Creek Plan Not a Promise," *Reno Gazette-Journal,* August 7, 1992.

p. 158 tribal timber industry: Data are based on interviews with Ken Smith, Louis Pitt, Jody Calica, Ed Mannion, and Bill Donaghu, Warm Springs, September 1991; and Louis Pitt, by telephone, June 1995. For an overview of economic development on the Warm Springs reservation, see Robert H. White, *Tribal Assets,* 187–251.

p. 159 "the rocky crests": Eli Gifford and R. Michael Cook, eds., *How Can One Sell the Air? Chief Seattle's Vision,* 32.

p. 161 number of Indian slaves: "Chief's 1854 Lament Linked to Ecological Script of 1971," *New York Times,* April 21, 1992.

p. 161 "The ground beneath": Gifford and Cook, op. cit., 75.

5. Listening for the Ancestors

Interviews: Karl Reinhard, Hugh Genoways, and Tom Myers, Lincoln, Nebraska, May and October 1991; Dennis Hastings, Doran Morris, Sr., and Wynema Morris, Macy, Nebraska, May and October 1991; Donald J. Ortner, Washington, D.C., December 1990; W. Richard West and Douglas Owsley, Washington, D.C., April 1991; Robert Peregoy, by telephone, June 1991; Diana Fane, Brooklyn, New York, April, 1991; Curtis Hinsley, Flagstaff, Arizona, November 1991; Edmund J. Ladd, Santa Fe, New Mexico, November 1991; Peter Welsh, Phoenix, Arizona, November 1991; Harry Walters, Chinle, Arizona, November 1991.

p. 162 It is a fine morning: Descriptions of the drive to Macy and the reburial of the Omaha remains are based on the author's notes.

p. 164 The Omahas' origins: Alice C. Fletcher and Francis LaFlesche, *The Omaha Tribe,* 70ff; also Russell Thornton, *American Indian Holocaust and Survival,* 92.

p. 165 a remarkable transformation: Interviews with Karl Reinhard and Tom Myers.

p. 166 Many years ago [extract]: Letter from W. A. Massengale to Doran L. Morris, Sr., August 10, 1989.

p. 167 *Waxthe'xe,* the True Omaha: For the significance of the sacred cottonwood pole, see Fletcher and LaFlesche, op. cit., 217–19, 223–25.

p. 168 tribe's land base: Janet A. McDonnell, *The Dispossession of the American Indian 1887–1934,* 90.

p. 168 Of the tribe's 4,700 members: Data are drawn from *The Omaha Tribe of Nebraska Overall Economic Development Plan,* 1990, 60.

p. 169 "Family violence, child abuse": Ibid, 63–65.

p. 170 In 1989, President Bush signed: *National Museum of the American Indian Act,* 1989.

p. 171 "duplicate or abundant objects": Policy directive, March 5, 1991.

p. 172 To many Indians: Douglas H. Ubelaker and Lauryn Guttenplan Grant, "Human Skeletal Remains: Preservation or Reburial?" 1989 *Yearbook of Physical Anthropology* 32, 257–58, 266. Indian views from an advocacy perspective are discussed at length in Roger C. Echo-Hawk and Walter R. Echo-Hawk, *Battlefields and Burial Grounds.*

p. 172 "These medicine bundles": Repatriation Demanded Across the Country," *Indian Country Today,* September 22, 1993.

p. 173 In this view, contemporary Indians: Ubelaker and Grant, op. cit.

p. 173 "The bone robber barons": Gerald Vizenor, *Crossbloods,* 67.

p. 173 "always been available": Vine Deloria, Jr., "A Simple Question of Humanity," *Native American Rights Fund Legal Review,* Fall 1989.

p. 173 "This is an issue": Telephone interview with Bob Peregoy.

p. 174 Somewhat defensively, anthropologists: Ubelaker and Grant, op. cit., 249–52.

p. 174 At times, Indians: Francis Parkman, *The Oregon Trail,* 121.

p. 175 I explicitly assume [extract]: Ubelaker and Grant, op. cit., 260.

p. 176 the remains were eloquent: Karl J. Reinhard et al., *Progress Report of Skeletal Analysis Related to LB340 Legislation* (unpublished paper), April 27, 1990; also Kim Hachiya, "Omahas of Tonwantonga," *Visions,* Fall/Winter 1990, 5–9.

p. 179 Historians generally hold: Thornton, op. cit., 91–95; also William H. McNeill, *Plagues and Peoples,* 190.

p. 179 They were necessarily [extract]: George Catlin, *Letters and Notes on the Manners, Customs and Conditions of North American Indians,* Volume II, 257–59.

p. 180 "It is said that": Fletcher and LaFlesche, op. cit., 86–87.

p. 180 The survivors determined: Thornton, op. cit., 92–93.

p. 181 Blackbird was buried: Fletcher and LaFlesche, op. cit. 82–83, regard this version of the chief's interment as apocryphal.

p. 181 "Whilst visiting this mound": Catlin, op. cit., 5–6.

p. 182 "Strange to say": Quoted in Robert E. Bieder, *Science Encounters the Indian,* 58–59.

p. 182 "most symmetrical": Ibid., 61.

p. 183 "peculiar and eccentric": Ibid., 85.

p. 183 "They are not": Ibid., 70.

p. 183 "However much the": Ibid., 76.

p. 183 It is rather [extract]: Ibid., 66.

p. 184 "permit me to": Ibid., 92.

p. 184 "It is unpleasant": Ibid., 67.

p. 184 between 300,000 and 2.5 million: Christopher Vecsey, ed., *Handbook of American Indian Religious Freedom,* 67.

p. 184 the total number: Interview with Douglas Owsley.

p. 185 "Ours is a New World": Quoted in Diana Fane et al., *Objects of Memory and Myth,* 21.

p. 185 a virtual mania: Described by Curtis M. Hinsley in *Collecting Cultures and Cultures of Collecting: The Lure of the American Southwest, 1880–1915* (paper presented at the Brooklyn Museum, October 26, 1991).

p. 186 "lovely trait": Quoted by Curtis M. Hinsley in "Zunis and Brahmins," *History of Anthropology* 6, 203.

p. 186 "where things speak": Quoted in Fane, op. cit., 21.

p. 186 "To what extent": Ibid., 46.

p. 187 "The people were crazy": Ibid., 59.

p. 187 "a cryer was sent": Ibid., 60.

p. 187 Culin was determined: Ibid., 62.

p. 187 mischievous and unpredictable: Interview with Edmund J. Ladd.

p. 188 "A mask or statue": James Clifford, *The Predicament of Culture,* 136–37; generally, 117–51 contains a brilliant discussion of the Surrealists' fascination with the primitive. See also Robert Sivio, "Quiet Effort to Regain Idols May Alter View of Indian Art," *New York Times,* August 13, 1990.

p. 188 Paul Klee owned a: Clifford, op. cit., 209.

p. 188 A skilled pot hunter: For background on looting, see "Ancient Secrets Under Siege," *Houston Chronicle,* July 14, 1990; "Of Masks and Marauders," *Art and Antiques,* October 1990; "Native America . . . Looted!" *Condé Nast Traveler,* July 1992.

p. 189 "The rest": Interview with Father Dale Jamison, November 1991.

p. 189 There had always been Zunis: Interview with Edmund J. Ladd; also *New York Times,* August 13, 1990.

p. 191 halted the auction: *New York Times,* August 13, 1990.

p. 191 twelve wampum belts: "New York Returning Wampum Belts to Onondagas," *New York Times,* August 13, 1989.

p. 192 In July of that year: "Indian Artifacts to Be Returned," *Omaha World Herald,* July 16, 1989.

p. 193 "[It's] not just": T. J. Ferguson and Wilfred Eriacho, "Ahayuda Zuni War Gods: Cooperation and Repatriation," *Native Peoples,* Fall 1990, 6–12.

6. Predators, Victims, and Mother Earth

Interviews: Ola Cassadore Davis, New York, November 1992; Mike Davis and Ernest Victor, Jr., San Xavier Del Bac, Arizona, August 1992; William Belvado, Vera Cummings, and Norma Jean Kinney, San Carlos, Arizona, August 1992; Peter Strittmatter, Tucson, Arizona, November 1991; Jaap Baars and Chris Corbelly, Mount Graham, Arizona, August 1992; Brock Evans, by telephone, March 1994; Gerald Clifford, Manderson, South Dakota, June 1991 and July 1992; Mario Gonzalez, Rapid City, South Dakota, June 1991; Gregg Bourland, Eagle Butte, South Dakota, July 1992; John Around Him, Kyle, South Dakota, June 1991; William K. Powers, by telephone, November 1993.

p. 204 Dean James P. Morton's voice: Descriptions of the gatherings at the

Cathedral of St. John the Divine and the American Indian Community House are based on the author's notes.

p. 206 "the historical base": Leaflet distributed by the Friends of Mount Graham, 1992.

p. 207 dropped out of school: "Apache Woman Fights to Preserve Sacred Site," *Indian Country Today*, January 14, 1993.

p. 208 Environmentalists were already: "Irony on Mount Graham," *Arizona Republic*, September 29, 1991.

p. 208 Although court-mandated research: "Red Squirrels Are Living Outside Refuge, Study Says," *Arizona Daily Star*, February 7, 1991.

p. 208 "on the threshold of extinction": Quoted in "Red Squirrel Population Is Now Holding its Own, Census Indicates," *Arizona Daily Star*, May 16, 1990.

p. 209 "spiritual termination": Henrietta Mann, director of the Association on American Indian Affairs' Religious Freedom Coalition, "Hottest Religious War of Century Gets Still Hotter," quoted in *Lakota Times*, December 31, 1991.

p. 209 "an insult to": Jack Forbes, director of Native American studies at the University of California Davis, quoted in *Navajo-Hopi Observer*, September 18, 1991.

p. 209 "sheering the top": Suzan Shown Harjo in the *Lakota Times*, January 7, 1993.

p. 210 As the original environmentalists: See Arthur Versluis, *Sacred Earth*, and Jerry Mander, *In the Absence of the Sacred*, for typical renderings of this view.

p. 210 "Native Americans tend": Margaret Knox, "Their Mother's Keepers," *Sierra* magazine, April 1993.

p. 210 assortment of intertwined misconceptions: James A. Clifton, *The Invented Indian*, 32–37.

p. 211 "re-earthing" ceremonies: Theodore Roszak, *The Voice of the Earth*, 244–45.

p. 211 "Images of noble savagery": Ibid., 222.

p. 211 "original simplicity was": Quoted in "View from the Shore," *Northwest Indian Quarterly*, Fall 1990, 61.

p. 211 "There is only": Kirkpatrick Sale, *The Conquest of Paradise*, 369.

p. 211 There is no certainty: Ake Hultkranz, *Native Religions of North America*, 24; conventional mythologies about Indians and the earth are brilliantly dissected by Sam D. Gill in *Mother Earth*.

p. 212 tribes often exhausted the resources: Shepard Krech III, "Ecology and the American Indian," *Ideas*, Summer 1994.

p. 212 In heavily populated Mexico: Robert Royal, *1492 and All That*, 93–95; William K. Stevens, "An Eden in Ancient America? Not Really," *New York Times*, March 30, 1993.

p. 212 "came into the Fort": George Catlin, *Letters and Notes on the Manners, Customs and Conditions of North American Indians*, Volume I, 256.

p. 212 According to a 1990 survey: Survey entitled "One Nation Under God," Christian Science Publishing Society, 1995.

p. 213 "That's where you went wrong": Oren Lyons to Bill Moyers, in *The Faithkeeper* (video).

p. 213 "Mount Graham is more": "History Has Many Faces; Some Carved in Mountains," *National Catholic Reporter,* June 18, 1989.

p. 213 The impact of: "Ohio State Pullout May Kill Largest Mount Graham Scope Project," *Arizona Daily Star,* September 8, 1991; *Order of the Day,* City Council of Florence, Italy, June 1, 1991; *Business of the Day,* City Council of Rome, Italy, April 28, 1992; "MSU Drops Out of Mount Graham Project," *Indian Country Today,* March 30, 1994.

p. 215 Mount Graham was chosen: Interviews with Peter Strittmatter and Jaap Baars.

p. 216 In 1985, the University of Arizona wrote: *Draft Environmental Impact Statement: Notification of Native American Organizations* and *Summaries of Contact: San Carlos Apache Tribe and Pueblo of Zuni* (background papers), Steward Observatory, 1992.

p. 216 the Apaches were newcomers: Francis Jennings, *The Founders of America,* 69–70; Edward H. Spicer, *Cycles of Conquest,* 229ff.

p. 216 "firm and total opposition": San Carlos Apache Tribal Council, July 10, 1990.

p. 217 "How could poor": Quoted in Carol Ann Bassett, "Fighting for the Heavens," *Tucson Weekly,* April 22–28, 1992.

p. 217 "Because our traditional": Deposition in United States District Court, Phoenix, Arizona, in *Apache Survival Coalition v. U.S. and James Abbott,* April 9, 1992.

p. 218 "It is apparent": Statement by Franklin Stanley to the Arizona Board of Regents, March 27, 1992.

p. 218 To many of the Indian leaders: The description of the Religious Rights Summit is based on the author's notes.

p. 219 "so-called religious ceremonies": Quoted in Sharon O'Brien, *American Indian Tribal Governments,* 150.

p. 220 Supreme Court ruled: *Employment Division, Department of Human Resources of Oregon v. Smith,* 1990.

p. 220 Indian leaders estimate: Dan Baum, "Sacred Places," *Mother Jones,* March–April 1992.

p. 220 "All of the mountains": Quoted in "The Blackfeet Nation (U.S.) and Petroleum Exploration," *The Eagle,* Late Winter 1993.

p. 221 In 1988, the Supreme Court: *Lyng v. Northwest Indian Cemetery Protective Association,* 1988.

p. 221 might have "devastating effects": Ibid.

p. 221 attacked the majority's "astonishing conclusions": Ibid.

p. 222 "For Indians all over": Donald Worster, *Under Western Skies,* 107.

p. 222 "The taking of": Quoted in "Land Theft Cited for United Nations," *Lakota Times,* April 3, 1991.

p. 222 Taken altogether, commercial activities: Edward Lazarus, *Black Hills—White Justice,* 419.

p. 222 the Homestake Mine: Worster, op. cit., 123.

p. 226 "a North American bible": Quoted in Introduction to John G. Neihardt, *Black Elk Speaks,* xiii.

p. 226 in the vision: Neihardt, op. cit., 20–47.

p. 226 a Catholic catechist: The full story of Black Elk's conversion and missionary work is told in Michael F. Steltenkamp, *Black Elk*, especially 62–77 and 80–82.

p. 226 "Anywhere is the center": Quoted in Neihardt, op. cit., 43.

p. 227 "old man waiting": Neihardt, op. cit., xvi.

p. 227 Neihardt consciously rejected: Steltenkamp, op. cit., 87.

p. 227 "My father wanted": Quoted in ibid., 20.

p. 228 The whites created [extract]: Worster, op. cit., 120–21.

p. 228 "Only someone with": Quoted in "Sioux Want Hills Land, Disagree on How to Get It," *Lakota Times,* April 1, 1992.

p. 228 not a single tribal leader: Worster, op. cit., 142–43.

p. 228 Indeed, their words: Little Bear, Red Cloud, and Spotted Tail are quoted in Worster, op. cit., 124.

p. 229 It was not until 1920: Lazarus, op. cit., 138.

p. 230 In 1942, the U.S. Court of Claims: Ibid., 175–77.

p. 230 New life was breathed: A detailed discussion of the deliberations of both the Court of Claims and the Supreme Court will be found in Lazarus, op. cit., 366–402.

p. 231 "If they voted": Ibid., 405.

p. 231 "the foundation of Indian religion": Quoted in Worster, op. cit., 108.

p. 231 "Star charts" purported: Illustrative of such scholarship is Ronald Goodman, *Lakota Star Knowledge.*

p. 232 "the sacred center": *The Sioux Nations Black Hills Bill, S705,* also known as the "Bradley Bill," as introduced in the U.S. Senate, March 10, 1987.

p. 232 "Star charts, petroglyphs": David B. Miller, "Historians View of S.705—The Sioux Nations Black Hills Bill," in *The Wicazo sa Review: Indian Studies Journal* (special issue on the Black Hills), Spring 1988.

p. 234 "Where the old ways": Eric Hobsbawm and Terence Ranger, *The Invention of Tradition,* 8.

p. 235 "at the cutting edge": Quoted in Bassett, op. cit.

p. 235 "If you put": Ibid.

p. 235 "If you are": Ibid.

p. 235 Then, to everyone's astonishment: Quotes from Karen Long, Norma Jean Kinney, and Buck Kitcheyan are from unpublished copies of their statements in the author's possession.

p. 238 "At stake is": "Give Religion Back to the Tribes," *Denver Post,* July 28, 1991.

7. "A Scene Most Resembling Hell"

Interviews: Robbie Daniels, Frank Gonzalez, and Nick Begay, Gallup, New Mexico, November 1991; Gregg J. Bourland, Greg Ducheneaux, Eagle Butte, South Dakota, July 1992; Gene Thin Elk, Pine Ridge reservation, July 1992.

p. 240 Inside the sweat lodge: The description of this gathering is based on the author's notes.

p. 241 A bottle sold: Data are drawn from a superb series of articles on Indian alcoholism in Gallup called "The Killing Season," featured in the *Albuquerque Tribune,* September 27, to October 1, 1988.

p. 242 Begay's prowl car: The narrative of Begay's tour of duty is based on the author's notes.

p. 246 "The most truthful": Susan Sontag, *Illness as Metaphor,* 3.

p. 247 The appetite of [extract]: Quoted in Francis Prucha, *The Great Father,* 115.

p. 247 "the most severe": *Final Report of the American Indian Policy Review Commission,* May 17, 1977.

p. 247 "after a century": *Native Americans and Alcohol* (Indian Health Service report), 1985.

p. 247 67 percent of: According to a 1984 study by the Alcoholism Research Group, nearly 70 percent of adult Americans drink at least once a year, and 7 percent drink daily, quoted by W. B. Clark and M. E. Hilton in *Alcoholism in America,* 53–81. The national 1991 Epidemiological Catchment Area Study found that 13.8 percent of adults meet the criteria for a lifetime diagnosis of alcoholism and alcohol abuse. Dr. Prem Peter, a psychiatrist and expert in addictions at New York Medical College, estimates the rate of alcoholism among Americans as a whole to be about 12 percent; interview, July 1995.

p. 247 Estimates of the extent: "Relationship Between Prevalence of Alcohol Problems and Socioeconomic Conditions Among Oklahoma Native Americans," State of Oklahoma, 1981; "Ethnic Differences in Alcohol Use," *Journal of Social Biology,* Fall–Winter 1985; *The Omaha Tribe of Nebraska Overall Economic Development Plan,* 1990; "Alcoholism as a Mental Health Problem of Native Americans," *Archives of General Psychiatry,* November 1975; *Western Washington Native American Behavioral Risk Factor Survey,* 1989.

p. 248 Probably the most comprehensive analysis: James O. Whittaker, "Alcohol and the Standing Rock Sioux Tribe," *Journal of Studies on Alcohol* Vol. 43, No. 3, 1982.

p. 248 The cumulative effect: *Native Americans and Alcohol,* op. cit.; "Alcohol Abuse Among Native Americans," *Journal of Community Health,* Fall 1988; "Leaders: Find a Solution for Number One Killer," *Lakota Times,* October 16, 1990; *Trends in Indian Health* (Indian Health Service report), 1991; Margaret M. Gallaher et al., "Pedestrian and Hypothermia Deaths Among Native Americans in New Mexico," *Journal of the American Medical Association,* March 11, 1992; "FAS Conference Explores Ways to Reduce Syndrome," *Lakota Times,* September 2, 1992.

p. 248 one treatment program: Information paper distributed by Medicine Wheel, Inc., Tecumseh, Kansas, 1991.

p. 249 tribal council proclaimed a "war": Cheyenne River Sioux tribal council resolution 313-87, November 4, 1987.

p. 249 "the disease of alcoholism": Cheyenne River Sioux tribal council resolution 10-91, January 14, 1991.

p. 249 "the effects of": Ibid.

p. 249 "it has become": Ibid.

p. 250 the tribe affirms: Interview with Gregg J. Bourland.

p. 252 "alcoholism becomes": George E. Vaillant, *The Natural History of Alcohol*, 44; for a discussion of the problem of defining alcoholism, see 15–49.

p. 252 "a chronic and progressive disease": Harold Kaplan and Benjamin Sadock, *Comprehensive Textbook of Psychiatry*, 6th ed., 775.

p. 252 "A tree is known": Donald W. Goodwin, *Is Alcoholism Hereditary?* 77.

p. 252 a six-year study: Ibid., 65–84.

p. 253 "It is interesting": Ibid., 77.

p. 253 More recent biochemical research: Marc A. Schukit, "Genetics and the Risk for Alcoholism, " *Journal of the American Medical Association*, November 8, 1985; Schukit, "Two Decades of Alcoholism Genetics Research Reviewed," *Psychiatric Times*, February 1990.

p. 253 Other studies undertaken: "The Genetics of Alcoholism," *Alcohol Alert*.

p. 254 genetic structural differences: Schukit, "Genetics and the Risk for Alcoholism."

p. 254 examining a gene: Michael P. Conneally, "Association Between the D2 Dopamine Receptor Gene and Alcoholism," *Archives of General Psychiatry*, July 1991.

p. 254 "The Lakota are": Quoted in "Curley: Alcoholism Neither Is Nor Is Not a Disease," *Lakota Times*, December 18, 1991.

p. 254 "There is nothing": Quoted in Jerry Reynolds, "Border Run Drinking Style Reinforces Old Stereotypes," *Lakota Times*, October 2, 1991.

p. 255 "a history of discriminatory": Barry Willer, *Prevention of Chemical Dependency Among Native American Families and Youth*.

p. 255 "Tribe after tribe": Michael Dorris, *The Broken Cord*, 83–84.

p. 256 "as good an excuse": Ibid., 84.

p. 256 "We know it": Quoted in Clark Wissler, *Indians of the United States*, 295.

p. 256 Intoxicants were not wholly unknown: Wissler, op. cit., 296.

p. 256 European colonists usually introduced: James Axtell, *The European and the Indian*, 257–59.

p. 256 But Indian demand: Peter C. Mancall, *Deadly Medicine*, 42ff; also Francis Prucha, *American Indian Policy in the Formative Years*, 102–38, generally.

p. 256 *mni wakan*: For definitions, see Dorris, op. cit., and Edward Lazarus, *Black Hills—White Justice*, 12.

p. 256 French missionaries reported: James Axtell, *The Invasion Within*, 65.

p. 257 "running after and": Quoted in J. C. Furnas, *The Life and Times of the Late Demon Rum*, 28.

p. 257 "they have recd": Quoted in Anthony F. C. Wallace, *The Death and Rebirth of the Seneca*, 200.

p. 257 Now that the party [extract]: Quoted in Bernard W. Sheehan, *Seeds of Extinction*, 236.

p. 257 "Little does the spirit": Quoted in Brian W. Dippie, *The Vanishing American*, 36.

p. 258 "Father, we care": Ibid., 36.

p. 258 "No ardent spirits": Quoted in Prucha, *American Indian Policy in the Formative Years*, 102–38, especially 127.

p. 258 "the Indians are furnished": Ibid., 125.

p. 258 "treacherous, filthy": Quoted in Robert F. Berkhofer, Jr., *The White Man's Indian,* 105.

p. 259 a draconian program: Quotations that follow are from the *Draft Plan of Operation for War on Alcoholism,* 1991.

p. 261 letter to Ducheneaux: Letter from Gregg J. Bourland to Greg Ducheneaux, February 24, 1992. Ducheneaux was eventually fired by Bourland, in January 1993. Ducheneaux's brother Wayne was defeated in an attempt to unseat Bourland as chairman in 1995.

p. 262 "Perhaps the most startling": Whittaker, op. cit.

p. 263 Similar figures have: "The Myth of the 'Drunken Indian,' " *Washington Post,* September 22, 1992.

p. 263 perhaps as low as 10 percent: This is an estimate shared by many professionals in the field of alcoholism treatment, in the absence of scientific studies; interview with Dr. Prem Peter, July 1995.

p. 263 history offers a precedent: W. J. Rorabaugh, *The Alcoholic Republic,* an excellent study of historical drinking patterns in America; for statistics, 233.

p. 264 among the Alabama-Coushattas: Interviews with Perry Williams, Alabama-Coushatta tribal council chairman, and Dick Cordis, reservation IHS administrator, May 1992.

p. 267 Some of us [extract]: Gene Thin Elk in *Sacred Seventh Direction* (video).

p. 267 "We can have": Ibid.

p. 267 "What part of": Gene Thin Elk in *Natural/Unnatural Worlds* (video).

p. 267 "There's nothing wrong": Ibid.

p. 267 "We have to": Interview with Gene Thin Elk.

8. "The Hollowness of a Person Needs to Be Filled"

Interviews: Henry Real Bird, Janine Pease-Windy Boy, Tim Bernardis, Joe Medicine Crow, Dale Old Horn, Crow Agency, Montana, October 1991; Don McCabe, Chinle, Arizona, November 1991; Ella Irving, Pine Ridge, South Dakota, June 1991; Reuben Snake, Winnebago, Nebraska, October 1991; Marvin Buzzard, Lawrence, Kansas, May 1991.

p. 272 This land should have brought: Janet A. McDonnell, *The Dispossession of the American Indian 1887–1934,* 61–65, 68–69; also, interview with Richard Bowler, editor of the *Big Horn County News,* Hardin, Montana, October 1991.

p. 273 The college's mission statement: *Catalog,* Little Big Horn College, 1990–93, 3.

p. 274 "a colossal, pulverizing engine": Quoted in Robert F. Berkhofer, Jr., *The White Man's Indian,* 175.

p. 274 most hopeful single development: *Tribal College* magazine, Winter 1991, 11–17.

p. 275 Indian students who transfer: Huntly Collins, "Retaining Culture and Students: Tribal Colleges Offer Native Americans Hope," *Philadelphia Inquirer,* May 13, 1991.

p. 275 similarly improved likelihood: Data in this and the following paragraph are drawn mainly from *Tribal Colleges* (Carnegie Foundation report), 60–62; also telephone interview with Paul Boyer, author of the report, June 1995.

p. 280 "the Education of": Quoted in *Tribal Colleges,* op. cit., 7.

p. 280 "cure the Natives": Quoted in James Axtell, *The European and the Indian,* 98.

p. 280 "purge all the": Ibid.

p. 280 "Few conceive aright": Ibid., 95.

p. 280 But you, who [extract]: Quoted in Ernest L. Boyer, op. cit., 9.

p. 281 "In the present state": Quoted in George A. Schultz, *An Indian Canaan,* 34–35.

p. 282 "this whole reservating": Quoted in Francis Prucha, *The Great Father,* 235.

p. 282 quarter million Indians be spread: Ibid., 236.

p. 282 "is born a blank": Quoted in Brian W. Dippie, *The Vanishing American,* 118.

p. 282 "A great general": Francis Prucha, ed., *Americanizing the American Indians,* 260–61.

p. 282 "When one Indian": Quoted in *Lawrence Journal,* September 21, 1884.

p. 283 taught carpentry, blacksmithing: *Lawrence Daily Gazette,* September 8, 1885.

p. 283 A thorough training [extract]: *Topeka Daily Capital,* March 16, 1890.

p. 284 I was stripped [extract]: *Indian Leader,* October 30, 1925.

p. 285 tied to a stairpost: Interview with Reuben Snake.

p. 285 But the fundamental flaw: Ibid., 224, 240–43.

p. 290 "Mary"—she prefers to keep her real name out of print: Student interview, Little Big Horn College, October 1992.

p. 292 In 1978, Congress mandated: Ernest L. Boyer, op. cit., 36–37.

p. 292 In 1994, tribal colleges received: cited by Paul Boyer, telephone interview, June 1995.

p. 294 federal agents finally seized: "Ex-Crow Chairman Surrenders to Serve 27 Months in Prison," *Lakota Times,* April 17, 1991.

p. 295 The anxiety shows: Description of the tribal council debate is based on the author's notes.

p. 295 The tribal council is about to vote: "College Asks Tribe for $5 million Grant Again," *Big Horn County News,* October 9, 1991.

p. 298 "Indian people have contributed": *Lakota Times,* March 26, 1992.

p. 298 Indians are now commonly taught: The case for this notion is made in Bruce E. Johansen, *Forgotten Founders,* and has been widely popularized in books such as *Indian Givers* by Jack Weatherford; an excellent critique of the meager documentary evidence, by Elizabeth Tooker, will be found in James A. Clifton, ed., *The Invented Indian,* 107–28.

p. 298 "At most, his voyage": *Smithsonian Runner,* March–April 1992.

p. 298 "were far superior": Quoted in "Early Indians Had a Superior Society," *Lakota Times,* February 5, 1991.

p. 299 "Why should we adapt": Student interview, Little Big Horn College, October 1991.

9. "Our Lives Have Been Transmuted, Changed Forever"

Interviews: Phillip Martin, Harlan Majors, Robert Benn, Lester Dalme, Sam Schisler, William Richardson, Choctaw reservation, Mississippi, June 1992; Dennis Hastings, Macy, Nebraska, May 1991; Micki Hutchinson, Isabel, South Dakota, July 1992; Ivan Makil, Salt River Pima-Maricopa reservation, Arizona, November 1991; Ramon Roubideux, Rapid City, South Dakota, July 1992; Steve Aberle, Glencross, South Dakota, July 1992; John Chapela, Gallup, New Mexico, November 1991; Robin Powell and Elmer Savilla, by telephone, November 1994.

p. 303 By 1995, sales: Telephone interview with William Richardson, June 1995.

p. 303 "They're willing to buy": Interview with the author.

p. 304 Some Choctaws hold: Carolyn K. Reeves, ed., *The Choctaw Before Removal*, 6–12.

p. 304 an instinct for business: Ibid., 34, 40.

p. 304 Choctaws who remained behind: Interview with Bob Ferguson, tribal historian, June 1992.

p. 310 "Some of the current": Speech by Phillip Martin to the annual meeting of the Association on American Indian Affairs, May 12, 1986.

p. 312 more than $800 million: Francis Prucha, *American Indian Treaties*, 230–31.

p. 312 "The only fair": Quoted in ibid., 230.

p. 312 an additional $818 million: Ibid., 232.

p. 312 roughly $50 billion: Mark N. Trahant et al., "Fraud in Indian Country," *Arizona Republic*, October 4, 1987; also, "Indian Country," *Arizona Republic*, January 21, 1990. Of the $3 billion in direct federal spending on Indians each year, approximately $1 billion each is spent by the Bureau of Indian Affairs and the Indian Health Service. The remainder is spread among many federal agencies, with the largest amounts being appropriated by the departments of Education, Housing and Urban Development, and Agriculture. An additional $3 billion in profits from the management of properties held in trust by the federal government is also transferred to Indians each year.

p. 312 "For all its many flaws": Charles Wilkinson, *American Indians, Time and the Law*, 4–5.

p. 313 "There is no reason": Quoted in "Standing Ovation for Deer," *Indian Country Today*, July 21, 1993.

p. 315 Now picture the scene: The narrative of events is based partly on interviews with tribal councilmen Duane "Chili" Yazzie and Daniel Tso, local journalists Mark Trahant and Betty Reid, and BIA counsel Tom O'Hara, in Window Rock, Arizona, 1991, and with journalist Bill Donovan and John Chapela, a prominent Navajo lawyer, in Gallup, New Mexico, November 1991.

p. 315 something larger than life: MacDonald's remarkable life story is recounted in detail in his autobiography, *The Last Warrior*.

p. 316 "As long as you allow": As quoted by Bill Donovan to the author.

p. 316 prompted by revelations: Trahant, op. cit.; "Extravagance, Hint of Scandal in Mark MacDonald's Leadership," *Arizona Republic*, January 15, 1989.

p. 316 MacDonald had accepted: *Final Report of the Special Committee on Investigations of the Select Committee on Indian Affairs of the United States Senate,* 1989, 183–91.

p. 316 "Big Bo" was: Ibid., 191–97.

p. 317 MacDonald admitted taking: Tribal council minutes, February 14, 1989.

p. 317 Inside, MacDonald repeatedly: Ibid.

p. 317 "No one will": Quoted in ibid.

p. 317 "Ronald Reagan had": Ibid.

p. 317 "It hurts my heart": Ibid., February 17, 1989.

p. 318 Councilman Leo Begay: Ibid.

p. 318 Our government is [extract]: Ibid.

p. 319 seeking precedent, the court ruled: *The Navajo Nation v. Peter MacDonald,* April 13, 1989; also interview with Tom Tso, chief justice of the Navajo Supreme Court, November 1991.

p. 320 reports of official corruption: "White Earth Woman Says She Forged Election Ballots," *News from Indian Country,* October 1990; "Alex Lunderman Out at Rosebud," *Lakota Times,* May 20, 1992; "Crow Creek Chairman Welcomes Investigation," *Lakota Times,* April 15, 1992; "Normalcy Slowly Returning" (to Pyramid Lake), *Nevada Appeal,* May 25, 1993; also *Final Report of the Special Committee on Investigations,* op. cit., 198–202.

p. 322 "It's not really": Quoted in "Newspaper Editor Canned by Council," *Indian Country Today,* April 6, 1994.

p. 322 "It is very": Letter from Richard LaFramboise to Robin Powell, April 8, 1994.

p. 322 "The issue here": "It's the People's Right to Know," *Indian Country Today,* May 18, 1994.

p. 323 the May 1994 Albuquerque "Listening Conference": The description of the conference is based on the author's notes.

p. 326 hemorrhaging jobs and people: Data are from Frank J. Popper and Deborah E. Popper, "The Future of the Great Plains" (draft paper); and Frank J. Popper, "The Strange Case of the Contemporary American Frontier," *Yale Review,* Autumn 1986. The changing rural culture of the Great Plains is vividly chronicled by Richard Critchfield in *Trees, Why Do You Wait?*

p. 328 "Every penny goes": Telephone interview with Gregg J. Bourland, July 1995.

p. 329 Instead of a [extract]: Arthur M. Schlesinger, Jr., *The Disuniting of America,* 16.

p. 329 "A point will": Thornton, *American Indian Holocaust and Survival,* 236–37.

p. 332 "Our lives have": Quote by Rayna Green from author's notes.

Epilogue

Interviews: Rosalyn Hoag, Nancy Milligan, by telephone, April 1995; William Richardson, Choctaw reservation, Mississippi, June 1992; Ken Smith, Warm Springs reservation, Oregon, October 1991; Thomas Killion, Washington, D.C., April 1992.

p. 334 By early 1995: Details of Salamanca's evolution are based on interviews with Hoag and Milligan.

p. 335 Then hell broke loose: "Three killed in Seneca Dispute," *Indian Country Today,* March 30, 1995; and "Death and Politics Leave Seneca in Disarray," *Indian Country Today,* April 6, 1995.

p. 336 "We are entering": Statement by Douglas Endreson delivered at the National Tribal Leaders Forum, Washington, D.C., May 11, 1992.

p. 338 "domestic dependent nations": *Cherokee Nation v. Georgia,* U.S. Supreme Court, 1832.

p. 339 nearing its peak: Saturation of the gambling market is analyzed at length by Robert Goodman, *Legalized Gambling as a Strategy for Economic Development,* 117–33.

p. 339 "gaming is probably": "Tribes 'Will Not Stand' for Further Gaming Restrictions," *International Gaming and Wagering Business,* January 5, 1994.

p. 340 A federal study: Report of the Task Force on Indian Economic Development, July 1986, in Francis Prucha, ed., *Documents of United States Indian Policy,* 305–8.

Selected Bibliography

The American Indian and the Media. Minneapolis: The American Indian Media Image Task Force, 1991.

ANDERSON, WILLIAM L., ed. *Cherokee Removal: Before and After.* Athens, Georgia: University of Georgia Press, 1991.

The Arctic National Wildlife Refuge: Its People, Wildlife Resources, and Oil and Gas Potential. Anchorage, Alaska: Arctic Slope Consulting Engineers, 1990.

ATHEARN, ROBERT G. *The Mythic West in Twentieth Century America.* Lawrence, Kansas: University Press of Kansas, 1986.

AXTELL, JAMES. *Beyond 1492: Encounters in Colonial North America.* New York: Oxford University Press, 1992.

——. *The European and the Indian: Essays in the Ethnohistory of Colonial North America.* New York: Oxford University Press, 1981.

——. *The Invasion Within: The Contest of Cultures in Colonial North America.* New York: Oxford University Press, 1985.

BARNETT, CATHERINE. "Of Masks and Marauders." *Art & Antiques,* October 1990.

BARTON, LOIS. *A Quaker Promise Kept: Philadelphia Friends' Work with the Allegany Senecas 1795–1960.* Eugene, Oregon: Spencer Butte Press, 1990.

BASSETT, CAROL ANN. "Fighting for the Heavens." *Tucson Weekly,* April 22–28, 1992.

BASSO, KEITH H. *Portraits of "The Whiteman": Linguistic Play and Cultural Symbols Among the Western Apache.* New York: Cambridge University Press, 1979.

BAUM, DAN. "Sacred Places." *Mother Jones,* April 1992.

BERKHOFER, ROBERT F., JR. *The White Man's Indian.* New York: Vintage Books, 1979.

BIEDER, ROBERT E. *Science Encounters the Indian, 1820–1880.* Norman, Oklahoma: University of Oklahoma Press, 1986.

BIERHORST, JOHN. *In the Trail of the Wind: American Indian Poems and Ritual Orations.* New York: Sunburst, 1987.

BILLINGTON, RAY. *Land of Savagery, Land of Promise: The European Image of the American Frontier in the 19th Century.* Norman, Oklahoma: University of Oklahoma Press, 1985.

"The Blackfeet Nation (U.S.) and Petroleum Exploration." *The Eagle.* (Naugatuck, Connecticut.) Late Winter 1993.

BLU, KAREN I. *The Lumbee Problem: The Making of an American Indian People.* New York: Cambridge University Press, 1980.

BLY, ROBERT. *Iron John: A Book About Men.* New York: Vintage, 1992.

BOLT, CHRISTINE. *American Indian Policy and American Reform.* London, England: Unwin Hyman Ltd., 1990.

BOYER, PAUL. "We Just Can't Fail: Little Big Horn College President Janine Pease-Windy Boy Talks About Teaching and Tribal Development." *Tribal College,* Spring 1991.

BRANDON, HENRY. *Indians.* New York: American Heritage, 1989.

BROWN, DEE. *Bury My Heart at Wounded Knee.* New York: Pocket Books, 1981.

BROWN, JOSEPH EPES, ed. *The Sacred Pipe: Black Elk's Account of the Seven Rites of the Oglala Sioux.* Norman, Oklahoma: University of Oklahoma Press, 1953.

BROWNE, MALCOLM W. "As Deadlines Near, Scientists Seek Data from Indian Bones." *New York Times,* September 25, 1990.

BRUCE, CHRIS, et al. *Myth of the West.* New York: Rizzoli, 1990.

BRUCKNER, PASCAL. *The Tears of the White Man: Compassion as Contempt.* New York: Free Press, 1986.

BUCHANAN, CHESTER C., and Coleman, Mark E. *The Cui-ui.* National Audubon Society Wildlife Report, 1987.

CAMPISI, JACK. *The Mashpee Indians: Tribe on Trial.* Syracuse, New York: Syracuse University Press, 1991.

CAPOEMAN, PAULINE K., ed. *Land of the Quinault.* Taholah, Washington: Quinault Indian Nation, 1990.

CARTER, IRL. "Gambling with Their Lives: American Indians and the Casinos." *CURA Reporter,* Center for Urban and Regional Affairs, University of Minnesota, August 1992.

CATLIN, GEORGE. *Letters and Notes on the Manners, Customs and Conditions of North American Indians,* Volumes I and II. New York: Dover Publications, 1973.

Chronological List of Actions, &c., With Indians from January 15, 1837 to January, 1891. The Old Army Press, 1979.

CLARK, W. B., and HILTON, M. E., eds. *Alcoholism in America.* Albany, New York: State University Press of New York, 1991.

CLIFFORD, JAMES. *The Predicament of Culture.* Cambridge: Harvard University Press, 1988.

CLIFTON, JAMES A. *Being and Becoming Indian.* Chicago: Dorsey Press, 1989.

———, ed. *The Invented Indian: Cultural Fictions and Government Policies.* New Brunswick, New Jersey: Transaction Publishers, 1990.

CLOWSER, DON C. *Dakota Indian Treaties.* Deadwood, South Dakota: Don Clowser, 1974.

COLLIER, JOHN. *From Every Zenith*. Denver, Colorado: Sage Books, 1963.

———. *Indians of the Americas: The Long Hope*. New York: New American Library, 1947.

COLLINS, HUNTLY. "Retaining Culture and Students: Tribal Colleges Offer Native Americans Hope." *Philadelphia Inquirer*, May 13, 1991.

CONNEALLY, P. MICHAEL. "Association Between the D2 Dopamine Receptor Gene and Alcoholism." *Archives of General Psychiatry*, July 1991.

CONNELL, EVAN S. *Son of the Morning Star*. New York: Perennial Library, 1984.

COOK, SHERBURNE F. *The Conflict Between the California Indian and White Civilization*. Berkeley, California: University of California Press, 1976.

COOPER, JAMES FENIMORE. *The Last of the Mohicans*. New York: Bantam, 1981.

CORNELL, STEPHEN. *The Return of the Native: American Indian Political Resurgence*. New York: Oxford University Press, 1988.

COUGHLIN, ELLEN K. "Returning Indian Remains." *The Chronicle of Higher Education*, March 16, 1994.

CRITCHFIELD, RICHARD. *Trees, Why Do You Wait? America's Changing Rural Culture*. Washington, D.C.: Island Press, 1991.

CROSBY, ALFRED W., JR. *The Columbian Exchange: Biological and Cultural Consequences of 1492*. Westport, Connecticut: Greenwood Press, 1973.

CROW DOG, MARY. *Lakota Woman*. New York: Harper Perennial, 1991.

Cui-Ui Recovery Plan (Second Revision). Portland, Oregon: U.S. Fish and Wildlife Service, 1992.

CUSHING, FRANK H. *My Adventures in Zuni*. Palmer Lake, Colorado: Filter Press, 1967.

CUSTER, GEORGE ARMSTRONG. *My Life on the Plains*. Norman, Oklahoma: University of Oklahoma Press, 1988.

DEBO, ANGIE. *And Still the Waters Run*. Princeton, New Jersey: Princeton University Press, 1940.

———. *The Rise and Fall of the Choctaw Republic*. Norman, Oklahoma: University of Oklahoma Press, 1989.

———. *The Road to Disappearance*. Norman, Oklahoma: University of Oklahoma Press, 1941.

DELORIA, VINE, JR. *Custer Died for Your Sins*. Norman, Oklahoma: University of Oklahoma Press, 1969.

———. "Sacred Lands and Religious Freedom," *Native American Rights Fund Legal Review*, Summer 1991.

DIPPIE, BRIAN W. *The Vanishing American: White Attitudes and U.S. Indian Policy*. Middletown, Connecticut: Wesleyan University Press, 1985.

DOOLING, D. M., ed. *The Sons of the Wind: The Sacred Stories of the Lakota*. New York: HarperCollins, 1992.

DORRIS, MICHAEL. *The Broken Cord*. New York: Harper Perennial, 1989.

DRIMMER, FREDERICK. *Captured by the Indians*. New York: Dover, 1985.

DRINNON, RICHARD. *Facing West: The Metaphysics of Indian Hating and Empire Building*. New York: Schocken Books, 1990.

———. *Keeper of Concentration Camps: Dillon S. Myer and American Racism*. Berkeley, California: University of California Press, 1987.

EASTMAN, CHARLES A. *From the Deep Woods to Civilization.* Lincoln, Nebraska: University of Nebraska Press, 1977.

———. *Indian Boyhood.* Lincoln, Nebraska: University of Nebraska Press, 1991.

ECHO-HAWK, ROGER C., and ECHO-HAWK, WALTER R. *Battlefields and Burial Grounds: The Indian Struggle to Protect Ancestral Graves in the United States.* Minneapolis, Minnesota: Lerner Publications, 1994.

ECHO-HAWK, WALTER R. "Tribal Efforts to Protect Against Mistreatment of Indian Dead." *Native American Rights Fund Legal Review,* Winter 1988.

EHLE, JOHN. *Trail of Tears: The Rise and Fall of the Cherokee Nation.* New York: Anchor Books, 1988.

ERDRICH, LOUISE. *The Bingo Palace.* New York: HarperCollins, 1994.

———. *Love Medicine.* New York: Bantam Books, 1989.

EWERS, JOHN C. "The Emergence of the Plains Indian as the Symbol of the North American Indian," in *Annual Report of the Smithsonian Institution.* Washington, D.C.: Smithsonian Institution, 1964.

FANE, DIANA, et al. *Objects of Memory and Myth: American Indian Art at the Brooklyn Museum.* (Catalogue.) New York: The Brooklyn Museum, 1991.

FEDULLO, MICK. *Light of the Feather: A Teacher's Journey into Native American Classrooms and Culture.* New York: Anchor Books, 1992.

FEHRENBACH, T. R. *Comanches: The Destruction of a People.* New York: Knopf, 1974.

FERACA, STEPHEN E. *Why Don't They Give Them Guns? The Great American Indian Myth.* Lanham, Maryland: University Press of America, 1990.

FERGUS, CHARLES. *Shadowcatcher.* New York: Soho Press, 1991.

FERGUSON, T. J., and ERIACHO, WILFRED. "Ahayuda Zuni War Gods: Cooperation and Repatriation." *Native Peoples,* Fall 1990.

Final Report of the Special Committee on Investigations of the Select Committee on Indian Affairs of the United States Senate, November 1989.

FLEMMING, PAULA R., and LUSKEY, JUDITH. *The North American Indians in Early Photographs.* New York: Dorset Press, 1988.

FLETCHER, ALICE C., and LAFLESCHE, FRANCIS. *The Omaha Tribe,* Volumes I and II. Lincoln, Nebraska: University of Nebraska Press, 1972.

FLORES, PHILIP J. "Alcoholism Treatment and the Relationship of Native American Cultural Values to Recovery." *The International Journal of the Addictions,* Vol. 20, Nos. 11 and 12, 1985–1986.

FLORIO, JOHN, trans. *The Essayes of Montaigne.* New York: Modern Library, 1933.

FRENCH, LAURENCE, and HORNBUCKLE, JIM, eds. *The Cherokee Perspective.* Boone, North Carolina: The Appalachian Consortium Press, 1981.

FREY, RODNEY. *The World of the Crow Indians.* Norman, Oklahoma: University of Oklahoma Press, 1987.

FRIEDERICI, GEORG, et al. *Scalping and Torture.* Ohsweken, Canada: Iroqrafts Ltd., 1985.

FRIEDMAN, HERBERT. *The Astronomers' Universe.* New York: Ballantine Books, 1990.

FURBER, BRADLEY B. "Two Promises, Two Propositions: The Wheeler-Howard Act as a Reconciliation of the Indian Law Civil War." *University of Puget Sound Law Review,* Vol. 14:211.

FURNAS, J. C. *The Life and Times of the Late Demon Rum.* New York: Capricorn Books, 1973.

FUSON, ROBERT H., trans. *The Log of Christopher Columbus.* Camden, Maine: International Marine Publishing, 1992.

GALLAHER, MARGARET M., et al. "Pedestrian and Hypothermia Deaths Among Native Americans in New Mexico." *Journal of the American Medical Association,* March 11, 1992.

GEERTZ, ARMIN. "Native American Art and the Problem of the Other." *European Review of Native American Studies,* Vol. 5, No. 2, 1991.

"The Genetics of Alcoholism." *Alcohol Alert.* National Institute on Alcohol Abuse and Alcoholism, October 1982.

GIAGO, TIM. *The Aboriginal Sin.* San Francisco: The Indian Historian Press, 1978.

————. *Notes from Indian Country,* Volume I. Pierre, South Dakota: State Publishing Company, 1984.

————. "Tribes Shouldn't Get Too Cozy with Casino Cash, Living-Room Gambling Is on Its Way." *Indian Country Today,* May 11, 1994.

GIFFORD, ELI, and COOK, R. MICHAEL, eds. *How Can One Sell the Air? Chief Seattle's Vision.* Summertown, Tennessee: The Book Publishing Company, 1992.

GILDART, ROBERT C. "Gwich'in: We Are the People." *Native Peoples,* Winter 1993.

GILL, SAM D. *Mother Earth.* Chicago: University of Chicago Press, 1991.

GOMEZ, DAVID, et al. "The Killing Season." (Special series on Indian alcoholism in Gallup, New Mexico.) *The Albuquerque Tribune,* September 27 to October 1, 1988.

GOODMAN, ROBERT. *Legalized Gambling as a Strategy for Economic Development.* Northampton, Massachusetts: United States Gambling Study, 1994.

GOODMAN, RONALD. *Lakota Star Knowledge.* Rosebud, South Dakota: Sinte Gleska College, 1990.

GOODWIN, DONALD W. *Is Alcoholism Hereditary?* New York: Oxford University Press, 1979.

GORE, AL. *Earth in the Balance.* New York: Plume, 1993.

GREEN, JESSE, ed. *Zuni: Selected Writings of Frank Hamilton Cushing.* Lincoln, Nebraska: University of Nebraska Press, 1981.

HACHIYA, KIM. "Omahas of Tonwantonga: Research Team Uncovers the Story of a Village in Decline." *Visions,* Fall/Winter 1990.

HAEDERLE, MICHAEL. "War Gods Are Finally at Peace." *Los Angeles Times,* August 12, 1991.

HAGAN, WILLIAM T. *Quanah Parker, Comanche Chief.* Norman, Oklahoma: University of Oklahoma Press, 1993.

HASSRICK, ROYAL B. *The George Catlin Book of American Indians.* New York: Watson-Guptill, 1977.

————. *The Sioux.* Norman, Oklahoma: University of Oklahoma Press, 1989.

HAUPTMAN, LAURENCE M., and WHERRY, JAMES D., eds. *The Pequots of Southern New England.* Norman, Oklahoma: University of Oklahoma Press, 1990.

HAUSLE, STEPHANIE A. "99 Years: The Salamanca Lease." *Turtle Quarterly,* Winter 1990.

HECHT, ROBERT A. *Oliver LaFarge and the American Indian.* Metuchen, New Jersey: The Scarecrow Press, 1991.

HINSLEY, CURTIS M. "Zunis and Brahmins: Cultural Ambivalence in the Gilded Age," in *History of Anthropology 6*, George Stocking, ed. Madison, Wisconsin: University of Wisconsin Press, 1989.

The History Leading to Tribal Government Gaming. Prior Lake, Minnesota: Tribal Government Gaming Issues, 1992.

HOBSBAWM, ERIC, and Ranger, Terence, eds. *The Invention of Tradition.* Cambridge, England: Cambridge University Press, 1986.

HOIG, STAN. *The Sand Creek Massacre.* Norman, Oklahoma: University of Oklahoma Press, 1987.

HOPKINS, SARAH WINNEMUCCA. *Life Among the Paiutes.* Bishop, California: Chalfant Press, 1969.

HUDSON, M. F. *Senator Francis G. Newlands: His Work.* Carson City, Nevada: Appeal Publishing, 1908.

HYDE, GEORGE E. *Red Cloud's Folk: A History of the Oglala Sioux Indians.* Norman, Oklahoma: University of Oklahoma Press, 1987.

"If We Keep Ignoring Realities, We'll Turn Drought into Disaster." (Editorial.) *Reno Gazette-Journal,* October 13, 1992.

Important American Indian Art (catalogue). New York: Sotheby's, June 12, 1992.

The Indian Civil Rights Act: A Report of the United States Commission on Civil Rights. Washington, D.C.: United States Government Printing Office, 1991.

Indian Tribes and a National Indian Legislative Agenda: A Compendium of Regional Tribal Leaders' Forum Reports. Oakland, California: American Indian Resources Institute, 1991.

Indian Tribes as Sovereign Governments: A Sourcebook on Federal-Tribal History, Law and Policy. Oakland, California: American Indian Resources Institute, 1988.

IVERSON, PETER. *The Navajo Nation.* Albuquerque, New Mexico: University of New Mexico Press, 1983.

JACKSON, HELEN. *A Century of Dishonor.* New York: Indian Head Books, 1993.

JAIMES, ANNETTE M., ed. *The State of Native America: Genocide, Colonization and Resistance.* Boston: South End Press, 1992.

JENNINGS, FRANCIS. *The Founders of America.* New York: Norton, 1994.

———. *The Invasion of America: Indians, Colonialism and the Cant of Conquest.* New York: Norton, 1976.

JOHANSEN, BRUCE E. *Forgotten Founders: How the American Indian Helped Shape Democracy.* Boston: The Harvard Common Press, 1982.

JOHNSON, DIRK. "Census Finds Many Claiming New Identity: Indian." *New York Times,* March 5, 1991.

———. "Indians' Water Quest Creates New Foe: Environmentalists." *New York Times,* December 28, 1991.

———. "Population Decline in Rural America: A Product of Advances in Technology." *New York Times,* September 11, 1990.

JOHNSON, KIRK. "An Indian Tribe's Wealth Leads to the Expansion of Tribal Law." *New York Times.* May 22, 1994.

———. "Gambling Helps Tribe Invest in Education and the Future." *New York Times,* February 21, 1995.

————. "Tribe's Promised Land Is Rich but Uneasy." *New York Times,* February 20, 1995.

JOSEPHY, ALVIN M., JR. *The Indian Heritage of America.* Boston: Houghton Mifflin, 1991.

KAMMER, JERRY. *The Second Long Walk: The Navajo-Hopi Dispute.* Albuquerque, New Mexico: University of New Mexico Press, 1980.

KARP, IVAN, and LAVINE, STEVEN D. *Exhibiting Cultures: The Poetics and Politics of Museum Display.* Washington, D.C.: Smithsonian Institution Press, 1990.

KATZ, WILLIAM L. *Black Indians: A Hidden Heritage.* New York: Atheneum, 1986.

KILBORN, PETER L. "Sad Distinction for the Sioux: Homeland Is No. 1 in Poverty." *New York Times,* September 20, 1992.

KING, DUANE H., ed. *The Cherokee Indian Nation.* Knoxville, Tennessee: University of Tennessee Press, 1989.

KLEINFELD, N. R. "Legal Gambling Faces Higher Odds." *New York Times,* August 29, 1993.

KNACK, MARTHA, and STEWART, OMER C. *As Long as the River Shall Run. An Ethnohistory of Pyramid Lake Indian Reservation.* Berkeley, California: University of California Press, 1984.

KNOX, MARGARET. "Their Mother's Keepers." *Sierra,* April 1993.

KRECH, SHEPARD, III. "Ecology and the American Indian." *Ideas,* National Humanities Center, Summer 1994.

KROEBER, THEODORA. *Ishi in Two Worlds: A Biography of the Last Wild Indian in North America.* Berkeley, California: University of California Press, 1961.

LAZARUS, EDWARD. *Black Hills—White Justice: The Sioux Nation Versus the United States 1775 to the Present.* New York: HarperCollins, 1991.

LEMONICK, MICHAEL D. *The Light at the Edge of the Universe.* New York: Villard Books, 1993.

LENDER, MARK E., and MARTIN, JAMES K. *Drinking in America: A History.* New York: The Free Press, 1987.

LIMERICK, PATRICIA. *The Legacy of Conquest: The Unbroken Past of the American West.* New York: Norton, 1988.

LITTLE EAGLE, AVIS. "The Sticky Issue of Enrollment." *Indian Country Today,* January 7, 1993.

LOCKE, RAYMOND F. *The Book of the Navajo.* Los Angeles: Mankind Publishing, 1989.

LOPEZ, BARRY. *The Rediscovery of North America.* New York: Vintage, 1992.

LOWIE, ROBERT H. *The Crow Indians.* Lincoln, Nebraska: University of Nebraska Press, 1983.

LUCHETTI, CATHY. *Under God's Spell: Frontier Evangelists 1772–1915.* New York: Harcourt Brace Jovanovich, 1989.

LUHAN, CAROL C. "Alcohol-Related Deaths of American Indians." *Journal of the American Medical Association,* March 11, 1992.

The Lumbee Petition. (Unpublished.) Pembroke, North Carolina: Lumbee River Legal Services, Inc., 1987.

LYONS, OREN, et al. *Exiled in the Land of the Free: Democracy, Indian Nations and the U.S. Constitution.* Santa Fe, New Mexico: Clear Light Publishers, 1992.

MacDonald, Peter (with Ted Schwartz). *The Last Warrior: Peter MacDonald and the Navajo Nation.* New York: Orion Books, 1993.

Maffeo, Sabino. *In the Service of Nine Popes: 100 Years of the Vatican Observatory.* Rome, Italy: Vatican Observatory Foundation, 1991.

Mancall, Peter C. *Deadly Medicine: Indians and Alcohol in Early America.* Ithaca, New York: Cornell University Press, 1995.

Mander, Jerry. *In the Absence of the Sacred: The Failure of Technology and the Survival of the Indian Nations.* San Francisco: Sierra Club Books, 1990.

Mankiller, Wilma. *Mankiller: A Chief and Her People.* New York: St. Martin's Press, 1993.

Marquis, Thomas B. *Memoirs of a White Crow Indian (Thomas Leforge).* Lincoln, Nebraska: University of Nebraska Press, 1974.

Matthews, Anne. *Where the Buffalo Roam.* New York: Grove Press, 1992.

Matthiessen, Peter. *Indian Country.* London, England: Flamingo, 1985.

———. *In the Spirit of Crazy Horse.* New York: Penguin, 1991.

McClearn, Gerald E., et al. "Genetics and the Human Encounter with Alcohol." *Social Biology,* Fall/Winter 1985.

McDonnell, Janet A. *The Dispossession of the American Indian 1887–1934.* Bloomington, Indiana: University of Indiana Press, 1991.

McLuhan, T. C. *Dream Tracks: The Railroad and the American Indian 1890–1930.* New York: Abrams, 1985.

———. *Touch the Earth: A Self-Portrait of Indian Existence.* New York: Touchstone, 1971.

McMillan, Doug, et al. "Facing the Truth About Water." (Special series on the Truckee River watershed.) *Reno Gazette-Journal,* August 21–25, 1988.

McNeill, William H. *Plagues and People.* New York: Anchor Books, 1989.

McNickle, D'Arcy. *Native American Tribalism: Indian Survivals and Renewals.* New York: Oxford University Press, 1973.

Means, Russell. "Fighting Words on the Future of the Earth." *Mother Jones,* December 1980.

Medicine Crow, Joseph. *From the Heart of the Crow Country.* New York: Crown, 1992.

Melville, Herman. *Moby Dick.* New York: Random House, 1930.

Membrino, Joseph R. "Indian Reserved Water Rights, Federalism and the Trust Responsibility." *Land and Water Law Review,* Vol. 27, No. 1, 1992.

Merrell, James. *The Indians' New World: Catawbas and Their Neighbors from European Contact Through the Era of Removal.* New York: Norton, 1991.

———. "The Racial Education of the Catawba Indians." *The Journal of Southern History,* August 1984.

Miner, Craig, and Unrau, William E. *The End of Indian Kansas: A Study in Cultural Revolution, 1854–1871.* Lawrence, Kansas: University Press of Kansas, 1990.

Minnesota Gambling 1993. St. Paul, Minnesota: MN Planning, 1993.

Minugh, Carol J., ed. *Indian Self-Governance.* Kenmore, Washington: Center for World Indigenous Studies, 1989.

Momaday, N. Scott. *House Made of Dawn.* New York: Perennial Library, 1989.

MOORE, JOHN H., ed. *The Political Economy of North American Indians.* Norman, Oklahoma: University of Oklahoma Press, 1989.

MORNINGSTAR, HEATHER. *How to Enroll in an Indian Tribe.* Denver, Colorado: Arrowstar Publishing, 1993.

MOYERS, BILL. *The Faithkeeper.* (Videotape.) New York: Mystical Fire Video, 1991.

NABOKOV, PETER, ed. *Native American Testimony.* New York: Viking, 1991.

NAPPE, TINA. "Negotiating the Future of Wildlife: Saving Wetlands and Fish Along the Truckee River." (Abstract.) Bend, Oregon: The Chiles Award Papers, The High Desert Museum.

NEIHARDT, JOHN G. *Black Elk Speaks.* Lincoln, Nebraska: University of Nebraska Press, 1979.

————. *The End of the Dream and Other Stories.* Lincoln, Nebraska: University of Nebraska Press, 1991.

NEWLANDS, FRANCIS G. *An Address to the People of Nevada on Water Storage and Irrigation.* (Pamphlet.) Reno, Nevada: Reno Gazette Press, 1890.

NICKLASON, FRED H. *The Early Career of Henry L. Dawes, 1816–1871.* (Unpublished doctoral dissertation.) Yale University, 1967.

NORTON, JACK. *Genocide in Northern California.* San Francisco: The Indian Historian Press, 1979.

———— et al. "The California Indians." Special issue of *The American Indian Quarterly,* Fall 1989.

O'BRIEN, DAN. *In the Center of the Nation.* New York: Atlantic Monthly Press, 1991.

O'BRIEN, SHARON. *American Indian Tribal Governments.* Norman, Oklahoma: University of Oklahoma Press, 1989.

OLSON, JAMES C. *Red Cloud and the Sioux Problem.* Lincoln, Nebraska: University of Nebraska Press, 1965.

OLSON, PAUL A., ed. *The Book of the Omaha.* Lincoln, Nebraska: Nebraska Curriculum Development Center, 1979.

OPPELT, NORMAN T. *The Tribally Controlled Indian Colleges.* Tsaile, Arizona: Navajo Community College Press, 1990.

PARKER, A. C. *The Code of Handsome Lake, the Seneca Prophet.* Ohsweken, Canada: Iroqrafts Ltd., 1990.

PARKER, WATSON. *Gold in the Black Hills.* Lincoln, Nebraska: University of Nebraska Press, 1982.

PARKMAN, FRANCIS. *The Oregon Trail.* Boston: Little, Brown, 1891.

PASSELL, PETER. "Foxwoods, a Casino Success Story." *New York Times,* August 8, 1994.

PEARCE, ROY H. *Savagism and Civilization: A Study of the Indian and the American Mind.* Berkeley: University of California Press, 1988.

PERDUE, THEDA, ed. *Cherokee Editor: The Writings of Elias Boudinot.* Knoxville, Tennessee: University of Tennessee Press, 1983.

PEREGOY, ROBERT. "Nebraska Lawmakers Enact Precedent-Setting Indian Burial Legislation." *Native American Rights Fund Legal Review,* Fall 1989.

PETERSON, MERRILL D., ed. *Thomas Jefferson: Writings.* New York: The Library of America, 1984.

PEVAR, STEPHEN L. *The Rights of Indians and Tribes: The Basic ACLU Guide to*

Indian and Tribal Rights. Carbondale, Illinois: Southern Illinois University Press, 1992.

PORTER, JOSEPH C. *Paper Medicine Man: John Gregory Bourke and His American West*. Norman, Oklahoma: University of Oklahoma Press, 1989.

POWERS, WILLIAM K. *Oglala Religion*. Lincoln, Nebraska: University of Nebraska Press, 1977.

————. *Yuwipi: Vision and Experience in Oglala Ritual*. Lincoln, Nebraska: University of Nebraska Press, 1984.

PRESTON, DOUGLAS J. "Skeletons in Our Museums' Closets." *Harper's Magazine*, February 1989.

Proceedings of the Fourth Annual Meeting of the Lake Mohonk Conference of the Friends of the Indian. Philadelphia: Sherman and Co., 1886.

Proceedings of the Fifth Annual Meeting of the Lake Mohonk Conference of the Friends of the Indian. Philadelphia: Sherman and Co., 1887.

PRUCHA, FRANCIS. *American Indian Policy in the Formative Years*. Lincoln, Nebraska: University of Nebraska Press, 1970.

————. *American Indian Treaties: The History of a Political Anomaly*. Berkeley, California: University of California Press, 1994.

————, ed. *Americanizing the American Indians: Writings by the "Friends of the Indian" 1880–1900*. Lincoln, Nebraska: University of Nebraska Press, 1978.

————, ed. *Cherokee Removal: The "William Penn" Essays and Other Writings by Jeremiah Evarts*. Knoxville, Tennessee: University of Tennessee Press, 1981.

————, ed. *Documents of United States Indian Policy*. Lincoln, Nebraska: University of Nebraska Press, 1990.

————. *The Great Father: The United States Government and the American Indians*. Lincoln, Nebraska: University of Nebraska Press, 1986.

————. *The Indians in American Society*. Berkeley, California: University of California Press, 1985.

QUADE, VICKI. "Who Owns the Past? Interview with Walter Echo-Hawk." *Human Rights*, Winter 1989–1990.

RAWLS, JAMES J. *Indians of California*. Norman, Oklahoma: University of Oklahoma Press, 1984.

REEVES, CAROLYN K., ed. *The Choctaw Before Removal*. Jackson, Mississippi: University Press of Mississippi, 1985.

REINHOLD, ROBERT. "Farmers in West May Sell Something More Valuable Than Any Crop: Water." *New York Times*, April 6, 1992.

————. "New Age for Western Water Policy: Less for the Farm, More for the City." *New York Times*, October 11, 1992.

REISNER, MARC. *Cadillac Desert: The American West and Its Disappearing Water*. New York: Penguin, 1987.

RENO, PHILIP. *Mother Earth, Father Sky and Economic Development*. Albuquerque, New Mexico: University of New Mexico Press, 1981.

RENSI, RAY C., and WILLIAMS, H. DAVID. *Gold Fever: America's First Gold Rush*. Atlanta, Georgia: Georgia Humanities Council, 1988.

Report of the United States Commission on Civil Rights. Washington, D.C.: U.S. Government Printing Office, 1981.

REYNOLDS, JERRY. "Border Run Drinking Style Reinforces Old Stereotypes." *Lakota Times,* October 2, 1991.

RIDINGTON, ROBIN. "Omaha Survival: A Vanishing Tribe That Would Not Vanish." *The American Indian Quarterly,* Winter 1987.

ROBERTS, DAVID. *Once They Moved like the Wind: Cochise, Geronimo and the Apache Wars.* New York: Simon and Schuster, 1993.

ROESSEL, FAITH. "Federal Recognition—A Historical Twist of Fate." *Native American Rights Fund Legal Review,* Summer 1989.

RONDA, JAMES P. *Lewis and Clark Among the Indians.* Lincoln, Nebraska: University of Nebraska Press, 1988.

RORABAUGH, W. J. *The Alcoholic Republic.* New York: Oxford University Press, 1981.

ROSZAK, THEODORE. *The Voice of the Earth.* New York: Touchstone, 1993.

ROUCHE, BERTON. *The Neutral Spirit: A Portrait of Alcohol.* Boston: Little, Brown, 1960.

ROUSSEAU, JEAN-JACQUES. *Discourse on Inequality.* (Harvard Classics, Vol. 34.) New York: The Collier Press, 1910.

ROYAL, ROBERT. *1492 and All That: Political Manipulations of History.* Washington, D.C.: Ethics and Public Policy Center, 1992.

RUSCO, ELMER. "John Collier: Architect of Sovereignty or Assimilation?" *The American Indian Quarterly,* Winter 1991.

SALE, KIRKPATRICK. *The Conquest of Paradise: Christopher Columbus and the Columbian Legacy.* New York: Plume, 1991.

SANDOZ, MARI. *Cheyenne Autumn.* New York: Avon Books, 1964.

SARF, WAYNE M. *God Bless You, Buffalo Bill: A Layman's Guide to History and the Western Film.* East Brunswick, New Jersey: Associated University Presses, 1991.

SAVAGE, WILLIAM W., JR., ed. *Indian Life: Transforming an American Myth.* Norman, Oklahoma: University of Oklahoma Press, 1976.

SCHLESINGER, ARTHUR M., JR. *The Disuniting of America: Reflections on a Multicultural Society.* New York: Norton, 1992.

SCHMIDT, WILLIAM E. "Wisconsin Spring: New Fishing Season, Old Strife." *New York Times,* April 5, 1990.

SCHNEIDER, PAUL. "Other People's Trash: A Last-Ditch Effort to Keep Corporate Garbage Off the Reservation." *Audubon,* July–August 1991.

SCHULTZ, GEORGE A. *An Indian Canaan: Isaac McCoy and the Vision of an Indian State.* Lincoln, Nebraska: University of Nebraska Press, 1972.

SEAVER, JAMES E. *A Narrative of the Life of Mrs. Mary Jemison.* Syracuse, New York: Syracuse University Press, 1990.

Selected Consensus Health Status Indicators Among IHS Areas. Rockville, Maryland: U.S. Department of Health and Human Services, 1991.

SELF, R. D. "Chronology of New Echota." *Early Georgia,* Spring 1955.

SHATTUCK, GEORGE C. *The Oneida Land Claims: A Legal History.* Syracuse, New York: Syracuse University Press, 1991.

SHEEHAN, BERNARD W. *Seeds of Extinction: Jeffersonian Philanthropy and the American Indian.* Chapel Hill, North Carolina: University of North Carolina Press, 1973.

SIDER, GERALD M. *Lumbee Indian Histories: Race, Ethnicity, and Indian Identity in the Southern United States.* New York: Cambridge University Press, 1994.

SILKO, LESLIE M. *Ceremony.* New York: Penguin, 1986.

SLOTKIN, RICHARD. *The Fatal Environment.* New York: HarperPerennial, 1994.

SONTAG, SUSAN. *Illness as Metaphor.* New York: Vintage Books, 1979.

SPICER, EDWARD H. *Cycles of Conquest: The Impact of Spain, Mexico and the United States on the Indians of the Southwest, 1533–1960.* Tucson, Arizona: University of Arizona Press, 1989.

SPITTAL, W. G., ed. *Scalping and Torture: Warfare Practices Among North American Indians.* Ohsweken, Canada: Iroqrafts Ltd., 1985.

The State of Native American Youth Health. Minneapolis, Minnesota: University of Minnesota, Division of General Pediatrics and Adolescent Health, 1992.

STEGNER, WALLACE. *Beyond the Hundredth Meridian.* New York: Penguin, 1992.

———. *Where the Bluebird Sings to the Lemonade Springs.* New York: Penguin, 1993.

STEINER, STAN. *The Vanishing White Man.* Norman, Oklahoma: University of Oklahoma Press, 1987.

STELTENKAMP, MICHAEL F. *Black Elk: Holy Man of the Oglalas.* Norman, Oklahoma: University of Oklahoma Press, 1993.

STEVENS, WILLIAM K. "An Eden in Ancient America? Not Really." *New York Times,* March 30, 1993.

STEWART, OMER C. *Peyote Religion: A History.* Norman, Oklahoma: University of Oklahoma Press, 1987.

Stillwater National Wildlife Refuge and Stillwater Wildlife Management Area. (Briefing Paper.) U.S. Fish and Wildlife Service, 1991.

STOWELL, CYNTHIA D. *Faces of a Reservation: A Portrait of the Warm Springs Indian Reservation.* Oregon Historical Society Press, 1987.

SURO, ROBERTO. "Quiet Effort to Regain Idols May Alter Views of Indian Art." *New York Times,* August 13, 1990.

Survey of Conditions of Indians in the United States. (U.S. Senate report.) Washington, D.C.: U.S. Government Printing Office, 1930.

SUTTON, IMRE, ed. *Irredeemable America: The Indians' Estate and Land Claims.* Albuquerque, New Mexico: University of New Mexico Press, 1985.

SUZUKI, DAVID, and KNUDTSON, PETER. *Wisdom of the Elders: Sacred Native Stories of Nature.* New York: Bantam Books, 1993.

SWARTZLANDER, DAVID. "Historical Society Head Labeled Racist." *Lincoln Journal,* October 5, 1988.

TEDLOCK, DENNIS, and TEDLOCK, BARBARA. *Teachings from the American Earth: Indian Religion and Philosophy.* New York: Liveright, 1975.

THIN ELK, GENE. *Natural/Unnatural Worlds.* (Video.) Vermillion, South Dakota: Lakota Concepts, Inc., 1990.

———. *Sacred Seventh Direction.* (Video.) Vermillion, South Dakota: Lakota Concepts, Inc., 1990.

THORNTON, RUSSELL. *American Indian Holocaust and Survival: A Population History Since 1492.* Norman, Oklahoma: University of Oklahoma Press, 1990.

Toward a National Indian Legislative Agenda for the 1990's. Oakland, California: American Indian Resources Institute, 1992.

TRAFZER, CLIFFORD E. *The Kit Carson Campaign.* Norman, Oklahoma: University of Oklahoma Press, 1990.

TRAHANT, MARK N., et al. "Fraud in Indian Country: A Billion-Dollar Betrayal." (Special series.) *The Arizona Republic,* October 4–11, 1987.

———. "Indian Country." *The Arizona Republic,* January 21, 1990.

Trends in Indian Health. Washington, D.C.: Indian Health Service, 1991.

Tribal Colleges: Shaping the Future of Native America. Princeton, New Jersey: The Carnegie Foundation for the Advancement of Teaching, 1989.

TURNER, FREDERICK W., III. *The Portable North American Indian Reader.* New York: Penguin, 1977.

UBELAKER, DOUGLAS H. "North American Indian Population Size, A.D. 1500 to 1985." *American Journal of Physical Anthropology* 77, 1988.

——— and Grant, Lauryn Guttenplan. "Human Skeletal Remains: Preservation or Reburial?" *Yearbook of Physical Anthropology,* 1989.

UNDERHILL, LONNIE E., and LITTLEFIELD, DANIEL F., JR. *Hamlin Garland's Observations on the American Indian 1895–1905.* Tucson, Arizona: University of Arizona Press, 1976.

UTLEY, ROBERT M. *Custer Battlefield: A History and Guide to the Battle of the Little Bighorn.* Washington, D.C.: National Park Service, 1988.

———. *The Indian Frontier of the American West 1846–1890.* Albuquerque, New Mexico: University of New Mexico Press, 1984.

VAILLANT, GEORGE E. *The Natural History of Alcohol.* Cambridge, Massachusetts: Harvard University Press, 1983.

VECSEY, CHRISTOPHER, ed. *Handbook of American Indian Religious Freedom.* New York: Crossroad, 1991.

——— and Starna, William A. *Iroquois Land Claims.* Syracuse, New York: Syracuse University Press, 1988.

VERSLUIS, ARTHUR. *Sacred Earth: The Spiritual Landscape of Native America.* Rochester, Vermont: Inner Traditions International, 1992.

"View from the Shore: American Indian Perspectives on the Quincentenary," *Northeast Indian Quarterly,* Fall 1990.

VIOLA, HERMAN J. *After Columbus.* Washington, D.C.: Smithsonian Books, 1990.

VIZENOR, GERALD. *Crossbloods: Bone Courts, Bingo and Other Reports.* Minneapolis: University of Minnesota Press, 1990.

WADDELL, JACK O., and EVERETT, MICHAEL W., eds. *Drinking Behavior Among Southwestern Indians.* Tucson, Arizona: University of Arizona Press, 1980.

WALD, MATTHEW L. "Nuclear Storage Divides Apaches and Neighbors." *New York Times,* November 11, 1993.

WALDMAN, CARL. *Atlas of the North American Indian.* New York: Facts on File, 1985.

WALL, STEVE, and ARDEN, HARVEY. *Wisdomkeepers.* Hillsboro, Oregon: Beyond Words Publishing, Inc., 1990.

WALLACE, ANTHONY F. C. *The Death and Rebirth of the Seneca.* New York: Vintage Books, 1972.

WASHBURN, WILCOMB E. *The American Indian and the United States: A Documentary History.* New York: Random House, 1973.

We Are Choctaw. Philadelphia, Mississippi: Mississippi Band of Choctaw Indians, 1981.

WEATHERFORD, JACK. *Indian Givers: How the Indians of the Americas Transformed the World*. New York: Crown Publishers, 1988.

WELCH, JAMES. *The Death of Jim Loney*. New York: Penguin, 1987.

WELLMAN, PAUL I. *Death on the Prairie: The Thirty Years' Struggle for the Western Plains*. Lincoln, Nebraska: University of Nebraska Press, 1987.

Western Washington Native American Behavioral Risk Factor Survey; Final Report. Washington, D.C.: Indian Health Service, 1989.

WEXLER, MARK. "Sacred Rights." *National Wildlife*, June–July 1992.

WHITE, RICHARD. *"It's Your Misfortune and None of My Own": A New History of the American West*. Norman, Oklahoma: University of Oklahoma Press, 1993.

WHITE, ROBERT H. *Tribal Assets: The Rebirth of Native America*. New York: Henry Holt, 1990.

WHITTAKER, JAMES O. "Alcohol and the Standing Rock Sioux Tribe: A Twenty-Year Follow-Up Study." *Journal of Studies on Alcohol*, Vol. 43, No. 3, 1982.

The Wicazo sa Review: Indian Studies Journal. (Special issue on the Black Hills.) Spring 1988.

Wild Life on the Plains and the Horrors of Indian Warfare. (Reprint.) New York: The Arno Press, 1969.

WILKINS, DAVID E. *A Handbook of Navajo Government*. Tsaile, Arizona: Navajo Community College Press, 1987.

WILKINSON, CHARLES F. *American Indians, Time and the Law*. New Haven, Connecticut: Yale University Press, 1987.

———. *The Eagle Bird: Mapping a New West*. New York: Pantheon, 1992.

———. *The Truckee River Watershed*, Books I–III. (Compendiums of published documents.) Advanced Natural Resources Seminar, University of Colorado School of Law, Spring 1992.

WILLER, BARRY. *Prevention of Chemical Dependency Among Native American Families and Youth*. (Report.) Buffalo, New York: Division of Community Psychiatry, State University of New York at Buffalo, 1989.

WILSON, AMANDA. "Hazardous and Solid Waste Dumping Grounds Under RCRA's Indian Law Loophole." *Santa Clara Law Review*, Winter 1990.

WILSON, EDMUND. *Apologies to the Iroquois*. New York: Farrar, Straus and Cudahy, 1960.

WISSLER, CLARK. *Indians of the United States*. New York: Anchor, 1989.

WOODS, WILTON. "American Indians Discover Money Is Power." *Fortune*, April 19, 1993.

WOODWARD, GRACE S. *The Cherokees*. Norman, Oklahoma: University of Oklahoma Press, 1988.

WORSTER, DONALD. *Rivers of Empire: Water, Aridity, and the Growth of the American West*. New York: Oxford University Press, 1992.

———. *Under Western Skies: Nature and History in the American West*. New York: Oxford University Press, 1992.

Acknowledgments

M Y INTEREST in Indians was kindled many years ago by numerous men and women whose work, usually with the Association on American Indian Affairs, helped lay the foundation for much of the current revival of tribal culture. During my research for this book, Pauline and Wayne Tyndall and Alfred W. "Buddy" Gilpin of Macy, Nebraska, and Ella Irving of Pine Ridge, South Dakota, were living bridges between the past and the present. They offered both kindness and encouragement. Others, including the late Alfreda Janis, Oliver LaFarge, and John Woodenlegs, were sorely missed. They all taught me early in life that Indians have much to say and that they deserve to be heard.

Dr. Elizabeth Clark Rosenthal, a longtime board member of the Association, was a constant source of inspiration, provocative ideas, and pointed criticism. Her friendship and affection sustained me through more than one bout of discouragement, as did her conviction that a fresh and iconoclastic examination of the concerns of modern Indians would benefit both Indians and other Americans alike. The reservoir of understanding that she has gained from a lifetime spent in and around Indian communities was often a reminder that many of the truths of history lie in its contradictions.

I owe many debts to the tribal governments and officials without whose cooperation this book could never have been written, in particular: Gregg J. Bourland of the Cheyenne River Sioux Tribe; Joe De la Cruz of the Quinault Nation; Merlyn D. Dixon of the Fallon Paiute-Shoshone Tribes; Ralph Goff of the Campo Band of Indians; Zane Jackson and Ken Smith of the Confederated Tribes of Warm Springs; Elwood Lowery of the Pyramid Lake Paiute Tribe; Ivan Makil of the Salt River Pima-Maricopa Tribe; Phillip Martin of the Mississippi Band of Choctaws; Doran L. Morris, Sr., of the Omaha Nation; Jeff Parker of the Bay Mills Chippewa Community; Harold Salway of the Pine Ridge Sioux Tribe; Jonathan L. Taylor of the Eastern Band of Cherokees; and the offices of Wilma Mankiller of the Cherokee Nation, and Peterson Zah of the Navajo Nation.

I would also like to thank Barbara Bratone and Kristen Simone of the American Indian College Fund; Jeralyn de Coteau, Don B. Miller, Steven Moore, and Robert Peregoy of the Native American Rights Fund; former Under Secretary of the Interior for Indian Affairs Forrest Gerard; Tim Giago, the publisher of *Indian Country Today* (formerly the *Lakota Times*); Frank Gonzalez, chief of the Gallup, New Mexico, Police Department; Gary Kimble, the executive director of the Association on American Indian Affairs; Arlinda Locklear of the Lumbee Tribe; Bob Martin, president of Haskell Indian College; Robert S. Pelcyger of Fredericks and Pelcyger, Boulder, Colorado; Dr. Prem Peter of the faculty of New York Medical College; Mark Pinsky of the *Orlando Sentinel;* Peter Strittmatter, director of the Steward Observatory of the University of Arizona; and my cousins, Grace Bordewich and Nancy Bordewich Bowers of Carson City, Nevada.

James A. Clifton, scholar-in-residence in the Department of Anthropology of Western Michigan University; Robbie Daniels, director of substance abuse at the Indian Health Service hospital in Gallup, New Mexico; Bill Donovan of Gallup, New Mexico; Diana Fane, curator of African, Oceanic and New World art at the Brooklyn Museum; Ray Fogelson of the University of Chicago; Dennis Hastings, the Omaha tribal historian; Curtis M. Hinsley of the Department of History at Northern Arizona University; Edmund J. Ladd, curator of ethnology at the Museum of Indian Arts and Culture; Ruth Locklear and Cynthia Locklear Hunt of Pembroke, North Carolina; James H. Merrell of the Department of History at Vassar College; Wynema Morris, business manager of the Omaha Nation; Dan O'Brien of Rapid City, South Dakota; Donald J. Ortner, Douglas Owsley, Douglas H. Ubelaker, and Thomas W. Killion of the National Museum of Natural History; Janine Pease-Windy Boy, president of Little Big Horn Community College; Henry Real Bird of Garryowen, Montana; Leon Red Dog of Eagle Butte, South Dakota; Holly Reckord and George Roth of the Branch of Acknowledgement and Recognition of the Bureau of Indian Affairs; Karl Reinhard of the Department of Anthropology at the University of Nebraska; William T. Richardson, director of the Office of Economic Development of the Mississippi Band of Choctaws; Ramon A. Roubideaux of Rapid City, South Dakota; former Under Secretary of the Interior for Indian Affairs Ross O. Swimmer; Tom Tso, former chief justice of the Navajo Supreme Court; Don Vetter, the public information officer for Washoe County, Nevada; Peter Welsh, chief curator of the Heard Museum; Charles F. Wilkinson of the University of Colorado Law School; and Duane "Chili" Yazzie of the Navajo Tribal Council were exceptionally generous with their time and thoughts, which in many ways helped this book to be better than it would otherwise have been.

Others who freely gave of their advice and ideas included: Dan Agent; Ronald M. Anglin; John Around Him; Sharon Bass and Dennis O'Malley; Bruce Bernstein; Richard Bowler; Jody Calica; Pauline Capoeman; Jim Court; Steve Crawford; Kitty Belle Deernose; Bob DePerro; Tom Dardis; Fred Dressler; William DuBois; Greg Ducheneaux; Wayne Ducheneaux; Jim Ellsbury; Joe Ely; Michael Everett; Christian Feest; Linda S. Ferber; Bob Ferguson; C. Clinton Fixin; David Franz; Rick Gallego; Hugh Genoways; Mario Gonzalez; James Gunnerson; Richard Handler; Suzan Shown Harjo; Bill Harlan; Benson Heath; Robert Hecht; George Heron; Gordon Hunter; Peter Iverson; John Jeffries; Dwayne H. King; Stan Knick; Steve Lacy; Bob Maas; Jim Mannion; Francis Mason; Charles and Steven Marsh; Howard Martin; Donald A. McCabe; Douglas C. McChristian; Lyman McConnell; Martha McLeod; Randy Morrison; Thomas Muskrat; Tom Myers; Tina Nappe; Ron Nichols; Frank Popper; William K. Powers; John Ratje; Betty Reid; Robin Ridington; Joseph Rivera; R. Bruce Ross; Karin Sandness; Wayne Sarf; Carl Shaw; Nat Shaw; Jane Smiley; Tom Strekel; Clem F. Sylestine; Gene Thin Elk; Tommy Thompson; Katheryn L. Tierney; Mark Trahant; Mark Van Norman; Harry Walters; Merle Watt; Bill Wells; W. Richard West, Jr.; Dan Wildcat; Richard B.

Wilks; Perry Williams; Mervyn Wright; Milo Yellow Hair; Akhtar Zaman; and many more.

Paul Sheehan and Jack Barschi often took time to read the manuscript and to make many incisive suggestions. They have improved this volume in countless ways, large and small.

This book might never have come to fruition without the enthusiastic support of Casey Feutsch, my first editor at Doubleday, and of my current editor, Roger Scholl of Anchor Books. They both have my profound gratitude. I am also indebted to Kenneth Y. Tomlinson and Christopher Willcox of *Reader's Digest,* whose kindness in accommodating the demands of this book is deeply appreciated. My agent, Carl D. Brandt, has been an ever reassuring and good-humored presence during what must often have seemed like an interminable endeavor.

No one, however, has contributed more to this book than my wife Jean and daughter Chloe, whose endless forbearance can only be rewarded, however inadequately, by the final product.

Index